Joseph Smith and
the Origins of
The Book of Mormon

by

DAVID PERSUITTE

McFarland & Company, Inc., Publishers
Jefferson, North Carolina, and London

MP

Except in a few places that have been noted, the spelling, grammar, punctuation, and emphasis of the quoted sources have been retained. The use of *sic* has been avoided except where there might be some doubt as to the original reading.

Second printing with corrections, 1991

Library of Congress Cataloguing in Publication Data

Persuitte, David, 1939–
   Joseph Smith and the origins of The Book of Mormon.

   Bibliography: p.
   Includes index.
   1. Book of Mormon—Authorship.   2. Smith, Joseph, 1805–1844.   3. Smith, Ethan, 1762–1849.   View of the Hebrews.   I. Title.   II. Title: Joseph Smith and The Book of Mormon.
BX8627.P43   1985   289.3′22   84-42734

ISBN 0-89950-134-6

Manufactured in the United States of America

McFarland   Box 611   Jefferson NC 28640

Acknowledgments

I would like to give particular thanks to Wesley P. Walters and H. Michael Marquardt for critically examining the drafts of this book and for supplying me with many pieces of important information. Without their patient help and encouragement, I could not have done my work nearly so effectively.

I would also like to thank Jay Adams and many others who gave their help in one way or another. Thanks are due also to Charles Parker and the other members of the Poultney, Vermont, Historical Society, and to several other historical societies and libraries around the country. Finally, I would like to give special thanks to R. Wise for whetting my curiosity about Mormon origins.

Table of Contents

Foreword

Vern L. Bullough

Mormonism, or more correctly, the teachings of the Church of Jesus Christ of Latter-day Saints, is now believed by more than seven million people and is one of the fastest growing religions in the world. Unlike most religions, however, Mormonism began at a time when written records were available, and these can be examined to check claims and counterclaims about the historical record of the church relating to its origins. Obviously, none of these records can prove or disprove that Joseph Smith received revelations from God; that is a matter ultimately of faith. But they can demonstrate that Smith was very much a person of his time, influenced by conditions and events of his environment.

The key to Mormonism is *The Book of Mormon*. According to the Mormons, the book was translated from gold plates unearthed by the young Joseph Smith in the Hill Cumorah in the town of Manchester, near the village of Palmyra, New York, not far from present-day Rochester. Those plates, Smith declared, had been stored in the hill by an ancient person named Moroni, and described the story of the descendants of some Israelites who had come to the New World before the birth of Jesus. According to *The Book of Mormon*, these early settlers were part of the Lost Ten Tribes of Israel, and Jesus appeared to them after his death and resurrection in Jerusalem.

For much of its history, there was little objective scholarship about Mormonism. Mormons wrote pro-Mormon history, and those non-Mormons who became interested in the subject were more often concerned with debunking it than with looking at it objectively. Over the last few decades, however, there has been a reexamination of the origins of Mormonism by professional scholars, both Mormon and non-Mormon. David Persuitte's study belongs to this latter category and should help us to better understand where some of the concepts of Mormonism came from.

Persuitte, in his research of early Mormon beginnings, came across references to a book entitled *View of the Hebrews; or the Tribes of Israel in America*. The book was written by an East Poultney, Vermont, minister named Ethan Smith and was first published by him some seven years before Joseph Smith's *Book of Mormon* appeared. Persuitte argues that the two books have similar descriptions, concepts, and religious ideas; so much so that he could only conclude that the author of *The Book of Mormon* had acquired many of his ideas, perhaps even his inspiration from Ethan Smith's book. Whether he has proved his case or not will be up to the reader to decide. His book does more, however, than simply compare *View of the Hebrews* and *The Book of Mormon*. Persuitte also tries to set Joseph Smith in his time and place. Only by books such as this can we understand what Mormonism is all about. For those interested, both in the development of Mormonism and of religion in general, this book should prove fascinating.

Buffalo, N.Y.
September 1983

Introduction

"This Joe Smith is undoubtedly one of the greatest characters of the age." So remarked a New York State newspaper editor when the founder of Mormonism was near the height of his career. Though the comment may have been lightly made, it certainly was not far from the truth. Many present-day historians would agree that Joseph Smith *was* one of the greatest "characters" of the early nineteenth century, even if only in the colloquial sense of the word. To so categorize the Mormon leader one might simply point out that he established what is probably the most successful of the many new religious movements appearing during the past few centuries. In a different vein, one could also readily assert that few others of his time were as colorful and as fascinating as he was.

But what is especially significant about Joseph Smith is that he became one of the most controversial and enigmatic figures ever to appear in American history. Ample testimony for this aspect of his character can be found in the array of literature that has been published about him during the past century and a half. That literature includes works by scores of writers who have passionately clashed with each other in turning out completely different explanations of how the man that Mormons refer to as a "prophet" was able to accomplish what he did and what motivated him. Some of these writers proclaimed that he had the spirit of the Lord within him; others swore that he was possessed by the devil. Some felt that he swayed people by means of a kind of powerful animal magnetism; others cynically declared that he proved that any proposition, no matter how foolish, would soon gather a multitude of credulous supporters.

Since it presents such contradictory and emotional views, the literature about Joseph Smith is often a source of frustration to anyone trying to learn how he founded the Mormon religion. Among all the beliefs, theories, and speculations that have been expressed about him, only one thing seems to be reasonably certain. Without *The Book of Mormon*, Joseph Smith most likely would never have been able to do what he did. And that raises an important point. If one is going to make a proper study of how Joseph Smith founded the Mormon religion, one must also make a study of *The Book of Mormon*. More specifically, to understand how Joseph Smith actually became the Mormon prophet, one must first understand how *The Book of Mormon* came to be. But therein lies a problem.

1

The literature about the origin of *The Book of Mormon*, like that about Joseph Smith, is permeated with contradiction and controversy. It all began, of course, with Smith's own explanation for the origin of the book. The Mormon prophet first published his latter-day "revelation" in 1830, declaring that he had translated it by a "gift of God" from a set of inscribed gold plates he had found. According to him, the book was a divinely revealed history of ancient America which showed that the Bible and Christianity had become corrupted, and which gave him the authority to restore the true church of God to the world.

Understandably enough, those claims set into motion a long-lasting debate between the believers and the nonbelievers in the new religion. On the one hand, the believers argued from the very beginning that *The Book of Mormon* had to be an actual revelation from God because Joseph Smith was only an "ignorant" backwoods "boy" who would have been incapable of making it up himself. In later years, the believers even "proved" that no one living in the early nineteenth century could possibly have written *The Book of Mormon* and that it was an accurate history of the ancient inhabitants of America. On the other hand, some of the nonbelievers "proved" that Joseph had written the book under the influence of the devil to lead the faithful astray. Other nonbelievers "proved" various conflicting theories of how Joseph had come by the book. These theories often involved the proposition that Joseph and some of his friends had conspired to enrich themselves by means of a religious fabrication.

So it went through the years. Over the past century and a half, believers and nonbelievers in *The Book of Mormon* have written scores of volumes defending their respective stands. Yet, despite this mass of literature (or perhaps because of it), the origin of Joseph Smith's latter-day "revelation" has until now remained a mystery enshrouded in the unyielding mists of time.

When I began doing research on Mormonism several years ago, I came across a few vague references to a book that had been written by a New England minister named Ethan Smith. The title of the book was *View of the Hebrews; or the Tribes of Israel in America*. Though the references gave little information on the matter, they indicated that *The Book of Mormon* had some similarities with *View of the Hebrews* — a rather interesting circumstance, since Ethan Smith's book was first published seven years before the initial publication of Joseph Smith's new revelation from God. Finding nothing further on the subject at the time, and my curiosity aroused, I acquired a copy of Ethan Smith's book and began to compare it extensively with *The Book of Mormon*. The similarities in descriptions, concepts, and religious ideas that I subsequently found between the two books were quite remarkable and numerous. They were so remarkable and numerous that I could only conclude that the author of *The Book of Mormon* had acquired an essential measure of his material and ideas, perhaps even his very "inspiration," from Ethan Smith's book. I found, in short, that *The Book of Mormon* appeared to have had its conceptual origins in *View of the Hebrews*.

To add to the significance of this find, I later learned that a considerable amount of other evidence relating to the origins of Mormonism has turned up during the past few decades. Some of this resolves several long-standing disputes about Joseph Smith's early life; some of it answers many questions about *The Book of Abraham*, another of Joseph Smith's works. When all this material is gathered together, it sheds abundant light upon the path that Joseph Smith took to originate the Mormon religion. Unfortunately, however, much of this new evidence has not hitherto been gathered together effectively and widely published.

In writing this book, I have chosen to make full use of the documentation and to let the evidence speak for itself. If I did otherwise, I would be merely repeating mistakes that earlier writers on Mormonism have frequently made. It is one thing to say, for example, that *View of the Hebrews* was the primary source of material for *The Book of Mormon*; it is quite another thing to prove it. By providing an extensive comparative analysis of the two books, I feel that I have proved it quite conclusively. Be that as it may, it should be emphasized that Joseph was also dependent upon other sources, and we will note some of these as well. All this material will show that *The Book of Mormon* was a product of the early nineteenth century rather than a history of ancient America.

Except in a few cases that I have noted, I have retained the spelling, grammar, and emphasis that occurs in my sources. I have also refrained from using *sic*, except where there might be some doubt as to the original reading. To do differently would detract from the rustic flavor of some of the excerpts.

A final note: There are some differences in wording and punctuation between the first and subsequent editions of *The Book of Mormon*. Most of these differences are not crucial to the meaning of the affected parts; nevertheless, in order to be as close as possible to the sense, tone, and grammar of the original version as dictated by Joseph Smith, I have used the first edition for all of the *Book of Mormon* quotations. Consequently, the references for those quotations will have the page numbers for that edition. For reader convenience, however, the references will also include the book, chapter, and verse of the current edition published by the Mormon church that is headquartered in Utah. This church, properly known as the Church of Jesus Christ of Latter-day Saints, is the largest of the several independent Mormon denominations in existence today, and its version of *The Book of Mormon* is presently the most widely used.

Prologue

East Poultney, Vermont, at first glance appears to be not much different from numerous other small villages that dot the countryside of the Green Mountain State. There is the traditional white frame church on the central village green, a scattering of assorted buildings, and a lingering trace of a bygone time when life was simpler and more placid. The setting would be familiar to most of the tourists who might pass through the village on their way to the mountains or to nearby Lake St. Catherine, so few would find any compelling reason to stop there.

Still, an observant tourist might notice and pause to investigate two or three small, time-worn buildings among the houses surrounding the village green. Dating from the early nineteenth century, these old structures are museums now, and one of them provides the village with a bit of fame. In 1826, a fourteen-year-old boy came to Poultney (as East Poultney was then called) to work as an apprentice in the print shop of the *Northern Spectator*, which was then located in the building. The boy was Horace Greeley, and his apprenticeship in the shop led to his career as a noted nineteenth century journalist and political leader.

Though there is nothing to indicate it to the casual tourist, that same building can be considered to have a much greater historical importance. In 1823 and in 1825, the press of the *Northern Spectator* printed the first and second editions, respectively, of a book that is virtually unheard of today, but which, as will be shown, appears to have inspired a system of religious belief that presently claims more than seven million adherents. The book was *View of the Hebrews; or the Tribes of Israel in America*, by Ethan Smith, who at that time was the pastor of the Poultney Congregational Church. This was not the first book that Ethan Smith had written, nor was it to be his last, but it was to be — though he did not know it — his most significant.

As the title of the book indicates, Pastor Smith was presenting a view of the Hebrews. This view dealt primarily with the dispersion of the Hebrews from their homeland and with their prophesied restoration to that homeland prior to the Millennium. More specifically, Pastor Smith was concerned with the whereabouts of the Ten Lost Tribes of Israel. He was convinced that certain biblical prophecies included the Ten Tribes in the restoration, and he therefore believed that those tribes had to have a distinct existence somewhere

5

VIEW OF THE HEBREWS;

OR THE

TRIBES OF ISRAEL IN AMERICA.

EXHIBITING

CHAP. I. THE DESTRUCTION OF JERUSALEM. CHAP. II. THE CER-
TAIN RESTORATION OF JUDAH AND ISRAEL. CHAP. III. THE
PRESENT STATE OF JUDAH AND ISRAEL. CHAP. IV. AN
ADDRESS OF THE PROPHET ISAIAH TO THE UNITED
STATES RELATIVE TO THEIR RESTORATION.

SECOND EDITION, IMPROVED AND ENLARGED.

By Ethan Smith,

PASTOR OF A CHURCH IN POULTNEY (VT.)

" *These be the days of vengeance.*"
" *Yet a remnant shall return.*"
" *He shall assemble the outcasts of Israel; and gather together the
dispersed of Judah.*"

PUBLISHED AND PRINTED BY SMITH & SHUTE,
POULTNEY. (VT.)
....
1825.

The title page for the 1825 edition of Ethan Smith's *View of the Hebrews.*

in the world in order for those prophecies to be fulfilled. But *where* were the Israelites? For the Vermont minister, this question had a certain urgency since he was sure that the "latter days" were at hand.

Influenced by some earlier books that had been published on the subject, Ethan Smith had come to believe that one did not have to look very far for the Israelites. Those earlier books had suggested that the American Indians were descended from the Ten Tribes, a proposition that Pastor Smith found very appealing. The Vermont minister therefore consolidated in his own book much of the "evidence" that had already been published in support of the idea, adding to it a large amount of new "evidence" that he himself had gathered. He also included his own thoughts on the subject — one of which was his theory on what had happened to the "Israelites" after their arrival in the New World. And finally, of particular importance, he tied his book together with a religious viewpoint that had certain implications for his fellow Americans.

The ideas and religious views that Ethan Smith presented on the origin of the American Indians might well have gained the attention of a certain young man who was then living in Poultney. The name of this young man was Oliver Cowdery. A few years later, as Joseph Smith's most important scribe, he would assist in the "translation" of *The Book of Mormon*. Moreover, he would be one of the gold plate "witnesses" and he would become Second Elder in the church that Joseph Smith would establish. And that brings up an interesting point: There is no absolute proof that Oliver Cowdery played a part in authoring (as opposed to "translating") *The Book of Mormon*, but it is noteworthy that he lived in the same small town which saw the publication of the book that appears to have been the most important source of material and ideas for Joseph Smith's "Gold Bible."

Oliver Cowdery surely must have been aware of Ethan Smith's book. As pastor of the Poultney Congregational Church, Ethan Smith would have been known by most of the inhabitants of the town. Moreover, there were several lengthy advertisements in the *Northern Spectator* for the first edition of *View of the Hebrews*. We can also assume that the book was much discussed in the town, especially since the first edition had a "speedy sale," as Pastor Smith noted in the second edition. Furthermore, Oliver Cowdery was a literate individual and he likely would have been interested in any book published in his hometown.

What is even more significant is that the records of the Poultney Congregational Church indicate that a "Mr Cowdry" had three of his children baptized in that church on August 2, 1818. This "Mr Cowdry" was not identified any further, but the names of the children were given. They were "Rebeka Maria, Lucy, and Phebe."[1]* Interestingly enough, Oliver Cowdery's mother had died in 1809, and his father had married Mrs. Keziah Pearce Austin in 1810. Of this union, three children were born: Rebecca, Lucy, and Phoebe.[2] The entry in the record states that the children were baptized "on the faith of their mother." Mrs. Cowdery was formally enrolled as a member of the church (as indicated elsewhere in the records), Mr. Cowdery was not. Mr. Cowdery must have considered himself nominally a Congregationalist, however, since

See Chapter Notes, beginning on page 270.

in those days children were traditionally baptized in the faith of the father.[3] In any case, these records indicate that the Cowdery family had an association with the same church that Ethan Smith was to become pastor of in 1821 — only three years after the baptism of the girls.[4] It is reasonable to expect, then, that Oliver Cowdery eventually became acquainted firsthand with Ethan Smith.

Since Pastor Smith wrote his book to convince his fellow Americans of the religious importance of his ideas about the American Indians, we can speculate that he also used his pulpit to expound upon them. In the congregation, Oliver Cowdery might thus have heard and been deeply impressed by something like the following:

> An address is found in ... Isaiah, which is apprehended to be of deep interest to America....
>
> Should it be proved a *fact*, that the aborigines of our continent are the descendants of the ten tribes of Israel; it would heighten the probability to a moral certainty, that we are the people especially addressed, and called upon to restore them; or bring them to the knowledge of the gospel, and do with them whatever the God of Abraham designs shall be done.
>
> The great and generous Christian people, who occupy much of the land of those natives, and who are on the ground of their continent, and hence are the best prepared to meliorate their condition, and bring them to the knowledge and order of the God of Israel, must of course be the people to whom this work is assigned.
>
> Ye friends of God in the land addressed; can you read this prophetic direction of the ancient prophet Isaiah, without having your hearts burn within you? Surely you cannot, if you view it as an address of the Most High to you. God here exalts you, in the last days, the age of terror and blood, as high as the standard to be raised for the collection of the seed of Abraham....
>
> If these views be correct, Christians in this land may well bless God that it is their happy lot to live in this land shadowing with wings; this protecting realm, an asylum of liberty and religion.... Our children coming upon the stage may live to see the *meaning* and *fulfillment* of this prophetic chapter....
>
> Ho thou nation of the last days.... Rejoice, then, ye distinguished people in your birthright, and engage in the work by Heaven assigned....
>
> Look at the origin of those degraded natives of your continent, and fly to their relief.... Send them the heralds of salvation.... Teach them the story of their ancestors; ... of Abraham, Isaac, and Jacob. — Teach them their ancient history.[5]

Oliver Cowdery left Poultney for New York State "about" the year 1825,[6] the same year in which the second edition of *View of the Hebrews* was published. Five years later, after having worked together on the "translation" of *The Book of Mormon*, he and Joseph Smith would set out to "engage in the work by Heaven assigned" in seeming compliance with Ethan Smith's exhortation.

Part One

Angels, Peepstones, and Gold Plates

Joseph Smith (1805–1844); oil by Adrian Lamb (1971) after an unidentified artist. By permission of National Portrait Gallery, Smithsonian Institution, Washington, D.C.; gift of the Reorganized Church of Jesus Christ of Latter-Day Saints, Independence, Mo.

Chapter 1

"A Romancer of the First Water"

Anyone thumbing through a copy of the first edition of *The Book of Mormon* might be drawn to a statement on the title page reading, "BY JOSEPH SMITH, JUNIOR, AUTHOR AND PROPRIETOR." Although similar statements of authorship appear on most books, this particular declaration is curious because it seems to contradict the claims that Joseph Smith made about the origin of his latter-day "revelation." Indeed, it seems to imply that *The Book of Mormon* was his own creation rather than being an authentic "history" of ancient America. The Mormon prophet himself appears to have belatedly realized what the statement implied, since in the next edition he amended it to read: "TRANSLATED BY JOSEPH SMITH, JUN."

While the change better conformed to Joseph's claims for the book, the question remains as to whether the initial attribution was the more accurate. This is not to say that credence can be attached to the amended byline. There is evidence to show that *The Book of Mormon* had its origin in Joseph Smith's time instead of in ancient America as the founder of Mormonism claimed. Still, this in itself does not prove that Joseph Smith was the author of the book. Someone else might have authored it and Smith might have subsequently gone through the motions of "translating" it for the sake of appearances. The proper question to ask, then, is *who* authored *The Book of Mormon*? Was it Joseph Smith? or was it one of his contemporaries?

To form an opinion on that question, one must first form an opinion on another: Did Joseph Smith have the ability to author *The Book of Mormon*? In order to advance their own beliefs on theories about the origin of Joseph Smith's latter-day "revelation," many writers, Mormon and non-Mormon, have maintained that Joseph did not have such an ability. Yet, many individuals have made a name for themselves in literature despite having inauspicious origins.

Nevertheless, the question remains: Is it reasonably possible that Joseph Smith *did* have the capability of composing *The Book of Mormon*? Furthermore, just who *was* Joseph Smith?

Joseph Smith, Jr., was born in Sharon, Vermont, on December 23, 1805, the fourth child in a family that eventually had nine children. Joseph's father was a farmer and sometime schoolteacher who appears to have made some bad investments which resulted in the impoverishment of the family.

THE

BOOK OF MORMON:

AN ACCOUNT WRITTEN BY THE HAND OF MOR-MON, UPON PLATES TAKEN FROM THE PLATES OF NEPHI.

Wherefore it is an abridgment of the Record of the People of Nephi; and also of the Lamanites; written to the Lamanites, which are a remnant of the House of Israel; and also to Jew and Gentile; written by way of commandment, and also by the spirit of Prophesy and of Revelation. Written, and sealed up, and hid up unto the LORD, that they might not be destroyed; to come forth by the gift and power of GOD, unto the interpretation thereof; sealed by the hand of Moroni, and hid up unto the LORD, to come forth in due time by the way of Gentile; the interpretation thereof by the gift of GOD; an abridgment taken from the Book of Ether.

Also, which is a Record of the People of Jared, which were scattered at the time the LORD confounded the language of the people when they were building a tower to get to Heaven: which is to shew unto the remnant of the House of Israel how great things the LORD hath done for their fathers; and that they may know the covenants of the LORD, that they are not cast off forever; and also to the convincing of the Jew and Gentile that JESUS is the CHRIST, the ETERNAL GOD, manifesting Himself unto all nations. And now if there be fault, it be the mistake of men; wherefore condemn not the things of GOD, that ye may be found spotless at the judgment seat of CHRIST.

BY JOSEPH SMITH, JUNIOR,

AUTHOR AND PROPRIETOR.

PALMYRA:

PRINTED BY E. B. GRANDIN, FOR THE AUTHOR.

1830.

The title page for the first edition of *The Book of Mormon*.

Attempting to get a new start in life, the Smith family relocated itself several times in New England and then migrated to Palmyra, in western New York, in 1816. The family moved again about two years later, settling down this time just over the town line into Manchester (though their new home was still closer to Palmyra village proper than to Manchester village proper).

One of Joseph's acquaintances in the early years at Manchester was a printer's assistant named Orsamus Turner. In a book dealing with the settlement of western New York that he wrote several years later, Turner included some incidental recollections of Joseph and his family:

> Joseph Smith, the father of the prophet Joseph Smith, Jr., was from the Merrimack river, N.H. He first settled in or near Palmyra village, but as early as 1819 was the occupant of some new land on "Stafford street" in the town of Manchester, near the line of Palmyra.... The elder Smith had been a Universalist, and subsequently a Methodist; was a good deal of a smatterer in Scriptural knowledge: but the seed of revelation was sown on weak ground; he was a great babbler, credulous, not especially industrious, a money digger, prone to the marvelous; and withal, a little given to difficulties with neighbors, and petty law suits....
>
> ... Mrs. Smith was a woman of strong uncultivated intellect; artful and cunning; imbued with an illy regulated religious enthusiasm....
>
> ... Joseph Smith, Jr., ... was lounging, idle; ... and possessed of less than ordinary intellect. The author's own recollections of him are distinct ones. He used to come into the village of Palmyra with little jags of wood, from his backwoods home; sometimes patronizing a village grocery too freely; sometimes find an odd job to do about the store of Seymore Scovall; and once a week he would stroll into the office of the old Palmyra Register, for his father's paper. How impious, in us young "dare *Devils*" to once in a while blacken the face of the then meddling inquisitive lounger — but afterwards Prophet, with the old fashioned balls, when he used to put himself in the way of the working of the old fashioned Ramage press!...
>
> But Joseph had a little ambition; and some very laudable aspirations; the mother's intellect occasionally shone out in him feebly, especially when he used to help us solve some portentous questions of moral or political ethics, in our juvenile debating club, which we moved down to the old red school house on Durfee street, to get rid of the annoyance of critics that used to drop in upon us in the village; and subsequently, after catching a spark of Methodism in the camp meeting, away down in the woods, on the Vienna road, he was a very passable exhorter in the evening meetings.[1]

As was common with many others who gave descriptions of the young man who was to become the Mormon prophet, Turner (who had his own theory on the origin of *The Book of Mormon*) did not give Joseph* much credit for his intellectual ability. But Turner's grudging admission that "the mother's intellect occasionally shone out in him feebly" perhaps shows that

---

**To preclude confusion of the two Smiths, Joseph and Ethan, Joseph will henceforth be referred to by his first name.*

Joseph had a mind that was a little bit better than some of those who knew him were willing to report. Incidentally, since Turner left the Palmyra area in 1822, Joseph could not have been more than sixteen years old at the time.

It is interesting to note that Turner stated that Joseph was "a very passable exhorter" in the Methodist meetings. At the time, the Methodist preachers traveled circuits in those areas where their congregations had not yet constructed churches. As he traveled along his circuit, each preacher would preach in any convenient place: in a log cabin, in a tavern, or in the woods. Occasionally, the preacher would hold a "camp meeting," a large gathering which sometimes lasted several days. In various localities along his circuit, each preacher would also establish a "class" which he placed under a local "class leader." An "exhorter" was a young man with some ability at public speaking who was urged by the circuit preacher or the class leader to "exercise his gifts" in the meetings.[2] Joseph therefore must have had a certain amount of talent in this respect.

An interesting word picture of Joseph was drawn by Daniel Hendrix, who, as a young man, lived in Palmyra and knew him. He also assisted in setting the type and reading proofs of the first edition of *The Book of Mormon*:

> I was a very young man in a store in Palmyra, N.Y., from 1822 until 1830, ... and among the daily visitors at the establishment was Joseph Smith Jr. Every one knew him as Joe Smith.... Joe was the most ragged, lazy fellow in the place, and that is saying a great deal. He was about 25 years old. I can see him now, in my mind's eye, with this torn and patched trousers, held to his form by a pair of suspenders made out of sheeting, with his calico shirt as dirty and black as the earth, and his uncombed hair sticking through the holes in his old battered hat. In winter I used to pity him, for his shoes were so old and worn out that he must have suffered in the snow and slush; yet Joe had a jovial, easy, don't care way about him that made him a lot of warm friends. He was a good talker, and would have made a fine stump speaker if he had had the training. He was known among the young men I associated with as a romancer of the first water. I never knew so ignorant a man as Joe was to have such a fertile imagination. He never could tell a common occurrence in his daily life without embelishing the story with his imagination; yet I remember that he was grieved one day when old Parson Reed told Joe that he was going to hell for his lying habits.
>
> Mrs. Smith, Joe's mother, was a staunch Presbyterian, and was a great admirer of her son, despite his shiftless and provoking ways. She always declared that he was born with a genius, and did not have to work. "Never mind about my son Joseph," said she one day, when my employer had rallied her upon her heir's useless ways, "for the boy will be able some of these fine days to buy the whole of Palmyra and all the folks in it. You don't know what a brain my boy has under that old hat."...[3]

As a boy, Joseph had only a meager formal schooling. He attended school when his farm chores permitted and he received supplementary instruction from his parents at home. Undoubtedly, it was this meager formal schooling, rather than a mental deficiency, that led some of his contemporaries to state that Joseph had "less than ordinary intellect." The condescending attitude of these acquaintances is perhaps understandable, but the amount of formal schooling that Joseph had is hardly a true indication of his inherent mental abilities. For that matter, the comments that Daniel Hendrix made (and others made similar comments) would indicate that Joseph actually had an active and inquisitive mind.

Still, many writers have held that Joseph could not have authored *The Book of Mormon* because of his limited education. But that argument is fallacious in several respects. In the first place, it presupposes that *The Book of Mormon* contains material that its author could have acquired only through a higher education. In actuality, though, the book does not contain any such material; it is long on verbal ramblings, but short on hard facts. Secondly, one does not need to have a university education to be a story teller—and more than anything else, *The Book of Mormon* tells a story. Finally, a higher education can certainly imbue one with a more polished literary style, but Joseph's limited formal education seems to have been reflected in the literary style of the first edition of *The Book of Mormon*. That edition contains many errors in grammar as well as tediously frequent run-on sentences.

In any case, it appears that Joseph was quite aware of his limited education and tried to do something about it a few years before he brought out *The Book of Mormon*. Of his own volition he went to school in 1826 when he was twenty years old and away from home. He certainly was not required to go to school at that age; his doing so must have been from his own desire to increase his learning—perhaps to prepare himself for the task of composing his "history" of ancient America. Joseph was staying in Bainbridge, New York, at the time, and there are some comments about him in a biographical sketch of Asa B. Searles, one of his schoolmates:

> Going to South Bainbridge, he [Searles] lived there four or five years, and attended school where his brother Lemuel taught. Joe Smith, the coming prophet, was a fellow pupil, with whom, uncle Asa says, he had many a wrestle; but young Smith was a large, strong fellow and could handle any of the boys. He was lazy, but kindhearted, had a large brain and a good deal of ability.[4]

Searles' comment that Joseph "had a large brain and a good deal of ability" is a further indication of Joseph's actual intelligence.

Another indication of Joseph's actual intellectual ability was provided by C.G. Webb, an early convert to Mormonism. Webb had been personally acquainted with Joseph for eleven years, but eventually became disillusioned with "the Prophet" and his church. In his later years, he made these interesting comments during an interview with Wilhelm Wyl:

> Joseph was the calf that sucked three cows. He acquired knowledge very rapidly, and learned with special facility all the tricks of the scoundrels who worked in his company. He soon outgrew his teachers. He studied Hebrew, he wanted to be fit for his place and enjoy the profits and power alone. He learned by heart a number of Latin, Greek and French

commonplace phrases, to use them in his speeches and sermons.... Joseph
kept a learned Jew in his house for a long time for the purpose of studying
Hebrew with him; the Jew used to teach his language in a room of the
"temple" to Joseph and a number of the elders.... I taught him the first rules
of English Grammar in Kirtland in 1834. He learned very rapidly, while
Heber C. Kimball never came to understand the difference between noun
and verb.[5]

Certainly, Webb's description is not one of somebody with "less than
ordinary intellect." Moreover, Wyl added to Webb's comments by interjecting,
"It was probably his rapidly augmenting knowledge of the sciences, that made
[Joseph] say, a few months before his death: *I know more than the whole
world.*'"

Since Joseph had only a limited formal education before he brought out
The Book of Mormon, he did not have much of a chance to develop his pen-
manship or his spelling ability. This was noted by Orson Pratt, an early
Mormon writer, who stated that Joseph "could read without much difficulty,
and write a very imperfect hand."[6] His imperfect handwriting, coupled with
his talent for speaking (noted by Hendrix and Turner), sheds light upon the
reason Joseph chose the method that he did of getting *The Book of Mormon* on
paper. Rather than writing it down himself, he dictated it (and most of his
other works, as well) to a scribe. Joseph's poor writing hand, but good
speaking ability, also brings to mind remarks made by some of the characters
in *The Book of Mormon*:

And now I, Nephi, cannot write all the things which were taught among
my people; neither am I mighty in writing, like unto speaking....[7]
And I said unto him, Lord, the Gentiles will mock at these things,
because of our weakness in writing; ... and thou hast made us that we could
write but little, because of the awkwardness of our hands.[8]

Joseph likewise was not "mighty in writing, like unto speaking." This
similarity between Joseph and some of the characters in *The Book of Mormon*
might be more than just a coincidence. If he were the author of the book, it
would not be surprising if he had projected something of himself into the characters he invented.

Some Mormon writers have maintained that Joseph lived in an isolated
backwoods area that was virtually devoid of books. Consequently, they say,
it would have been impossible for him to have acquired all the material that he
would have needed to write *The Book of Mormon.* But, in fact, that was
hardly the case. In the first place, there were several roads connecting the
towns of western New York with each other and with the eastern cities. More
importantly, Dewitt Clinton's Erie Canal passed one block away from the
main street of Palmyra. This canal connected Palmyra with the Hudson River
(and thereby New York City) as early as 1823, and with Lake Erie by 1825.
Bringing much business and trade to the area, the canal in fact caused Palmyra
to become a boom town of sorts.

Books were not lacking in the Palmyra-Manchester area, either. Even some Mormon writers seem to have done their homework concerning this, and in so doing have contradicted their less diligent colleagues. Milton V. Backman, Jr., for example, states that the Palmyra library was organized in the winter of 1822–1823, and that the Manchester library was organized in 1817. He further states that the T.C. Strong bookstore had an advertisement in the *Palmyra Register* during October of the year 1817 offering three hundred volumes for sale, and that in the year 1815 a store owner in the neighboring community of West Bloomfield advertised that he had more than a thousand volumes for sale.[9] To this can be added the fact that P. Tucker placed an advertisement in the *Wayne Sentinel* (published in Palmyra) of June 2, 1824, in which he listed by title approximately two hundred and fifty books that he had, among others, in his new bookstore.

Actually, Joseph by no means had to have access to a vast library in order to acquire the material he would have needed to write *The Book of Mormon*. He in fact would have found most of what he needed in the newspapers and in the popular books of the day. These sources frequently contained speculations about ancient American peoples and civilizations — particularly about the builders of the large man-made earthen mounds that the settlers found scattered from New York State to the Mississippi River. Some of these mounds were located near the Smith farm; popular speculations about them could easily have fired Joseph's imagination and made their way into *The Book of Mormon*.

Even Joseph's mother indicated that her son had an interest in ancient America several years before he brought out *The Book of Mormon*. The start of the process that was to lead to the "Nephite record" might be indicated by the following anecdote that she related. Her dating of the anecdote is somewhat vague, but the time frame appears to have been in 1823 or 1824:

> During our evening conversations, Joseph would occasionally give us some of the most amusing recitals that could be imagined. He would describe the ancient inhabitants of this continent, their dress, mode of travelling, and the animals upon which they rode; their cities, their buildings, with every particular; their mode of warfare; and also their religious worship. This he would do with as much ease, seemingly, as if he had spent his whole life with them.[10]

If this account is accurate, the "recitals" that Joseph gave his family would corroborate the tales of his fertile imagination that some of his acquaintances reported. The recitals might also indicate that, even at an early age, this "romancer of the first water" was familiar with the speculative literature about the Indian "antiquities."

The Book of Mormon is more than just a story about ancient America, of course. It also contains a large amount of religious thought. But religion and a knowledge of the Bible played an important part in the lives of early American country folk, and Joseph's family was no exception in this respect. Joseph's father appears to have been somewhat of a cynic as far as organized religion was concerned, but, even so, he was "a good deal of a smatterer in Scriptural knowledge." Joseph's mother had more of a conventional religious outlook than did her husband. She had a deep concern about the religious upbringing of her family, and she gave Joseph and his siblings instruction in religion during their early years. Moreover, as Orsamus Turner noted, Joseph himself caught "a spark of Methodism in the camp meeting." Joseph, remember, would have been no older than sixteen at the time.[11]

When Joseph grew somewhat older, his awareness of religion would have been heightened by some religious "excitement" that began to be felt in the Palmyra area in 1824. Characterized by revivals and mass conversions, this "excitement" was one of many upheavals in religion that occurred in early America. In western New York, the religious fervor brought on by these upheavals was so intense that many people became inured to religious emotion — so much so, that the roving evangelists began to call the area the "burned-over district." It was probably no coincidence that Joseph brought out his new "revelation" shortly after the occurrence of this particular religious excitement. He undoubtedly saw many examples of the emotional involvement that people could have with religion, and one might conjecture that his observations of the excitement would have influenced him in the composition of *The Book of Mormon.* Such a conjecture might be reinforced by the fact that one of the characters in Joseph's "history" of ancient America makes a "prophecy" about that particular religious excitement.[12]

The picture that one gets of Joseph during his early years, then, is of a young man with only a limited education, but of a young man with an inquisitive mind and an active imagination. Moreover, this young man lived in a time when speculations about ancient America were common in the press, and in a time when religious emotions ran high. When one puts everything together, it almost seems that something like *The Book of Mormon* would be a natural result.

But, of course, none of this is proof that Joseph was the author of *The Book of Mormon.* Someone else could have composed the book and Joseph might merely have made a show of "translating" it and presenting it to the world. It is also possible that Joseph jointly authored it with another person, perhaps even with more than one person.

All things considered, it seems quite likely that Joseph did have at least one collaborator. Of course, if there were any such collaboration, its participants would have carefully erected a screen to obscure it. Nevertheless, there are a few clues that might suggest that such an alliance did exist. As we noted in the Prologue, for example, Oliver Cowdery lived in Poultney, Vermont, at the same time that *View of the Hebrews* was published there. He would thus have had the chance to become acquainted with the book that was, as the evidence appears to indicate, to be the primary source of material for *The Book of Mormon.*

There are other clues that might suggest the existence of a collaboration. For example, in March of 1829, while he was in the process of dictating *The Book of Mormon,* Joseph took time out to give the following "revelation":

> ... I the Lord am God, and I have given these things unto my servant Joseph...; and he has a gift to translate the book, and I have commanded him that he shall pretend to no other gift, for I will grant him no other gift.[13]

This is the reading as it was given in *A Book of Commandments for the Government of the Church of Christ*, which was a collection of Joseph's "revelations" that was published in 1833, but which had been compiled as early as 1831. The strange thing about this "revelation" is that the "Lord" limited Joseph to only the "gift" of translating *The Book of Mormon*, and that the "Lord" commanded Joseph to "pretend" to no other gift. It would not have made much sense for Joseph to have deliberately limited himself in such a manner, especially if he were planning to organize a church. But this limitation might make sense if he had some partners who had imposed it upon him in order to prevent him from gathering too much power to himself. If this were the case, Joseph was later able to assert himself against these partners. Taking advantage of the fact that only a few copies of the *Book of Commandments* were salvaged after a mob set fire to the shop that was printing it, Joseph changed the revelation to read:

> ... I, the Lord, am God, and I have given these things unto you, my servant Joseph Smith, jun,...; And you have a gift to translate the plates and this is the first gift that I bestowed upon you, and I have commanded that you should pretend to no other gift, until my purpose is fulfilled in this; for I will grant you no other gift until it is finished.[14]

With this change in wording, Joseph was able to claim that he had received other gifts from the Lord after he finished "translating" *The Book of Mormon*. Relating to this, David Whitmer (who was deeply involved in the establishment of the church, but who later had a falling out with Joseph and joined a splinter Mormon sect) had this to say about the change:

> The way this revelation has been changed, ... it would appear that God had broken His word...; commanding Brother Joseph to pretend to no other gift but to translate the Book of Mormon, and then the Lord had changed and concluded to grant Joseph the gift of a Seer to the Church.[15]

Whitmer's objection to Joseph's changing the revelation might be more pointed if Whitmer himself had been "behind the curtain" as one of the collaborators who imposed the original revelation upon Joseph. Whitmer and Cowdery, moreover, were close friends during the period in which Joseph was "translating" *The Book of Mormon*.

So, if one has difficulty in believing that Joseph would have been able to compose *The Book of Mormon* entirely by himself, it can be kept in mind that he might have had some collaborators. Still, most likely it was Joseph, with his story-telling ability, who welded everything together to make *The Book of Mormon* whole. Furthermore, it was Joseph who dictated the book, and it was he who was described as its "Author and Proprietor" in its first edition (and in its initial advertisement). Finally, despite the hints suggesting that there was a collaboration, it cannot be proven that such a collaboration existed. For these reasons, and for the sake of simple convenience, we shall use Joseph Smith's standpoint when we investigate how the author of *The Book of Mormon* apparently derived his ideas from certain early nineteenth century sources.

In the final analysis, it is the evidence for the literary origins of *The Book of Mormon* that is important. This evidence is valid regardless of whether Joseph Smith had any collaborators.

Chapter 2

Visions and Revivals

The Book of Mormon by no means constitutes the sum of the Mormon religion. To survive as an institution, any religion requires a body of beliefs, doctrines, and ceremonies within a social organization that can attract and hold followers. Mormonism is no exception. Over the years, that American-born religion has accumulated a mass of its own distinctive religious accessories. Among non-Mormons, one of the better known Mormon doctrines has been polygamy, primarily because of the notoriety it received in the days of Brigham Young in Utah. Polygamy, however, is no longer sanctioned by the Utah church, though some small splinter Mormon sects and individuals still practice it. Some other doctrines include celestial marriage, baptism of the dead, and the so-called "Negro Doctrine." The Utah church has recently abrogated the Negro Doctrine, but still holds to the others mentioned.

Although certain other individuals played a part in its formation, Joseph Smith was the chief architect of the Mormon religious structure. He gave the church most of its beliefs and doctrines, and instituted most of its ceremonies. In particular, Joseph incorporated pre-eminently into the church hierarchy of belief the tenet that he, as a youth, experienced certain visions which supernaturally foreshadowed the coming forth of *The Book of Mormon* and the establishment of the church.

But if, as the evidence seems to indicate, *The Book of Mormon* was not produced by a supernatural means and was, instead, a product of Joseph's imagination, then such must also have been the case with the visions. And there is a substantial amount of evidence which seems to show that the visions were indeed a creation of Joseph's mind. What is particularly important about this evidence, however, is that it demonstrates the evolutionary nature of early Mormonism and resolves much of the confusion arising from the conflicting accounts of Joseph's early years. In order to prepare for our investigation of those years, we should examine this evidence.

In 1820, at the age of fourteen, Joseph was supposed to have experienced what came to be known as his "first" vision. Several years later, he dictated an account of the vision to one of his scribes and it was subsequently published in the *Times and Seasons* (a Mormon periodical) in 1842:

21

Some time in the second year after our removal to Manchester, there was in the place where we lived an unusual excitement on the subject of religion. It commenced with the Methodists, but soon became general among all the sects in the region of country, indeed the whole district of country seemed affected by it, and great multitudes united themselves to the different religious parties, which created no small stir and division amongst the people, some crying, "lo, here," and some "lo, there;" some were contending for the Methodist faith, some for the Presbyterians, and some for the Baptists....

I was at this time in my fifteenth year. My father's family was proselytized to the Presbyterian faith, and four of them joined that church, namely, my mother, Lucy, my brothers Hyrum [and] Samuel Harrison, and my sister Sophronia.[1]

Joseph went on to relate that he wanted to know which of the contending "sects" he should join and that he went into the woods to ask guidance of the Lord. There, he claimed, God the Father and Jesus the Son appeared to him:

It was ... early in the spring of eighteen hundred and twenty.... After I had retired into the place where I had previously designed to go, ... I kneeled down and began to offer up the desires of my heart to God. I had scarcely done so when immediately I was seized upon by some power which entirely overcame me.... I saw a pillar of light exactly over my head.... When the light rested upon me I saw two personages (whose brightness and glory defy all description) standing above me in the air. One of them spake unto me, calling me by name, and said, (pointing to the other,) "This is my beloved Son, hear him."

... I asked the personages who stood above me in the light, which of all the sects was right (for at this time it had never entered into my heart that all were wrong,) and which I should join. I was answered that I must join none of them, for they were all wrong, and the personage who addressed me said that all their creeds were an abomination in his sight; that those professors were all corrupt.... He again forbade me to join with any of them: and many other things did he say into me which I cannot write at this time.[2]

Finally, Joseph stated that the vision became the cause of great persecution against him:

I soon found however that my telling the story had excited a great deal of prejudice against me among professors of religion and was the cause of great persecution which continued to increase, and though I was an obscure boy only between fourteen and fifteen years of age and my circumstances in life such as to make a boy of no consequence in the world; yet men of high standing would take notice sufficient to excite the public mind against me and create a hot persecution, and this was common among all the sects: all united to persecute me.[3]

In his narrative, Joseph claimed that the followers of the various religious "sects" were "all united to persecute" him because he had told the story of the vision soon after he experienced it. But, in fact, it appears that no one at that time and for a long time thereafter was aware that he was supposed to have had the vision. In her 1945 biography of Joseph Smith, Fawn Brodie pointed out this inconsistency and presented the results of her research on the matter.[4] As far as she could determine, there was no mention of the 1820 vision in any of the writings or publications of either the proponents or the opponents of Mormonism until the year 1840. In that year, Orson Pratt gave an account of the vision in his pamphlet, *Remarkable Visions*, which was published in Scotland. Joseph did not publish the story of the vision himself until 1842. In fact, Joseph's 1842 publication could be considered the first publication of the vision in its full significance since Pratt did not include the words, "This is my beloved Son," in his 1840 account. Therefore, the 1842 publication was the first to intimate that Joseph had seen the Father and the Son in the vision.

For some time after Mrs. Brodie first published her findings, other researchers attempted to find a pre–1840 mention of the "first" vision. The wider the search reached, the more it appeared that Mrs. Brodie was correct in her conclusion. Considering the fact that the story of Joseph's "second" vision (as it was later called), was well known and frequently published during the 1830s, this lack of mention of the "first" vision in Mormon literature during the period before 1840 was quite remarkable and revealing. This situation is all the more remarkable in light of the fact that Joseph's "first" vision eventually came to be used by the church as evidence for its authority.

The non-Mormon literature of the period before 1840 also appears quite ignorant of the 1820 vision. By 1840, several anti-Mormon books, tracts, and articles had been published, and the newpaper editors of the day often provided accounts of the new religion to entertain or to inflame their readers. But in none of this material is there any mention of the 1820 vision. For that matter, there was apparently no mention of the "first" vision in any non-Mormon publication until 1843, and the source for that case was Joseph Smith himself in an interview with the editor who published it.[5]

Such a lack of mention of the vision is quite peculiar in light of the fact that Joseph claimed that "men of high standing would take notice sufficient to excite the public mind" against him because of his reporting the vision shortly after it supposedly occurred. If the public mind in 1820 was aware that Joseph claimed to have seen God and His Son, it seems unusual that no one made any mention of it for so many years, especially in light of the sentiment against the founder of Mormonism. If the story of this vision had been publicly known before 1840, the anti-Mormons of the time surely would have seized upon it as another example of Joseph's religious "imposture."

Eventually, about twenty years after Fawn Brodie published her findings, two previously unpublished accounts of the vision were uncovered in the archives of the Utah church. In 1965, Paul R. Cheesman, a Brigham Young University student, brought the first of these to light in a thesis that he wrote as an apparent rebuttal to Mrs. Brodie's argument. This account was written in 1832 and is in Joseph's own hand. Instead of supporting the validity of the vision as Joseph published it in 1842, though, it presents serious problems because of many differences it has from the later "official" version. For example, in this early version Joseph had the vision occur in his "sixteenth year" rather than when he was fourteen. Also, he made no mention of a religious "excitement" or revival. He related instead that he had studied the Bible from the age of twelve and had concluded from his study that none of the religious denominations of his day were right—this, even before he was supposed to have had the vision. But this is in flat contradiction with his later account. In that account he said that it never entered his heart that all of the denominations were wrong until the Lord told him so in the vision. Finally, instead of both God and Jesus appearing to Joseph in this version, only Jesus appeared.[6]

The other account of the first vision appears in a journal that was written in the year 1835, and is in the handwriting of one of Joseph's scribes. This version also has many variations from the "official" version. In this account, Joseph had the vision occur when he was fourteen years old. But again, there is no mention of a "religious excitement." And instead of God and His Son appearing in this version, two "personages" appear without being identified. One of these personages testified that "Jesus Christ is the Son of God." This would indicate that the two personages were not supposed to be God and Jesus. (In the same journal, there is a brief subsequent mention of the vision. It states simply that Joseph had a "visitation of angels when he was about 14 years old.")[7]

The problems that these accounts of the 1820 vision raise for Joseph's "testimony" far outweigh any support they may give it. Moreover, the finding of these accounts by no means demolishes Mrs. Brodie's basic argument. There has not yet been found any pre–1840 published mention of that vision or any other mention of it in any of the writings of any of the church members of the time. Far from being a matter of public record, it seems that any knoweldge of the "first" vision prior to 1840 was held solely within the private sphere of Joseph Smith and a few close associates.

Even after the story of the "first" vision was finally published in 1840, there was confusion among many Mormons over just what was Joseph's first vision. For several decades after Joseph's death, Mormon writers often described the 1823 vision of the angel who told Joseph about the plates, rather than the 1820 vision of God and His Son, as Joseph's first religious experience. In these cases, the writers seem to have been carrying on a tradition that had been prevalent among the Mormons during the 1830s.[8]

This lack of mention of the 1820 vision in any publication before 1840 is not the only problem about that vision. Many other difficulties arise when one tries to square Joseph's story of the vision with the events of the time and with other Mormon narratives. An analysis of the first Mormon history provides an example. This history was written by Oliver Cowdery with Joseph Smith's collaboration, and was published in installments in the *Latter Day Saints' Messenger and Advocate*. In the December, 1834, issue, Oliver related that the following occurred in the "fifteenth year" of Joseph's life:

> One Mr. Lane, a presiding Elder of the Methodist church, visited Palmyra, and vicinity.... There was a great awakening, or excitement raised on the subject of religion.... Large additions were made to the Methodist,

Presbyterian, and Baptist churches. — Mr. Lane's manner of communication was peculiarly calculated to awaken the intellect of the hearer, ... and in common with others, our brother's mind became awakened.

For a length of time the reformation seemed to move in a harmonious manner, but ... a general struggle was made by the leading characters of the different sects, for proselytes. Then strife seemed to take the place of that apparent union and harmony..., and a cry — I am right — you are wrong — was introduced in their stead.

In this general strife for followers, his mother, one sister, and two of his natural brothers were persuaded to unite with the Presbyterians.[9]

Oliver closed out this installment by describing Joseph as wondering which of the contending denominations to join. So far, this all sounds quite like Joseph's account of events leading up to the 1820 vision. But in the next installment, Oliver had this to say:

You will recollect that I mentioned the time of a religious excitement, in Palmyra and vicinity to have been in the 15th year of our brother J. Smith Jr's, age — that was an error in the type — it should have been the 17th. — You will please remember this correction, as it will be necessary for the full understanding of what will follow in time. This would bring the date down to the year 1823.[10]

So, according to Oliver, these events took place in the year 1823. Oliver went on to state:

... while this excitement continued, he continued to call upon the Lord in secret for a full manifestation of divine approbation, and for, to him, the all important information, if a Supreme Being did exist, to have an assurance that he was accepted of him.[11]

Here, in 1835, Oliver Cowdery related that in 1823 Joseph Smith was not sure that a Supreme Being existed. However, Joseph claimed later (in his account published in 1842) that he had met that Supreme Being face to face in an 1820 vision.

Oliver went on to relate that Joseph experienced a vision as a result of his calling upon the Lord. But the one that Oliver described was not the appearance of the Father and His Son. Rather, it was what was later to be known as the "second" vision — the 1823 appearance of the angel who told Joseph about the gold plates.

Oliver Cowdery's early history of the church, then, causes several difficulties for Joseph's later account of the 1820 vision. Not only did Oliver make no mention of the 1820 vision, he presented the 1823 vision as if it were Joseph's initial religious experience. Furthermore, Oliver gave the 1823 vision a setting that has a remarkable similarity to the setting of the 1820 vision that Joseph later described. Both accounts place the respective visions in the context of a religious "excitement" that caused Joseph to question which of the contending sects was right. Both accounts begin the excitement with the

Methodists and then have it spread to the Presbyterians and Baptists. Oliver also reported that Joseph's mother, a sister, and two brothers joined the Presbyterian Church during the 1823 revivals. Yet, in his later account, Joseph stated that these family members joined that church during the "excitement" which he said occurred in 1820.

Since Oliver wrote his history with Joseph's collaboration, Joseph at that time must have placed these events in the context of the 1823 vision. However, Joseph changed all this when he dictated his own history of the church a few years later. He transferred the original setting of the 1823 vision to 1820, placed it in the context of the vision that was supposed to have occurred then, and deleted it from the 1823 vision.

Because of the implications of these changes, Mormon writers have disputed that Joseph actually made them. Some of these writers have maintained that Joseph was not with Oliver during the period when the latter was composing his history. Oliver, they say, was therefore working without the necessary information and consequently made errors. But this goes against Oliver's clear statements that Joseph *was* assisting with the history.[12] Furthermore, a study of the *History of the Church* shows that the two men were frequently together during the period. In any event, if Oliver's history had such gross "errors," why then did Joseph not give a correction in a subsequent issue of the *Messenger and Advocate*? His not having done so indicates that Oliver's history must have met with his approval at that time.

Some Mormon writers have tried other ways of explaining the discrepancies. One approach they have taken has been to propose that there were actually two revivals: one in 1820, and another in 1823. This, they seemed to feel, would explain the similarities in the two accounts. But Wesley P. Walters, a Presbyterian minister who has done much research on Mormonism, published a study which "conclusively" proves that "the revival did not occur until the fall of 1824 and that no revival occurred between 1819 and 1823 in the Palmyra vicinity."

There are several arguments by which Pastor Walters advances his case, and we shall mention some of the more important ones.[13] First, Oliver Cowdery happened to state that the "religious excitement," or the "great awakening" had started among the Methodists when Mr. Lane, a presiding Elder of the Methodist Church, visited Palmyra and initiated the revival. Mr. Walters notes that "in ... 1819, Rev. Lane ... was assigned to serve the Susquehanna District in Central Pennsylvania, over 150 miles from Palmyra." The Reverend Lane "served in this area for 5 years and not until July of 1824 did he receive an appointment to serve as Presiding Elder of the Ontario District in which Palmyra is located." Pastor Walters also came across the Reverend Lane's own account of the revival, written while the revival was still in progress, and published in the *Methodist Magazine* only a few months later. From that account, the revival began in 1824, not in 1823 or in 1820.[14]

Oliver Cowdery also noted that the revival fever spread from the Methodists to the Baptists and the Presbyterians. Pastor Walters makes note of some narratives that William Smith, Joseph's brother, gave of the revival. William stated that not only Reverend Lane took part in the revival, but also a Reverend Stockton of the Presbyterian Church. Pastor Walters notes that

Reverend Benjamin B. Stockton was pastor of a church in Skaneatea, New York, from 1818 to 1822: "The earliest contemporary reference to his ministry in the Palmyra area is in connection with a wedding November 26, 1823, just a week after Alvin Smith's death.... He was not installed as pastor of the Presbyterian Church until February 18, 1824." Alvin Smith, incidentally, was one of Joseph Smith's brothers.

The 1824 revival brought "large additions" (to use the term Oliver Cowdery used for his 1823 revival) to the various denominations. Pastor Walters verified this by examining the church records. But, concerning Joseph's description of the 1820 vision, Mr. Walters states the following:

> When we turn to the year 1820, however, the "great multitudes" are conspicuously missing. The Presbyterian Church in Palmyra certainly experienced no awakening that year. Reverend James Hotchkin's history records revivals for that church as occurring in the years 1817, 1824, 1829, etc., but there is nothing for the year 1820. The record of Presbytery and Synod give the same picture.... Since these reports always rejoice at any sign of a revival in the churches, it is inconceivable that a great awakening had occurred in their Palmyra congregation and gone completely unnoticed.
>
> The Baptist Church records also show clearly that they had no revival in 1820, for the Palmyra congregation gained only six by baptism, while the neighboring Baptist churches of Lyons, Canandaigua, and Farmington showed net losses of 4, 5, and 9 respectively....
>
> The Methodist figures, though referring to the entire circuit, give the same results, for they show net losses of 23 for 1819, 6 for 1820, and 40 for 1821. This hardly fits Joseph Smith's description of "great multitudes" being added to the churches of the area. In fact, the Mormon Prophet could hardly have picked a poorer year in which to place his revival as far as the Methodists were concerned. For some time prior to 1820 a sharp controversy had existed in the denomination, which in the Genesee Conference had resulted in a decline and a "loss of spirituality" throughout the entire conference....
>
> Another significant lack of information concerning an 1820 revival lies in the area of the religious press. The denominational magazines of that day were full of reports of revivals, some even devoting separate sections to them. These publications carried more than a dozen glowing reports of the revival that occurred at Palmyra in the winter of 1816–17. Likewise, the 1824–25 revival is covered in a number of reports. These magazines, however, while busily engaged in reporting revivals [elsewhere] during the 1819 to 1821 period, contain not a single mention of any revival taking place in the Palmyra area during this time. It is unbelievable that every one of the denominations which Joseph Smith depicts as affected by an 1820 revival could have completely overlooked the event. Even the Palmyra newspaper, while reporting revivals at several places in the state, has no mention whatever of any revival in Palmyra or vicinity in either 1819 or 1820. The only reasonable explanation for this massive silence is that no revival occurred in the Palmyra area in 1820.[15]

Even if it could be shown that a revival had occurred in the Palmyra area in 1820, difficulties for Joseph's first vision would remain. There are too many other discrepancies. For example, Joseph stated that his mother, a sister, and two of his brothers joined the Presbyterian Church in 1820 as a result of the religious "excitement." But Joseph's brother, William, stated:

> In 1822 and in 1823, the people in our neighborhood were very much stirred up with regard to religious matters by the preaching of a Mr. Lane, an Elder of the Methodist Church, and celebrated throughout the country as a "great revival preacher."
>
> My mother, who was a very pious woman and much interested in the welfare of her children, both here and hereafter, made use of every means which her parental love could suggest, to get us engaged in seeking for our soul's salvation.... She prevailed on us to attend the meetings.... This extraordinary excitement prevailed not only in our neighborhood but throughout the whole country. Great numbers were converted. It extended from the Methodists to the Baptists, from them to the Presbyterians....
>
> After the excitement had subsided, in a measure, each sect began to beat up for volunteers.... The consequence was that my mother [and] my brothers Hyrum and Samuel ... joined the Presbyterian Church. Joseph, then about seventeen years of age, had become seriously inclined, though not "brought out," as the phrase was, began to reflect and inquire, which of all these sects was right.[16]

William placed this revival in 1823 rather than in 1824, but this was probably to conform to Joseph's original scenario for the second vision. Still, it would seem that, according to William's recollection, the formal enrollment of the family members in the Presbyterian Church was due to the revival started by Reverend Lane—a revival that historically occurred in 1824. Further, William related that the seventeen-year-old Joseph asked which of the sects was right; but according to Joseph in his later account of the first vision, he had been told at the age of fourteen by the Lord that none of them were right.

Joseph's mother herself indicated that she and the others did not join the Presbyterian Church until some time after 1820. According to her:

> Shortly after the death of Alvin, a man commenced laboring in the neighborhood, to effect a union of the different churches, in order that all might be agreed, and thus worship God with one heart and with one mind.
>
> This seemed about right to me, and I felt much inclined to join in with them; in fact, the most of the family appeared quite disposed to unite with their numbers; but Joseph, from the first, utterly refused even to attend their meetings, saying, "Mother, I do not wish to prevent your going to meeting, or any of the rest of the family's; or your joining any church you please; but do not ask me to join them. I can take my Bible, and go into the woods, and learn more in two hours, than you can learn at meeting in two years, if you should go all the time."
>
> To gratify me, my husband attended some two or three meetings, but peremptorily refused going to any more, either for my gratification, or any other person's.[17]

In the preliminary manuscript for her biography, Joseph's mother made some comments not in the final version that provide additional information and clarify certain points. She related the story of Alvin's death, then:

> About this time their was a great revival in religion and the whole neighborhood was very much aroused to the subject and we among the rest flocked to the meeting house to see if their was a word of comfort for us that might releive our overcharged feelings[.][18]

Then, after describing what Joseph had said about going into the woods with his Bible, Lucy related the following:

> My husband also declined attending the meetings after the first but did not object to myself and such of the children as choose going or becoming church members if we wished[.][19]

In these narratives, Joseph's mother makes it clear that she and others in her family did not become formal members of the Presbyterian church until after the revival had begun, and that did not take place until after Alvin's death. She indicated that it was because of Alvin's death that some family members, including herself, subsequently took an interest in the revival and joined the church. Since the date of Alvin's death was November 19, 1823, Joseph's mother and the others had to have joined the church after that date.[20] This would have put these events roughly into 1824, the year in which Wesley P. Walters placed the revival from his examination of contemporary records.

The quoted accounts by Joseph's mother reveal some other interesting facts. She stated that her husband attended only "two or three meetings" and refused to go to any more, and that Joseph refused to attend any meetings at all. She did not say that Joseph refused to attend the meetings because he had received a commandment from the Lord in 1820 that he not join any of the "sects." If he did refuse to attend the meetings because of such a commandment, she surely would have mentioned it. Why, then, did Joseph refuse to attend the meetings? And why did Joseph's father refuse to go to any more after he had attended only "two or three"?

Something that William Smith said possibly provides an answer to those questions. During an interview, William was asked why Joseph sought guidance as to which church to join. William answered:

> Why there was a joint revival in the neighborhood between the Baptists, Methodists and Presbyterians and they had succeeded in stirring up quite a feeling, and after the meeting the question arose which church should have the converts. Reverend Stockton was the president of the meeting and suggested that it was their meeting and under their care and they had a church and they ought to join the Presbyterians, but as father did not like Reverend Stockton very well, our folks hesitated....[21]

During this same interview, William had already mentioned why his father did not like Reverend Stockton and the Presbyterian Church:

He did not like it because a Reverend Stockton had preached my brother's
funeral sermon and intimated very strongly that he had gone to hell, for
Alvin was not a church member, but he was a good boy and my father
did not like it.[22]

This seems to be the reason why Joseph's father, after going to only two
or three meetings to gratify his wife, refused to attend any more. The Reverend Stockton's intimations about Joseph's dead brother might have affected
Joseph even more strongly. The minister's lack of Christian charity towards
Alvin could have caused Joseph to refuse to go to any meetings and to tell his
mother, "I can take my Bible, and go into the woods and learn more in two
hours, than you can learn at meeting in two years, if you should go all the
time."

The important point about William's statement is that it confirms
Lucy's narrative that the revival and the enrollment of the family members in
the Presbyterian Church did not take place until after Alvin's death. So despite
Joseph's later statement that the family members joined the church as a result of a revival supposedly occurring in 1820, it seems that they actually
joined that church because of an 1824 revival. Since the enrollment of the
family in the church plays a central role in the setting that Joseph described for
his first vision, this discrepancy undermines the whole foundation of that vision.

In his narrative of the 1820 vision, Joseph claimed that the Lord had
told him not to join any of the "sects," for they were all an "abomination" to
Him. If Joseph did have that vision, then his mother and the two brothers,
Hyrum and Samuel, apparently did not agree with the Lord; they not only
joined the Presbyterian Church, but remained active in it until — as the "Session Records" of the church show — about September of the year 1828, when
they began to "neglect worship and the sacrament of the Lord's supper."[23]

If the Lord did tell Joseph that all sects were an abomination, the rest of
the family would have had reservations about joining an institution that was
so harshly condemned in a divine visitation. Their apparent disregard for the
sentiments of the Lord is heightened by the fact that they remained active in
the church until September of 1828 — a full year after Joseph supposedly
received the gold plates that would bring the "true" church of God to the
world. All of this seems to indicate that Joseph did not convey to his family a
divinely revealed message that would have inhibited them from joining the
Presbyterian Church or from remaining members in it for as long as they did.

If it was unusual for his family to take lightly the word of the Lord, it
was even more so for Joseph himself. We have already noted that by 1822
Joseph had caught "a spark of Methodism in the camp meeting, away down in
the woods, on the Vienna road." Since the Methodists did not acquire that
property until July of 1821, Joseph's "spark of Methodism" can probably be
assigned after that date.[24] This would indicate that Joseph became involved
with one of the "sects" after the Lord supposedly told him not to join any of
them.

That was not the only time Joseph had taken part in a church after purportedly experiencing his first vision. Fayette Lapham, a local resident,
mentioned that Joseph had once gone to the Baptist Church. Lapham related

that around 1830 he had "heard that some ancient records had been discovered that would throw some new light on the subject of religion." Being interested, he and a friend set out to investigate. Arriving at the residence of the Smith family and finding that Joseph was not there, they asked Joseph's father to tell them the story of the discovery of the plates. The elder Smith complied, and while doing so described some early events in his son's life, including the digging of a well that it is known Joseph had dug in 1822. About two years after digging the well (Lapham related the father as saying), Joseph "became concerned as to his future state of existence, and was baptized, becoming a member of the Baptist Church."[25] Two years after 1822 would be 1824, the year of the revivals started by Mr. Lane.

Joseph's connection with the Baptist Church seems to be verified by another source. In an article about the history of the Manchester Baptist Church which was partly based upon reminiscences of conversations with some old Manchester townsmen (including his grandfather), Mitchell Bronk related the following:

> Writers on Mormonism have paid too much attention to Palmyra and not enough to Manchester in connection with Joe Smith — my old townsmen never dignified him with "Joseph!" But Gold Bible Hill (Cumorah, forsooth!) is in Manchester, not Palmyra, and the Smith family lived in our town.... What concerns us here, however, is the fact that Joe occasionally attended the stone church; especially the revivals, sitting with the crowd — the "sinners" — up in the gallery. Not a little of Mormon theology accords with the preaching of Elder Shay.[26]

So it appears that Joseph did join one of the sects during the 1824 revival. Like his father, Joseph apparently could not reconcile himself to Presbyterianism because of Reverend Stockton's lack of charity to Alvin. Nevertheless, it seems that Joseph did not rule out all of the established denominations, despite the supposed commandment from the Lord that he not join any of the sects. In addition there is even stronger evidence that Joseph took steps to join the Methodist Episcopal Church during the summer of 1828. (This will be discussed in a later chapter).

In contrast with accounts of the 1820 vision, those of the 1823 experience were published comparatively early, though still not until many years afterwards. According to a statement he published in 1842, Joseph went to bed on the evening of the twenty-first of September, 1823, and prayed to be forgiven for his sins and follies. He asked for a manifestation that he might know his standing before God — then:

> I discovered a light appearing in the room, which continued to increase until the room was lighter than at noon-day, when immediately a personage appeared at my bedside, standing in the air.... He called me by name, and said unto me that he was a messenger sent from the presence of God to me, and that his name was Nephi; that God had a work for me to do.... He said there was a book deposited, written upon gold plates, giving an account of the former inhabitants of this continent, and the source whence

they sprang.... Also that there were two stones in silver bows, and these stones fastened to a breastplate, constituted what is called the Urim and Thummim, deposited with the plates, and the possession and use of these stones were what constituted Seers in ancient or former times, and that God had prepared them for the purpose of translating the book.... Again, he told me that when I got those plates of which he had spoken (for the time that they should be obtained was not then fulfiilled) I should not show them to any person, neither the breastplate, with the Urim and Thummin, only to those to whom I should be commanded to show them....[27]

There are several questions concerning the 1823 vision. In the above version, the angel who visited Joseph was supposed to be Nephi, one of the characters in *The Book of Mormon*. In other accounts the angel was supposed to be Moroni, another of the characters. It is Moroni's name that is in current use, though for many years after Joseph's death there was some confusion in the matter.

The many variations in the accounts of the second vision show that it, like the first vision, evolved over the years. The biography that Joseph's mother wrote provides a good example. In her preliminary manuscript, rather than describing the two as distinct events, Lucy Smith told of a single vision that Joseph was supposed to have experienced. Lucy's report of this vision contains a confused combination of elements present in other versions of both the first and the second visions, as well as of elements found in no other account. Here is her narration of the story:

> In the spring after we moved onto the farm we were sitting till quite late conversing upon the subject of the diversity of churches that had risen up in the world and the many thousand opinions in existence as to the truths contained in scripture.... After he ceased conversation [Joseph] went to bed and was pondering in his mind which of the churches were the true one, but he had not laid there long until he saw a bright light enter the room where he lay. He looked up and saw an angel of the Lord standing by him. The angel spoke: "I perceive that you are enquiring in your mind which is the true church. There is not a true church on Earth. No, not one, and has not been since Peter took the keys of the melchisedic priesthood after the order of God into the kingdom of heaven. The churches that are now upon the Earth are all man made churches. There is a record for you, but you cannot get it until you learn to keep the commandments of God.... The record is ... on the Hill of cumorah 3 miles from this place...."[28]

Notice that, instead of the Lord telling Joseph that there is no true church on the earth, an angel tells him. Moreover, that same angel tells him about the ancient records buried in the hill Cumorah. Lucy could have been confused by trying to make sense of her recollections of Joseph's altering stories of the visions. She apparently gave up the effort because, in the published version of her biography, she quoted Joseph's accounts of the two visions that had appeared in the *Times and Seasons* in 1842. This might have been not so much her doing as that of Martha Knowlton Coray, her collaborator, who may have realized that Lucy's variant vision would cause some difficulties.

From this, one would gather that even the members of Joseph's own family had no clear memories of being told about the visions at the time Joseph was supposed to have experienced them. The descriptions that the family gave of the visions appear to have been picked up piecemeal as Joseph altered his stories over a period of time. If Joseph actually did have these visions, the testimony of his family would have afforded a clearer and more convincing witness than the record seems to indicate.

To the changing statements of the family, we can add those made by several individuals who knew Joseph while he was living in Palmyra. In narrating what Joseph and his family told them before the publication of *The Book of Mormon*, many of these acquaintances said that no religious significance had been attached to the "finding" of the plates at first. Moreover, soon after the publication of *The Book of Mormon*, the editor of the Palmyra *Reflector* stated that it was "well known that Jo Smith never pretended to have any communion with angels, until a long period after the *pretended* finding of his book."[29]

From such evidence, we can come to some reasonable conclusions about how Joseph may have developed his stories of the visions. Evidence to be presented in later chapters will indicate that Joseph initially used a nonreligious explanation of how he came by the plates for *The Book of Mormon*. For that matter, *The Book of Mormon* itself apparently began as a nonreligious book. It was only later, after he began to conceive of turning the book into a new revelation from God, that he put forth a religious explanation of how he came by the plates.

Even after turning *The Book of Mormon* into a religious book, Joseph continued to develop his stories of how he came to be the Mormon prophet. The 1823 vision apparently sufficed for the early church. But, as his stature as a religious leader grew, Joseph could have come to feel that he needed a greater manifestation of his authority. Therefore, during the 1830s he began to work up a new vision story. The end of the decade could have seemed the time to present it to his followers. He was well established then as a religious leader and far removed from his New York State hometown where the vision was supposed to have taken place. He could have felt that the realities of time and place gave him the license and the liberty to present a story from his youth that would enhance his position.

To present this new story, Joseph had to change the setting of the already established vision. This was necessary because he had presented the 1823 vision as his initial religious experience and he wanted his new vision to have taken place earlier. Therefore, Joseph removed from the 1823 vision those events that were supposed to have been the cause of his initial overture to the Lord—the revival and the resultant controversy over which was the correct church—and placed them in the setting of his new vision. This explains why the setting of the 1823 vision that Oliver Cowdery described is similar to the setting of the 1820 vision Joseph later described. Joseph also apparently felt that he had to clear a path prior to telling his followers the story of the new vision. Perhaps that was why he had Pratt publish a version of the story in Scotland and why he himself told a version of it in the so-called "Wentworth Letter" in the

March 1, 1842, *Times and Seasons,* but giving no indication in either of these versions that he had seen the Father and the Son.

The alterations that Joseph made in the stories of the visions illustrate the changes that he made in several aspects of Mormonism. He undoubtedly sought to strengthen the early church with some of these, but instead weakened it. Many of Joseph's followers seem to have wondered how God could be so inconsistent, and the resultant controversies caused dissent within the church and helped to shape the events that led to Joseph's early death. The Mormon prophet might have done better if he had been more consistent—but then, he would not have been nearly so interesting.

Chapter 3

The Prophet in His Own Country

For the past century and a half, there has been considerable disagreement over what Joseph Smith did in the years before he brought out *The Book of Mormon*. Mormon believers, of course, have accepted what Joseph said about his activities during those years; i.e., that he had experienced certain visions and that he was preparing himself for his divine mission. On the other hand, those not so willing to accept these things have charged that Joseph was engaged in more mundane and less respectable undertakings. Not willing to let such charges pass unanswered, the believers in turn have accused Joseph's detractors of inventing stories to slander and persecute the Prophet.

One of the problems in resolving that dispute has been a scarcity of documented evidence that would reveal exactly what Joseph was doing during the years in question. It was only after Joseph published *The Book of Mormon* that belated accounts of his early years began to appear.

One of the more important sources appeared in 1834. This was Eber D. Howe's *Mormonism Unvailed*, which was one of the first of many anti-Mormon books. Besides giving his report of the rise of Mormonism, Howe also included several affidavits and statements about Joseph that had been collected from residents of the Palmyra area and from Joseph's in-laws and acquaintances in the Harmony (now Oakland), Pennsylvania, area. (Joseph married Emma Hale, of Harmony, in January of 1827, and spent some time there.) This material could not be considered flattering to the Mormon prophet. For example, the following is an excerpt from a statement that was jointly signed by fifty-one citizens of Palmyra:

> We, the undersigned, have been acquainted with the Smith family, for a number of years, while they resided near this place, and we have no hesitation in saying, that we consider them destitute of that moral character, which ought to entitle them to the confidence of any community. They were particularly famous for visionary projects, spent much of their time in digging for money which they pretended was hid in the earth; and to this day, large excavations may be seen in the earth, not far from their residence, where they used to spend their time digging for hidden treasures. Joseph Smith, Senior, and his son Joseph, were in particular considered entirely destitute of *moral character and addicted to vicious habits*.[1]

35

One of Joseph's neighbors, Parley Chase, made the following affidavit:

> I was acquainted with the family of Joseph Smith, Sen., both before and since they became Mormons, and feel free to state that not one of the male members of the Smith family were entitled to any credit, whatsoever. They were lazy, intemperate and worthless men, very much addicted to lying. In this they frequently boasted of their skill. Digging for money was their principal employment. In regard to their Gold Bible speculation, they scarcely ever told two stories alike. The Mormon Bible is said to be a revelation from God, through Joseph Smith Jr., his Prophet, and this same Joseph Smith Jr. to my knowledge, bore the reputation among his neighbors of being a liar. The foregoing can be corroborated by all his former neighbors.[2]

Besides the above statements, there are others in Howe's book. In all, more than ninety individuals who knew Joseph gave, or witnessed, statements concerning his character and activities. Some of these were quite detailed.

At this point, it would be proper to ask whether the statements can be given any credence. The statements have not been without criticism from Mormons, of course. Some Mormon writers have charged that Philastus Hurlbut, an apostate Mormon who collected some of the statements for Howe, had fabricated them for the signers.[3] But this is not very likely. In the first place, most of the statements were sworn to before judges or justices of the peace. Secondly, Hurlbut did not collect the statements from Joseph's in-laws and acquaintances in the Harmony, Pennsylvania, area. These statements were first published in the May 1, 1834, *Susquehanna Register*, and subsequently republished by Howe in *Mormonism Unvailed*. The statement that Joseph's father-in-law, Isaac Hale, made is particularly important since it deals with several significant events leading up to the production of *the Book of Mormon*.

Since the signers of the statements were convinced that *The Book of Mormon* was a hoax perpetrated by Joseph Smith to enrich himself, it is reasonable to suppose that they might have exaggerated any idiosyncrasies that Joseph and his family had displayed. The problem that we have to deal with is finding out just how much exaggeration, if any, there is in the statements. Fortunately, there is a large amount of independent evidence, much of it recently found, to help us in discerning the facts.

To begin with, Howe's collection of statements was not the first to give such critical descriptions of Joseph Smith and his family. For example, in the years 1830 and 1831, Obadiah Dogberry,[4] the editor of the Palmyra *Reflector*, published several articles which give support to the statements that Howe later published in his 1834 book. Moreover, Dogberry's articles can hardly be said to have been colored or fabricated by Hurlbut.

In one of his articles, Dogberry stated:

> Joseph Smith, senior, the father of the personage of whom we are now writing, had by misfortune or otherwise been reduced to extreme poverty before he migrated to western New York.... We have never been able to

learn that any of the family were ever noted for much else than ignorance and stupidity, to which might be added, so far as it may respect the elder branch, a propensity to superstition and a fondness for everything *marvelous.*

We have been credibly informed that the mother of the prophet had connected herself with several religious societies before her present illumination; ... but how far the father of the prophet, ever advanced in these particulars, we are not precisely informed, it however appears quite certain that the prophet himself never made any serious pretentions to religion until his late pretended revelation.

We are not able to determine whether the elder Smith was ever concerned with money digging transactions previous to his emigration from Vermont, or not, but it is a well authenticated fact that soon after his arrival here he evinced a firm belief in the existence of hidden treasures, and that this section of country abounded in them. — He also revived, or in other words propagated the vulgar, yet popular belief that these treasures were held in charge by some *evil* spirit, which was supposed to be either the DEVIL himself, or some one of his most trusty favorites.[5]

In another article, Dogberry stated:

It is well known that Jo Smith never pretended to have any communion with angels, until a long period after the *pretended* finding of his book, and that the juggling of himself or father, went no further than the pretended faculty of seeing wonders in a "peep stone," and the occasional interview with the spirit, supposed to have custody of hidden treasures....[6]

In the various descriptions of Joseph Smith and his family, the tag "money digger" frequently appears. This term was applied to persons who tried to dig up treasures that supposedly had been buried throughout the land by pirates, Spaniards, or the ancient inhabitants of the country. In the Palmyra area, there was a group of men, including several members of the Smith family, who spent much of their time in this pursuit. Joseph, in particular, played a key role in these money digging operations. His job was to "search" for the treasures by using a technique similar to water dowsing, except that he used a "peepstone" instead of a forked stick. By placing the peepstone in his hat and gazing at it much like a fortune teller would gaze into a crystal ball, he would "locate" the treasure and direct the diggers where to dig.

Mormons have usually denied that Joseph ever searched for buried treasures in such a manner. The stories of his using a peepstone, they have frequently said, were simply fabrications designed to malign the Prophet and to discredit their religion. Nevertheless, the evidence shows overwhelmingly that Joseph did use a peepstone to search for buried treasures. Moreover, much of this evidence provides important information about Joseph's character and about the origin of *The Book of Mormon*. Because the origin and development of *The Book of Mormon* were so closely entangled with Joseph's money digging activities, a knowledge of them is necessary in order to understand how *The Book of Mormon* came to be.

From many of the statements given, it would appear that it was Joseph's father who first started the family in the business of money digging. The proclivity of the elder Smith in this respect was well illustrated by one of his neighbors:

> I, Peter Ingersoll, first became acquainted with the famly of Joseph Smith, Sen. in the year of our Lord, 1822. — I lived in the neighborhood of said family, until about 1830; during which time the following facts came under my observation.
>
> The general employment of the family, was digging for money. I had frequent invitations to join the company, but always declined being one of their number.... I was once ploughing near the house of Joseph Smith, Sen., about noon, he requested me to walk with him a short distance from his house, for the purpose of seeing whether a mineral rod would work in my hand.... When we arrived near the place at which he thought there was money, he cut a small witch hazel bush and gave me direction how to hold it. He then went off some rods, and told me to say to the rod, "work to the money," which I did.... While the old man was standing off some rods, throwing himself into various shapes, I told him the rod did not work.... On my return, I picked up a small stone and was carelessly tossing it from one hand to the other.... He put the stone ... into his hat, and stooping forward, he bowed and made sundry manuevers, quite similar to those of a stool pigeon. At length he said, in a faint voice, "if you knew what I had seen, you would believe." ... His son Alvin then went through with the same performance, which was equally disgusting.[7]

Contemporary newspaper accounts of the digging activities would, of course, verify the later reports. Unfortunately, there are none that are known. Still, despite this lack, there is other evidence from sufficiently varied sources which leaves little doubt that Joseph did engage in such an activity. One of the most recently found examples is a letter that was written by the Reverend John Sherer of Colesville, New York. It was addressed to the American Home Missionary Society, and has a date of November 18, 1830. The following is an extract:

> I will relate a circumstance that has given me pain — A member of the church in Sandford, a young female, has renounced her connexion with the church, and joined another in Colesville founded by Joseph Smith. This man has been known, in these parts, for some time, as a kind of juggler, who has pretended, through a glass, to see money underground &c &c.[8]

Colesville is in south central New York some distance from Palmyra and near Bainbridge where Joseph spent some time. Thus this letter presents an independent verification of Joseph's money digging activities by showing that those activities were not restricted to the Palmyra-Manchester area.

This letter is also important because it is one of the earliest known documents to mention Joseph's use of a "glass" to look for buried money. (Other documents indicate that Joseph liked to call his peepstone a glass.) It predates Obadiah Dogberry's *Reflector* articles describing Joseph's use of the peepstone. That series of articles began in February of 1831. A series of *Reflector* articles in June and July of 1830 referred to Joseph's money digging, but did not go into detail about methodology.

The company of money diggers that the Smiths belonged to was not unique. Newspapers of the time occasionally gave accounts of other money diggers and also of individuals known as "seers" who made their living by this profession. Such a seer's usual method of operation was to hire himself out to those interested in finding buried treasures on their land. One of these seers seems to have had some influence upon Joseph. In one of his articles in the Palmyra *Reflector*, Obadiah Dogberry mentioned a "juggler" named Walters who was employed by the local company of money diggers. "Juggler" then denoted someone who manipulated people for fraudulent purposes. The current term would be "con man."

> ...and it also is equally well known that a vagabond fortune-teller by the name of Walters, who then resided in the town of Sodus, and was once committed to the jail of this county for *juggling*, was the constant companion and bosom friend of these money digging imposters.
>
> There remains but little doubt, in the minds of those at all acquainted with these transactions, that Walters, who was sometimes called the conjurer, and was paid three dollars per day for his services by the money diggers in the neighborhood, first suggested to Smith the idea of finding a book. Walters, the better to carry on his own deception with those ignorant & deluded people who employed him, had procured an old copy of Cicero's Orations, in the Latin language, out of which he read long and loud to his credulous hearers, uttering at the same time an unintelligible jargon, which he would afterwards pretend to interpret, and explain, as a record of the former inhabitants of America, and a particular account of the numerous situations where they had deposited their treasures previous to their final extirpation.[9]

In June and July of 1830, Dogberry had published a parody of *The Book of Mormon*, which he called the "Book of Pukei." This parody began:

> And it came to pass in the latter days, that ... the idle and slothful said one to another, let us send for Walters the Magician, who has strange books, and deals with familiar spirits; peradventure he will inform us where the *Nephites* hid their *treasures....*

Walters came and set the "idle and the slothful" to digging until they "became weary of their mighty labors" and decided that they had been deceived. Walters, hearing this, slipped away "lest the *strong* arm of the law" should bring him to justice.

> Now the rest of the acts of the magician, how his *mantle* fell upon the *prophet* Jo Smith, Jun. and how Jo. made a league with the *spirit*, who afterwards turned out to be an angel, and how he obtained the "Gold Bible,"

Spectacles, and breast plate—will they not be faithfully recorded in the Book of Pukie?

And it came to pass, that when the mantle of Walters the Magician had fallen upon Joseph, sirnamed the prophet, who was the son of Joseph; that the "idle and slothful" gathered themselves together, in the presence of Joseph, and said unto him, "lo! we will be thy servants forever...."[10]

The sarcasm of the parody aside, Dogberry had suggested that the mantle of Walters the juggler had fallen upon Joseph. Whether so or not, Joseph did use his peepstone to direct the money diggers where to dig as Walters had done.

Joseph might well have felt it reasonable to take the mantle of Walters upon himself. Since his father had recruited Joseph and his brothers to assist during the treasure hunting, it is possible that his faculty with a peepstone began in part with his desire to let others do the hard digging. Alva Hale, who was to become Joseph's brother-in-law, told his cousin, Joseph Lewis, something about one of Joseph's money digging expeditions which suggests that such might have been the case. Hale said that:

Joe Smith never handled one shovel of earth in those diggings. All that Smith did was to peep with stone and hat, and give directions where and how to dig, and when and where the enchantment moved the treasure. That Smith said if he should work with his hands at digging there, he would lose the power to see with the stone.[11]

These particular diggings took place in the vicinity of Harmony, Pennsylvania, near where Hale lived.

From the numerous statements given by those who were familiar with his treasure hunting, Joseph acquired quite a reputation for his work, but he was not particularly successful at enriching those who hired him. His usual reason for not finding the treasure was that it was under the protection of a "spirit" or a "devil" who "moved" it through the ground to keep it away from the diggers. A similar concept appears in *The Book of Mormon*:

Yea, we have hid up our treasures, and they have slipped away from us because of the curse of the land. O that we had repented in the day that the word of the Lord came unto us; for behold the land is cursed, and all things are become slippery, and we cannot hold them. Behold we are surrounded by demons....[12]

This is another example indicating that Joseph put something of his own character and environment into *The Book of Mormon*.

Among the numerous other accounts of Joseph's use of a peepstone in the money digging operations is this detailed description of his methodology given by Joseph Capron:

The family of Smiths held Joseph Jr. in high estimation on account of some supernatural power, which he was supposed to possess. This power he pretended to have received through the medium of a stone of peculiar quality. The stone was placed in hat, in such a manner as to exclude all light, except that which emanated from the stone itself. This light of the stone, he pretended, enabled him to see anything he wished. Accordingly he discovered ghosts, infernal spirits, mountains of gold and silver, and many other invaluable treasures deposited in the earth. He would often tell his neighbors of his wonderful discoveries, and urge them to embark in the money digging business. Luxory and wealth were to be given to all who would adhere to his council.... I will mention one circumstance.... The sapient Joseph discovered, north west of my house, a chest of gold watches; but as they were in the possession of the evil spirit, it required skill and stratagem to obtain them. Accordingly, orders were given to stick a parcel of large stakes in the ground, several rods around, in a circular form ... over the spot where the treasures were deposited. ... Samuel F. Laurence, with a drawn sword in his hand, marched around to guard any assault which his Satanic majesty might be disposed to make. Meantime, the rest of the company were busily employed in digging for the watches. They worked as usual till quite exhausted. But, in spite of their defender, Laurence, and their bulwark of stakes, the devil came off victorious, and carried away the watches.[13]

Thus, Joseph Smith, in the years before he published *The Book of Mormon*, gave his neighbors and acquaintances impressions of himself that were quite different from his own later descriptions of those years. These contemporary witnesses did not see him as a religious young man who had visions of God and his Son, and who was preparing himself for the day when he would receive a new revelation. They saw instead a young schemer who sent superstitious money diggers after will-o'-the-wisp treasures.

Joseph's treasure hunting operations might at first seem simply ludicrous, but it is incongruous for the founder of a religion to have played upon the superstitions of credulous money diggers as did Joseph. Moreover, Joseph eventually embarked upon a money digging foray that got him into serious trouble. As we shall see, some recently found evidence relating to this trouble now seems to prove conclusively that he did use a peepstone to search for buried treasures — this, despite almost a century and a half of Mormon denials.

Chapter 4

The 1826 Trial

In October of 1825, Josiah Stowel, a farmer from South Bainbridge (now Afton), located in the south-central part of the state, visited a relative in the Palmyra area. This Simpson Stowel seems to have been one of the money diggers with whom the Smiths searched for buried treasures. He told Josiah about Joseph's ability with the peepstone and introduced the two men.

Simpson Stowel may have previously described Josiah Stowel's Bainbridge farm within Joseph's hearing. At any rate, Joseph used his peepstone to show off his clairvoyant "powers" by describing the farm. The demonstration impressed the farmer so much that he asked the young seer to go with him to Pennsylvania to help find a lost gold mine that the Spaniards were supposed to have worked. Joseph agreed to do so, and he and his father went along with Stowel and some others to Harmony, Pennsylvania, near which, according to legend, the mine was located. While there, they boarded with Isaac Hale, who provided the following description of events:

> I first became acquainted with Joseph Smith, Jr. in November, 1825. He was at that time in the employ of a set of men who were called "money diggers;" and his occupation was that of seeing, or pretending to see by means of a stone placed in his hat, and his hat closed over his face. In this way he pretended to discover minerals and hidden treasure. His appearance at this time, was that of a careless young man—not very well educated, and very saucy and insolent to his father. Smith, and his father, with several other 'money-diggers' boarded at my house while they were employed in digging for a mine that they supposed had been opened and worked by the Spaniards, many years since. Young Smith gave the 'money-diggers' great encouragement, at first, but when they had arrived in digging, to near the place where he had stated an immense treasure would be found—he said the enchantment was so powerful that he could not see. They then became discouraged, and soon after dispersed. This took place about the 17th of November, 1825; and one of the company gave me his note for $12.68 for his board, which is still unpaid.
>
> After these occurrences, young Smith made several visits at my house, and at length asked my consent to his marrying my daughter Emma. This I refused, and gave my reasons for so doing; some of which were, that he

was a stranger, and followed a business that I could not approve; he then left the place.[1]

After departing from Harmony, Joseph and Stowel went to Stowel's Bainbridge farm, about twenty-five miles to the north. While there, as noted in Isaac Hale's affidavit, Joseph made several trips back to Harmony to court Hale's daughter, Emma. During much of the remaining time, Joseph and Stowel continued to look for buried treasure in the Bainbridge area. This treasure hunting went on for several months until some of Stowel's relatives, distressed by the way Stowel was squandering his money, brought charges against Joseph. What follows are some notes made during his trial:

STATE OF NEW YORK V. JOSEPH SMITH. Warrant issued upon written complaint upon oath of Peter G. Bridgeman, who informed that one Joseph Smith of Bainbridge was a disorderly person and an imposter.

Prisoner brought before Court March 20, 1826. Prisoner examined: says that he came from the town of Palmyra, and had been at the house of Josiah Stowel in Bainbridge most of time since; had small part of time been employed in looking for mines, but the major part had been employed by said Stowel on his farm, and going to school. That he had a certain stone which he had occasionally looked at to determine where hidden treasures in the bowels of the earth were; that he professed to tell in this manner where gold mines were a distance under ground, and had looked for Mr. Stowel several times, and had informed him where he could find these treasures, and Mr. Stowel had been engaged in digging for them. That at Palmyra he pretended to tell by looking at this stone where coined money was buried in Pennsylvania, and while at Palmyra had frequently ascertained in that way where lost property was of various kinds; that he had occasionally been in the habit of looking through this stone to find lost property for three years, but of late had pretty much given it up on account of its injuring his health, especially his eyes, making them sore; that he did solicit business of this kind, and had always declined having anything to do with this business.

Josiah Stowel sworn: says that prisoner had been at his house something like five months; had been employed by him to work on farm part of time; that he pretended to have skill of telling where hidden treasures in the earth were by means of looking through a certain stone; that prisoner had looked for him sometimes; once to tell him about money buried in Bend Mountain in Pennsylvania, once for gold on Monument Hill, and once for a salt spring; and that he positively knew that the prisoner could tell, and did possess the art of seeing those valuable treasures through the medium of said stone; that he found the [word illegible] at Bend and Monument Hill as prisoner represented it; that prisoner had looked through said stone for Deacon Attleton for a mine, did not exactly find it but got a p— [word unfinished] of ore which resembled gold, he thinks; that prisoner had told by means of this stone where a Mr. Bacon had buried money; that he and prisoner had been in search of it; the prisoner had said it was in a certain root of a stump five feet from the surface of the earth, and with it would be found a tail feather; that said Stowel and prisoner thereupon commenced digging, found a tail feather, but money was gone; that he supposed the money moved down. That prisoner did offer his services; that he never deceived him; that prisoner looked through stone and described Josiah Stowel's house and outhouses, while at Palmyra at Simpson Stowel's, correctly; that he had told about a painted tree, with a man's head painted upon it, by means of said stone. That he had been in company with prisoner digging for gold, and had the most implicit faith in prisoner's skill.

Arad Stowel sworn: says that he went to see whether prisoner could convince him that he possessed the skill he professed to have, upon which prisoner laid a book upon a white cloth, and proposed looking through another stone which was white and transparent, hold the stone to the candle, turn his head to look, and read. The deception appeared so palpable that witness went off disgusted.

McMaster sworn: says he went with Arad Stowel, and likewise came away disgusted. Prisoner pretended to him that he could discover objects at a distance by holding this white stone to the sun or candle; that prisoner rather declined looking into a hat at his dark colored stone, as he said that it hurt his eyes.

Jonathon Thompson says that prisoner was requested to look for chest of money; did look, and pretended to know where it was; and prisoner, Thompson, and Yeomans went in search of it; that Smith arrived at spot first; was at night; that Smith looked in hat while there, and when very dark, and told how the chest was situated. After digging several feet, struck something sounding like a board or plank. Prisoner would not look again, pretending that he was alarmed on account of the circumstances relating to the trunk being buried [which] came all fresh to his mind. That the last time he looked he discovered distinctly the two Indians who buried the trunk, that a quarrel ensued between them, and that one of said Indians was killed by the other, and thrown into the hole beside the trunk, to guard it, as he supposed. Thompson says that he believes in the prisoner's professed skill; that the board he struck his spade upon was probably the chest, but on account of an enchantment the trunk kept settling away from under them when digging; that notwithstanding they continued constantly removing the dirt, yet the trunk kept about the same distance from them. Says prisoner said that it appeared to him that salt might be found at Bainbridge, and that he is certain that prisoner can divine things by means of said stone. That as evidence of the fact prisoner looked into his hat to tell him about some money witness lost sixteen years ago, and that he described the man that witness supposed had taken it, and the disposition of the money: And therefore the Court find the Defendant guilty. Costs: Warrant, 19c. Complaint upon oath, 25½c. Seven witnesses, 87½c. Recognisances, 25c. Mittimus, 19c. Recognisances of witnesses, 75c. Subpoena, 18c. —$2.68.[2]

These notes of the trial are extremely important because of what they reveal about Joseph's activities and character. First, they support the various statements of those who asserted that Joseph used a peepstone to look for buried treasure. In contrast with those statements these trial notes were written down four years before *The Book of Mormon* was published; hence, it cannot be said that the witnesses were prejudiced against Joseph, or fabricated stories about him, because of that book. According to the notes, even Joseph himself stated that he used a stone to search for buried treasure. He defended himself by claiming that he actually had the ability to see things with the stone and that he was not trying to deceive anyone. Even Josiah Stowel and Jonathon Thompson, who were friendly to Joseph, and who believed that he had such an ability, confirmed that Joseph looked for buried treasures with a stone. *

Secondly, from these trial notes, and also from the other descriptions of Joseph's money digging activities, it would seem that Joseph was engaging in a confidence scheme in which he hired himself out to look for buried treasure. The problem of questionable intent arises because of an "enchantment" that caused the treasure to "move" through the earth and elude the diggers.

The implications of this are quite dramatic insofar as Joseph's character is concerned — not to mention his possible motivation in bringing out *The Book of Mormon*. Is it any wonder, then, that Mormons have vehemently denied that Joseph ever searched for buried treasures by using a peepstone, or that he was ever brought to trial for so doing? Mormon writers have argued that the material relating to the trial and to Joseph's use of a peepstone for money digging was fabricated to malign Joseph, but they have also freely acknowledged that the implications would be staggering if such a trial actually took place. Therefore, since the question of the historical reality of the trial is of such importance, it is imperative that we ascertain that reality.

Determining the reality of the trial entails finding and evaluating as many references to it as possible. To begin, we might take a look at what Joseph himself said about the trip to Pennsylvania. The following is from his autobiography that was published in 1842:

> In the month of October eighteen hundred and twenty-five I hired with an old gentleman, by the name of Josiah Stoal who lived in Chenango county State of New York. He had heard something of a silver mine having been opened by the Spaniards in Harmony Susquehanna county State of Pennsylvania, and had previous to my hiring with him been digging in order if possible to discover the mine. After I went to live with him he took me among the rest of his hands to dig for the silver mine, at which I continued to work for nearly a month without success in our undertaking, and finally I prevailed with the old gentleman to cease digging after it. Hence arose the very prevalent story of my having been a money digger.[3]

Joseph did not mention the trial, nor did he mention the precise reason Stowel had brought him all the way from Palmyra, New York, to Harmony, Pennsylvania. From this account, one would gather that Stowel had simply hired him to work as a digger. But if that were the case, one would wonder why Stowel brought Joseph so far to work as a laborer when he could have

---

*If summaries of testimony by Joseph and the two other witnesses seem confused about assertions that Joseph was a "seer," it is because the notetaker took it upon himself to add "pretended" to the descriptions of Joseph's use of the peepstone.

hired someone in Harmony. Stowel must have hired Joseph for some other purpose; i.e., to use his talent as a seer. Alva Hale, remember, stated that Joseph "never handled one shovel of earth in those diggings," and that "all Smith did was to peep with stone and hat, and give directions where and how to dig." Alva was specifically describing the digging operations near his home in Pennsylvania. Even Joseph's mother stated that Stowel hired Joseph for something other than manual labor:

> A short time before the house was completed, a man by the name of Josiah Stoal, came from Chenango county, New York, with the view of getting Joseph to assist him in digging for a silver mine. He came for Joseph on account of having heard that he possessed certain keys, by which he could discern things invisible to the natural eye.[4]

The "certain keys" by which Joseph could "discern things invisible to the natural eye" were, of course, his peepstone and hat. Joseph's own mother thus provides an independent verification of the notes of the trial.

In his autobiography, Joseph also stated that he prevailed upon Stowel to cease the treasure hunt within a month after it began. But if the digging in Pennsylvania had ceased in November, why was it not until March that the charges were finally brought against Joseph, and why were the charges brought in the adjacent state of New York? The answer is that Joseph and Stowel went on to do more digging in the Bainbridge area as the notes of the trial indicate.

Joseph also claimed that it was this trip which gave rise to the stories of his being a money digger. But if the trip did trigger those stories, then one would expect that his Palmyra neighbors would have mentioned the trip in their statements. Yet, those neighbors reported nothing about this particular expedition; rather, they dwelled upon Joseph's Palmyra digging activities. Moreover, according to the trial notes, Joseph admitted in his testimony that he had used his peepstone and hat in the Palmyra area. The trip to Pennsylvania does not appear to have been what started the stories of his being a money digger. Why, then, did he try to make it appear that it had?

It would seem that Joseph did not have much choice in the matter. For one thing, it was on this trip that he met the woman who was to become his wife. He could hardly ignore that important meeting, and in his narrative he had to account for the reason he was in Pennsylvania when he met her. In addition, when Joseph was organizing his church in the Bainbridge area in 1830, he was put on trial on two more occasions. In at least one of these 1830 trials, as we shall see, the matter of the 1826 trial was brought up and many of his converts heard testimony about his money digging activities in Pennsylvania. Although Joseph probably would have liked to have denied all his former money digging activities, these facts simply would not allow it—the Pennsylvania episode was too well known within his own church for him to ignore it completely. He therefore probably felt it prudent to mention at least that particular episode, and to try to present it as innocently as possible to account for the stories of his being a money digger.

Though Joseph made no mention of the trial, Oliver Cowdery did do so in his 1835 history that was published in the *Messenger and Advocate*:

... a gentleman from the south part of the state, (Chenango County,) employed our brother as a common laborer, and accordingly he visited that section of country; and had he not been accused of digging down all, or nearly so, the mountains of Susquehanna, or causing others to do it by some art of micromancy, I should leave this for the present, unnoticed.... This gentleman, whose name is Stowel, resided in the town of Bainbridge, on or near the head waters of the Susquehanna river. Some forty miles south, or down the river, in the town of Harmony, Susquehanna County, Pa. is said to be a cave ... where a company of Spaniards, a long time since, ... excavated from the bowels of the earth ore, and coined a large quantity of money; ... leaving part still in the cave, ... and accordingly, our brother was required to spend a few months with some others in excavating the earth, in pursuit of this treasure....

On the private character of our brother I need add nothing further, at present, previous to his obtaining the records of the Nephites, only that while in that country, some very officious person complained of him as a disorderly person, and brought him before the authorities of the county; but there being no cause of action he was honorably acquited.[5]

In this account Cowdery did not mention Joseph's use of the peepstone and hat (the "certain keys") in the digging operation. Rather, he stated that Stowel had hired Joseph to work as a laborer, which is what Joseph later implied. Cowdery did not say that the trial was in connection with the money digging, but only that Joseph was complained of as a disorderly person. (Notably, this was one of the complaints against Joseph in the trial notes.) The problem with Cowdery's account is that it describes a different outcome for the trial than the trial notes do. According to Cowdery, Joseph was acquitted, but the notes indicate that he was found guilty. Still, Cowdery's account does confirm that a trial did take place. Some Mormon writers have held that Cowdery was referring to one of the 1830 Bainbridge trials; but this is in conflict with Cowdery's statement that the trial occurred before Joseph had acquired the gold plates — the "records of the Nephites."

Although Cowdery substantiated the occurrence of the trial, his attempts to vindicate Joseph must not be taken seriously. He was not in Pennsylvania with Joseph when the money digging occurred, nor was he present at the trial. As Cowdery had previously stated, he was dependent upon Joseph for many details about Joseph's early life. Joseph therefore could have supplied Cowdery with a whitewashed version of the money digging and the trial.

All of which brings us back to the notes supposed to have been made during Joseph's trial. These notes give summaries of the testimonies that were given and therefore provide important information concerning Joseph's money digging. But, since Mormon writers have declared that the notes are a fabrication, we should relate what is known about them and examine the evidence for their validity.

In 1870 a woman named Emily Pearsall, from Bainbridge, New York, was preparing to go on a mission to Salt Lake City under Bishop Daniel Tuttle of the Episcopal Church. Miss Pearsall was related to the justice of the peace who had presided over Joseph's 1826 trial, and the justice's docket book had been handed down in her family. Thinking that the pages containing the notes of the trial might prove useful, she tore them out of the docket book and brought them with her to Salt Lake City. In 1871, she showed the notes to Charles Marshall, a visiting British journalist. Marshall copied the notes, then included them in an article that he wrote and had published in *Fraser's Magazine* in 1873 after his return to England. Miss Pearsall died in 1872, and Bishop Tuttle came into possession of the notes. Not knowing that Marshall had already published the notes in England, Bishop Tuttle published them in 1883 in the *New Schaff-Herzog Encyclopedia* with the announcement that they had never before been published.

The fact that Bishop Tuttle did not know that Marshall had already published the trial notes is of importance, for it shows that the two men did not take liberties in copying the notes. If one of them had changed the testimonies in order to make Joseph look worse, it could be discerned by comparison with the version published by the other. The two versions are, in fact, almost exactly alike. The very slight differences between them can be attributed to a difficulty in reading the handwriting of the original. Also, Bishop Tuttle did omit the court costs and Marshall left out a very short testimony by Horace Stowel.[6]

In the January, 1886, issue of the *Utah Christian Advocate*, the Methodists provided an additional publication from the original copy of the notes. The text of this publication corroborates that of the two previous publications, and contains each of the above-mentioned items that Marshall and Tuttle had omitted. The original copy of the notes eventually disappeared, possibly destroyed in a fire in the Salt Lake City Episcopal Church.

Despite such earlier publications, the notes of the trial did not become significantly known until 1945 when Fawn Brodie, using the *New Schaff-Herzog Encyclopedia* as her source, included them in her biography of Joseph Smith[7] —whereupon Mormon leaders and writers denounced the notes and declared them to be a fraud. For example, in the "Church Section" of the *Deseret News* for May 11, 1946, a scathing review of the Brodie book included this statement about the notes: "This record could not possibly have been made at the time as the case proceeded. It is patently a fabrication of unknown authorship and never in the court records at all."

In none of the publications of the trial notes, nor in any of the other writings of Bishop Tuttle relating to them, was the name of the presiding justice of the peace in Joseph's trial mentioned. The justice's name came to light in 1947 when an independent account of the trial was found in the *Chenango Union* of May 3, 1877. (Bainbridge is in Chenango County.) Claiming to have been an eyewitness, a Dr. William Purple described the trial in a letter to the newspaper:

> More than fifty years since, at the commencement of his professional career, the writer spent a year in the present village of Afton, in this county. It was then called South Bainbridge....
>
> In the year 1825 we often saw in that quiet hamlet, Joseph Smith, Jr....
> He was an inmate of the family of Deacon Isaiah Stowell.... Here, in the estimation of the Deacon, he confirmed his conceded powers as a seer, by

means of the stone which he placed in his hat.... Mr. Stowell, with his ward and two hired men, who were, or professed to be, believers, spent much time in mining near the State line on the Susquehanna and many other places....

In February, 1826, the sons of Mr. Stowell, who lived with their father, were greatly incensed against Smith, as they plainly saw their father squandering his property in the fruitless search for hidden treasures, and that the youthful seer had unlimited control over the illusions of their sire. They made up their minds that "Patience had ceased to be a virtue," and resolved to rid themselves and their family from this incubus, who, as they believed, was eating up their substance and depriving them of their anticipated patrimony. They caused the arrest of Smith as a vagrant, without visible means of livelihood. The trial came on in the above mentioned month before Albert Neely, Esq., the father of Bishop Neely of the state of Maine. I was an intimate friend of the Justice, and was invited to take notes of the trial, which I did.[8]

Considering the number of years since the trial, many of the details that Dr. Purple related closely matched the trial notes that Emily Pearsall brought to Salt Lake City. His account also gave a substantial amount of additional information. This included the name of the justice of the peace, Albert Neely. Dr. Purple also stated Stowel's sons had "caused" Joseph's arrest.

With the finding of the Purple account, Mormon writers again cried "fraud" and declared that Dr. Purple had fabricated his version of the trial from the notes that had been published in *Fraser's Magazine* a few years earlier. Dr. Purple, however, made no mention of the *Fraser's Magazine* publication, apparently unaware of its existence. There are some differences between Dr. Purple's account and the notes of the trial. For example, Dr. Purple referred to Josiah Stowell as Isaiah Stowell, and he placed the trial in February instead of in March. These differences would not be likely if he had access to *Fraser's Magazine*, but would be quite understandable if he were trying to recollect events from fifty years earlier.

But this meant little to those who believed that Joseph Smith was a prophet of God. Since there appeared to be no existing documentation from the trial itself, they were quite sure that all of the later accounts were spurious. In summing up the Mormon position at that time, Francis Kirkham said this:

A careful study of all facts regarding this alleged confession of Joseph Smith in a court of law that he had used a seer stone to find hidden treasure for purposes of fraud, must come to the conclusion that no such record was ever made, and therefore, is not in existence.[9]

Not long after Kirkham made this statement, it was found that the 1826 Bainbridge trial had been mentioned as early as 1831 in a letter appearing in the *Evangelical Magazine and Gospel Advocate*, published in Utica, New York. The letter was signed with the initials A.W.B., which have been identified as those of A.W. Benton, a citizen of Bainbridge at the time of the trial. Here is an excerpt from the letter:

Messrs. Editors — In the sixth number of your paper I saw a notice of a sect of people called Mormonites; and thinking that a fuller history of their founder, Joseph Smith, Jr., might be interesting ..., I will take the trouble to make a few remarks on the character of that infamous imposter. For several years preceding the appearance of his book, he was about the country in the character of a glass-looker: pretending, by means of a certain stone, or glass, which he put in a hat, to be able to discover lost goods, hidden treasures, mines of gold and silver, &c. Although he constantly failed in his pretensions, still he had his dupes who put implicit confidence in all his words. In this town, a wealthy farmer, named Josiah Stowell, together with others, spent large sums of money in digging for hidden money, which this Smith pretended he could see, and told them where to dig; but they never found their treasure. At length the public, becoming wearied with the base imposition which he was palming upon the credulity of the ignorant, for the purpose of sponging his living from their earnings, had him arrested as a disorderly person, tried and condemned before a court of Justice. But, considering his youth, (he then being a minor,) and thinking he might reform his conduct, he was designedly allowed to escape. This was four or five years ago. From this time he absented himself from this place, returning only privately, and holding clandestine intercourse with his credulous dupes, for two or three years.[10]

Note that Benton stated that Joseph was charged as a "disorderly person." This is one of the charges against Joseph in the trial notes. Benton also remarked that Joseph was "designedly allowed to escape" because of his youth. Wesley P. Walters has suggested that this was "perhaps an off-the-record proposition ... giving Joseph the option of leaving the area shortly or face sentencing."[11] In other words, Joseph was possibly told to "get out of town." If this were the case, it would explain why the trial notes made no mention of a sentence imposed upon Joseph. Some Mormon writers have made an issue of this lack of a sentence, and have declared that such a lack proves the record fraudulent.

Even with the finding of the Benton letter, Mormon writers continued to disparage the trial evidence. One of these, Dr. Hugh Nibley, proposed that Benton had been confused about one of Joseph's 1830 Bainbridge trials and had placed it earlier in time. Building on that, Dr. Nibley theorized that someone had used Benton's letter to fabricate the later accounts of the trial.[12] However, since Benton wrote his letter in 1831, it hardly seems likely that he would have back-dated five years a trial that had taken place just the previous year. Moreover, Benton played a part in one of the 1830 trials, so he surely would not have been confused about when they took place. In any case, apparently feeling that he had an explanation for the trial notes, Dr. Nibley went on to say, "If this court record is authentic, it is the most damning evidence in existence against Joseph Smith."[13]

In 1971, Wesley P. Walters, who had been doing considerable research on the trial record, made several trips to New York State in search of new evidence. In July of that year, accompanied by Mr. Fred Poffarl, he found what he was looking for. In the basement of the Chenango County Jail, where

The Justice Neely bill that Wesley P. Walters found in 1971. The entry for Joseph Smith's trial is in the center. It reads: "Same [i.e., People] V. Joseph Smith / The Glass looker / March 20, 1826. Misdemeanor. To my fees in examination of the above Cause, 2.68".

old county documents were kept, Mr. Walters found several bundles of court bills, "badly water soaked and mildewed":

> When I opened the 1826 bundle and got part way through the pile of Bainbridge bills ..., I came upon, first, the J.P. bill of Albert Neely and then upon the Constable's bill of Phillip M. DeZeng. On Mr. Neely's bill was the item of the trial of "Joseph Smith the Glass Looker" on March 20, 1826, and a cost to the county from Mr. Neely of $2.68. On the bill of Mr. DeZeng were the charges for arresting and keeping Joseph Smith, notifying two justices, subpoenaing 12 witnesses, as well as a mittimus charge for 10 miles travel "to take him," with no specification as to where he was taken on the Mittimus....
>
> In my opinion, the bills are authentic, of the same paper quality and ink quality as the other 1826 and 1830 bills and appeared to me to have remained tied up and untouched since the day they were bound up and placed in storage.[14]

On the justice of the peace bill that Pastor Walters found (see page 51), the trial date of March 20, 1826, and the justice's charges of $2.68 both exactly match up the corresponding items in the trial notes that Emily Pearsall brought to Salt Lake City. Also, Joseph is called a "Glass Looker," just as A.W. Benton had labeled him in his 1831 letter. (From other sources it would appear that Joseph preferred that title for himself.) The justice's name at the top and bottom of that bill, and on several others that Mr. Walters found, is that of Albert Neely. That is the same name that Dr. Purple gave for the justice of the peace who presided over Joseph's trial. The constable's bill that Mr. Walters found in association with the justice's bill provides further confirmation of the trial record.

All this by no means exhausts the evidence for the validity of the trial notes. Before moving on, we should examine several other important pieces of evidence.

The docket book pages containing the notes were brought to Salt Lake City by Emily Pearsall, supposedly a relative of the justice of the peace for Joseph's trial. That information was provided by Bishop Tuttle in the following statement:

> The Ms. was given me by Miss Emily Pearsall who, some years since, was a woman helper in our mission and lived in my family, and died here. Her father or uncle was a Justice of the Peace in Bainbridge, Chenango Co., New York, in Jo. Smith's time, and before him Smith was tried. Miss Pearsall tore the leaves out of the record found in her father's house and brought them to me.[15]

According to the *History and Genealogy of the Pearsall Family in England and America*, Emily Pearsall was the daughter of Robert Pearsall and Flavia Newton, who lived "at Walnut Grove, Bainbridge, Chenango Co., N.Y."[16] The entry for Miss Pearsall reads:

Emily Pearsall, born January 25, 1833; died November 5, 1872, at the home of Bishop D.S. Tuttle, Salt Lake City, Utah, where she had gone as an Episcopal missionary. She was unmarried.[17]

Emily Pearsall's father had a sister named Phebe; their parents were Thomas Pearsall and Phebe Sutton.[18] The entry for Phebe Pearsall reads:

Phebe Pearsall, born July 11, 1809 ...; married Albert Neely.[19]

Therefore, Miss Emily Pearsall was indeed the niece of Albert Neely. And Albert Neely, according to Dr. Purple and to the justice of the peace bill found by Pastor Walters, was the presiding justice of the peace in Joseph's trial. This should be sufficient evidence to show that Miss Pearsall did have access to Neely's docket book, and that the notes are genuine.

A further verification of the trial notes comes from the fact that all of the participants mentioned in them have been found to have actually lived at the time of the trial. For instance, Peter G. Bridgeman, who brought the charges against Joseph, was found to have been Josiah Stowell's nephew.[20] Apparently Bridgeman was acting on behalf of Stowell's sons, who, according to Dr. Purple, were concerned that their father was squandering his money upon the treasure hunting under Joseph.

Another individual mentioned in the notes, Simpson Stowel, was found to have lived near Joseph's home. A deed for a land sale that he made on January 29, 1827, has been found. It describes him as "Simpson Stowel of the town of Manchester."[21]

Even Joseph's seemingly innocuous remark that he had been attending school in Bainbridge has been verified and is further proof of the veracity of the notes. In Chapter 1, we quoted the *History of Lee County*, Illinois, which related that Asa B. Searles had lived in Bainbridge, New York, as a youth, and had attended school there with Joseph Smith.

Another bill that Wesley Walters found confirms that Dr. Purple was in Bainbridge about the time of the trial. This was for the issuing of a search warrant "on application of William D. Purple" to search for his stolen coat.[22] It adds to the credibility of Dr. Purple's account of the trial, which in turn supports the notes.

Finally, in 1977, Wesley P. Walters brought to light two more items relating to Joseph's money digging operations in the Bainbridge area. One of these was in a letter written by the Reverend John Sherer, of the neighboring village of Colesville, which was quoted in the previous chapter. Dated November 18, 1830, it stated that Joseph was "known, in these parts, for some time, as a kind of juggler, who has pretended, through a glass, to see money underground."

The other document is a letter written by Joel K. Noble, who happens to have been the presiding justice of the peace in one of Joseph's 1830 trials. Dated March 8, 1842, this letter was written to Jonathon B. Turner and was intended for publication in Turner's *Mormonism in All Ages*, but apparently arrived too late for inclusion in that book. The following excerpt has been punctuated for clarity:

> Jo. Smith (Mormon) came here when about 17–18 y. of age in the capacity of Glass Looker or fortuneteller.... Jo. engaged the attention of a few indiv[iduals] Given to the marvelous. Duge for money, Salt, Iron Oar, Golden Oar, Silver Oar, and almost any thing, every thing, until Civil authority brought up Jo. standing (as the boys say) under the Vagrant act. Jo. was condemned. Whisper came to Jo. "off, off" — took Leg Bail.... Jo. was not seen in our town for 2 Years or more (except in Dark Corners).[23]

In this letter, Noble stated that Joseph was arrested under the Vagrant Act. Wesley Walters points out that according to the laws in effect at the time of Joseph's trial, the various types of vagrancy were brought together under the heading "Disorderly Persons." Included in this heading were "all jugglers, and all persons pretending to have skill in physiognomy, palmistry, or the like crafty sciences, or pretending to tell fortunes, or to discover where lost goods may be found."[24] According to the trial notes, Joseph was charged as a "disorderly person." The testimony made it clear that he was a "juggler," and that he pretended to be able to find hidden treasures and lost goods with his peepstone. He was thus engaged in an activity illegal in New York State. Incidentally, Noble was in error about Joseph's age. Joseph would have been twenty years at the time of the trial.

Noble's letter not only provides further confirmation that Joseph was brought to trial and found guilty; it also indicates that Pastor Walters was correct in his speculation that Joseph was given the option of leaving town or facing a sentence. Joseph "took Leg Bail," according to Noble, and got out of town, which explains why no sentence was imposed upon him. This might also explain a seeming contradication in the Purple account when it is compared with the trial notes. Purple stated that "as the testimony of Deacon Stowell could not be impeached, the prisoner was discharged." Possibly what happened was that Stowell interceded on behalf of Joseph and requested that he not be imprisoned or fined. Justice Neeley might then have complied with Stowell's request but ordered Joseph to leave town. Thinking back over the fifty years since the trial, Dr. Purple might have vaguely remembered this, and, being confused by it, thought that Joseph had been "discharged." Nevertheless, Stowell's testimony, however well disposed towards Joseph, still indicates that Joseph was involved in juggling. Because of that, Justice Neely would have had no recourse but to find him in violation of the laws of New York State. This is confirmed by the trial notes, by A.W. Benton's letter, and by Justice Noble's letter.

Despite Mormon denials, the evidence thus indicates that Joseph did engage in a confidence scheme in which he would hire himself out to search for buried treasure with the aid of a peepstone. There is also sufficient documentation to show that this activity resulted in his arrest, trial, and conviction on charges of his being "a disorderly person and an imposter."

The support for these conclusions has now accumulated to such an extent that even some Mormon writers have conceded that Joseph did use a peepstone and that he was brought to trial, though most Mormons are still not aware of the facts. But these writers still tend to underplay the significance of the conclusions that can be derived from the evidence. For example, in a book published in 1977, one writer tries to show that money digging was actually a respectable pastime in the early nineteenth century.[25]

At the time, some individuals may have thought that money digging was a respectable activity, but the contemporary newspapers usually described condescendingly those who practiced it. In any case, Joseph was not a simple digger; rather, he was a "seer." And, even if it had been considered respectable to dig for money, it was actually illegal for one to juggle the money diggers, as Joseph did, for one's own gain. It was for doing this that Joseph was arrested, tried, and found guilty.

Chapter 5

A Record from the Earth?

When he set out on the road to Palmyra after the 1826 trial, Joseph was likely already on the path that was to lead to the creation of *The Book of Mormon*. There are some indications that he had taken the first step — probably without even realizing where it would lead — during the previous year when he claimed to have divined the hiding place of some ancient gold plates. At the time, he apparently attributed no religious significance to them and said only that they contained a short history of the ancient inhabitants of America and the locations of their buried treasure. He might have made that claim only to enhance himself in the eyes of the money diggers and had no thoughts about doing anything more with it. When the money diggers asked Joseph why he did not dig up the plates, he explained that they were in the charge of a spirit who would not surrender them until the proper time. Joseph might have used this explanation in order to keep their interest by giving them the hope that he would eventually be able to gain possession of the plates and the treasures they described.

Joseph appears to have kept his discussions about the plates within the circle of money diggers. His father, however, was more garrulous — Orsamus Turner called him a "babbler." During this period he supplied most of the information concerning Joseph's claims about the plates. A few years later, several individuals retold the stories that the elder Smith had circulated. For example, the following is from one of the articles that Obadiah Dogberry published in the Palmyra *Reflector*:

> In the commencement, the imposture of the "book of Mormon," had no regular plan or features. At a time when the money digging ardor was somewhat abated, the elder Smith declared that his son Jo had been the *spirit*, (which he then described as a little old man with a long beard,) and was informed that he (Jo) under *certain* circumstances, eventually should obtain great treasures, and that in due time he (the spirit) would furnish him (Jo) with a book, which would give an account of the Ancient inhabitants (antideluvians,) of this country, and where they had deposited their substance, consisting of costly furniture, &c. at the approach of the great deluge, which had ever since that time remained secure in his (the spirits) charge, in large and spacious *chambers*, in sundry places in this vicinity....

It will be borne in mind that no *divine* interposition had been dreamed of at the period.[1]

The Book of Mormon might have remained no more than an intangible promise to a group of money diggers if Joseph had not come across a copy of *View of the Hebrews*. It was Ethan Smith's book that seems to have provided the young seer with the concepts to get his imagination to work on transforming the expectations of the treasure hunters into the foundation of a church.

Although *View of the Hebrews* was published in the small town of Poultney, Vermont, the book appears to have had a wide distribution and might well have been available in the Palmyra area.[2] Even if Ethan Smith's book was not readily available around Joseph's home town, there was a reasonable period of time in which Oliver Cowdery could have supplied Joseph with a copy. Oliver had left Poultney for New York State "about" the year 1825, the same year in which the second edition of Ethan Smith's book was published. Though Joseph later claimed that he did not meet Oliver until the spring of 1829, he might have said that to preclude any appearance of collusion. It is also possible that some other individuals were involved in the collaboration and that Oliver worked with them first and not directly with Joseph until later.

There is another reason to suspect that Oliver and Joseph might have been acquainted before the time they later said they had first met. It is not generally known, even among Mormons, that Oliver and Joseph were related. Oliver's mother, Rebecca Fuller Cowdery, was the great-granddaughter of John Fuller and Mehitabel Rowley, who were also the second great-grandparents of Lucy Mack, Joseph's mother. In addition, Mary Gates, a cousin of Joseph's maternal grandmother (Lydia Gates Mack), was married to Nathaniel Cowdery, Jr., the brother of William Cowdery, Oliver's grandfather.[3]

There may have been yet another connection between the Cowdery family and the Smith family. Around the year 1800, Oliver Cowdery's father was involved in an episode known as the "Wood Scrape," which took place in the vicinity of Middletown, Vermont, near Poultney. Likewise involved in the Wood Scrape was a fellow named Wingate, who also used the name Winchell. In reading about the doings of this Wingate/Winchell, one gets the impression that they are remarkably like those of Walters the juggler, whose mantle descended upon Joseph Smith, Jr. Moreover, the notion that Walters might have been Wingate/Winchell is substantiated by reports from Middletown residents who had moved to the Palmyra neighborhood and who knew Wingate/Winchell. They reported that Wingate/Winchell had shown up in Palmyra and was involved in the money digging business with Joseph's father. This was shortly before Joseph himself took up being a seer for the money diggers. (The Wood Scrape is discussed in more detail in Appendix A.)

Finally, it should be noted that Oliver, like Joseph, claimed to have an ability in the art of divination. Rather than using a peepstone, though, Oliver used the more common forked stick, or divining rod.[4] This mutual interest in divination might have formed the basis of an early association of the two men, during which Oliver might well have loaned Joseph a copy of *View of the Hebrews*.

Regardless of how Joseph acquired a copy of *View of the Hebrews*, the book apparently gave him some new ideas. Perhaps at first he simply saw the book as a source of information about ancient America that he could use to impress the money diggers — much of the material that Ethan Smith presented would have been useful for such a pupose. But after Joseph read the book, some of Ethan Smith's speculations apparently began to work on his imagination. The minister had proposed that the ancient inhabitants of America did have a book and Joseph might have conjectured that finding such a book would cause considerable interest and excitement among his contemporaries.

Following this line of reasoning, it would seem that, in time, Joseph began to think about actually producing a book he could claim was a "history" of the ancient Americans. The material that Ethan Smith gave in support of his theories could well have excited the young seer and spurred his imagination along those lines. Moreover, the memories of the Bainbridge trial would have given Joseph even greater impetus for developing the idea. He might have felt that such a book, unlike his money digging operations, would give him a source of income that would not be fraught with the possibility of further confrontations with the law.

As Joseph developed his idea, it appears he became convinced that, with his ability as a story teller and with the material in *View of the Hebrews*, he could produce a suitable book. For its plot, there was Ethan Smith's speculations on what had happened to the ancestors of the Indians after their arrival in the New World. Furthermore, his reputation as a seer would help to explain how he had found and translated the book. All he had to do was to make his history convincing enough for its readers. The popular interest in ancient America would then assure good sales.

For Joseph, as for most authors, the ideas for his book did not come all at once. The testimonies of the Palmyra townspeople show that Joseph evolved his concepts as he went along. For example, Parley Chase had said that Joseph's family "scarcely ever told two stories alike" concerning the "Gold Bible." And again, Obadiah Dogberry had stated, "In the commencement, the imposture of the 'book of Mormon' had no regular plan or features."

At this point, Joseph probably did not think of making his book into a new revelation from God. But as he pored over *View of the Hebrews*, Ethan Smith's religious ideas apparently began to permeate his own thoughts. Of particular importance was Ethan Smith's belief in the "Hebrew" ancestry of the Indians and its religious significance for the American people. The Vermont minister had climaxed his book with an exhortation that emphasized America's role in converting the Indians to Christianity and in making known to them their "heritage" in the Hebrew family. According to his interpretation of scripture, this was to be one of the required events that were to take place in the "latter days" prior to the Millennium, which he believed was close at hand.

Ethan Smith had also urged the "generous" American people to assist in accomplishing the task he set before them. The Vermonter's exhortation would have been especially pertinent to Joseph at that time; his neighborhood had seen the throes of the great religious excitement which we described earlier. The revivals and the religious conversions that Joseph had seen could have prodded him into thinking about the possibility of the "generous" American people flocking to a new religion based upon the concepts presented in Ethan Smith's book. Joseph might therefore have come to see in *View of the Hebrews* a possible way out of his grinding poverty by turning his simple history of ancient America into a new revelation from God.

It took time for Joseph to develop the ideas for his book. When he first claimed to have received the gold plates, he probably still intended only to produce a popular book that he could sell for a profit — a book with little, if any, religious orientation. As Joseph Capron stated:

> At length, Joseph pretended to find the Gold Plates. This scheme, he believed, would relieve the family from all pecuniary embarrassment. His father told me, that when the book was published, they would be enabled, from the profits of the work, to carry into successful operation of the money digging business. He gave me no intimation, at that time that the book was to be of a religious character, or that it had anything to do with revelation. He declared it to be a speculation, and said he, "when it is completed, my family will be placed *on a level* above the generality of mainkind"!!⁵

At this stage in the development of *The Book of Mormon*, Joseph still clung to the methodology that he used in the money digging operations. He initially declared that a spirit (rather than an angel) had informed him of the existence of the plates, and he claimed to have used his peepstone to divine where the plates were hidden. Later on, after he had transformed his ancient history into a new revelation and presented a more religious account of how he had come by the plates, the early claims about the peepstone were not entirely forgotten — not even by some Mormons. For example, Martin Harris, who paid for the publication of *The Book of Mormon* and was one of the gold plate "witnesses," stated that Joseph found the plates with his "stone":

> "Joseph Smith, jr., found at Palmyra, N.Y., on the 22nd day of September, 1827, the plates of gold.... These plates were found at the north point of a hill two miles north of Manchester village. Joseph had a stone which was dug from the well of Mason Chase, twenty-four feet from the surface. In this stone he could see many things to my certain knowledge. It was by means of this stone he first discovered these plates...."⁶

Harris went on to relate that the stone was the same one that Joseph used in his treasure hunting operations.

Despite the fact that the present-day Mormon establishment virtually ignores Joseph's use of a peepstone and gives it no part in the finding of the plates, such was not the case in the very early church. By way of illustration, an early Mormon named Hosea Stout made the following entry in his journal under the date of 25 February, 1856:

> President [Brigham] Young exhibited the Seer's stone with which the Prophet Joseph discovered the Plates of the Book of Mormon, to the regents this evening.⁷

The evidence indicates that Joseph evolved the stories of how he came by the plates. Initially, these stories were firmly rooted in the gimmickry that he used in the money digging operations. It was not until after he developed the religious aspect of his book that he forsook his peepstone and claimed a purely spiritual basis for his finding the plates. Even then, it took some time for the church to cast off an acknowledgment of the peepstone.

The early tales of how Joseph was supposed to have come to know about the plates are quite interesting when they are compared with the later "official" version. Besides being essentially non-religious, these early stories usually had a fairy-tale quality about them. Willard Chase, for example, related the following:

> In the month of June, 1827, Joseph Smith, Sen., related to me the following story: That some years ago, a spirit had appeared to Joseph his son, in a vision, and informed him that in a certain place there was a record on plates of gold, and that he was the person that must obtain them, and this he must do in the following manner: On the 22nd of September, he must repair to the place where was deposited this manuscript, dressed in black clothes, and riding a black horse with a switch tail, and demand the book in a certain name, and after obtaining it, he must go directly away, and neither lay it down nor look behind him. They accordingly fitted out Joseph with a suit of black clothes and borrowed a black horse. He repaired to the place of deposit and demanded the book which was in a stone box, unsealed, and so near the top of the ground that he could see one end of it, and raising it up, took out the book of gold; but fearing some one might discover where he got it, he laid it down to place back the top stone, as he found it; and turning round, to his surprise there was no book in sight. He again opened the box, and in it saw the book, and attempted to take it out but was hindered. He saw in the box something like a toad, which soon assumed the appearance of a man, and struck him on the side of the head. —Not being discouraged at trifles, he again stooped down and strove to take the book, when the spirit struck him again, and knocked him three or four rods.... After recovering from his fright, he enquired why he could not obtain the plates; to which the spirit made reply, because you have not obeyed your orders. He then enquired when he *could* have them, and was answered thus: come one year from this day, and bring with you your oldest brother, and you shall have them.... Before the expiration of the year, his oldest brother died; which the old man said was an *accidental providence!*
>
> Joseph went one year from that day, to demand the book, and the spirit enquired for his brother, and he said that he was dead. The spirit then commanded him to come again, in just one year, and bring a man with him. On asking who might be the man, he was answered that he would know when he saw him.
>
> Joseph believed that one Samuel T. Lawrence was the man alluded to by the spirit, and went with him to a singular looking hill, in Manchester, and shewed him where the treasure was. Lawrence asked him if he had ever discovered anything with the plates of gold; he said no: he then asked him to look in his stone, to see if there was anything with them. He looked ...

and soon saw a pair of spectacles, the same with which Joseph says he translated the Book of Mormon.... Not long after this, Joseph altered his mind, and said L. was not the right man, nor had he told him the right place. About this time he went to Harmony in Pennsylvania, and formed an acquaintance with a young lady, by the name of Emma Hale, who he wished to marry.[8]

It is interesting to note that on page 81 of her "Preliminary Manuscript" Lucy Smith related a story about her son's first visit to the hill which does not appear in her final draft. This version of the visit has more of a religious context than the one Chase narrated, but the two are still quite similar. The following extract has been punctuated for clarity:

He put forth his hand and took [the plates] up, but when he lifted them from their place the thought flashed across his mind that there might be something more in the box that could be a benefit to him in a pecuniary point of view. In the excitement of the moment he laid the record down in order to cover up the box least some one should come along and take away whatever else might be deposited there. When he turned again to take up the record it was gone, but he knew not nor did he know by what means it was taken away. He was much alarmed at this. He kneeled down & asked the Lord why it was that the record was taken from him. The angel appeared to him and told him that he had not done as he was commanded in that he laid down the record in order to secure some imaginary treasure that rema[ined]. After some further conversation ... Joseph was then permitted to raise the stone again and there he beheld the plates the same as before. He reached forth his hand to take them, but was thrown back to the ground.

Fayette Lapham (whom we quoted in Chapter Two concerning Joseph's connection with the Baptist Church) also related that Joseph's father had given him an account of how Joseph came to learn about the plates. In this version, Joseph had a dream about a "very large and tall man ..., dressed in an ancient suit of clothes, and the clothes were bloody." The man said there was treasure buried not far away and that "he had now arrived for it to be brought to light." The man also said that when the treasure was deposited, "in order to prevent his making an improper disclosure, he was murdered or slain on the spot, and the treasure had been in his charge ever since." The remainder of the tale is similar to the one Willard Chase related except that Lapham made no mention of the toad or of Samuel Lawrence. (Samuel Lawrence was one of the money diggers who worked with Joseph.) Lapham related, as Chase did, about Joseph's fruitless first two trips to the place where the plates were supposed to be buried, and also about the commandment that Joseph return after one more year with the right person:

Joseph asked, "How shall I know the person?" and was told that the person would be known to him at sight. During that year, Joseph went to the town of Harmony, in the State of Pennsylvania, at the request of someone who wanted the assistance of his divining rod and stone in finding hidden treasure.... While there, he fell in company with a young woman; and, when he first saw her, he was satisfied that she was the person appointed to go with him to get the treasure he had so often failed to secure. To insure success, he courted and married her.[9]

As different as these versions of the story are from the official version, Joseph must be considered to have actually told something like them in the years before he brought out *The Book of Mormon*. Not only do these versions generally support each other, several other individuals told similar stories. Of particular importance is a recently found document that was penned by Joseph Knight, a close friend of Joseph's from Colesville and an early convert to Mormonism. The document is a history of Joseph Smith which Knight wrote sometime between the years 1833 and 1847. Unfortunately, at least one of the beginning pages of the manuscript is missing. The remainder begins at the point Joseph first went to the hill to get the plates. The tale generally follows the versions given above, including the disappearance of the plates after Joseph set them down, the command to Joseph to return with his brother in one year, the brother's death, and the commandment to return after one more year with the right person. Knight continued:

> Joseph says, "who is the right person?" The answer was, "you will know." Then he looked in his glass and found it was Emma Hale, Daughter of old Mr. Hail of Pensylvany, a girl that he had seen Before, for he had Bin Down there Before with me.[10]

Since Knight was Joseph's friend and had no animosity towards the Mormon prophet, he is unlikely to have fabricated this tale out of rancor. What is more likely is that Joseph himself told Knight this story not long after it was supposed to have happened. Along with the other versions Knight's account lends considerable credence to the suggestion that Joseph evolved the story of how he obtained the plates. These accounts apparently reflect the tale that Joseph was telling at about the time he made up his mind to compose a history of the ancient inhabitants of America, but before he transformed it into a new revelation. Notably, still present in these versions is his peepstone, or glass — the instrument of divination in his money digging operations.

These versions also appear to show that Joseph's relationship with Emma Hale was pivotal in the evolution of *The Book of Mormon*. Before that relationship developed, Joseph apparently used his tale of the gold plates only to tantalize the money diggers. But, as his feelings for Emma grew stronger, Joseph probably realized that he had a questionable future as a seer in the money digging business. Moreover, Joseph was probably cut deeply when Emma's father expressed his disapproval of that business and refused Joseph permission to marry his daughter. It would not be surprising, then, that his desire to marry Emma would have motivated Joseph to think up a surer and a more respectable way to make money. The result might have been that he began to consider seriously any thoughts he had about composing a history of ancient America. Once he made up his mind to do this, Joseph might even have used his book project to further his relationship with Emma and perhaps to induce her to marry him. He might have done this by insisting that she was the "right person" and that he could not proceed without her.

That autumn, Joseph set out for Pennsylvania to put his ideas into action. At this point, we can again take up Isaac Hale's description of events, going back in time a little for continuity:

> After these occurrences, young Smith made several visits at my house, and at length asked my consent to his marrying my daughter Emma. This I refused, and gave my reason for so doing; some of which were, that he was a stranger, and followed a business that I could not approve; he then left the place. Not long after this, he returned, and while I was absent from home, carried off my daughter, into the state of New York, where they were married without my approbation or consent.[11]

The several visits that Joseph made to Hale's house took place while he was working for Stowel in Bainbridge during the early part of 1826. He "left the place" after the trial in March of that year, then returned that autumn to marry Emma. Willard Chase gave this interesting description of Joseph's trip back to Harmony:

> In the fall of 1826, he wanted to go to Pennsylvania to be married; but being destitute of means, he now set his wits to work, how he should raise money, and get recommendations, to procure the fair one of his choice. He went to [Samuel] Lawrence with the following story, as related to me by Lawrence himself. That he had discovered in Pennsylvania, on the bank of the Susquehanna River, a very rich mine of silver, and if he would go there with him, he might have a share in the profits;.... Lawrence then asked Joseph if he was not deceiving him; no said he, for I have been there and seen it with my own eyes, and if you do not find it so when we get there, I will bind myself to be your servant for three years. By these grave and fair promises Lawrence was induced to believe something in it, and agreed to go with him. L. soon found that Joseph was out of money, and had to bear his expenses on the way. When they got to Pennsylvania, Joseph wanted L. to recommend him to Miss H., which he did, although he was asked to do it.... L. then wished to see the silver mine, and he and Joseph went to the river, and made search, but found nothing. Thus Lawrence had his trouble for his pains, and returned home lighter than he went, while Joseph had got his expenses borne, and a recommendation to his girl.[12]

Isaac Hale stated in his affidavit that he opposed the marriage because Joseph was a "stranger," and that Joseph "followed a business" that Hale "could not approve." This business was, of course, Joseph's juggling the money diggers with the peepstone. At the time that Joseph dictated his account of these events, however, his standing as a religious leader and his desire to downplay his former money digging activities caused him to change the reason Hale opposed the marriage. The following is the account that Joseph gave immediately after his version of the Pennsylvania episode:

During the time that I was thus employed I was put to board with a Mr. Isaac Hale of that place; it was there that I first saw my wife (his daughter) Emma Hale. On the eighteenth of January eighteen hundred and twenty-seven we were married while I was yet employed in the services of Mr. Stoal.

Owing to my still continuing to assert that I had seen a vision, persecution still followed me, and my wife's father's family were very much opposed to our being married. I was therefore under the necessity of taking her elsewhere, so we went and were married at the house of Squire Tarbill, in south Bainbridge, Chenango County, New York. Immediately after my marriage I left Mr. Stoal's and went to my father's and farmed with him that season.[13]

When he dictated this, Joseph apparently felt that it would have been more fitting if the opposition to his marrying Emma were due to "persecution" because of his "still continuing to assert" that he had "seen a vision." The vision referred to was the "first" vision, which, as we found, seems to have been almost unheard of until 1840, some fourteen years after Joseph's courtship of Emma.

Perhaps to make it appear that nothing untoward had happened in Bainbridge earlier in 1826, Joseph seems to have tried to create the impression that he worked for Josiah Stowel up until the time of his marriage to Emma. But, the evidence indicates that Joseph left Bainbridge for Palmyra shortly after the trial in March and that except possibly for a few times in secret he did not return until late that fall. After all, he had taken "leg bail" to escape sentencing, and if he had remained in Bainbridge he would have found himself invited back into the jail. Moreover, if Joseph had continued to work for Stowel, the farmer's sons would certainly have reported to Justice Neely that the "Glass Looker" was still around. Any dealings that Joseph had with Stowel during this time must therefore have been in "dark corners," as Justice Noble put it. This would be confirmed by A.W. Benton's statement that Joseph returned "privately, and holding clandestine intercourse with his dupes." Furthermore, Joseph's close friend and early convert, Joseph Knight, provides some strong evidence that Joseph was not working for Stowel when he married Emma. This is what Knight had to say about Joseph's return to Bainbridge:

Joseph then went to Mr. Stowels whare he had lived sometime Before. But Mr. Stowel Could not pay him money for his work very well and he came to me perhaps in November and worked for me until about the time that he was Married, which I think was in February. And I paid him the money and I furnished him with a horse and Cutter to go and see his girl Down to Mr. Hails. And soon after this he was Married and Mr Stowel moved him and his wife to his fathers in Palmyra Ontario County.[14]

So Joseph worked for Joseph Knight in the neighboring village of Colesville that fall. Stowel obviously could not "very well" openly pay Joseph to work for him because of the possibility that it would be reported to Justice Neely. But Stowel did give Joseph money (in secret, probably) to move back to Palmyra, perhaps to prevent further embarrassment to himself or to Joseph.

Joseph and Emma stayed in Palmyra for several months to give Isaac Hale's temper a chance to cool. Finally, Emma decided that she wanted to pick up some of her things in Harmony. The following is from Isaac Hale's account:

> After they arrived at Palmyra N.Y., Emma wrote to me inquiring whether she could have her property, consisting of clothing, furniture, cows, &c. I replied that her property was safe, and at her disposal. In a short time they returned, bringing with them a Peter Ingersol, and subsequently came to the conclusion that they would move out, and reside upon a place near my residence.
>
> Smith stated to me, that he had given up what he called "glass-looking," and that he expected to work hard for a living, and was willing to do so. He also made arrangements with my son Alva Hale, to go to Palmyra, and move his (Smith's) furniture &c. to this place. He then returned to Palmyra....[15]

Since he passed over it, Isaac Hale evidently felt that the conversation that occurred between him and Joseph was personal. Peter Ingersoll, however, was under no such constraint. He related this:

> In the month of August, 1827, I was hired by Joseph Smith, Jr. to go to Pennsylvania to move his wife's household furniture up to Manchester, where his wife then was. When we arrived at Mr. Hale's, in Harmony, Pa. from which place he had taken his wife, a scene presented itself, truly affecting. His father-in-law (Mr. Hale) addressed Joseph, in a flood of tears: "You have stolen my daughter and married her. I had much rather have followed her to her grave. You spend your time in digging for money — pretend to see in a stone, and thus try to deceive people." Joseph wept, and acknowledged he could not see in a stone now, nor never could; and that his former pretensions in that respect, were all false. He then promised to give up his old habits of digging for money and looking into stones. Mr. Hale told Joseph, if he would move to Pennsylvania and work for a living, he would assist him in getting into business. Joseph acceded to this proposition. I then returned with Joseph and his wife to Manchester.[16]

This was apparently the only time that Peter Ingersoll and Isaac Hale met; yet, the general points of the two narratives are in close agreement. The validity of the statements would be further confirmed by the fact that they were separately made and collected.

Ingersoll went on to narrate an interesting anecdote about the return trip:

> On our journey to Pennsylvania, we could not make the exact change at the toll gate near Ithaca. Joseph told the gate tender, that he would "hand" him the toll on his return, as he was coming back in a few days. On our return, Joseph tendered him 25 cents, the toll being 12½. He did not recognize Smith, so he accordingly gave him back the 12½ cents. After we had passed the gate, I asked him if he did not agree to pay double gateage on our

return? No, said he, I agreed to "*hand*" it to him, and I did, but he handed it back again.[17]

When Joseph returned to Palmyra, he did indeed intend "to give up his old habits of digging for money." But he was not yet finished with his peepstone, nor did he mean to go into a business set up for him by his father-in-law. Instead, it seems that Joseph was prepared to show the world just how good a story-teller he was.

Chapter 6

"I Shall Proceed to Do a Marvelous Work"

In September of 1827, after returning to Palmyra from Harmony, Joseph appears to have set into motion the plan for producing his history of ancient America. The first step would require laying the groundwork to provide answers for any questions that might be asked later and to make more convincing his claims about the book. If he was going to translate some ancient records, he would have to get them first. That would entail appearing to take the gold plates from the place where they were supposed to be hidden. He would especially have needed to go through such a procedure if he had previously told Emma that she was the "right person" to be with him when he got the plates. Therefore, to set the stage for the initial step in the creation of his book, he told his family and a few of his friends that the spirit would allow him to get the plates on the twenty-second day of the month.

When the chosen day came, it seems Joseph began to worry about the possibility uninvited guests would ruin his scenario. He was astute enough to realize that if the money diggers learned of what he had said about his getting the plates, they might remember his old promise to them and show up in an attempt to get their share of the treasure. Joseph was particularly worried about Samuel Lawrence, one of the more tenacious members of the company. Joseph Knight, a friend whom Joseph told about the plates, mentioned the situation and Joseph's reaction to it:

> Nothing material took place untill toard fall the forepart of September. I went to Rochester on Buisness and returned by Palmyra to be there about the 22nt of September. I was there several Days. I will say there [was] a man near By By the name Samuel Lawrence. He was a Seear [Seer] and he had Bin to the hill and knew about the things in the hill and he was trying to obtain them. ... Now Joseph was some affraid of him that he mite be a trouble to him. He therefore sint his father up to Sams as he Called him near night to see if there was any signs of his going away that night. He told his father to stay till near Dark and if he saw any signs of his going you till him if I find him there I will thrash the stumps with him. So the old man came a way and saw no thing like it.[1]

When he dictated his autobiography several years later, Joseph made

67

no mention of his worries about the money diggers, probably because he wanted to downplay his former treasure hunting proclivities. Significantly, Knight's account also substantiates Willard Chase's story about Joseph's having previously brought Samuel Lawrence, probably in 1825, to the hill where the plates were supposed to have been buried. When he brought Lawrence to the hill, Joseph may have intended simply to tantalize the treasure hunter with the promise of the riches that the plates would help uncover.

Satisfied that Lawrence would not show up at the hill and disrupt the scenario he had planned, Joseph borrowed Joseph Knight's horse and wagon (unbeknownst to Knight, who was a bit perturbed at the disappearance of his property until he found out the purpose) and departed with Emma to "get" the plates. When they returned some time later, Joseph's mother observed that they did not have the plates with them. Joseph later related that he had hidden them in a space he had dug in a rotted birch tree. Emma did not see the plates either. After they had arrived at the hill, Joseph had made her stay by the wagon while he proceeded on foot to where the plates were supposed to be buried.

Still, Joseph supposedly did not return empty handed. His mother claimed that he brought back with him the "spectacles" with which he was to translate the plates. She gave the following description of them:

> I ... took the article of which he spoke into my hands, and, upon examination, found that it consisted of two smooth three cornered diamonds set in glass, and the glasses were set in silver bows, which were connected with each other in much the same way as old fashioned spectacles.[2]

However, other individuals who claimed to have seen the spectacles gave different descriptions of them. Martin Harris, for example, described them so:

> The two stones set in a bow of silver were about two inches in diameter, perfectly round, and about five-eights of an inch thick at the center; but not so thick at the edges where they came into the bow. They were joined by a round bar of silver, about three-eights of an inch in diameter, and about four inches long, which, with the two stones, would make eight inches.
> The stones were white, like polished marble, with a few grey streaks....[3]

Possibly there never was a set of spectacles. Joseph might simply have made up a description of them to give family and acquaintances, who, trying to appear more intimately involved with the bringing forth of the new religion, in turn claimed to have actually seen them. If, on the other hand, the spectacles actually existed, Joseph, or perhaps a collaborator, probably manufactured them so he could claim that he used them to translate the plates. If so, they were made more likely with tin than with silver.

Reflecting the way his ideas evolved over time, Joseph changed his claims about the spectacles. At first, they were supposed to be a magical device to allow him to translate the plates. Several years later Joseph gave them a religious connotation by calling them the "Urim and Thummim" after the biblical objects of that name. Because of this, the term "Urim and Thummim" does not appear in *The Book of Mormon.* Instead, the spectacles are called "interpreters" in that book. Apparently the first use of the term Urim and Thummim was in the year 1833 — more than five years after Joseph was supposed to have found them.[4]

Now that his plan was set into motion, Joseph was nearly ready to produce the translation of his "ancient record." Apparently he was also looking ahead to the day when he would have the problem of financing the printing of the book. He could not possibly have paid the printing costs himself, but there was a possible source of funds in the person of Martin Harris, a well-to-do farmer for whom he had occasionally worked. What G.W. Stodard said of Harris is typical of what many others said:

> I have been acquainted with Martin Harris, about thirty years. As a farmer, he was industrious and enterprising, so much so, that he had, (previous to his going into the Gold Bible speculation) accumulated in real estate, some eight or ten thousand dollars. Although he possessed wealth, his moral and religious character was such, as not to entitle him to respect among his neighbors. He was fretful, peevish, and quarrelsome.... Yet he was a public professor of some religion. He was first an orthodox Quaker, then a Universalist, next a Restorationist, then a Baptist, next a Presbyterian, and then a Mormon. By his willingness to become all things to all men, he has attained a high standing among his Mormon brethren.[5]

Another Palmyra resident, the Reverend John A. Clark, told of a visit that Harris had made to his house in the fall of 1827. He mentioned Harris's switching of religions, and then:

> At this time, however, in his religious views he seemed to be floating upon the sea of uncertainty. He had evidently quite an extensive knowledge of the Scriptures, and possessed a manifest disputatious turn of mind. As I subsequently learned, Mr. Harris had always been a firm believer in dreams, and visions, and supernatural appearances, such as apparitions and ghosts, and therefore was a fit subject for such men as Smith and his colleagues to operate upon.[6]

Joseph apparently reasoned that Harris was just the sort of person that he could induce to provide the financial backing for his book. Still, the printing would cost a lot of money, and Joseph needed a strong argument to convince Harris to make the investment. It was out of this need that Joseph probably got his first push to enlarge the religious aspect of his book. Harris was a man who was in search of something religious, and Joseph seems to have concluded that if his book could provide the promise of that something, he would be able to convince him to part with some of his money. Joseph asked his mother to go to the farmer, inform him about the finding of the plates, and invite him to their place for a discussion (about which Joseph would have prompted his family). The following is from the account that Harris gave of his visit to the Smith farm:

... I waited a day or two, ... took my breakfast, and ... went directly to old Mr. Smith's. I found that Joseph had gone away to work for Peter Ingersol to get some flour.... When Joseph came home ... I took him by the arm and led him away from the rest, and requested him to tell me the story, which he did as follows, He said: 'An angel had appeared to him, and told him it was God's work.' ... Joseph had before this described the manner of his finding the plates. He found them by looking in the stone found in the well of Mason Chase. The family had likewise told me the same thing.

Joseph said the angel told him he must quit the company of the money-diggers. That there were wicked men among them. He must have no more to do with them. He must not lie, nor swear, nor steal. He told him to go and look in the spectacles, and he would show him the man that would assist him. That he did so, and saw myself, Martin Harris, standing before him. That struck me with surprise. I told him I wished him to be very careful about these things. 'Well,' said he, 'I saw you standing before me as plainly as I do now.' I said, if it is the devil's work I will have nothing to do with it; but if it is the Lord's you can have all the money necessary to bring it before the world.... Now you must not blame me for not taking your word. If the Lord will show me that it is his work, you can have all the money you want...."[7]

In this account, which he gave many years after the events described therein, Harris said an "angel" had appeared to Joseph. Apparently Harris was employing the term that was in use at the time he related the account. It is likely that Joseph had actually said that "a spirit," rather than "an angel," had appeared to him. It is also likely that he did not say it was "God's work." Over the years it would have been very easy for Harris to modify unconsciously his memory of the meeting to reflect his later religious outlook.

In any case, Harris had his share of doubts. Possibly he was concerned because most of the other treasures that Joseph claimed to have divined with his peepstone were supposed to have been under the control of evil spirits or devils. He did not want to pay for the devil's work, so he insisted on being shown that Joseph's book was of the Lord. Because of this, Joseph probably felt compelled to enlarge the religious aspect of his book even more. He needed a substantial amount of money to get it published, and he could have all the money he wanted if he could convince Harris that the book was the Lord's work.

It is not known exactly what Joseph said to Harris to convince him to back the book, but he might have obtained some novel religious ideas from *View of the Hebrews*. Certainly, Ethan Smith's exhortation to the American people would have been inspiring enough. Pastor Smith had argued that the task he set before the American people would need to be accomplished before the Millennium could arrive. Moreover, in the fore part of Ethan Smith's book was a statement that it was "designed" for "hastening the progress of the millennial glory." Interestingly enough, when Harris visited with the Reverend John A. Clark not long after meeting with Joseph, he told Clark that the "Golden Bible ... would be found to contain such disclosures as would ... speedily bring on the glorious millennium."[8]

It is also possible that Harris did not fully believe Joseph's claims about the plates, but felt that paying for the book's publication would not compromise his religious principles. Joseph might have reassured Harris by voicing an argument similar to the following, which he later included in *The Book of Mormon*:

> ... wherefore I shew unto you the way to judge: for every thing which inviteth to do good, and to persuade to believe in Christ, is sent forth by the power and gift of Christ; wherefore ye may know with a perfect knowledge, it is of God; but whatsoever thing persuadeth men to do evil, and believe not in Christ, and deny him, and serve not God, then ye may know with a perfect knowledge it is of the devil....[9]

Joseph, of course, would have assured Harris that his book would "persuade" its readers "to believe in Christ." Harris might therefore have concluded that the book could be considered "the Lord's work" and not that of the devil.

Be that as it may, Harris also appears to have come to the conclusion that Joseph's project had definite possibilities for profit and that he would be rewarded for investing in the book. For example, the Reverend John Clark had this to say when he described the visit that Harris made to his house that autumn of 1827:

> The whole thing appeared to me so ludicrous and purile, that I could not refrain from telling Mr. Harris, that I believed it a mere hoax got up to practice upon his credulity, or an artifice to extort from him money; for I had already, in the course of the conversation, learned that he had advanced some twenty-five dollars to Jo Smith as a sort of premium for sharing with him in the glories and profits of this new revelation. For at this time, his mind seemed to be quite as intent upon the pecuniary advantage that would arise from the possession of the plates of solid gold of which this book was composed, as upon the spiritual light it would diffuse over the world.[10]

Harris's own wife, Lucy, was even more cynical about her husband's involvement with Joseph's book:

> Martin Harris was once industrious, attentive to his domestic concerns, and thought to be worth about ten thousand dollars.... About a year previous to the report being raised that Smith had found gold plates, he became very intimate with the Smith family, and said he believed Joseph could see in his stone anything he wished....
> ... His whole object was to make money by it.... One day, while at Peter Harris' house, I told him he had better leave the company of the Smiths, as their religion was false; to which he replied, if you would let me alone, I could make money by it.[11]

Abigail Harris made a statement that confirmed what Lucy Harris said:

> ... Martin Harris and his wife were at my house. In conversation about the Mormonites, she observed, that she wished her husband would quit them,

as she believed it was all false and a delusion. To which I hea[r]d Mr. Harris
reply: *"What if it is a lie; if you will let me alone I will make money out of
it!.* I was both an eye and an ear witness of what has been stated above....[12]

With Harris's backing, the prospects for the book appeared good. But it
was not all smooth going. Within a few days after Joseph first claimed to have
obtained the plates, reports of the find circulated throughout the
neighborhood and caused a good deal of excitement. Joseph's mother related
that her husband had heard of a gathering of men in a nearby house who were
intent on finding where Joseph had hidden the plates, and who had even hired
a "conjurer" to help them. Concerned about the threat that the men posed for
the plates, the elder Smith went to the house to see if he could learn their plans:

> Making an errand, he went in and sat down near the door, leaving it a
> little ajar, in order to overhear their conversation. They stood in the yard
> near the door, and were devising plans to find "Joe Smith's gold bible," as
> they expressed themselves....
>
> Presently, the woman of the house, becoming uneasy at the exposures
> they were making, stepped through a back door into the yard, and called
> to her husband, in a suppressed tone, but loud enough to be heard dis-
> tinctly by Mr. Smith, "Sam, Sam, you are cutting your own throat." At this
> the conjurer bawled out at the top of his voice, "I am not afraid of any-
> body — we will have them plates in spite of Joe Smith or all the devils in
> hell."[13]

The "Sam" that the woman of the house called to was probably Samuel
Lawrence, which would indicate that Joseph's fears about the money digger
were well founded. Still, Joseph must have decided to make the best of the
situation and even tried to have some fun at the expense of those who were
looking for the plates. He obtained a wooden box and, claiming that he had
put the plates in it, moved it around to various places of concealment in order
to keep the treasure hunters guessing. These tactics did not endear Joseph to
his old money digging companions. They angrily demanded that he give them
their due share of the treasure according to the promises previously made. As
Martin Harris explained:

> There was a company in that neighborhood, who were digging for money
> supposed to have been hidden by the ancients. Of this company were old
> Mr. Stowel — I think his name was Josiah — also old Mr. Beman, also Samuel
> Lawrence, George Proper, Joseph Smith, Jr., and his father, and his brother
> Hiram Smith. They dug for money in Palmyra, Manchester, also in Penn-
> sylvania, and other places....
>
> The money-diggers claimed that they had as much right to the plates as
> Joseph had, as they were in company together. They claimed that Joseph
> had been traitor, and had appropriated to himself that which belonged to
> them. For this reason Joseph was afraid of them and continued concealing
> the plates....[14]

Eventually, the demands of the money diggers for the gold plates became so great that Joseph felt compelled to leave Palmyra. (When he described these events in his autobiography years later, Joseph did not say he had to leave because of the money diggers. He stated instead that he had to leave because of persecution by unnamed individuals.) Deciding to move to Pennsylvania as his father-in-law had suggested the previous summer, he wrote to Emma's brother to come with a wagon to transport their belongings. After Alva brought Joseph and Emma back to Harmony, the couple moved into a house on the Hale farm. Returning to Isaac Hale's account:

> Soon after this, I was informed they had brought a wonderful book of Plates down with them. I was shown a box in which it is said they were contained, which had to all appearances, been used as a glass box of the common window glass. I was allowed to feel the weight of the box, and they gave me to understand that the book of plates was then in the box — into which, however, I was not allowed to look.
>
> I inquired of Joseph Smith Jr., who was to be the first who would be allowed to see the Book of Plates? He said it was a young child. After this, I became dissatisfied, and informed him that if there was anything in my house of that description, which I could not be allowed to see, he must take it away; if he did not, I was determined to see it. After that, the Plates were said to be hid in the woods.[15]

Soon after they had arrived in Harmony, Joseph began "translating" the plates while Emma took down his dictation. The plates were supposed to be still hidden in the woods, but Joseph claimed that the power of the spectacles was so great he could read the plates just as if they were before him.

At this time, Joseph apparently still had not yet gone so far as to think seriously of making his book into a new revelation from God, nor of using it to found a new religion. Rather, the book was supposed to be ostensibly a history of ancient America that would arouse public curiosity and make a profit. It is likely that Joseph was including in his book a large amount of religious material that he had derived from *View of the Hebrews*, but he was evidently using this material merely to invoke greater reader interest and to satisfy Martin Harris. Furthermore, he apparently had not yet seriously considered presenting a religious basis for his finding the plates. The beginnings of a religious basis that he had given to Harris were for the farmer's benefit, and he apparently saw no reason to give the same story to Emma's relatives. Emma's cousins, Joseph and Hiel Lewis, for example, related the following:

> He said that by a dream he was informed that at such a place in a certain hill, in an iron box, were some gold plates with curious engravings, which he must get and translate, and write a book; that the plates were to be kept concealed from every human being for a certain time, some two or three years; that he went to the place and dug till he came to the stone that covered the box, when he was knocked down; that he again attempted to remove the stone, and was again knocked down; this attempt was made the third time, and the third time he was knocked down. Then he exclaimed,

"Why can't I get it?" or words to that effect; and then he saw a man standing over the spot, which to him appeared like a Spaniard, having a long beard down over his breast to about here, (Smith putting his hand to the pit of his stomach) with his (the ghost's) throat cut from ear to ear, and the blood streaming down, who told him that he could not get it alone; that another person whom he, Smith, would know at first sight, must come with him, and then he would get it. And when Smith saw Miss Emma Hale, he knew that she was the person....

In all this narrative, there was not one word about "visions of God," or of angels, or heavenly revelations. All his information was by that dream, and that bleeding ghost.[16]

This story is quite similar to those that Joseph's father had told separately to Willard Chase and to Fayette Lapham, and to the one that Joseph's friend, Joseph Knight, related. These diverse sources provide substantial evidence that Joseph actually did then recount such tales and that they represent a stage in the development of *The Book of Mormon* from a nonreligious book to one supposed to be a new revelation from God.

In February of 1828, Martin Harris made a trip to Harmony. It is not clear why he made it, but perhaps he was worried about his investment and wanted to be sure that Joseph could actually produce the book. Whatever the reason for Harris's visit, Joseph gave the farmer a piece of paper containing some "reformed Egyptian" characters which he said he had copied from the plates. Harris, in turn, took the paper to New York City to get an opinion from "the learned."

As with so many other episodes in the story of the production of *The Book of Mormon*, the various accounts of Harris's search for an opinion of the characters have their share of contradiction and controversy. Nevertheless, as a result of his trip, Harris apparently became convinced that Joseph could do what he set out to do. When he returned to Palmyra, he paid another visit to the Reverend John Clark, who described the farmer's feelings on the matter:

> After his return he came to see me again, and told me that, among others, he had consulted Professor Anthon, who thought the characters in which the book was written very remarkable, but he could not decide exactly what language they belonged to. Martin had now become a perfect believer. He said he had no more doubt of Smith's commission, than of the divine commission of the apostles. The very fact that Smith was an obscure and illiterate man, showed that he must be acting under divine impulses: —"God had chosen the foolish things of the world to confound the wise...."[17]

According to Harris in this account, Professor Anthon[18] could not translate the characters, nor could he state to which language they belonged. The same was reported in several other early accounts of the Harris visit to Anthon. However, not long after Joseph established his church, Mormon missionaries began saying that Anthon had declared that the characters were "reformed Egyptian." They also stated that Joseph had supplied his translation of the characters, and that Anthon had affirmed that the translation was correct. Because Mormon missionaries were using these claims to gain proselytes, Eber D. Howe wrote to Professor Anthon and asked him for the facts concerning the Harris visit. Howe subsequently published Anthon's answer in *Mormonism Unvailed.* The following is an excerpt:

> The whole story about my having pronounced the Mormonite inscription to be "reformed Egyptian hieroglyphics" is *perfectly false.* Some years ago, a plain, and apparently simple-hearted farmer, called upon me with a note from Dr. Mitchell of our city, now deceased, requesting me to decypher, if possible, a paper, which the farmer would hand me, and which Dr. M. confessed he had been unable to understand. Upon examining the paper in question, I soon came to the conclusion that it was all a trick, perhaps a *hoax.* When I asked the person, who brought it, how he obtained the writing, he gave me ... the following account: A "gold book," ... had been dug up in the northern part of the state of New York, and along with the book an enormous pair of *"gold spectacles"!....* Whoever examined the plates through the spectacles, was enabled not only to *read* them, but fully to *understand* their meaning. All this knowledge, however, was confined at that time to a young man, who had the trunk containing the book and spectacles in his sole possession. This young man was placed behind a curtain, ... and, thus concealed from view, ... decyphered the characters of the book.... Not a word, however, was said about the plates having been decyphered "by the gift of God." ... The farmer added, that he had been requested to contribute a sum of money towards the publication of the "golden book".... As a last precautionary step, however, he had resolved to come to New York, and obtain the opinion of the learned about the meaning of the paper which he brought with him, and which had been given him as a part of the contents of the book, although no translation had been furnished at the time by the young man with the spectacles. On hearing this odd story, I ... began to regard it as a part of a scheme to cheat the farmer of his money, and I communicated my suspicions to him.... He requested an opinion from me in writing, which of course I declined giving, and he then took his leave carrying the paper with him. This paper was in fact a singular scrawl. It consisted of all kinds of crooked characters in columns, and had evidently been prepared by some person who had before him at the time a book containing various alphabets. Greek and Hebrew letters, crosses and flourishes, Roman letters inverted or placed sideways, were arranged in perpendicular columns, and the whole ended in a rude delineation of a circle divided into various compartments, decked with various strange marks, and evidently copied after the Mexican Calender given by Humboldt, but copied in such a way as not to betray the source whence it was derived.... I ... well remember that the paper contained anything else but *"Egyptian Hieroglyphics."*[19]

When he dictated his autobiography several years later, Joseph gave what he called Martin Harris's version of the Anthon visit. Incidentally, when Joseph dictated this account, Harris had been excommunicated from the church several months earlier:

I went to the city of New York and presented the characters which had been translated, with the translation thereof to Professor Anthony, a gentleman celebrated for his literary attainments; — Professor Anthony stated that the translation was correct, more so than any he had before seen translated from the Egyptian. I then showed him those which were not yet translated, and he said that they were Egyptian, Chaldeac, Assyriac, and Arabic, and he said they were the true characters. He gave me a certificate certifying to the people of Palmyra that they were true characters, and that the translation of such of them as had been translated was also correct. I took the certificate and put it into my pocket, and was just leaving the house, when Mr. Anthony called me back, and asked me how the young man found out that there were gold plates in the place where he found them. I answered that an angel of God had revealed it unto him.

He then said to me, let me see that certificate. I accordingly took it out of my pocket and gave it to him, when he took it and tore it to pieces, saying that there was no such thing as ministering of angels, and that if I would bring the plates to him, he would translate them. I informed him that part of the plates were sealed, and that I was forbidden to bring them, he replied, 'I cannot read a sealed book.' I left him and went to Dr. Mitchell, who sanctioned what Professor Anthony had said respecting both the characters and translation."[20]

It should be emphasized that this is not Harris himself saying what happened on the trip, but rather Joseph saying that it was what Harris said. Actually, this account is suspect because it not only contradicts Anthon's account of the visit, it also contradicts many other earlier accounts, including the one that Harris gave to Clark. These accounts held that Anthon (and Mitchell, for that matter) was not able to translate the characters. Even if the characters were Egyptian, it is unlikely that Anthon could have translated them; the study of the Egyptian writing system was then in its infancy.

Adding to the confusion is a piece of paper with some scrawled characters copied on it that is presently in the possession of the Reorganized Church of Latter Day Saints. (See the plate on page 77.) The characters purportedly are the ones that Harris brought to Anthon, but they do not match the description that Anthon gave of them. The characters on this transcript are lined up horizontally rather than in vertical columns as Anthon described, and they do not end in a "rude delineation of a circle divided in various compartments."[21] It is possible that the characters are some of the same ones that Harris brought to Anthon, but were copied on another piece of paper in a different arrangement.

Competent philologists have examined copies of this scrap of paper and they agree that it is not an Egyptian inscription and that it is not written in any other known script. Moreover, the characters are completely unlike anything that has been left behind by any of the ancient American Indian civilizations purportedly described in The Book of Mormon. The characters, in fact, appear to be simply a hodge-podge of random scribblings and of figures and characters taken from various sources, including even some that could have been taken from the same alphabet that speakers of English use. Therefore, because the various forms of Egyptian writing are considerably better known

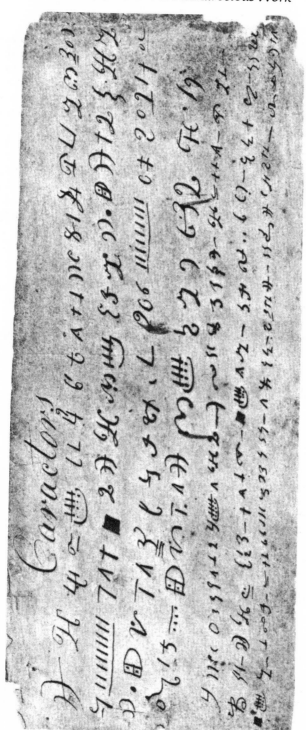

Characters that Joseph Smith supposedly copied from the gold plates.

now than they were in Anthon's time, and can presently be translated, it can be quite reasonably stated that Anthon could not possibly have translated the characters, much less verified any "translation" that Joseph might have given.

The problem, then, is to try to discern what actually happened during the trip that Harris made to New York City to get a learned opinion about the characters, and why Harris became convinced that Joseph could do the job of translating them. What now seems likely is that Joseph engineered the whole thing for Harris's benefit, and that he got his inspiration for the scenario from Isaiah 29:11. That verse in Isaiah mentions a book that is delivered to one who is learned, but who could not read it.

Obviously, despite the fact that he later said that "Professor Anthony" stated that his "translation" was correct, Joseph would have known that any scholar that Harris went to with the characters would not have been able to translate them. In fact, it was believed in the very early church that the "learned" could not translate the characters. After all, according to *The Book of Mormon* only those who were supplied with the "means" could make a translation of the characters:

> And now behold, we have written this record according to our knowledge in the characters, which are called among us reformed Egyptian, being handed down and altered by us, according to our manner of speech.... But the Lord knoweth ... that none other people knoweth our language; and ... therefore he hath prepared means for the interpretation thereof.[22]

Thus, when he dictated *The Book of Mormon*, Joseph claimed that those who engraved the plates wrote in a language that was unknown to all other people, and only by means of the "interpreters" could the record be translated.

Why, then, did Joseph later claim that Anthon could translate the characters and verify a translation that Joseph himself had supplied? And what really happened on the trip to "the learned" that convinced Harris to back Joseph's book?

The answer to the first question lies in the sensitivity of the early church to the charges of the unbelievers that *The Book of Mormon* was a fraud and that Joseph Smith had no real ability to translate ancient languages. In defense of their prophet, the Mormon missionaries apparently began to manufacture stories to the effect that the learned had confirmed that Joseph did correctly translate the characters. It would appear that Joseph himself went along with the new stories in order to magnify his standing as a translator. The result of this was the highly artificial account of the Harris trip that Joseph gave in his autobiography.

Why then did the trip to "the learned" dispel any doubts that Harris may have had? First, as we know, Anthon could not have translated the characters. Second, since he had invented them, Joseph knew that Anthon could not translate the characters. Third, Joseph told Harris what to expect when the learned tried to translate them. Fourth, what Joseph told Harris to expect came to pass: the learned could not read the characters and Joseph could (or so he claimed). But Joseph was just an ignorant young man. Harris concluded, therefore, that "God had chosen the foolish things of the world to confound the wise."

It seems, then, that Joseph may have manipulated the situation for Harris's sake. Moreover, when Harris returned from visiting Anthon, Joseph showed him Isaiah 29:11–12, which reads:

> And the vision of all is become unto you as the words of a book that is sealed, which *men* deliver to one that is learned, saying, Read this, I pray thee: and he saith, I cannot; for it *is* sealed: And the book is delivered to him that is not learned, saying, Read this, I pray thee: and he saith, I am not learned.

The passage apparently had given Joseph the idea for having Harris make the trip in the first place. And, when Harris returned, Joseph used the passage to make the farmer think he had fulfilled a biblical prophecy. Harris, of course, was the type of person who would be overwhelmed at having played such a role. As a result, he was convinced that Joseph could do the task he had set out to do.

While he was dictating *The Book of Mormon* some time later, Joseph included a "prophecy" about the Harris trip by working it up with the imagery of the Isaiah passage:

> But behold, it shall come to pass that the Lord God shall say unto him to whom he shall deliver the book, Take these words which are not sealed, and deliver them to another, that he may shew them unto the learned, saying: Read this, I pray thee. And the learned shall say, Bring hither the book, and I will read them.... And the man shall say, I cannot bring the book, for it is sealed. Then shall the learned say, I cannot read it. Wherefore it shall come to pass, that the Lord God will deliver again the book and the words thereof, to him that is not learned; and the man that is not learned, shall say, I an not learned.[23]

But, of course, a prophecy made after the fact is not really a prophecy; it is merely a historical comment. It should also be noted that Isaiah was not referring to an actual sealed book, but rather was making an allusion to the lost state of the city of Jerusalem: "... all that fight against her and her munitions, and that distress her, shall be as a dream of a night vision.... And the vision of all is become unto you as the words of a book that is sealed...."

In April of 1828, Harris returned to Harmony and relieved Emma of the task of taking down Joseph's dictation. He could not see Joseph during the process, because a blanket was hung up between the two men. As Joseph "translated" the plates on one side of the blanket, Harris sat at the table on the other side and wrote down the words that Joseph dictated. Joseph supposedly was using the spectacles to read the plates, but since the plates were still supposed to be secreted in the woods with Joseph translating them from a distance, there would have been no reason for the blanket — unless, of course, he actually had various materials hidden behind the blanket to assist him in developing the story he was telling. These materials probably consisted of an outline he had worked out for the story and books and notes to refer to. With these and his imagination and storytelling ability, Joseph would have been able to narrate his history. The process, however, was painstakingly slow. Joseph would have had to think out carefully what he was going to say in order to minimize any corrections or changes.

Joseph and Harris continued working in this manner for two months. By June, some 116 pages of manuscript were completed. Counting the time that Emma had taken the dictation, an average of less than one page of manuscript had been done per day. At this time, Harris asked Joseph for permission to take the 116 pages back to Palmyra in order to convince his wife of the worth of what he was doing. At first, Joseph refused, but he eventually relented and gave Harris his permission. Emma was due to have a child soon, and perhaps he thought that the dictation would be interrupted anyway.

It turned out that Joseph made a mistake in letting Harris take the 116 pages, but it was a mistake that redirected the course of his future.

Chapter 7

The Gold Bible

When his wife gave birth in June of 1828, Joseph received what was to be the first in a series of what must have been unsettling experiences. The infant "was still-born and very much deformed," according to Sophia Lewis, a relative of Emma's who was present at the birth.[1] To add to the shock that Joseph must have felt, Emma came close to losing her life during the delivery and remained in critical condition for several days.

The effect of these blows upon Joseph is perhaps illustrated by evidence showing he tried to join the Harmony Methodist Episcopal Church that same month. This attempt resulted in yet another ordeal. In a letter they sent to the *Amboy Journal* several years later, Emma's cousins, Joseph and Hiel Lewis, described what happened:

> He [Joseph Smith] presented himself in a very serious and humble manner, and the minister, not suspecting evil, put his name on the class book, in the absence of some of the official members, among whom was the under-signed, Joseph Lewis, who, when he learned what was done, took with him Joshua McKune, and had a talk with Smith. They told him plainly that such a character as he was a disgrace to the church, that he could not be a member of the church unless he broke off his sins by repentance, made public confession, renounced his fraudulent and hypocritical practices, and gave some evidence that he intended to reform and conduct himself some-what nearer like a christian than he had done. They gave him his choice, to go before the class, and publicly ask to have his name stricken from the class book, or stand a disciplinary investigation. He chose the former, and immediately withdrew his name. So his name as a member of the class was on the book only three days.[2]

Regardless of what motivated Joseph to try to join the Harmony Methodist Episcopal Church, his attempt to do so (and also his involvement with the Methodist and Baptist churches in the Palmyra area, mentioned earlier) conflicts with his later claims about his first vision. In that vision the Lord supposedly commanded Joseph to join none of the sects, for they were all an abomination in his sight. But this episode also provides clues to the development of Joseph's thinking and to the evolution of *The Book of Mormon*.

It is appropriate to pursue this subject further, noting the existence of additional evidence that Joseph sought to join the Harmony Methodist Episcopal Church, which was presented by no less a source than a Mormon elder. Attempting to rebut the statements that Joseph and Hiel Lewis made, Edwin Cadwell, who belonged to the Reorganized Church, sent the *Amboy Journal* a letter. Included in that letter was the following:

> Messrs. Lewis say Joseph joined the M.E. Church, but that "his name was on the (class) book only three days." A very short "probation" indeed. Now Mr. Morse [Cadwell's neighbor] says *he* was the "leader" of the said "class" and that to his certain knowledge Smith's name remained on the class book ... for about *six months*, when it was simply "dropped," as Smith did not seek to become a full member.[3]

Regardless of whether Joseph's name was on the book for three days or six months, Elder Cadwell confirmed that Joseph did seek to become a member of the Harmony Methodist Episcopal Church. In so doing, he unthinkingly undermined the credibility of Joseph's claims about the first vision.

But that was not the end of the exchange of letters. Joseph Lewis sent another letter to the *Amboy Journal* in answer to Elder Cadwell's letter. In it, Lewis reaffirmed what he had said previously, and gave further information. This included the year and month in which the episode took place. It was the same year and month in which Emma gave birth to their deformed and still-born son. The following is an extract from this letter:

> The facts are these: I with Joshua McKune, a local preacher at that time, I think in June, 1828, heard on Saturday, that Joe Smith had joined the church on Wednesday afternoon.... We thought it was a disgrace to the church to have a practicing necromancer, a dealer in enchantments and bleeding ghosts, in it. So on Sunday we ... talked with him some time ... before the meeting. Told him that his occupation, habits, and moral character were at variance with the discipline, that his name would be a disgrace to the church, that there should have been recantation, confession, and at least promised reformation — That he could that day publicly ask that his name be stricken from the class book, or stand an investigation. He chose the former, and did that very day make the request that his name be taken off the class-book, Michael B. Morse to the contrary notwithstanding. And if said Morse was leader at that time, and Smith's name remained on the class-book six months, the class leader carelessly or wickedly neglected his duty.[4]

If Joseph did indeed sincerely seek to become a member of the church because he was distressed over the outcome of his wife's childbirth, the choices that Joseph Lewis and the preacher gave him surely would have made his distress even more intense.

As unsettled as Joseph must have felt because of what had already happened, the frustrations that were to plague him during that June were not yet over. Another began when the date of Martin Harris's scheduled return came and went with no sign of the farmer. As the days wore on with no word, Joseph became increasingly concerned about his backer and the 116 pages of manuscript. Finally, after Emma had recovered sufficiently, Joseph made a trip to Palmyra to find out what happened. When he arrived, he learned from an abject Martin Harris that the 116 pages were missing. Harris suspected that his wife had taken them from the bureau drawer in which he had kept them, but nothing he said or did would make her return them or even admit to having taken them. When Joseph confronted Lucy Harris, she contemptuously challenged him to replace the missing pages the same way he had acquired them.

The loss of the manuscript left Joseph in a dilemma. If the missing 116 pages could not be found, he would have to make up the loss. But in what way? It appears that he had spontaneously dictated most of the material in the 116 pages; thus he would not have been able to reproduce it exactly if he tried to redictate it. Moreover, there was the possibility that the missing pages would be brought forward later to invite comparison with the replacement. That would ruin everything. The book that he was dictating was supposed to be a true history of the former inhabitants of America, and his method of translating that history would lose credibility if the two versions were different.

Joseph's dilemma marked a turning point in the nature of *The Book of Mormon*. Before that June, he had apparently made no really serious pretensions that his ancient history was a new revelation from the Lord, even though it may have contained many religious concepts from *View of the Hebrews*. In the following months, however, he greatly expanded the religious significance of the book, even to the point of claiming that it was a divine revelation. Joseph also represented himself as being a spokesman for God and began to develop his role as a prophet who was restoring the true religion of old. His newly acquired religious presence was so impressive that it even infected some of his family and caused them to forsake their affiliation with the Presbyterian Church.

One can only speculate on what caused Joseph to make this change, but surely the events of June of 1828 played a part in it. It would appear that seeing his stillborn and much deformed infant son, not to mention his wife's critical condition, had caused Joseph to get religion. But then when he had tried to act upon his religious impulses by joining the Harmony Methodist Episcopal Church, two members of the church rebuffed him and forced him to make an upsetting decision. Perhaps this lack of charity by professed Christians, one of whom was a preacher, made him recall what had happened a few years earlier at Alvin's funeral service. On that occasion, another preacher had showed a lack of Christian charity when he intimated very strongly that Joseph's much beloved brother had gone to hell for not belonging to any church.

As Joseph reflected on these events, his feelings about the religious institutions of the day might have turned deeply cynical. He might even have come to consider those institutions to be an abomination (the word he later used). Moreover, his reflection upon these things, and particularly upon his deformed and stillborn son, might have caused him to become cynical about God—perhaps even about the very existence of God. If this were the case, his cynicism and resentment might have been what caused him to enter boldly into areas that he previously had barely touched upon—areas in which he could use the religious impulses of others for his own benefit, just as he had previously used the get-rich-quick impulses of the money diggers. Once he entered these areas, Joseph apparently even felt no compunction about putting words into the mouth of God. And that was how Joseph found a way to get out of his dilemma.

In July, after he returned to Harmony, Joseph received his first "revelation" from the "Lord." This revelation chastised him for losing the 116 pages and revoked his translation privileges for a "season." This perhaps indicates that he needed time to work out his new plans. In a subsequent revelation, the Lord commanded Joseph not to retranslate the same section of the plates that he had translated before. By the design of Satan, according to the revelation, those who had taken the pages would alter them to keep the work from being accepted. Instead, Joseph was to translate from the plates of Nephi, which were in a different section, but which contained a more detailed account of the same things that he had previously translated.

But that was not all. "Behold," declared the Lord, "there are many things engraven on the plates of Nephi, which do throw greater views upon my gospel."[5] In other words, the lost 116 pages did not contain as much of a religious message as the material that Joseph would dictate in their place. Joseph had completed the transition. *The Book of Mormon* was no longer simply a "history" of ancient America; it was now a new "revelation" from God.

It is not known exactly when Joseph returned to his dictation. Some of his biographers have said it was not until that winter, but Joseph's mother indicated that it was in September or shortly thereafter. She related that she and her husband visited Joseph in Harmony about two months after he had returned there from his trip to Palmyra. Upon their arrival, as she described it, Joseph told them about the revelation he had received from the Lord. He then said, "... I have again commenced translating, and Emma writes for me, but the angel said that the Lord would send me a scribe, and I trust his promise will be verified."[6]

It should again be noted that from about this time Joseph's mother and the two brothers began to neglect worship and the sacrament of the Lord's supper in the Presbyterian Church. One might therefore conclude that it was probably during this visit that Joseph's parents, and consequently the rest of the family, first learned that Joseph was going to restore the "true" church of God.

As was noted before, it was from about this time that Joseph's mother and the two brothers began to neglect worship and the sacrament of the Lord's supper in the Presbyterian Church.[7] The falling away from the church by these family members at this time is very likely an indication that Joseph had begun to develop a religious slant to his ancient "history." Lucy Smith was a devoutly religious woman and she was deeply concerned that her family have its religious side. The fact that she herself had continued to attend the Presbyterian Church up to this point would indicate that she had no reason to do otherwise. If Joseph had had visions from the Lord several years earlier, especially one in which the Lord told Joseph that all of the "sects" were an "abomination," and if he had claimed that the gold plates contained a new revelation from God when he obtained them more than a year before, his family would have quit the church much sooner than they did. One would have to conclude either that his family did not believe him when he had made those pronouncements, or one would have to conclude that he never made them. If she had believed Joseph, Lucy certainly would not have gone to one of the churches that was so roundly condemned by the Lord.

Therefore it seems most likely that it was during this visit that Lucy and her husband made to Joseph in Harmony that they first learned that Joseph was going to "restore" the "true" church of God. Upon their return to Palmyra they would have informed the rest of the family of this momentous revelation and thus caused the "neglect" in worshipping at the Presbyterian Church.

Regardless of how long his "translation privileges" were revoked, Joseph would have used the time to work on and improve the outline of his book. Along with the practice he had in dictating the 116 pages, this extra time evidently served him well. When he began dictating again, the words came from his lips with some fluidity, if not always in the best prose form. With his new-found confidence, Joseph even dispensed with the blanket that had previously separated him from his scribe. The work went faster. Depending on whether he began dictating earnestly in September or sometime that winter when Martin Harris again took over the task of writing for him, he would have produced an average of from two to four pages per day up to the time the book was completed in the following July.

In March, Joseph produced another revelation from the Lord. It commanded him to translate a few more pages and then to stop for a season. The Lord continued, "I ... will provide means whereby thou mayest accomplish the thing which I have commanded thee."[8] A short time later, Oliver Cowdery came and took over from Harris the job of writing for Joseph.

Oliver had been boarding with Joseph's family in Manchester. Supposedly, the two had never met before and he ostensibly made the trip to Harmony because he was intrigued by the stories the family had told him about Joseph and the plates. In any case, the meeting between the two men resulted in the agreement that Oliver would henceforth be Joseph's scribe.

Still, the dictation was not all smooth going for Joseph. At times he was afflicted with what is now called writer's block, and his talent for creativity would fail. David Whitmer, a close friend of Oliver's from Fayette, New York, paid them a visit that spring and later described Joseph's explanation of these dry spells:

> At times when Brother Joseph would attempt to translate, he would look into the hat in which the stone was placed, he found that he was spiritually blind and could not translate. He told us that his mind dwelt too much on earthly things, and various causes would make him incapable of proceeding with the translation. When in this condition he would go out and pray, and when he became sufficiently humble before God, he could then proceed with the translation.[9]

As with many other authors who have had similar spells, Joseph found that the best cure for them is going out for a walk. The conscious mind then rests, while the subconscious mulls over the problem and finds an answer.

Peter Whitmer, David's father, had also visited Harmony. Impressed with what he saw, he invited Joseph to be his houseguest for the remainder of the translation process. Taking up the invitation, Joseph and Oliver went to Fayette in June, and completed the manuscript in a few weeks.

Despite the seeming success that Joseph had in convincing others of the worth of what he was doing, his father-in-law remained skeptical. The following concludes Isaac Hale's statement:

> The manner in which he pretended to read and interpret, was the same as when he looked for the money-diggers, with the stone in his hat, and his hat over his face, while the Book of Plates were at the same time hid in the woods!
>
> After this, Martin Harris went away, and Oliver Cowdery came and wrote for Smith, while he interpreted as above described....
>
> Joseph Smith Jr. resided near me for some time after this, and I had a good opportunity of becoming acquainted with him, and somewhat acquainted with his associates, and I conscientiously believe from the facts I have detailed, and from many other circumstances, ... that the whole "Book of Mormon" (so called) is a silly fabrication of falsehood and wickedness, got up for speculation, and with a design to dupe the credulous and unwary—and in order that its fabricators may live upon the spoils of those who swallow the deception.[10]

Note that Isaac Hale made no mention of seeing Joseph use the spectacles to translate the plates. Instead, he described Joseph as using the same method as when he looked for the money-diggers, with the stone in his hat, and his hat over his face. Most of the others who were present also stated that Joseph used his peepstone rather than the spectacles in the translation process. For example, David Whitmer said:

> I will now give you a description of the manner in which the Book of Mormon was translated. Joseph Smith would put the seer stone into a hat, and put his face into the hat, drawing it closely around his face to exclude the light; and in the darkness the spiritual light would shine. A piece of something resembling parchment would appear, and on that appeared the writing.[11]

In a letter she wrote to one of her sons several years later, Joseph's wife, Emma, also indicated that Joseph used the stone in his hat to translate the plates:

> In writing for your father, I frequently wrote day after day, often sitting at the table close by him, he sitting with his face buried in his hat, with the stone in it, and dictating hour after hour with nothing between us.[12]

According to an early Mormon publication, Martin Harris made a similar statement:

> Martin Harris related ... that the Prophet possessed a seer stone, by which he was enabled to translate as well as from the Urim and Thummim, and for convenience he then used the seer stone.... By aid of the seer stone, sentences would appear and were read by the Prophet and written by Harris....
>
> Martin said further that the seer stone differed in appearance entirely from the Urim and Thummim that was obtained with the plates.... Martin said there were not many pages translated while he wrote, after which Oliver Cowdery and others did the writing.[13]

As it turned out, Joseph did not pretend to use the Urim and Thummim, or spectacles, to translate any part of the published version of *The Book of Mormon*. In an interview, David Whitmer related the story of the loss of the 116 pages by Martin Harris, then continued with the following:

> This unpardonable carelessness evoked the stormiest kind of chastisement from the Lord, who took from the prophet the Urim and Thummim and otherwise expressed his condemnation. By fervent prayer and by otherwise humbling himself, the prophet, however, again found favor, and was presented with a strange, oval-shaped, chocolate-colored stone, about the size of an egg, only more flat, which it was promised, should serve the same purpose as the missing Urim and Thummim (the latter was a pair of transparent stones set in a bow-shaped frame and very much resembled a pair of spectacles). With this stone all of the present Book of Mormon was translated.[14]

Whitmer's statement concerning the translation of the published version of *The Book of Mormon* is substantiated by a statement that Joseph's wife made:

> Now the first that my husband translated, was translated by the use of the Urim and Thummim, and that was the part that Martin Harris lost, after that he used a small stone, not exactly black, but was rather a dark color.[15]

According to these statements, then, Joseph supposedly used the Urim and Thummim, or spectacles, to translate only the 116 pages that Martin Harris lost. Subsequently, in translating the version of *The Book of Mormon* that came to be published, Joseph used only the seer stone, or the peepstone as it was sometimes called. Joseph, however, was not given the stone after the loss of the 116 pages as David Whitmer reported. Joseph had actually had the stone for several years, and it was the same stone that he used in his money digging operations. Willard Chase related that this stone was found while Alvin and Joseph were digging a well:

> In the year 1822, I was engaged in digging a well. I employed Alvin and Joseph Smith to assist me.... After digging about twenty feet below the surface of the earth, we discovered a singularly appearing stone, which excited my curiosity. I brought it to the top of the well, and as we were examining it, Joseph put it into his hat, and then his face into the top of his

hat.... The next morning he came to me and wished to obtain the stone, alledging that he could see in it; but I told him I did not wish to part with it on account of its being a curiosity, but would lend it....

In April, 1830, I again asked Hiram for the stone which he had borrowed of me; he told me I should not have it, for Joseph made use of it in translating his Bible.[16]

Nowhere did Joseph make any mention of using the peepstone to translate *The Book of Mormon*. But that really should be no surprise; after he became the Mormon prophet he tried to downplay anything that had a close connection with his former money digging operations. He therefore declared that the translation was all done through the medium of the Urim and Thummim, and most modern Mormons accept this.

And that brings us to the question of what actually took place while Joseph was translating *The Book of Mormon*. To answer that question, we must indulge in a certain amount of speculation. For example, we have already conjectured that Joseph probably had some notes and books behind the blanket to help him in dictating the story when he was supposedly using the Urim and Thummim. We might further theorize that later, when he did away with the blanket, he used his hat and peepstone for much the same purpose. He might have pinned a piece of paper in the hat outlining what he intended to dictate at that session. He could have either glanced at the paper before he put the hat to his face, or let light shine through a slit in the hat and onto the paper so he could read it after he put the hat to his face. Perhaps when Joseph had to go out and pray, he actually had to pin the next installment in his hat.

In creating *The Book of Mormon*, Joseph seems to have used his fertile imagination to reshape, meld together, and project allegorically into ancient America an array of literary and social material that was a part of his own early American environment. That, perhaps, was one reason a large number of people accepted the book within a comparatively short time. The universal themes and the familiar contemporary ideas, such as the belief in the Hebrew ancestry of the Indians, allowed many of its readers to find something to which they could relate. Moreover, the initial success of the book (within fifteen years there were several tens of thousands of Mormon converts) paved the way for its future acceptance. The religious organization that resulted was able to keep up the momentum of gaining new believers even after some of the themes in the book were no longer relevant. In contrast, if *The Book of Mormon* had made its first appearance today instead of a century and a half ago, it probably would be looked upon as being only a rather tedious epic fantasy — but then, one never knows.

The story that *The Book of Mormon* tells begins in Jerusalem shortly before the Babylonian Captivity. Under the guidance of God, the family and followers of an Israelite patriarch named Lehi leave the city and eventually make their way to the New World. After arriving there, they divide into two factions. One faction, which is civilized and follows the way of God, is led by Nephi, one of Lehi's sons. Laman, another of Lehi's sons, leads the other faction, which consists of savage hunters who have forsaken the way of God. For hundreds of years there are numerous wars between the savage Lamanites and the civilized Nephites. Eventually, many of the Nephites also forsake the way of God and thus bring His wrath down upon themselves. At about the time of the Crucifixion, the Nephite cities are subjected to wholesale destruction as a divine punishment for the transgressions of the inhabitants. Jesus then appears to the people of the New World and preaches the gospel. This initiates an era of peace and religion, but it does not last long. Most of the Nephites again forsake the way of God, thus once more calling His wrath down upon themselves. The wars start up again, and finally, about A.D. 400, the Lamanites almost totally destroy the Nephites. Mormon, one of the few remaining Nephites who are faithful to the Lord, writes the history of his people upon plates of gold. He then hides the plates in the hill Cumorah, where Joseph was supposed to have found them centuries later. The Lamanites, meanwhile, become the Indians that the European settlers eventually find upon their arrival in the New World. Near the end of *The Book of Mormon*, in "The Book of Ether," there is a summary of the history of another group of people, called the Jaredites. These people were supposed to have come to the New World from the tower of Babel and, after several centuries of civil warfare, to have destroyed themselves at about the time Lehi and his followers came over.

The Book of Mormon shows more than just Joseph's creative ability and eclectic skill; it also shows that he had an understanding of the psychology of religious belief. Acquiring such an understanding probably came quite naturally to Joseph. Even before he produced *The Book of Mormon*, he demonstrated an innate ability to sway others. If he had not had such an ability, he would not have been able to induce the treasure hunters to do so much digging. In time, he was able to expand upon this personal skill by observing what made people accept religious conversion. The religious ferment that was brewing throughout the early American countryside while *The Book of Mormon* was apparently gestating in his mind probably gave him ample lessons in such things. Specifically, Joseph undoubtedly saw many conversions during the height of the 1824 religious excitement described earlier. Thus, the religious climate of the time could easily have helped Joseph assimulate an understanding of how he could motivate people to accept his new religion.

Joseph seems to have incorporated into *The Book of Mormon* much of what he learned about influencing people. *The Book of Mormon* is somewhat lulling, being long and tedious reading. Constantly running through its chapters is the theme that those who follow the way of God will prosper, while those who forsake God will be led to their destruction. That is the theme of the major plot and most of the subplots. The susceptible reader is therefore influenced to place himself in a position to be accepted by God. And, of course, the way for the reader to be accepted by God is for the reader to accept *The Book of Mormon* as His word. Joseph strengthened this pressure with the following request:

> And when ye shall receive these things, I would exhort you that ye would ask God, the Eternal Father, in the name of Christ, if these things are not true; and if ye shall ask with a sincere heart, with real intent, having faith in Christ, and he will manifest the truth of it unto you, by the power of the Holy Ghost....[17]

But in this is a psychological catch. If the reader did ask "with a sincere heart, with real intent," he would have already, at least subconsciously, committed himself to accepting the book. It would not be surprising, then, that such an individual would receive a witness to its truth.

Joseph also used other inducements to gain converts for his church. These included satisfying the need that most people have for a close relationship with others, promoting a sense of belonging to an exclusive community, and providing an authoritative system of belief. In short, he provided the same things that have led people to join religious denominations throughout time. Joseph, however, emphasized these even more strongly than did most of the traditional religions.

The Book of Mormon is a rather long book—it has about 275,000 words. But then, Joseph seems to have wanted a book that looked impressive, a book of epic proportions in which the reader would lose himself and be convinced that it was no run-of-the-mill novel. Yet, an analysis of Joseph's latter-day revelation reveals that it contains a large amount of padding. For one thing, the book imitates the language and style of the King James version of the Bible, often in an exaggerated form covering a good deal of space. The result is that several lines are taken up to say that which could have been said in one or two. Prophecies are repeated, thus taking up even more space. With the book thus filled out, it appears more voluminous.

If such padding was in an ordinary book, it would be considered simple wordiness. In *The Book of Mormon*, however, it results in an incongruity because Joseph had Mormon, the supposed writer of the history, lament that he did not have enough space on the plates to tell the full story of his people. In an attempt to expand the book (or perhaps because he was on occasion at a loss for ideas), Joseph even had Mormon include more than twenty complete chapters almost verbatim from the Bible—this, even though Mormon was supposed to have prophetically known that the recipients of his history would have the quoted chapters in their own Bible. In fact, these chapters from the Bible make up approximately one tenth of the content of *The Book of Mormon*. Such a waste of space would be rather odd if the book had actually been written by someone who was concerned with a limited writing space. On the other hand, it would not have been odd if he were trying to flesh it out in order to give it impressive proportions.

The first edition had other stylistic faults besides its wordiness. In fact, the editors of the succeeding editions felt compelled to make some changes, perhaps to make it appear more like a divine revelation. Because of these, the later editions do not give a completely accurate picture of Joseph's original prose style. For example, the first edition of *The Book of Mormon* was rather cumbersome to read because Joseph frequently ran his sentences together by overusing conjunctions such as "and." The editors of the later editions ameliorated this condition somewhat by dividing the chapters up into numbered verses and by adding periods so that the sentences were more manageable.

Reflecting Joseph's lack of formal education, the first edition of *The Book of Mormon* also had a large number of grammatical errors. For example, Joseph would insert an unnecessary article before participles: "... when the

Lamanites saw that Moroni was a coming against them..."; "And as I was a going thither...."[18] Joseph also used "no" when he should have used "any": "...they did not fight against God no more...."[19] He frequently formed his past participles incorrectly: "...and they had began to possess the land of Amulon, and had began to till the ground."[20] Finally, he often used the wrong form of the past tense: "...and this he done, that..."; "...they was angry with me...."[21] Most of the grammatical errors were corrected in subsequent editions, so the book seems more literate now than it did originally.

There were yet other stylistic faults in the first edition of *The Book of Mormon*. Joseph made excessive use of the phrase, "and it came to pass that." Perhaps he used this so that he could gather his thoughts before dictating what would follow, but the results were verbose and ludicrous. The editors of the later editions, apparently feeling the phrases detracted from the readability of the book, deleted many of them. The following is an example:

> Now it came to pass that after Alma had received his message from the angel of the Lord, he returned speedily to the land of Ammonihah. And it came to pass that he entered the city by another way, yea, by the way which was on the south of the city Ammonihah. And it came to pass that as he entered the city, he was an hungered...."[22]

In the modern Utah edition, only the first "it came to pass that" remains.

The faults of *The Book of Mormon* are not limited to those of style and grammar. Among the most apparent of other flaws are the quotations from the King James version of the Bible, which has many language characteristics befitting the time and place in which it was first published. Yet, that is the version of the Bible used in *The Book of Mormon* — a book that was supposedly written more than a thousand years before the time of King James. Joseph did modify some of the biblical verses, but most remain unchanged.

There are many other anachronisms and incongruities in the book. For example, its characters leave Palestine before the Babylonian Captivity and then build synagogues in the New World "after the manner of the Jews." But synagogues did not arise in the Old World until after the Babylonian Captivity had begun. According to *The Book of Mormon*, the pre-Columbian inhabitants of the Americas had such Old World domesticated plants and animals as wheat, barley, cattle, horses, and sheep (which the pre-Columbians in fact did not have) but the book makes virtually no mention of the New World domesticated plants and animals upon which they were in fact dependent.

But perhaps the greatest fault in *The Book of Mormon* is its implied claim that the Indians are of Hebrew descent. In Joseph's time this was not so serious because many people then believed that the Indians were descended from the Ten Tribes of Israel. Today, no non-Mormon archaeolgist or anthropologist gives serious consideration to the idea that the Indians are of Hebrew descent. We shall deal with this subject more fully in Appendix B.

Joseph was acutely aware that his book had defects. His solution to the problem seemingly was to try to intimidate those who would criticize his new revelation because of those defects. For example, possibly to cover his weakness in grammar and prose style, he had one of the characters in his book say:

Thou hast also made our words powerful and great, even that we cannot write them; wherefore, when we write, we behold our weakness, and stumble because of the placing of our words; and I fear lest the Gentiles shall mock at our words. And when I said this the Lord spake unto me, saying, Fools mock, but they shall mourn.[23]

And to cover any other defects in the book, Joseph had the same character say:

... and if there be faults, they be the faults of a man. But behold, we know no fault. Nevertheless, God knoweth all things; therefore he that condemneth, let him be aware lest he shall be in danger of hell fire.[24]

Despite these threats of hell fire, many critics pointed with delight to some of the faults of The Book of Mormon soon after its publication. Yet, Joseph's new revelation weathered the criticism and gained converts for the new church—slowly at first, but with remarkable success in a few years. The Book of Mormon remains the cornerstone of the Mormon religion. It was an ambitious literary work and because of it Joseph became a prophet revered by millions.

Chapter 8

"Send Them the Heralds of Salvation"

As Joseph neared the end of his dictation of *The Book of Mormon*, he began to think about some problems he would have to solve before the book could be published. A minor one, easily taken care of, was that of the missing 116 pages. His revelation concerning these would hinder their being used against him, but he would have to let the readers of his book know about it if it were to be effective. Toward that end, he prepared the following preface, which appeared only in the first edition:

TO THE READER —

As many false reports have been circulated respecting the following work, and also many unlawful measures taken by evil designing persons to destroy me, and also the work, I would inform you that I translated, by the gift and power of God, and caused to be written, one hundred and sixteen pages, the which I took from the Book of Lehi, which was an account abridged from the plates of Lehi, by the hand of Mormon; which said account, some person or persons have stolen and kept from me, notwithstanding my utmost exertions to recover it again — and being commanded of the Lord that I should not translate the same over again, for Satan had put it into their hearts to tempt the Lord their God, by altering the words, that they did read contrary from that which I translated and caused to be written; and if I should bring forth the same words again, or, in other words, if I should translate the same over again, they would publish that which they had stolen, and Satan would stir up the hearts of this generation, that they might not receive this work: but behold, the Lord said unto me, I will not suffer that Satan shall accomplish his evil design in this thing: therefore thou shalt translate from the plates of Nephi, until ye come to that which ye have translated, which ye have retained; and behold ye shall publish it as the record of Nephi; and thus I will confound those who have altered my words. I will not suffer that they shall destroy my work; yea, I will shew unto them that my wisdom is greater than the cunning of the Devil. Wherefore, to be obedient unto the commandments of God, I have, through his grace and mercy, accomplished that which he hath commanded me respecting this thing. I would also inform you that the plates of which hath been spoken, were found in the township of Manchester, Ontario county, New-York.

THE AUTHOR

The next problem Joseph faced was not so easy to solve: he was supposed to have translated the book from a set of gold plates, and people would naturally wonder if they existed. It was not likely that Joseph had any gold plates. All that anyone had seen was the box in which the plates were supposedly kept, or a cloth placed over what were supposed to be the plates as they were sitting on a table. If someone appeared overly inquisitive, Joseph had an explanation of why he could not allow the plates to be seen: God would strike anyone dead who looked upon them without authorization. It is interesting to note that several individuals said they hefted the box that was supposed to contain the plates. These individuals variously estimated the weight of the plates as being between thirty and sixty pounds. An actual set of gold plates of the same approximate dimensions as Joseph's were supposed to have been would have weighed almost two hundred pounds.[1]

Joseph would have realized that his claims about the plates would be subject to ridicule if he could not provide some kind of evidence for their existence. As a partial solution for the problem, he might have made up a set of dummy plates. Of course, these plates would not have been gold. Instead, they most likely would have been made out of pieces of tin sheeting. By placing these dummy plates under a cloth, Joseph could allow a few privileged persons to feel them through the material and discern their form and metallic nature, but they would have had only his word that they were of gold.

Even if he did make a set of dummy plates, Joseph apparently felt that they were not sufficient for his purpose. As long as it could be said that no one had seen any plates of gold, he could lose a great many potential believers in his new revelation. In order to make his claims convincing, he needed some testimonies asserting that he did have such a set of plates.

Joseph succeeded in having two groups of "witnesses" give the testimony he needed. The first group consisted of Oliver Cowdery, David Whitmer, and Martin Harris. The following is their statement as it appeared in the first edition of *The Book of Mormon*:

THE TESTIMONY OF THREE WITNESSES.

Be it known unto all nations, kindreds, tongues, and people, unto whom this work shall come, that we, through the grace of God the Father, and our Lord Jesus Christ, have seen the plates which contain this record, which is a record of the people of Nephi, and also of the Lamanites, his brethren, and also of the people of Jared, which came from the tower, of which hath been spoken; and we also know that they have been translated by the gift and power of God, for his voice hath declared it unto us; wherefore we know of a surety, that the work is true. And we also testify that we have seeen [sic] the engravings which are upon the plates; and they have been shewn unto us by the power of God, and not of man. And we declare with words of soberness, that an Angel of God came down from heaven, and he brought and laid before our eyes, that we beheld and saw the plates, and the engravings thereon; and we know that it is by the grace of God the Father, and our Lord Jesus Christ, that we beheld and bear record that these things are true; and it is marvelous in our eyes: Nevertheless, the voice of the Lord commanded us that we should bear record of it; wherefore, to be obedient unto the commandments of God, we bear testimony of these things. — And we know that if we are faithful in Christ, we shall rid our garments of the blood of all men, and be found spotless before the judgement seat of Christ, and shall dwell with him eternally in the heavens, And the honor be to the Father, and to the Son, and to the Holy Ghost, which is one God. Amen.

> OLIVER COWDERY,
> DAVID WHITMER,
> MARTIN HARRIS.

The second group consisted of eight individuals; their statement follows:

AND ALSO THE TESTIMONY OF EIGHT WITNESSES.

Be it known unto all nations, kindreds, tongues, and people, unto whom this work shall come, that Joseph Smith, Jr. the Author and Proprietor of this work, has shewn us the plates of which hath been spoken, which have the appearance of gold; and as many of the leaves as the said Smith has translated, we did handle with our hands; and we also saw the engravings thereon, all of which has the appearance of ancient work, and of curious workmanship. And this we bear record, with words of soberness, that the said Smith has shewn unto us, for we have seen and hefted, and know of a surety, that the said Smith has got the plates of which we have spoken. And we give our names unto the world, to witness unto the world that which we have seen: and we lie not, God bearing witness of it.

> CHRISTIAN WHITMER,
> JACOB WHITMER,
> PETER WHITMER, JR.
> JOHN WHITMER,
> HIRAM PAGE,
> JOSEPH SMITH, SEN.
> HYRUM SMITH,
> SAMUEL H. SMITH.

It should be noted that the words, "Joseph Smith, Jr. the Author and Proprietor," in the testimony of the eight witnesses were amended to read, "Joseph Smith, Jr. the translator," in the subsequent editions. Also, it is interesting that seven of the eight witnesses belonged either to the Smith family or to the Whitmer family, and that the remaining witness, Hiram Page, was married to a Whitmer.

Ever since *The Book of Mormon* was first published, the testimonies of the witnesses have caused a considerable amount of controversy. Nonbelievers, of course, have held that Joseph obviously could not have had an actual set of gold plates. But then, if Joseph had none, what really happened when the witnesses were supposed to have seen them?

Martin Harris provided perhaps the best answer to that question. During the printing of the first edition of *The Book of Mormon*, he was in the print shop while the type was being set for the testimony of the three witnesses. The printer, John Gilbert, asked him if he had seen the plates with his naked eye. "Martin looked down for an instant, raised his eyes up, and said, 'No, I saw them with a spiritual eye.'"[2]

While he was with a Mormon colony in Kirtland, Ohio, in 1838, Harris made some other statements that are very damaging to the testimonies of both groups of witnesses. Stephen Burnett, a Mormon who became disillusioned when he heard the statements, described them in a recently uncovered letter to a friend:

> I have reflected long and deliberately upon the history of this church & weighed the evidence for & against it—loth to give it up—but when I came to hear Martin Harris state in public that he never saw the plates with his natural eyes only in vision or imagination, neither Oliver nor David & also that the eight witnesses never saw them & hesitated to sign that instrument for that reason, but were persuaded to do it, the last pedestal gave away.... I therefore three weeks since in the Stone Chapel gave ... the reasons why I took the course which I was resolved to do, and renounced the Book of Mormon....
>
> I was followed by W. Parrish, Luke Johnson & John Boynton, all of who concurred with me, after we were done speaking M. Harris arose & said he was sorry for any man who rejected the Book of Mormon for he knew it was true, he said he had hefted the plates repeatedly in a box with only a tablecloth or a hankerchief over them, but he never saw them, only as he saw a city through a mountain. And said that he never should have told that the testimony of the eight was false, if it had not been picked out of [him] but should have let it passed as it was.[3]

From what Harris said, it is apparent that the three witnesses were not permitted to see any gold plates in the physical sense. Instead, their testimony was based upon seeing the plates in a vision. The account of the three witnesses itself indicates that such was the case since it describes an angel as having brought the plates before the witnesses. Yet, Joseph was supposed to have had the plates still in his possession at the time! If he did truly have them, then why were the three witnesses permitted to see them only in a vision? Moreover, contrary to the testimony of the three witnesses, the testimony of the eight has no mention of angels or of other supernatural overtones. It indicates instead that Joseph was supposed to have physically shown them the plates. If the eight were permitted to see the plates directly, why were the three treated differently? Harris's statements seem to make clear that no one saw any plates: how, then, did Joseph get the witnesses to sign the testimonies?

It appears that Joseph made some elaborate preparations before the three saw the plates in their "vision." First, as he translated *The Book of Mormon*, he "found" that there were to be three witnesses who would view the plates. He then received a revelation from the Lord giving Cowdery, Whitmer, and Harris the privilege of being those witnesses. Lastly, Joseph got the three men to pray very fervently to demonstrate to the Lord that they were worthy of the privilege. This certainly would have placed strong psychological and religious pressures upon the three — or at least upon whoever was not working with Joseph. If at least one of the three was a collaborator, he could have assisted in bringing about the vision. To prod the others, that witness might have declared with praises to the Lord that he had had a vision of the plates. Through an Emperor's New Clothes effect, or through religious hysteria, the remaining witnesses might then have declared they too had seen the plates.

The following is Joseph's narrative of the events:

> Not many days after the above commandment was given, we four viz: Martin Harris, David Whitmer, Oliver Cowdery and myself agreed to retire into the woods, and try to obtain by fervent and humble prayer, the fulfilment of the promises given in the revelation; that they should have a view of the plates &c. We ... knelt down [and] we began to pray in much faith, to Almighty God to bestow upon us a realization of these promises.... I commenced, by vocal prayer to our heavenly Father, and was followed by each of the rest in succession; we did not yet however obtain any answer, or manifestation of the divine favor in our behalf. We again observed the same order of prayer each calling on and praying fervently to God in rotation; but with the same result as before. Upon our second failure, Martin Harris proposed that he would withdraw himself from us, believing as he expressed himself that his presence was the cause of our not obtaining what we wished for; he accordingly withdrew from us, and we knelt down again, and had not been many minutes engaged in prayer when presently we beheld a light above us in the air of exceeding brightness, and behold an angel stood before us; in his hands he held the plates which we had been praying for these to have a view of....
>
> I now left David and Oliver, and went in pursuit of Martin Harris, who I found at a considerable distance, fervently engaged in prayer, he soon told me however that he had not yet prevailed with the Lord, and ernestly requested me to join him in prayer, that he also might realize the same blessings which we had just received. We accordingly joined in prayer, and ultimately obtained our desires, for before we had yet finished, the same vision was opened to our view; at least it was again to me...; whilst at the same moment, Martin Harris cried out, apparently in ecstacy of joy, "Tis enough; mine eyes have beheld," and jumping up he shouted, hosannah, blessing God, and otherwise rejoiced exceedingly.[4]

Martin Harris gave a somewhat different version. He said he did not have the vision until three days later:

> I never saw the golden plates, only in a visionary or entranced state.... When the time came for the three witnesses to see the plates, Joseph Smith, myself, David Whitmer and Oliver Cowdery, went into the woods to pray. When they had engaged in prayer, they failed at that time to see the plates or the angel who should have been on hand to exhibit them. They all believed it was because I was not good enough, or, in other words, not

sufficiently sanctified. I withdrew. As soon as I had gone away, the three others saw the angel and the plates. In about three days I went into the woods to pray that I might see the plates. While praying I passed into a state of entrancement, and in that state I saw the angel and the plates."[5]

If Joseph did have collaborators, they probably were Oliver Cowdery and David Whitmer. That being the case, they might have reasoned beforehand that they could manipulate Harris into being a third witness because of his religious idiosyncrasies. Therefore, when they sent Harris away because he was "not sufficiently sanctified," it might have been for the purpose of humbling and pressuring him. Then, when he was told the others had "seen" the plates in a vision, the pressure became overwhelming and he proclaimed that he also had seen the vision of the plates — perhaps because he did not want to appear unworthy.

When Joseph described the recurrence of the vision with Harris, he qualified it by saying, "at least it was again to me." Perhaps he said this in case Harris ever disavowed the vision. Joseph could then say that he had seen the vision even if Harris had not.

With these three saying that they had seen the plates, Joseph then persuaded the eight others to do likewise. Perhaps he used the testimony of the three witnesses as a lever to induce the eight to sign the "instrument" even though they "hesitated" to do so.

The three witnesses eventually left the church. Oliver Cowdery and David Whitmer were excommunicated because of considerable antagonism that developed between them and Joseph. Both of these men were opposed to the way Joseph was managing the church, and they also opposed some of his revelations. Perhaps this was because they were involved in a collaboration with Joseph and felt that they should have a greater say in church matters. Oliver subsequently joined the Methodist Church. In so doing, he declared that he was willing to make a statement of renunciation of his former religion. He also said he was "ashamed of his connection with Mormonism."[6] David Whitmer joined a splinter Mormon sect and declared that Joseph Smith was a "fallen prophet." Martin Harris had problems with the church as well. He frequently embarrassed church officials by saying the wrong things. That, along with some other problems that developed between him and Joseph, led to his excommunication from the church. Moreover, he eventually became a Shaker. Relating to this, Phineas Young wrote to Brigham Young in December, 1844, and stated, "Martin Harris is a firm believer in Shakerism, says his testimony is greater than it was for the Book of Mormon."[7]

After Joseph Smith's death, Oliver Cowdery and Martin Harris eventually took steps to return to the church, but they never regained their former status.

Mormon writers have made much of the fact that the three witnesses apparently never clearly disavowed their testimony about the gold plates during their period of disenfranchisement. One cannot, however, place great importance on this seeming steadfastness of the witnesses. If any of them had outspokenly denied his testimony, he would have exposed himself to the world as a base perjurer, and brought upon himself the wrath of those who had been converted to Mormonism because of that testimony.

With his signed statements attesting to the existence of the plates, and his manuscript finished, Joseph now had the task of getting the book printed. At first, he had some difficulty in this. Martin Harris seems to have had second thoughts about putting up money for the printing, but Joseph displayed a revelation from the Lord which chastised the recalcitrant farmer and caused him to mortgage his farm to get the funds. Joseph also had problems convincing Egbert B. Grandin, the editor of the *Wayne Sentinel*, to print the book. Grandin apparently did not want to associate himself with the project, but finally relented and agreed to take on the job.

In his memorandum about the printing of *The Book of Mormon*, John Gilbert, Grandin's typesetter, stated that Joseph's brother, Hyrum, brought the manuscript to the printing office in installments of twenty-four pages each day, returning in the evening to take them away. Gilbert found that the manuscript was virtually without punctuation, so he suggested that Hyrum let him keep it nights to punctuate it. At first, Hyrum refused, but then allowed Gilbert to do as he suggested (perhaps because Joseph had Cowdery make a second copy of the manuscript to prevent any more problems with missing pages). Concerning the manuscript itself, Gilbert said the following:

> Names of persons and places were generally capitalized, but sentences had no end. The character or short &, was used almost invariably where the word and, occurred, except at the end of a chapter. I punctuated it to make it read as I supposed the Author intended, but very little punctuation was altered in proof-reading.... Cowdery held and looked over the manuscript when most of the proofs were read.[8]

It took eight or nine months for the printing to be completed and a number of the 5,000 copies of the book to be bound. Finally, on March 26, 1830, the *Wayne Sentinel* carried an advertisement proclaiming that *The Book of Mormon* was "for sale, wholesale and retail, at the Palmyra Bookstore."

Joseph formally organized his church on April 6, 1830. Within a month he had about thirty members, most of whom were from southern New York State. A short time later, he received a revelation from the Lord which said, in part: "... the church which is in Colesville, Fayette and Manchester ... shall support thee.... And in temporal labors thou shalt not have strength, for this is not thy calling."[9]

To assure the future growth of his church, Joseph sent several of his converts out to proselytize. With an eye to fulfilling some of the prophecies in *The Book of Mormon*, he sent Oliver Cowdery and others west to preach among the Indians. Ethan Smith thus had his exhortation about the American Indians complied with, but for a purpose of which the Vermont minister would not have approved.

One of those accompanying Oliver was Parley Pratt, a convert to Mormonism from the reform movement begun by Alexander Campbell. Pratt detoured Oliver to Mentor, Ohio, in order to introduce him to a Campbellite preacher named Sidney Rigdon. With this step, he unknowingly made a significant contribution to the future success of Joseph's new religion.

The meeting of Cowdery and Rigdon could not have been at a more opportune time. Rigdon had recently quarreled with Campbell over church affairs, and because of this he was receptive to Oliver's proselytizing. But certain similarities between Campbellism and the new religion also helped Oliver to sway Ridgon — a result of Joseph's eclecticism. Moreover, the millennialism of the Mormon religion conformed to Rigdon's own ideas, which is not surprising since the ideas were in the air at the time Joseph was working on *The Book of Mormon*. The result of all this was that Rigdon not only accepted the new religion himself, but also converted his colony of Campbellites in nearby Kirtland.

While Cowdery and Pratt continued their mission to the west, Rigdon left for New York State to meet Joseph. In the course of their meeting, he convinced the Mormon prophet to leave New York and accompany him back to Ohio. Rigdon probably did not have to use much persuasion to get Joseph to leave New York. The founder of Mormonism had found that it was quite true that a prophet is not without honor save in his own country.

The people in Palmyra were displaying considerable hostility towards Joseph's attempts to establish a new religion. Even in southern New York, where most of his converts lived, the Mormon prophet found the inhabitants to be less than hospitable. A few months earlier, he had twice been brought to trial there, once in Bainbridge and once in Colesville.

When Joseph discussed these two 1830 trials in later years, he claimed that they were the result of religious persecution. His new religious activity indeed played a part in the trials, but as far as those who brought the charges against him were concerned, it was all a part of his juggling. In his 1831 letter to the *Evangelical Magazine and Gospel Advocate*, A.W. Benton gave a description of the 1830 Bainbridge trial and the reason it came about:

> During the past summer he [Joseph Smith] was frequently in this vincinity, and others of the baser sort, as Cowdery, Whitmer, etc., holding meetings, and proselyting a few weak and silly women, and still more silly men, whose minds are shouded in a mist of ignorance which no ray can penetrate, and whose credulity the utmost absurdity cannot equal.
>
> In order to check the progress of delusion, and open the eyes and understandings of those who blindly followed him, and unmask the turpitude and villany of those who knowingly abetted him in his infamous designs; he was again arraigned before a bar of justice, during last summer, to answer a charge of misdemeaner. This trial led to an investigation of his character and conduct, which clearly evinced to the unprejudiced, whence the spirit came which dictated his inspirations. During the trial it was shown that the Book of Mormon was brought to light by the same magic power by which he pretended to tell fortunes, discover hidden treasures, &c.[10]

Benton went on to relate that Josiah Stowel was placed on the stand and was asked about the earlier money digging operations:

> Did Smith ever tell you there was money hid in a certain place which he mentioned? Yes. Did he tell you, you could find it by digging? Yes. Did you dig? Yes. Did you find any money? No! Did he not lie to you then, and

deceive you? No! the money was there, but we did not quite get to it! How do you know it was there? Smith said it was!11

Benton's letter shows that this 1830 trial was prompted by Joseph's earlier money digging operations in the Bainbridge area, and was not purely a case of religious persecution. Many residents of the area knew that Joseph had engaged in a confidence scheme a few years before, and that he had been brought to trial and found guilty of engaging in that scheme. It is therefore not surprising that they concluded he was involved in yet another confidence scheme — this time by "sponging his living" from the earnings of the converts to his new religion. Benton himself ended his letter with such a conclusion by saying that *The Book of Mormon* was a "counterpart" of Joseph's "money-digging plan."

It appears that the 1830 Bainbridge trial came about through an attempt to re-charge Joseph with the complaint that was made against him in the 1826 trial so that he could be sentenced in accordance with the guilty verdict of that trial. (Joseph, remember, took "leg bail" in order to avoid sentencing in the 1826 trial.) As evidence for that, Justice of the Peace Joel K. Noble had this to say about the two 1830 trials in his letter to Jonathon Turner:

> After 2 years from the time of Jos first trial he appeared in our place bold as a lion again. Jo. was arrested, examination had. Jo. plead in bar Statute of Limitations. Jo. was no Sooner Set on teriferma than arrested again, brought before me in an adjoining County 6 miles distant.... Proof Jo. a Vagrant, idler, Lazy, (not drunkard) but now and then Drunk, Liar, Deceiver, Jo a nuicance to Good society.12

According to Noble's letter, then, Joseph had to plead in his 1830 Bainbridge trial that the statute of limitations had run out on the charges that were made against him in the 1826 trial. He would not have had to so plead unless he had been found quilty in the 1826 trial, nor unless an attempt was made to carry out a sentence in conformity with that verdict. Wesley P. Walters points out that the statute of limitations for a misdemeaner was three years, and it had been four years since the first trial.13 Noble reported that two years had passed, but he apparently meant that it was two years before Joseph began making himself seen openly in the area and not that the new trial occurred two years later.

Joseph Knight provided further information on the subject of the 1830 trials. He stated that "Doctor Benton" (the A.W. Benton mentioned above) swore out a warrant against Joseph "for as they said pertending to see underground." Knight further related that this charge could be brought against Joseph because of "a little Clause they found in the york Laws against such things."14 This again shows that the trials were related to Joseph's former money digging activities.

Partly because Joseph Knight hired two men well versed in law to defend Joseph Smith, these last two trials resulted in acquittals. Nevertheless, the Mormon prophet probably felt that he would continue to be harassed so long as he remained in New York. In January of 1831, followed by most of his

New York converts, Joseph left for Kirtland, Ohio, to establish his church there. This was the first of many migrations in his tumultuous career as a religious leader.

Part Two

Another Book of God?

Chapter 9

A Vermont Preacher's Theory

Ethan Smith wrote *View of the Hebrews* to inspire his fellow Americans to "engage in the work by Heaven assigned" concerning the American Indians. He seems to have had no thought of using it to start a new religion for his own gain, and he doubtlessly would have been chagrined if he had learned that a young money digger from New York State had apparently done just that for himself. Yet, with a little reflection, he might have realized that his book virtually invited someone who was opportunistic and imaginative to use it for such a purpose.

Joseph, of course, did not hold up a copy of *View of the Hebrews* in sight of everyone and proclaim that it was God's plan for the restoration of the true church. Instead, it appears he produced his own book by appropriating many of the religious ideas and concepts about the American Indians that he found in Ethan Smith's book. After doing this, he was then able to present his book as a new revelation from God and to use it in establishing a new religion — one that put into action much of what Ethan Smith had exhorted.

Now that might seem to be a quite reasonable explanation of how Mormonism originated; but saying that, and proving it, are two different things. To prove it, one needs to show that there is a substantial connection between *The Book of Mormon* and *View of the Hebrews*. One way to do that is to make an in-depth comparative analysis of Ethan Smith's book and Joseph Smith's latter-day revelation. If such an analysis reveals a significant number of similarities between the two books, then it can be reasonably said that the one had its origin in the other.

Let us begin by noting that Ethan Smith obtained much of the material for his book from previously published works which advocated the idea that the American Indians were of Hebrew origin. Joseph could have had access to these earlier books and perhaps have created *The Book of Mormon* from them. However, Ethan Smith also incorporated several of his own ideas into his book, and many of these ideas are reflected in *The Book of Mormon*. It is particularly notable that the basic plot of *The Book of Mormon* follows Ethan Smith's theory of what happened to the "Israelites" after their arrival in the New World. The Vermont minister summarized that theory in the following:

The probability then is this; that the ten tribes, arriving in this continent

104

with some knowledge of the arts of civilized life; finding themselves in a vast wilderness filled with the best of game, inviting them to the chase; most of them fell into a wandering idle hunting life. Different clans parted from each other, lost each other, and formed separate tribes. Most of them formed a habit of this idle mode of living, and were pleased with it. More sensible parts of these people associated together, to improve their knowledge of the arts; and probably continued thus for ages. From these the noted relics of civilization discovered in the west and south were furnished. But the savage tribes prevailed; and in process of time their savage jealousies and rage annihilated their more civilized brethren. And thus, as a holy vindictive Providence would have it, and according to ancient denunciations, all were left in an *"outcast"* savage state. This accounts for their loss of the knowledge of letters, of the art of navigation, and the use of iron [*View of the Hebrews*, 1825 ed., p. 172].*

Aside from the notion that the Indians were descended from the Ten Tribes of Israel as a whole, this summary of Ethan Smith's theory is also a somewhat brief but reasonably accurate summary of the basic story line of *The Book of Mormon.*

It is relatively unimportant that Joseph Smith seems to have modified Ethan Smith's theory by having only a part of the Ten Tribes of Israel as the ancestors of the Indians. There were several good reasons to do this, and we shall see why later on. What is important is that Ethan Smith's views are echoed throughout *The Book of Mormon.*

It may seem odd, but it was apparently Brigham H. Roberts, a prominent Mormon elder and scholar, who first noticed similarities between *View of the Hebrews* and *The Book of Mormon.* Roberts, however, did not make his findings known, except to some of the church authorities, before his death in 1933. Although the church authorities understandably did not take it upon themselves to publish Roberts' findings, the story leaked out from members of the church who knew of his work. A few years later, Fawn Brodie briefly mentioned the story about Roberts' study in her 1945 biography of Joseph Smith. She also examined Ethan Smith's book and suggested that Joseph was much influenced by it. However, beyond describing it briefly and pointing out a few similarities with *The Book of Mormon*, she carried the matter no further.[1]

Eventually, some of Roberts' findings came to light and were published in the January 1956 issue of the *Rocky Mountain Mason.* The Mormon elder had arranged these in the form of a short list of parallels between *The Book of Mormon* and *View of the Hebrews.* Moreover, he apparently considered that this material had serious implications for his church, since in his study he made this statement: "Query: could all this have supplied structural work for the Book of Mormon?"[2]

For all further references for both View of the Hebrews *and* The Book of Mormon *an abbreviated title of the book and the reference will appear at the end of the excerpt instead of in a footnote. This is to lessen the number of footnotes and to enable the reader to distinguish at a glance from which book the excerpts have been taken. The* Book of Mormon *quotations and page references are from the first edition, but the chapter and verse references are from the current Utah edition.*

In the years since Roberts' short study was published, several Mormon writers have taken it upon themselves to answer that question. As one might expect, they have fervently denied that *The Book of Mormon* had its origin in *View of the Hebrews* — something they found easy to do in the absence of any truly in-depth comparative analysis of the two books. Since, in this book, we attempt to remedy that absence, we should perhaps begin by taking a look at some of the arguments that these writers have made in support of their stand.

Francis Kirkham was one of the first of the Mormon writers to argue that *The Book of Mormon* did not have its origin in Ethan Smith's book. Because of the controversy that came about as a result of Fawn Brodie's book, he gave his pronouncements on the matter even before Roberts' list of parallels was first published. For good measure, he also included in his discussion two other early books that were suspected of being source material for *The Book of Mormon*. The following is the line of argument that he used:

> The table of contents of these three books and additional introductory and explanatory material which follows indicates that the Book of Mormon differs so widely in content and purpose that the knowledge of these books could have had little, if any influence on the material published in the Book of Mormon.[3]

One of the three books to which Mr. Kirkham referred was *View of the Hebrews*. The other two books were *The History of the American Indians*, by James Adair, published in 1775, and *A Star in the West*, by Elias Boudinot, published in 1816. Both of these espoused the idea of the Hebrew origin of the Indians. After making the quoted statement, Mr. Kirkham reproduced the table of contents and introductory material of these books, while totally ignoring the rest of their respective tests.

Another Mormon writer, Dr. Hugh Nibley, had this to say not long after the initial publication of Robert's short study:

> In the first place, only eighteen parallels are listed, and neither Mrs. Brodie nor Mr. Hogan [who published Roberts' short study] adds anything to the list. This then, is the best we can do for Ethan Smith's parallels.... In fact, Mr. Hogan in his recent treatment of the subject has unwittingly robbed the eighteen parallels of any significance by going to considerable pains to point out in his introduction that the ideas shared by Ethan and Joseph Smith were not original to either of them, but were as common in the world they lived in as the name Smith itself.... This being the case, why would Joseph Smith need to steal them from Ethan Smith.[4]

So Dr. Nibley thinks that, because neither Mrs. Brodie nor Mr. Hogan made any additions to Roberts' list, there are no more parallels to be found. That is, of course, an unwarranted assumption on his part. Moreover, Dr. Nibley has unwittingly robbed his own statements of any significance. In his endeavor to draw attention away from *View of the Hebrews*, he quoted Mr. Hogan as saying that "the ideas shared by Ethan and Joseph Smith were not original to either of them, but were as common in the world they lived in as the name Smith itself." But that is just the point. Those ideas were common in the world in which these two Smiths lived, the early nineteenth century, and not, except in Mormon circles, in the more knowledgeable world of today. Since those ideas also appear in *The Book of Mormon*, one has good reason to suspect that Joseph Smith's latter-day revelation originated in the early nineteenth century instead of in ancient America.

Several other Mormon writers have given their views on the relationship between the two books. It is not surprising that these writers' conclusions are little different from those of Kirkham and Nibley. As far as most of these writers are concerned, there are no significant similarities between *View of the Hebrews* and *The Book of Mormon*. But then, one wonders if they have tended to be somewhat less than honest in their evaluations. For an example, we might note what Roy E. Weldon has to say:

> Ethan Smith says: "Some have felt a difficulty arising against the Indians being of the Ten Tribes, from the ignorance of the mechanic arts, of writing and of navigation" (p. 17). The Book of Mormon has the ancient Americans using "machinery," great numbers of books, and ships capable of transporting several hundred people.[5]

Weldon's quote from *View of the Hebrews* is what Ethan Smith had said in leading up to the summary of his theory, given earlier in this chapter. By quoting only this excerpt, and not the theory itself, Weldon was apparently attempting to give his readers the impression that Ethan Smith's book is at odds with *The Book of Mormon* concerning the mentioned cultural traits. In Weldon's quote, however, Ethan Smith was speaking of the contemporary state of the Indians and not of their condition in ancient times. Moreover, the Vermont minister went on to say that it appeared the Indians had not always been bereft of the trappings of a higher civilization:

> But that the people who first migrated to this western world did possess some knowledge of the mechanic arts (as much doubtless, as was possessed by Israel when they disappeared in the east) appears from incontestible facts, which are furnished in Baron Humbolt, and in the American Archeology... [*V.H.*, pp. 171–172].

And then Ethan Smith postulated that the ancestors of the Indians had divided into savage and civilized factions, and that the savage faction eventually exterminated the civilized part (which, again, is *exactly* what *The Book of Mormon* describes). Moreover, Pastor Smith continued: "And thus, ... all were left in an '*outcast*' savage state. This accounts for the loss of the knowledge of letters, of the art of navigation, and of the use of iron" — and, of course, the "mechanic arts."

It is apparent that Weldon quoted Ethan Smith totally out of context. Contrary to the impression he was trying to give, the excerpt he presented from *View of the Hebrews* is quite compatible with the content of *The Book of Mormon*. On top of this, Weldon stated: "The only significant similarity between Ethan Smith's work and the Book of Mormon is the assertion that

American Indians are descended from the Hebrew people." We will leave it to
the reader to judge the validity of that remark.

In contradiction to Mr. Weldon, Sidney B. Sperry admitted to some
parallels between the two books:

> It is true that there are some obvious parallels between Ethan Smith's
> book and the Book of Mormon, but parallels can be drawn between the
> Nephite record and many other early American books. These parallels
> prove nothing concerning the origin of the Book of Mormon.[6]

The "many other early American books" to which Sperry referred are
apparently those of Adair, Boudinot, and others who tried to prove the
Hebrew origin of the Indians. Since Ethan Smith was heavily dependent upon
these other early books, it is not surprising that *The Book of Mormon* has
parallels with them.

Sperry went on to say:

> Attention should be called to the numerous differences between ideas
> found in the Book of Mormon and those found in Ethan Smith's book and
> other books similar in purpose to his. Where in Smith's book can be found
> a discussion of the atonement as distinctive as found in 2 Nephi 9:6–9?
> Where in Smith's book can be found a treatment of the doctrine of the
> opposition of all thing and the meaning of the fall such as in 2 Nephi 2:11–
> 25? ... And is there anything comparable in Ethan Smith's book to the
> dramatic three-day ministry of Jesus in 3 Nephi 11–26?[7]

In the omissions represented by the ellipsis, Sperry gives several other
examples of ideas of a religious or doctrinal nature that are found in *The Book
of Mormon* and not in *View of the Hebrews*. But how does an absence of these
things in Ethan Smith's book constitute "numerous differences" between the
ideas found in that book and those found in *The Book of Mormon*? It takes an
expression of an idea by one party to have a difference with an opposing idea
expressed by another party.

What Sperry really seems to be arguing is that Joseph Smith must have
acquired all of his ideas from *View of the Hebrews*, or else he must have
acquired none of them from that book. That sort of argument is clearly
ridiculous. Joseph was under no obligation to use *View of the Hebrews* as his
sole literary source. Anyone undertaking the writing of such a book as *The
Book of Mormon* would use any source that might help him — not to mention
his own imagination.

To be sure, there are some differences in ideas between the two books.
However, when the ideas in *The Book of Mormon* vary from those in *View of
the Hebrews*, they tend to do so through a logical extension or variation of
those that Ethan Smith expressed. There are even some statements in *The Book
of Mormon* that are in direct opposition to certain statements that Ethan Smith
made. Curiously, though, Joseph presented these statements in the form of an
argument, almost as if he were trying to refute what the Vermont minister was
saying. Actually, in light of what he was doing, Joseph was forced to oppose

Ethan Smith on these particular points. We shall see why in the next chapter. It suffices now to note that an opposition of ideas, as well as a concurrence, can indicate influence.

In the last example, given earlier, Sperry asked if Ethan Smith's book had "anything comparable" to the "three-day ministry of Jesus" described in *The Book of Mormon*. As a matter of fact, Ethan Smith provided a lengthy discussion of the very same subject that Mormons themselves use as evidence of such a ministry. That should qualify as being comparable. We shall investigate this particular subject further at the appropriate time.

Sperry concluded his discussion with the following:

> We submit that the style and purpose of *View of the Hebrews* is so different from that of the Book of Mormon that any fair-minded person who examines the two must have grave doubts that Joseph Smith was any more dependent upon Ethan Smith's book than upon a dozen other early American publications dealing with the American Indians.[8]

That argument is hardly valid. Suppose there is an author who wishes to write a historical novel about an era of which he knows little. He studies a comprehensive reference work on that era until he is quite versed in the people and times concerned. After spending some time thinking about what he has learned, he puts his imagination to work. Eventually, he finds that characters, scenes, and, finally, a story are beginning to emerge in his mind. As the story develops, he puts it down on paper in his own style and in a viewpoint that is applicable to his narrative. Now that style and viewpoint will certainly be different from that of the reference work consulted. But, even so, can it be properly said that the author was not dependent upon the reference work?

The same point applies to the question at hand. In presenting his theory on the origin of the American Indians, Ethan Smith wrote in an expository manner and in the style and viewpoint of an early American preacher. In composing *The Book of Mormon*, Joseph could have used Ethan Smith's book as a reference to familiarize himself with the theory of the Hebrew origin of the American Indians and to glean some religious ideas. Rather than using the style and viewpoint that Ethan Smith had used, Joseph used others that he considered appropriate. His having done so is not evidence against his having used *View of the Hebrews* as a source of ideas.

Sperry also declared, as did Kirkham, that *The Book of Mormon* and *View of the Hebrews* had completely different purposes. That is not a valid argument against the proposition that Joseph Smith's book had its origin in Ethan Smith's. After all, our theoretical novelist probably had an entirely different purpose in writing his novel than the author of the reference work had in writing his book; yet that did not keep the novelist from using the reference work as a source. Similarly, Joseph could have composed *The Book of Mormon* by using *View of the Hebrews* as a reference, but with a different purpose in mind than Ethan Smith had in writing his book. But are the purposes of these two works so different?

In fact, as far as the stated purpose of each is concerned, they are demonstrably not so far apart. It was Ethan Smith's purpose to inspire the American people to act on the following exhortation:

> Should we find ample conviction that our natives are of the lost tribes of Israel, and that the address is directed to us; we may ... imagine the prophet Isaiah ... uttering the following sentiments of the holy prophetic spirit;
>
> Ho thou nation of the last days...; instruct ... my ancient people...; especially that *outcast* branch of them, ... that degraded remnant..., by showing them what has been done for their nation; and what is yet to be done by the God of their fathers.... Teach them their ancient history; ... their being cast away; ... and the promises of their return.... That the Great Spirit ... calls them ... to come and receive his grace by Christ..., by [whom] you and multitudes of other Gentiles, have become children of [Abraham].... Unfold to them ... the entail of the covenant ... [*V.H.*, pp. 247–249].

Interestingly enough, we find Ethan Smith's "sentiments of the holy prophetic spirit" echoed on the title page of *The Book of Mormon* — wherein it says that book is

> . written to the Lamanites, which are a remnant of the House of Israel; and also to Jew and Gentile; written ... by the spirit of Prophesy.... Written ... to shew unto the remnant of the House of Israel how great things the Lord hath done for their fathers; and that they may know the covenants of the Lord, that they are not cast off forever; and also to the convincing of the Jew and Gentile and Jesus is the Christ ... [*B.M.*, title page].

There may be differences in style and standpoint between these two excerpts, but the essential expressions of purpose are virtually the same. The similarity is even more apparent if the relevant parts are arranged in parallel form. Note that most of the parts are even in the same sequence in the two books. In the few cases where they are not, I have enclosed those from *View of the Hebrews* in parentheses and shifted them so they match the corresponding passages in *The Book of Mormon*.

View of the Hebrews (pages 247–249)	*The Book of Mormon* (title page)
Should we ... find that our natives are (that degraded remnant) of the lost tribes of Israel,	... written to the Lamanites [the Native Americans], which are a remnant of the House of Israel;
and that the address is directed to us [American] (Gentiles);	and also to Jew and Gentile;
we may ... imagine the ... following sentiments of the holy prophetic spirit;	written ... by the spirit of Prophesy....

... instruct ... my ancient people...; especially that *outcast* branch of them, ... that degraded remnant..., by showing them what has been done for their nation; and what is yet to be done by the God of their fathers....

Written ... to shew unto the remnant of the House of Israel how great things the Lord hath done for their fathers;

(Unfold to them ... the entail of the covenant....) Teach them their ancient history; ... their being cast away; ... and the promises of their return....

and that they may know the covenants of the Lord, that they are not cast off forever;

That the Great Spirit ... calls them ... to come and receive his grace by Christ....

and also to the convincing of the Jew and Gentile that Jesus is the Christ....

The "nation of the last days" addressed by Ethan Smith was the United States of America — a "nation of Gentiles." Though it was not directly referred to in the given excerpt, there are several prophecies about America in the main part of *The Book of Mormon*. There it is called "a mighty nation among the Gentiles" that will be raised "upon the face of this land." It is significant that these prophecies are compatible with Ethan Smith's exhortations to the American people; both emphasize America's "heavenly assigned" role in the restoration of the Jews and the house of Israel. Moreover, as we shall see, Ethan Smith elsewhere espoused the cause of convincing the Jews that Jesus is the Christ, as does this excerpt from *The Book of Mormon*.

One wonders how Sperry and Kirkham could have arrived at the conclusion that the purposes of *The Book of Mormon* and *View of the Hebrews* are "so different" that the one could have had nothing to do with the other. A critical analysis shows that Joseph Smith apparently took Ethan Smith's exhortation and used it as the purpose for the appearance of his own book.

Ethan Smith's above mentioned reference to Isaiah raises a key point. The Vermont minister derived most of his ideas about the future restoration of the Indian "remnant of Israel" and the Jews from his interpretation of the prophecies of Isaiah. In fact, he quoted Isaiah the most of any of the Old Testament prophets. Significantly, Isaiah is also the most mentioned Old Testament book in *the Book of Mormon*. There is, however, a peculiarity about this when one compares Ethan Smith's book with Joseph's. Pastor Smith apparently was particularly intrigued with Isaiah 18 and devoted much of his book to his ideas about that chapter; yet, curiously, there is no mention of Isaiah 18 at all in Joseph Smith's latter-day revelation.

Some Mormon writers have made much of this seeming lack of correspondence. After all, if Joseph did get his ideas for *The Book of Mormon* from *View of the Hebrews*, then it seems that Isaiah 18 should have also been referred to in *The Book of Mormon*. But is it perhaps precisely because Ethan Smith made so much of Isaiah 18 that Joseph warily refrained from quoting it directly. Ethan Smith emphasized the expression, "land shadowing with wings," which appears in the first verse of Isaiah 18 in the King James Version. If Joseph had quoted this rather unusual expression, it would have immediately caught the eye of anyone reading *The Book of Mormon* who had also read *View of the Hebrews.* (I must admit I had hoped to find that expression in *The Book of Mormon.*) In addition, Ethan Smith asserted that some of the verses in Isaiah 18 were incorrectly translated. If Joseph had used the reading of these verses in the King James Version, and if Ethan Smith was correct about the errors, someone might have wondered about these latter-day defects appearing in *The Book of Mormon.* On the other hand, if Joseph had used Ethan Smith's "corrections," then someone might have noted that he had done so and suspect that *The Book of Mormon* had its origin in Ethan Smith's book—especially if Ethan Smith's "corrections" were themselves in error. With all these problems confronting him, Joseph had ample reason to refrain from referring to Isaiah 18 directly.

Nevertheless, even though Joseph did not directly quote Isaiah 18, Ethan Smith's thoughts about that chapter are reflected in *The Book of Mormon.* In fact, they permeate Joseph's latter-day revelation. A case in point: Ethan Smith derived his "sentiments" of the "prophetic spirit," which we saw were paralleled on the title page of *The Book of Mormon,* from his interpretation of Isaiah 18. The following from *View of the Hebrews* further illustrates the relationship between *The Book of Mormon* and Ethan Smith's interpretation of Isaiah 18:

> An address is found in the eighteenth chapter of the prophet Isaiah, which is apprehended to be of deep interest to America....
>
> The writer ... found it to be an address to some Christian people of the last days, just at the time of the final restoration of God's ancient people; an address to such a people ... in some region of the west; a call and solemn divine charge to them to awake and aid that final restoration.... It now appears to him ... that the Christian people of the United States of America are the subjects of the address....
>
> Should it be proved a *fact,* that the aborigines of our continent are the descendants of the ten tribes of Israel; it would heighten the probability to a moral certainty, that we are the people especially addressed, and called upon to restore them; or bring them the knowledge of the gospel ... [V.H., pp. 228-230].

As we have noted, and as we shall see in detail, this concept plays an important part in the content of *The Book of Mormon.*

Curiously, despite the fact that Isaiah 18 is not directly referred to in *The Book of Mormon,* an early Mormon writer by the name of Charles Thompson elaborated upon that chapter of Isaiah in his attempts to prove Joseph Smith's latter-day revelation true. Thompson was baptized as a Mormon in Kirtland, Ohio, in 1833, when that town was the headquarters of the Mormon church. While there, he would have had an ample opportunity to have discussions with Joseph Smith concerning *The Book of Mormon* and its evidences. In any event, Thompson went on a mission to New York State, where, in 1841, he published a book entitled *Evidences in Proof of the Book of Mormon*. In that book, Thompson referred to many of the same Indian traditions, archaeological findings, and biblical passages that Ethan Smith had referred to in *View of the Hebrews*. For example, Ethan Smith had made the following interpretation of the first verse of Isaiah 18:

> The land addressed, lies "beyond the rivers of Ethiopia." ... This address of Heaven must be to our western continent....
>
> Thou land "shadowing with wings." The above direction lands the prophetic vision at the point of the western continent, where the two great wings of North and South America meet as at the body of a great eagle. This at first might furnish the prophetic imagery of a land "shadowing with wings." The continent of those *two great wings* shall be found at last most interesting in relation to your Hebrew brethren [*V.H.*, pp. 237-238].

While in Charles Thompson's book we find:

> "Woe to the land shadowing with wings, which is beyond the rivers of Ethiopia." ... In looking beyond these rivers, from Jerusalem, upon the map of the world, the first land the eye lights upon, is North and South America, stretched out between the Pacific and Atlantic Oceans, from the South Temperate to the North Fridgid zones, and the form thereof is like the shadow of two great wings. Here, then, is the land, shadowing with wings....[9]

So both Ethan Smith and this early Mormon writer made the same interpretation of Isaiah 18:1 — even to the point of likening the continents of North and South America to "two great wings."

Of course it might be argued that Charles Thompson got his ideas directly from Ethan Smith's book rather than indirectly through Joseph Smith. However, despite the fact that one gets many echoes of *View of the Hebrews* by reading Thompson's book, Thompson nowhere mentions Ethan Smith's book. He did mention several others, including some that were published before *The Book of Mormon*, so if he knew about *View of the Hebrews* he probably would have mentioned it.

While on the subject of Isaiah 18, we should make an observation about the reading of the first verse of that chapter in the King James Version of the Bible. The first line in that version reads, "Woe to the land shadowing with wings," but the Revised Standard Version translates it as "Ah, land of whirring wings." The New English Bible, on the other hand, reads, "There is a land of sailing ships." The *Cambridge Bible Commentary on the New English Bible* notes that the "whirring wings" of the R.S.V. were understood to be references to the winged insects of the Nile, but in the N.E.B. they were understood literally as winged ships; i.e., boats with sails.[11] In any case, it would be a rather strange quirk if *The Book of Mormon* had its beginning in Ethan Smith's elaboration upon what turns out to be a faulty translation of the first verse of Isaiah 18 in the King James Version of the Bible.

There is one more argument that some Mormon writers have made against the idea that Joseph Smith used *View of the Hebrews* in writing *The Book of Mormon*. They admit to some parallels between the two books, but claim that the similarities are the result of the validity of *The Book of Mormon*. According to them, Ethan Smith simply perceived the evidence for the Hebrew origin of the Indians, and that same evidence proves *The Book of Mormon* true.

If the Indians had a Hebrew origin, that argument would certainly be a valid one. The problem is that most of Ethan Smith's evidence for the Indian's Hebrew origin was based on hearsay, rumor, and the distorted reports of individuals who, for religious reasons, wanted the Indians to be of the tribes of Israel. Ethan Smith's evidence must be balanced against the fact that an objective science of anthropology was scarcely developed at that time. Furthermore, no reputable non-Mormon archaeologist or anthropologist of today gives serious consideration to the idea that the Indians are of Hebrew descent. In fact, as will be shown in Appendix B, there is considerable evidence against such an ancestry.

In any case, it is curious that Ethan Smith published sufficient "evidence" to prove *The Book of Mormon* true before that book was published. This is even more so in light of the fact that some Mormon writers have claimed that neither Joseph Smith nor anyone else of his time had the necessary knowledge about ancient America to write *The Book of Mormon*.

In analyzing *The Book of Mormon* in relation to its sources, it is frequently helpful to look at things from the position of its author — to get into his mind, so to speak, and try to see how and why he brought together certain ideas and concepts that he found in the material he had at hand. At this point, therefore, we should reiterate what was said at the end of the first chapter. Joseph Smith, by the process of dictating *The Book of Mormon*, was intimately involved with its production. Also, there is no solid evidence that anyone other than Joseph was the author of the book, and he was named as its "Author and Proprietor" on the title page of its first edition. It is only natural then, for the sake of simple convenience and for the purpose of discussion, that we assume Joseph *was* the author. Therefore, we shall use Joseph's standpoint in our analysis of how the author derived his ideas from certain early nineteenth century sources.

This is not to mean that no one else was involved in authoring the book, but simply that, if there was, it is relatively unimportant for the purposes of our discussion. After all, the evidence that certain sources were used in creating *The Book of Mormon* is valid regardless of whether Joseph Smith was its sole author or whether it was written under other circumstances.

Chapter 10

The Idea and Its Development

Some of the greatest and best of divines have thought it would be strange, if nothing should be found in the prophetic scriptures having a special allusion to our western world, which by propitious Heaven was destined to act so distinguishing a part, both in the religious and political world, in the last days [*V.H.*, p. 228].

To understand how *View of the Hebrews* may have given Joseph the idea of creating *The Book of Mormon*, one must first understand that Ethan Smith's book expressed a viewpoint that had certain religious implications for the United States. The Vermont minister was not content with merely proving that the American Indians were descended from the Lost Tribes of Israel. He enthusiastically believed that the latter days were upon the earth, and he seemed sure that the finding of the Lost Tribes was but one of the events that would set the stage for the arrival of the Millennium. In his view, other events would be fulfilled when the Indians learned of their "heritage" in the Hebrew family, were converted to Christianity, and were restored to the land of their fathers along with the Jews. According to his interpretation of certain biblical prophecies, a great gentile nation would assist in accomplishing these things. That gentile nation, he zealously proposed, was America.

It would appear to be with a view of convincing the American people of their place in this divine plan that Ethan Smith wrote *View of the Hebrews*. Everything in his book seems designed for that end, and he brought it all together in the speech that he put into the mouth of the prophet Isaiah. That exhortation failed in its objectives, but it apparently had a considerable influence upon Joseph Smith as he was working out his ideas for *The Book of Mormon*. We have already seen some of the results of this influence; for example, that Joseph lifted from the exhortation the very statement of purpose that was put on the title page of *The Book of Mormon*. Here is another excerpt from the exhortation:

> Ho thou nation of the last days, ... save my ancient people...; especially that outcast branch of them, who were the natives of your soil.... Were not your fathers sent ... to be the instruments of gathering ... the remnants of my outcasts there, in the last days? Rejoice, then, ye distinguished people in your birth-right, and engage in the work by heaven assigned....

Look at the origin of those degraded natives of your continent, and fly to their relief. — Send them the heralds of salvation. Send them the word, the bread of life. You received that book from the seed of Abraham. ... And by them it was transferred from Jerusalem to the lost heathen world, and to you.... Restore it to them.... Learn them its history and their own. Teach them the story of their ancestors; the economy of Abraham, Isaac and Jacob.... Teach them their ancient history; their former blessings; their being cast away; the occasion of it; and the promises of their return. Tell them the time draws near, and they must now return to the God of their salvation.... That the Great Spirit above the clouds now calls them by you to come and receive his grace by Christ the true star from Jacob, the shiloh who has come, and to whom the people must be gathered [V.H., pp. 247–249].

By its own words, *The Book of Mormon* was designed to accomplish the very things that Ethan Smith had urged. In addition to the example already noted on its title page, one of its characters provides another in a prophecy about the coming forth of the book in the latter days:

And now, I would prophesy somewhat more concerning the Jews and the Gentiles. For after the book of which I have spoken shall come forth, and be written unto the Gentiles, ... there shall be many which shall believe the words which are written; and they shall carry them forth unto the remnant of our seed. And then shall the remnant of our seed know concerning us, how that we came out from Jerusalem, and that they are a descendant of the Jews. And the Gospel of Jesus Christ shall be declared among them; wherefore, they shall be restored unto the knowledge of their fathers, and also to the knowledge of Jesus Christ ... [B.M., p. 117; 2 Nephi 30:3–5].[1]

From these examples, there can be little doubt that Joseph produced *The Book of Mormon* with Ethan Smith's mission for the American people in mind. Of course, we have reason to believe that Joseph's motives were different from those of the Vermont minister. The Mormon prophet could have seen that Ethan Smith's mission for the American people had an enormous potential as a source of power and wealth for whoever could manipulate it for his own purpose.

Still, there is a long path from Ethan Smith's exhortation to Joseph Smith's latter-day revelation. That exhortation itself did not suggest that the way to its fulfillment was by having someone make up a religious history of the ancestors of the Indians. How, then, did Joseph get such an idea?

We can only guess. Perhaps it came as a matter of course from the claims he made about the gold plates he had supposedly located with his peepstone, plates that he said had been inscribed with an account of the ancient inhabitants of America and the places where they had hidden their treasures. To impress the money diggers with his knowledge of ancient America, Joseph might have told them some tales that he worked up from Ethan Smith's book — particularly from Ethan Smith's theory of what had happened to the "Israelites" after their arrival in the New World. Later, after

Joseph conceived of actually producing a book, Ethan Smith's religious views would naturally fit in.

Perhaps Ethan Smith's book itself motivated Joseph to think of finding a history of ancient America. In the first edition of his book, for example, Ethan Smith had said:

> The evidence discovered among the various tribes of Indians, of the truth of their Hebrew extraction, and of the divinity of their Old Testament, seems almost like finding, in the various regions of America, various scrapes of an ancient Hebrew Old Testament; — one in one wild; another in another, inscribed on some durable substance in evident Hebrew language and character, though much defaced by the lapse of ages. Surely such an event ... must silence the unbeliever in ancient revelation; and add a new and powerful item to the evidence already furnished upon so interesting a subject [*V.H.*, 1st edition (1823), p. 167].

Ethan Smith was using allegory here, but these words might well have suggested to Joseph the idea of a testament or record to be found in the wilds of America.

In the second edition of his book, Ethan Smith substituted the foregoing with the following:

> Some readers have said; if the Indians are of the tribes of Israel, some decisive evidence of the fact will ere long be exhibited. This may be the case. But what kind of evidence shall we expect? Must some miracle be wrought? It is generally thought the days of miracles are past.... Would evidence like the following be deemed as verging toward what would be satisfactory? Suppose a leading character in Israel—wherever they are— should be found to have had in possession some biblical fragment of ancient Hebrew writing. This man dies, and it is buried with him in such a manner as to be long preserved. Some people afterwards removing that earth, discover this fragment, and ascertain what it is—an article of ancient Israel [*V.H.*, p. 217].

Ethan Smith then went on to describe the finding of some dark yellow (perhaps suggesting gold to Joseph) fragments of parchment which were supposed to have had Hebrew characters written on them, but which were subsequently lost. Here again, there is the idea of a written record of the ancients being uncovered in modern times.

Elsewhere in his book, Ethan Smith related the tale of an old Indian that had been told to a Dr. West:

> An old Indian had informed him that his fathers in this country had not long since had a book which they had for a long time preserved. But having lost the knowledge of reading it ... they buried it with an Indian chief [*V.H.*, p. 223].

That is a rather explicit suggestion that the Indians had a book at one time. Yet Joseph would have found something in the appendix of the second edition that could have stimulated his imagination even more. In that appendix, Ethan Smith made comments about some of the criticisms that had been leveled against the first edition of his book:

> The Reviewer adds; "Neither does it appear that the Jewish scriptures were the first that God gave to man. On the contrary; there is strong proof that parts of the first books were compiled from earlier scriptures. And the ancestors of the Indians might have had a *book*, without being Hebrew" [*V.H.*, p. 280].

To which, Ethan Smith answered:

> ... if there is "strong proof" that eastern nations had possessed sacred writings before the writings of Moses, from which antecedent writings our natives may have brought down the tradition that their ancestors had a book of God, ... how strange it must be that none beside the Indians of America, and the Reviewer, have any knowledge of such a book of God.... Moses ... was inspired to write the book of God.... Now was there during all this time, in the other nations of the east, the knowledge of *another book of God* ... that the descendants of the northern barbarous nations might bring down many deep and correct impressions of it ... in so distant and extensive a region of the world as this continent? [*V.H.*, p. 280].

So there it is. If there had been nothing else in *View of the Hebrews* that might have given Joseph the idea, Ethan Smith's riposte to the reviewer was certainly quite adequate to have done so. Although the Vermont minister was arguing that the ancestors of the Indians had the "Book of Moses" rather than "another book of God," the seed of the idea was there. Joseph might well have wondered if there were any reason why it could not be said that the Indians were the descendants of the Hebrews as Ethan Smith had argued, and yet still have once had another book of God.

At this point, Joseph's active imagination would have taken over and begun to consider the possibilities. He might have wondered if it were possible that, in addition to the book of Moses, the ancestors of the Indians had one of their own revelations and history. If they did, what tales would it tell! The finding of such a treasure could bring new life to biblical prophecy and establish America as being part of God's great plan. A book such as that would surely make the "hearts burn within" those who read it, and inspire them to "engage in the work by heaven assigned."

The mass of material Joseph found in *View of the Hebrews* certainly would have been sufficient to urge him toward the creation of *The Book of Mormon*. Even if he originally intended only to produce a book that he could pass off as a simple history of the ancient Americans, he could have found Ethan Smith's religious views constantly tugging at his mind. Thus, when events finally induced him to transform his history into a new revelation from Heaven, the change most likely came quite easily.

Not so easy would be getting people to accept the new book of God.

They would tend to look with skepticism, if not with outright hostility, towards any competition with the traditional scriptures. Ethan Smith himself had expressed such a viewpoint:

> We are to expect no new revelation from heaven. And the days of miracles are thought to be past [*V.H.*, p. 168].

Here, the Vermont minister was reflecting on the possible means by which it could be known that the Indians were descended from the Israelites. In an excerpt that we examined previously, he made a similar statement:

> Some readers have said; If the Indians are of the tribes of Israel, some decisive evidence of the fact will ere long be exhibited. This may be the case. But what kind of evidence shall we expect? Must some miracle be wrought? It is generally thought the days of miracles are past [*V.H.*, p. 217].

These statements, of course, did not fit in with Joseph's scheme of things. In direct opposition to them, he intended to bring forth a new revelation from heaven showing that the Indians were "of" the tribes of Israel — a new revelation that would be translated by a miraculous means. The Mormon prophet therefore apparently felt compelled to dispute what Ethan Smith had said. (An opposition of ideas, as well as a concurrence, can indicate influence).

Since the Vermont minister had declared that no new revelation from heaven could be expected, and also that the Indians did not have another book of God, Joseph had his *Book of Mormon* character, Nephi, give an argument to the contrary in the form of a "prophecy":

> And ... many of the Gentiles shall say, A Bible, a Bible, we have got a Bible, and there cannot by any more Bible. But thus saith the Lord God: ... Thou fool, that shall say, A Bible, we have got a Bible and we need no more Bible. ... Know ye not that there are more nations than one? Know ye not that I ... remember those who are upon the isles of the sea.... Wherefore murmer ye, because that ye shall receive more of my word? ... And because that I have spoken one word, ye need not suppose that I cannot speak another....
>
> Wherefore, because that ye have a Bible, ye need not suppose that it contains all my words; neither need ye suppose that I have not caused more to be written [*B.M.*, pp. 115–116; 2 Nephi 29:3–10].

Then, apparently to dispute Ethan Smith's other statement, Joseph put these words into the mouth of his *Book of Mormon* character, Moroni:

> ... hath miracles ceased? Behold I say unto you, Nay ... [*B.M.*, p. 579; Mormoni 7:29].

Furthermore, Moroni presents a lengthy argument against the idea that the days of miracles were past. He concludes this argument with the following:

> And if there was miracles wrought, then why has God ceased to be a
> God of miracles, and yet be an unchangeable being? And behold I say
> unto you, He changeth not; if so, he would cease to be God; and he ceaseth
> not to be God, and is a God of miracles [B.M., p. 537; Mormon 9: 18].

Finally, alluding to the time when *The Book of Mormon* — a new revelation from heaven — would come forth, and again rebutting Ethan Smith, Joseph had Moroni prophesy:

> ... and it shall come in a day when it shall be said that miracles are done
> away ... [B.M. p. 534; Mormon 8:26].

But Joseph would have known these arguments would not be enough. He needed something that would cause people to have greater reason to look to his new book of God as a source of revelation. Interestingly enough, it might have been *View of the Hebrews* that showed him which direction to take. Ethan Smith had argued that some of the scriptures were imperfectly translated:

> Isaiah xviii. verse 1; "*Ho, land shadowing with wings,...*" Our translators render this address, "Wo to the land." — But this is manifestly incorrect, as the best expositors agree. The Hebrew particle here translated *Wo to*, is a particle of friendly calling, as well as denouncing [V.H., p. 237].

> Verse 2. concluded. "*Saying, go ye swift messengers, to a nation scattered and peeled, to a people...*" 'Saying,' before the command *Go*, is interpolated in our translation, and destroys the sense; as though the nation said this to her swift messengers; whereas it is what God says to the nation addressed [V.H., pp. 239–240].

In some of the other publications of the time, Joseph would have found yet more reason to believe that the scriptures were imperfectly translated. For example, David Millard, a minister in a "Christian connection" church in West Bloomfield, near Palmyra, stated in the preface of a book he published in 1818:

> I have made our English translation of the scriptures my rule, believing it to be correct. Many *Trinitarians*, in order to prove their system, have labored hard to render the *original* materially different from our common English translation of the scriptures. One writer speaks of a work to be published, and in recommending it to the public says, "the work, in my opinion, corrects several *errors in our common translation of the scriptures.*"[2]

Although Millard did not agree that there were errors in the traditional translation of the Bible, his remarks showed that many other people did believe such errors existed.

Alexander Campbell provided another example. In the preface of a new translation of the New Testament that he published in 1828, he had this to say:

But some are so wedded to the common version that the very defects of it have become sacred, and an effort, however well intended, to put them in possession of one incomparably superior in propriety, perspicuity, and elegance, is viewed very much in the light of making "a new Bible," or of altering and amending the "very word of God."[3]

What was said in these two works had also been said in several others of that period. Joseph undoubtedly knew that many people believed there were errors or defects in the Bible, for he played upon that belief in his new revelation. As he envisioned it, *The Book of Mormon* would restore the purity of the original scriptures. That would help justify the appearance of his book.

But Joseph also picked up some additional ideas about a restoration from *View of the Hebrews.* According to Ethan Smith, it was time to restore the word of God to the Indians. As he said:

Send them the word, the bread of life.... Restore it to them [*V.H.*, p. 249].

Ethan Smith also gave the reason that a restoration should occur at that time:

The restoration there predicted is to be in *"the latter days"* [*V.H.*, p. 230].

Here, Ethan Smith was speaking of the literal restoration of Judah and Israel (including, as he saw it, the American Indians). The Vermont minister, and many others, believed that the "latter days" were upon the earth, and it was time to begin the process of restoration. In that belief, Joseph could have found the justification he needed. If the latter days were indeed upon the earth, it was time for the restoration of all things—including the true word of God to the Christians as well as to the Indians. Moreover, it would also be time to restore the true church of God. What would be more natural than to "restore" God's "true" church along with His "true" word.

The concept of a restoration was perhaps further emphasized in Joseph's mind by some ideas expressed by Alexander Campbell. He was preaching that Christianity had fallen into an apostate condition and that there needed to be a restoration to the ancient order of things. He stated:

A RESTORATION *of the ancient order of things* is all that is necessary.... No attempt "to reform the doctrine, discipline, and government of the church" can promise a better result.... Celebrated as the *era of the Reformation* is, we doubt not but that the *era of the Restoration* will as far transcend it in importance....

The constitution and law of the primitive church shall be the constitution and law of the Restored Church.

We contend that all Christian sects are more or less apostatized from the institutions of the Saviour....[4]

These ideas of Alexander Campbell's are perfectly at home in the church that Joseph founded. As in Campbell's church, the concepts about the restoration of the ancient order of things and about the apostasy of the modern churches play an important part in Mormon doctrine. Campbell, in fact, considered Joseph's church to be a "gross satanic imitation" of his restorationist movement.

Joseph may even have acquired the idea for the name of his church from him. In his publication, *The Christian Baptist*, Campbell had given his opinion on a dispute that was taking place at the time:

> Look into the New Testament. There the church is the *Church of Christ*.... Look out of the New Testament, and look into the creeds and confessions. Here we see a Baptist church, a Methodist church, and a Presbyterian church....
>
> When we give a *name* and a *creed* to a church, other than the name of Christ, ... that church acquires immediately ... a character altogether different from what the *Church of Christ* really possesses....[5]

> Sectarianism ... robs the saint of the name of his Saviour; and of his authority too, by giving him the name of a sect.... Paul was greater than John the Baptist, (Matth. xi, ii.) yet he would not permit any of Christ's disciples to call themselves by his name, or by the name of Apollos, or of Peter.... God makes it the duty of every Christian to oppose every sectarian name and creed....[6]

Echoing this dispute of Joseph's own time, some *Book of Mormon* characters ask Jesus how the church should be named:

> And they said unto him, Lord, we will that thou wouldst tell us the name whereby we shall call this church; for there are disputations among the people concerning this matter. And the Lord said unto them, Verily, ... have they not read the scriptures, which saith ye must take upon you the name of Christ, which is my name? ... and how be it my church, save it be called in my name? for if a church be called in Moses' name then it be Moses' church: or if it be called in the name of a man then it be the church of a man; but if it be called in my name then it is my church ... [*B.M.*, p. 507; 3 Nephi 27:3–8].

And we also find in *The Book of Mormon*:

> And they which were baptized in the name of Jesus, were called the church of Christ [*B.M.*, p. 507; 3 Nephi 26:21].

When Joseph first organized his church, he called it simply the Church of Christ. It was not until later that he changed the name to the Church of Jesus Christ of Latter-day Saints.

With the ideas that the traditional scriptures had errors and that the modern churches were apostate, Joseph felt that he could justify bringing out the restored word of God and establishing the restored Church of Christ. But Joseph apparently also felt that he needed to provide an explanation of how the apostasy and the errors in scripture had come about. He needed something to place the blame upon, and he found it in the object of a popular prejudice of his time. Anti-Catholicism was quite prevalent in the Northeast, and particularly in New York State, in the years before he published *The Book of Mormon*. Even Ethan Smith reflected this prejudice:

> This old Indian had been informed something of the religion of the Roman Catholics; but he said he did not believe the great and good Spirit ever taught them any such nonsense [*V.H.*, p. 137].

> Capt. Carver says of the Indians "wholly unadulterated with the superstitions of the church of Rome" [*V.H.*, p. 155].

Many publications of the time presented inflammatory tirades against the Catholic Church. For example, in his *Wonders of Nature and Providence, Displayed* (which was available in the Manchester library), Josiah Priest devoted some forty pages to the horrors of the Inquisition. He described in detail some of the tortures that its victims had suffered, and were yet suffering in Spain where it was still going on. He also noted the thousands of people that had been killed both under the Inquisition and in the European religious wars between Catholics and Protestants. Concluding his account, he said:

> Well therefore, might the inspired penman say, that at mystic Babylon's destruction, "was found in her the blood of prophets, of saints, and of all that was slain upon the earth."[7]

Considering the anti-Catholic feelings of the time, it should not be surprising that Joseph would have come to think that the Catholic Church would fit his requirements for a villain. We therefore find Nephi giving this prophecy in *The Book of Mormon*:

> And it came to pass that I saw among the nations of the Gentiles, the foundation of a great church. And the angel said unto me, Behold the foundation of a church which is most abominable above all other churches, which slayeth the Saints of God, yea, and tortureth them and bindeth them down, and yoketh them with a yoke of iron, and bringeth them down into captivity [*B.M.*, p. 28; 1 Nephi 13:4–5].

Continuing to rely on the prejudice of his readers, Joseph reasoned that he could cast the Catholic Church as the cause of the corruption of the word of God and, consequently, the root of the apostasy of other churches. Joseph could have found these very ideas in a periodical that was published in Canandaigua, only a few miles from his home. Its name was the *Plain Truth* and its first issue appeared on March 8, 1822. Significantly, the first page of that first issue contains several ideas that are reflected in *The Book of Mormon*. For example, we find:

> In presenting the first number of PLAIN TRUTH to the public, we will remark, that the work is undertaken merely to expose the many errors now existing in the Christian world, which are passed off on the undiscerning, for "pure and undefiled religion."
>
> ... No Christian can deny that the Gospel of our blessed Savior, since the Apostolic days, has been clouded by *Popish superstition*, even to the present time. In what manner are the clouds to be dispersed, that we may behold the brightness of the "Son of Righteousness" — that we may behold the transcendent purity of the "Gospel of peace?"

Note that the writer in the *Plain Truth* held that many errors existed in the Christian world of his time and that he charged the Catholic Church with corrupting the gospel. In *the Book of Mormon*, we find that Joseph had his character, Nephi, see those very same things in a prophetic vision:

> And the angel of the Lord said unto me, Thou hast beheld that the Book ... contained the plainness of the Gospel of the Lord, of whom the twelve apostles bear record...; wherefore, these things go forth from the Jews in purity, unto the Gentiles...; and after that...; behold, ... thou seest the foundation of a great and abominable church, which is most abominable above all other churches; for behold, they have taken away from the Gospel of the Lamb, many parts which are plain and most precious; and also many Covenants of the Lord have they taken away; and all this have they done, that they might pervert the right ways of the Lord; ... and after that these plain and precious things were taken away, it goeth forth unto all the nations of the Gentiles; ... and because of these things which are taken away out of the Gospel of the Lamb, an exceeding great many do stumble ... [*B.M.*, p. 30; 1 Nephi 13:24-29].

Nephi then answers the question that the writer in the *Plain Truth* posed concerning the manner in which the clouds could be dispersed to reveal the purity of the gospel. *The Book of Mormon* would provide the means to make the gospel pure.

To be sure, the ideas about the corruption of the gospel, the errors in the Christian world, and the "blame" of the Catholic Church were hardly unique to the *Plain Truth*; Joseph found them in other sources also. However, note that the writer in the *Plain Truth* alluded to Malachi 4:2, but that he made a pun by changing "Sun of righteousness" into "Son of righteousness." Significantly, we find that the very same "pun" occurs in *The Book of Mormon* when Jesus "quotes" Malachi:

> But unto you that fear my name, shall the Son of righteousness arise with healing in his wings ... [*B.M.*, p. 505; 3 Nephi 25:2].

The pun, of course, can only be made in English since the words for "son" and "sun" sound completely different in both Greek and Hebrew.

Furthermore, this same page from the *Plain Truth* contains yet another likeness to *The Book of Mormon*. The *Plain Truth* writer quoted a letter in which a poor man was described as having scraped together money to give to his church. The writer then condemned this practice, saying:

> Here is an instance of a poor man who has been brought into the full belief of the efficacy of money in carrying souls to Heaven; and being told by some public preacher, (for he never found it in the Bible,) that he would be amply rewarded by his Maker, for all the money he might use in this way, the poor deluded fanatic has furnished, from his scanty stock.... If such a spell could be maintained over the *whole* of community, how long would it be before designing men, under the garb of Religion, would become perfect masters of every man's property, both personal and real?

In *The Book of Mormon*, Nephi makes a prophecy that the churches of Joseph's day would be guilty of the same thing:

> Because of pride, and because of false teachers, and false doctrine, their churches have become corrupted.... They rob the poor, because of their sanctuaries; they rob the poor, because of their fine clothing.... [*B.M.*, p. 113; 2 Nephi 28:12–13].

Finally, Joseph seems to have picked up an idea from what the writer in the *Plain Truth* said about "designing men, under the garb of Religion" becoming "perfect masters of every man's property." Perhaps these words gave him an idea about the possible monetary benefits he might accrue if he could put on the "garb of Religion." In any case, Joseph had his converts turn over all their property to his church soon after he established his new religion.

It appears that the virulent anti-Catholicism of his time was not the only prejudice that Joseph attempted to use to advantage in his book. As will be shown later, another bias played a significant part in the development of his ideas. When we add these to the early nineteenth century literary sources that are reflected in *The Book of Mormon*, it should be sufficient to demonstrate that the ideas appearing in that book were rooted in the cultural environment of the time.

And therein lies the answer to the question of whether or not Joseph Smith's latter-day revelation could have been a product of that time. Since the book reflects so many ideas that were common to, and indeed were peculiar to, the early nineteenth century, it can be readily said that it was a product of that time. All that remains for us to do now is to attempt to prove it by analyzing *The Book of Mormon* in relation to its sources.

Of those sources, Ethan Smith's *View of the Hebrews* is the most important. The in-depth comparative analysis of the two books in the following chapters will demonstrate this quite well. Before proceeding with that analysis, however, there are a few things that should be emphasized.

First, Joseph did not quote from Ethan's book word for word. In any case, *The Book of Mormon* would have needed to have the appearance of being original and not dependent upon any other contemporary work. Toward this end he seems to have put Ethan Smith's ideas into his own words, sometimes modifying the ideas slightly to disguise the source and to suit his own aims and needs. Because of this, one must often look beyond the actual wording in the comparisons and analyze the underlying ideas and meanings in order to see the relationship between the two books.

Second, Ethan Smith wrote in an expository style and from the standpoint of a minister of the early 1800s addressing his fellow American Christians. *The Book of Mormon* seems to imitate the style and language of the King James Bible written from the standpoint of the people who supposedly lived the story it tells. This difference in style and viewpoint further obscures the real relationship between the two books. Again, because of this, one must look at the ideas each book presents, rather than at the exact language and style.

Third, Ethan Smith made considerable use of the Bible. One might then ask if a corresponding use in *The Book of Mormon* came about because Joseph had used *View of the Hebrews* or because he had used the Bible itself. Joseph seems to have used both. In some cases, the interpretation of a biblical text clearly reflects Ethan Smith's comments. Other cases go beyond Ethan Smith's use and bring in considerable additional material.

That raises an additional point. Biblical references are copious in *The Book of Mormon*, but because of space limitations it is impossible for us to explore them except in those cases that specifically relate to *View of the Hebrews*. Numerous studies have already been made showing the use of the Bible in *The Book of Mormon*, so there is no need to repeat them here. It is more important for us to examine Joseph's apparent dependence upon early nineteenth century literary and cultural sources.

Part Three

The Comparisons

Chapter 11

To the Land of Promise

Although there are numerous conceptual similarities between Ethan Smith's *View of the Hebrews* and Joseph Smith's *The Book of Mormon*, they seem to disagree on a very basic point: exactly who the ancestors of the Indians were supposed to be. In contrast with the Vermont minister's proposal that they were the Ten Tribes of Israel, the Mormon prophet made them the family and followers of a Hebrew patriarch named Lehi. This apparent disagreement on such a basic point naturally raises the question, if Joseph Smith used Ethan Smith's book as his primary source why did he not follow Ethan's idea of who the ancestors of the Indians were?

We can begin to answer this by assuming that Joseph must have had some reason to modify Pastor Smith's views on the ancestry of the Indians. Of course we can only speculate about what that reason might have been but, by putting ourselves in his place, we can perhaps perceive why he might have wanted to make the change.

One of the first things that comes to mind is that Joseph would not have wanted his book to be an obvious plagiarism of *View of the Hebrews*. He might have thought that the borrowings would not be so apparent if he modified Ethan's proposals about the Indians' ancestors. This certainly would have been ample reason for him to make the change.

But there were further reasons for Joseph to modify Ethan's ideas. If he had used the Ten Tribes notion, he would have had to face some serious concerns, not least of which would be that he would have placed a heavy burden upon himself and the church he planned to establish. Ethan Smith had made it clear that certain biblical prophecies ordained that the Ten Tribes were to be returned to the Holy Land in the latter days. The natural consequence of this would have been that Joseph's church, as the restored "true" church of God, would have had the responsibility of seeing that the return was accomplished. But Joseph certainly was not about to take upon himself and his church the difficult and bizarre task of convincing the American Indians that they would have to leave their own land for a strange country across the sea. He surely felt instead that it would be a lot simpler and a lot more practical to modify Ethan's views and make the Indians a part of the Hebrew family that was not required to be restored to Palestine in the latter days.

Be that as it may, Joseph apparently felt that he still needed to act on

Ethan's call for the "restoration" of the Indians, the religious significance of which was too important to disregard. An example was Ethan's call for the Indians to be restored to the knowledge of their "heritage" in the Hebrew family. And, in a sense, Joseph did follow Ethan smith's ideas about the restoration of the Indians to Zion. The Indians would have their restoration completed, not with their return to their old Zion in Palestine, but with their acceptance into the new Zion that he planned to establish in America.

This is not to say that Joseph ignored Ethan's views on the restoration of the Ten Tribes. In fact, *The Book of Mormon* has several "prophecies" about those tribes which are in complete conformity with the spirit of those views. These prophecies declare that the "mighty nation among the gentiles" (i.e., America) would help in converting the Ten Tribes to Christianity and in restoring them to the land of their fathers. However, in *The Book of Mormon*, the Ten Tribes are said to be elsewhere on the earth, to be found when the time is ripe. For Joseph, this meant it would be a long time, if ever, before he and his church would have to confront the problem of returning the Ten Tribes to the land of their fathers.

Continuing to put ourselves in Joseph's place, we can perceive one more reason why the Mormon prophet could not use the Ten Tribes as the ancestors of the Indians. Ethan Smith had emphasized that those tribes had a stigma attached to them:

> The ten tribes revolted from the house of David, early in the reign of Rehoboam, son and successor of king Solomon. ... The revolting ten tribes submitted to another king, Jeroboam....
>
> The ten tribes thus went off to idolatry. A line of kings succeeded Jeroboam; but none of them, to the time of the expulsion, were true worshippers of the God of Israel. By their apostasy, folly, and idolatry, the ten tribes were preparing themselves for a long and doleful rejection, an outcast state for thousands of years. This Moses had denounced; Deut. xxviii. And this God fulfilled [*V.H.*, pp. 47–48].
>
> The casting out of the ten tribes for their impious idolatries, is full of instruction.... They should be excommunicated from the covenant, hurled from the promised land, and abandoned to a state of savage wretchedness, for two and a half millenaries. Their sin in those dark ages of the old dispensation was no trifle. Its consequence is held up as an awful warning to the world. It impresses the following language; "know thou and see that it is an evil thing and bitter that thou hast forsaken the Lord" [*V.H.*, p. 253].

These passages would have given Joseph pause for thought. Because of what he was trying to do, he may have felt that it would be more appropriate if the characters in his book were brought to the New World because of a blessing and a promise, instead of the result of being cast off as Ethan Smith had brought the Ten Tribes. Therefore one of the characters, shortly after arriving in America, emphasizes that they were not "cast off":

> ... we are not cast off; nevertheless, we have been driven out of the land of our inheritance ... [*B.M.*, p. 85; 2 Nephi 10:20].

Joseph must have felt that the Ten Tribes were unsuitable for his book because of the curse that was upon them. Those tribes had had their chance in the land of their fathers and had lost it.

For that matter, Ethan had declared that the Jews had also had their chance and had eventually lost it:

> But alas, we find recorded of this city, temple, and nation of the Jews, a fatal reverse. They found the sentiment in their sacred oracles fulfilled; "The Lord is with you while ye be with him; but if ye forsake him, he will cast you off."
>
> The Jews became carnal; crucified the Lord of Glory; and they fell under the denunciations and the full execution of his wrath [V.H., p. 14].

From this, Joseph could have concluded that the history of both the Jews and the Israelites revealed a pattern. Both had been with the Lord, both forsook the Lord, and then both were cast off by the Lord. Joseph would have found this interesting, but it did not help him solve the problem of who the people in his book should be. However, Ethan Smith had said yet something else that apparently did help the Mormon prophet on that matter:

> We find the same idea in Isai. lxiii. The chapter is introduced with the battle of the great day of God, which introduces the Millennium.... The events of the chapter then, are intimately connected with that period. They involve the restoration of God's ancient people. And we find a special branch of that ancient people pleading with God... — having been lost from the knowledge of the known descendants of Abraham, the Jews. Allusion is made to their ancient redemption; and to their subsequent and fatal rebellion, till God "was turned to be their enemy, and he fought against them;" — or cast them out of his sight. At last (at a period nearly connected with the great battle) they are waking up.... Here after a long period they awake as from the dead, and plead God's ancient love to their nation.... Here is a branch of the tribes ... who ... plead with God the entail of the covenant ... [V.H., p. 71-72].

Here again was the pattern of a people being with God, forsaking him, and being cast off — yet, with some rather interesting added ideas about the restoration in the "latter days" (the "period nearly connected with the great battle"). What may have especially interested Joseph was the idea that a "special branch" of the Hebrew people had been lost from the knowledge of the Jews. Ethan Smith had equated this special branch with the Ten Tribes, but the Mormon prophet saw how he could use it in his own book.

It appears that Joseph took the ideas in the above passage and integrated them with Ethan's theory of what had happened to the ancestors of the Indians. The story line from this integration of ideas worked out quite well for his purpose. As he conceived it, the ancient inhabitants of America would be a "special branch" (to use Ethan Smith's term) of the Hebrew people. Upon its arrival in the New World, this special branch would become lost from the knowledge of the Jews and would divide into savage and civilized factions. At first, the civilized faction would be "with" God (Ethan himself had suggested that in his theory). But then, the civilized faction would rebel against God till he was "turned to be their enemy, and he fought against them" and "cast" them off. That, perhaps, to Joseph would explain why the savage and idolatrous faction would eventually be able to annihilate them.

Moreover, the integration did not end there. Continuing to follow the above passage from *View of the Hebrews*, Joseph had his ancient Americans "awake as from the dead" in the "latter days" — symbolically, in *The Book of Mormon*, of course — and "plead with God the entail of the covenant" (again, to use Ethan's words).

At this point, the idea of a people calling to God seems to have caused Joseph to remember something that Ethan had said about the Indians:

> ... their little sons are obliged to ascend a hill fasting.... The little worshipper then rubs himself over with whitish clay....
>
> This has ... the appearance of descending from Hebrew tradition...; teaching their children to *fast* in *clay*, as "in dust and ashes;" and to cry to Jah [God] for pity and protection [*V.H.*, p. 161].

So, echoing both of the above passages from *View of the Hebrews* (and apparently chiding Ethan for saying the days of miracles were past), Joseph had Moroni say:

> Search the prophecies of Isaiah. Behold, I cannot write them. Yea, behold I say unto you, That those saints which have gone before me, which have possessed this land, shall cry; yea, even from the dust will they cry unto the Lord; and as the Lord liveth, he will remember the covenant which he hath made with them.... And ... out of the earth shall they come, by the hand of the Lord...; and it shall come in a day when it shall be said that miracles are done away; and it shall come even as if one should speak from the dead [*B.M.*, pp. 533–534; Mormon 8:23, 26].

Note that both Ethan Smith and Moroni referred to Isaiah and expressed similar ideas. In Ethan's book we find that the ancient inhabitants of America would "awake as from the dead" in the latter days and "plead with God the entail of the covenant." In *The Book of Mormon* we find that, "even as if one should speak from the dead," the ancient inhabitants of America would "cry unto the Lord" in the latter days and the Lord would "remember the covenant." Further, in both books there is a crying to God from the dust.

One might make an issue of the fact that the above passage from *The Book of Mormon* does not use the word "awake" in any form. But that point is moot. If the ancient Americans were to speak as from the dead, they would have to awake as from the dead first. In any case, though Joseph did not use "awake" in the above imagery, he did do so elsewhere. For example, Lehi reprimands his rebellious sons with the following words:

> Awake, my sons; ... and come forth out of obscurity, and arise from the dust [*B.M.*, pp. 61–62; 2 Nephi [1:23].

Note that there are hints of the Indian sons in the dust and of an unknown people awakening.

It is apparent that Joseph followed Ethan Smith's lead by making the characters of his book a "special branch" of the Hebrew people who were lost from the knowledge of the Jews. But how did he develop his specific ideas about those characters?

Again, it appears that *View of the Hebrews* supplied Joseph with some important concepts. The following, for example, is perhaps what caused him to begin thinking along certain lines:

> Tiglah-Pilnezer, king of Assyria, captured the tribes of Reuben and Gad, and the half tribe of Manasseh, who lay east of Jordan, and placed them in Halah, Harah, and Habor.... About twenty years after, (134 years before the Babylonian captivity of the Jews, and 725 years before Christ,) ... Shalmanezer, the succeeding king of Assyria, attacked Samaria, took the remainder of the ten tribes ... and placed them with their brethren in Halah and Habor ... [*V.H.*, p. 48].

As he continued reading, Joseph would also have come across this passage:

> Mr. Adair ... concludes thus; "...Had the nine tribes and a half of Israel, that were carried off by Shalmanezer, and settled in Median..." [*V.H.*, p. 80].

From these passages in *View of the Hebrews*, Joseph might have concluded that the Ten Lost Tribes were actually only nine and a half tribes, and that half the tribe of Manasseh was not taken captive. Moreover, having a certain amount of curiosity, he very likely wondered what had happened to that half tribe of Manasseh.

Something else Ethan said may have helped Joseph there. The Vermont minister had referred to a prophecy that Ezekiel had given:

> Both houses of the descendants of Abraham (viz. Israel and Judah,) are recovered, as will be seen....
>
> The re-union of the two branches of that people follows, by the figure of the two sticks taken by the prophet. On the one he writes, "For Judah, and for the children of Israel his companions." Upon the other; "For Joseph, the stick of Ephraim, and for all the house of Israel his companions."
>
> Lest any should say, the prediction which there seems to foretell the restoration of the ten tribes, as well as that of the Jews, were accomplished in the restoration of that few of the Israelites, who clave to the Jews under the house of David, and the ten tribes are irrecoverably lost; it is here expressed that the Jews and those Israelites, their companions, were symbolized by one stick; and Ephraim, all the house of Israel, (the whole ten tribes,) by the other stick. These sticks miraculously become one in the prophet's hand [*V.H.*, pp. 52–53].

By placing ourselves in the mind of the Mormon prophet, we can perceive how this passage could have aroused his curiosity. In the first part of the passage, he would have noted that one branch of the Hebrew family included Judah and "the children of Israel his companions," while the other branch included the biblical Joseph and "all the house of Israel his companions." But who were these children of Israel who were counted with Judah instead of with the remainder of the house of Israel? Could these "few of the Israelites who clave to the Jews under the house of David" have included at least some of the half tribe of Manasseh that were not cast off along with their idolatrous and apostate brethren. If so, and if they were not cast off, it must have been because they were faithful to the Lord and were being rewarded.

These ideas must have moved Joseph toward thinking of how he could have the half tribe of Manasseh provide the characters for his book. The apparent faithfulness of these children of Israel who clave to the Jews would be a good starting point. Because of that faithfulness, the Lord could reward them by bringing them to "the land of promise" in the New World. Yet, Joseph would have known he would have to be careful. He could not have all the "children of Israel" leave for the New World. History did not record such a movement, and most of these children of Israel were apparently known to have stayed with the Jews.

But again, Ethan Smith had said something else that may have provided a suggestion to the Mormon prophet:

> Pedro de Cicca de Leon, one of the conquerors of Peru, and who had travelled through many provinces of America, says of the Indians: "The people, men and women, although there are such a multitude of tribes or nations, in such diversities of climate, appear nevertheless like children of one father and mother" [*V.H.*, p. 88].

Here, then, was the answer. Since the American Indians were supposed to look like the children of one father and mother, why not make them actually such? Therefore, reasoning that one family would not be missed from the half tribe of Manasseh, that is what Joseph did. Apparently using ideas developed from *View of the Hebrews*, he made his characters the family and descendants of a man named "Lehi, who came out of the land of Jerusalem, who was a descendant of Manasseh, who was the son of Joseph..." (*B.M.*, p. 248; Alma 10:3).

According to *The Book of Mormon*, Lehi lived in "the land of Jerusalem" long after the Ten Tribes (or the nine and a half) had been cast off. Joseph must therefore have intended that Lehi and his family be included among that few of the Israelites who clave to the Jews, which were mentioned by Ethan in his elaboration of Ezekiel's prophecy.

But that is not all. Joseph had Lehi allude to the same prophecy. Here, Lehi is prophesying to one of his sons:

> Wherefore, the fruit of my ["thy" in later editions] loins shall write; and the fruit of the loins of Judah shall write; and that which shall be written by the fruit of thy loins, and also that which shall be written by the fruit of the loins of Judah, shall grow together ... in the latter days ... [*B.M.*, p. 67; 2 Nephi 3:12].

That which would be written by the descendants of Lehi's son was supposed to be *The Book of Mormon*; i.e., the stick of Ephraim, upon which was written, "For Joseph...." That which was to be written by the descendants of Judah was supposed to be the Bible; i.e., the stick of Judah. According to the nineteenth-century Joseph, these two books were to come together in the latter days. This he derived from Ezekiel's sticks that "became one in the prophet's hand." One might also note that, on an early advertising circular for *The Book of Mormon*, Joseph described his latter-day revelation as "the stick of Joseph taken from the hand of Ephraim."[1] Thus, with ideas that he garnered from *View of the Hebrews*, Joseph probably hoped to make it seem that *The Book of Mormon* fulfilled biblical prophecy.

And that brings us back to the seeming disagreement between the two books, which turns out not to be so great after all. In the final analysis, it seems Joseph still derived most of the essential ideas for his characters from concepts that he found in *View of the Hebrews*. From the foregoing, it is apparent that Joseph followed Ethan's view that the Indians had their ancestry in the tribes of Israel. To be sure, the Mormon prophet modified that view by using just a part of one of those tribes in that ancestry, but that tribe nevertheless was one of the Ten Tribes. Furthermore, it appears that Joseph even got his ideas for the modification from concepts found in *View of the Hebrews*.

It is even possible that Ethan provided Joseph a reason for not requiring that his Israelite family of Lehi (in their modern form as Indians) return to Palestine in the latter days. The Vermont minister stated the following:

> A *remnant* only of the ten tribes is to return. This is clearly taught. Isai. x 20–22.... That great numbers will return, there seems not room to doubt. But the actual proposition to return, will doubtless be a *free-will offering* of those whose hearts God shall incline [*V.H.*, p. 256].

If only a remnant of the Ten Tribes was required to return to Palestine, another part would not be. Joseph may have reasoned that this part could be the "special branch" of the Ten Tribes represented by the people of his book.

Furthermore, Joseph applied to his special branch of the Hebrew people most of the religious ideas that Ethan had applied to the Ten Tribes as a whole. Foremost among those ideas were the Vermont minister's interpretations of Isaiah. The following passage from *The Book of Mormon* illustrates this quite well. It is a part of what Nephi says shortly after he and his brethren arrive in the New World:

> Now it came to pass that I ... did read unto them which was written by the Prophet Isaiah.... Wherefore, I spake unto them, saying: Hear ye the words of the prophet, ye which are a remnant of the House of Israel, a branch of which have been broken off; hear ye the words of the prophet, which was written unto all the House of Israel, and liken it unto yourselves, that ye may have hope as well as your brethren, from whom ye have been broken off [*B.M.*, p. 52; 1 Nephi 19: 22–24].

Thus Joseph applied the words of Isaiah, as originally interpreted by

Ethan Smith, to the "special branch," the "remnant of the House of Israel," that he had created for his book.

Having decided on who the people of his book would be, Joseph now had to provide the justification for their leaving Jerusalem. Again, something he found in *View of the Hebrews* may have helped him:

> Mr. Adair gives his opinion, that the ten tribes, soon after their banishment from the land of Israel, left Media, and reached this continent from the north-west, probably before the carrying away of the Jews to Babylon [*V.H.*, p. 81].

This passage might have reminded Joseph that the Jews themselves were taken captive more than a hundred years after the tribes of Israel had met a similar fate. He would therefore have to get his family of Lehi away from Palestine before the Captivity occurred. Joseph solved the problem by having Lehi have a vision in which he was warned of the impending danger. Lehi and his family, along with a few others, thus leave Jerusalem and travel for a while in a southerly direction along the Red Sea.

At this point, Joseph seems to have gleaned some ideas for the journey from Ethan. The Mormon prophet doubtlessly wanted his book to appear to be supported by the evidence, so he frequently took advantage of some of the Indian traditions that he found mentioned in *View of the Hebrews*. For example, we find Ethan quoting this from one of his sources:

> The Indian tradition says that their forefathers in very remote ages came from a far distant country...; and that in process of time they removed eastward to their present settlements [*V.H.*, p. 152].

So, in *The Book of Mormon* we find:

> And it came to pass that we did again take our journey in the wilderness; and we did travel nearly eastward, from that time forth [*B.M.*, p. 42; 1 Nephi 17:1].

Following the direction reported in the Indian "tradition," Lehi's family would have left the Red Sea (where they were at the time), and would have had to cross the Arabian Desert. Joseph probably did not realize this, for he did not describe them as having any of the problems one might expect if they had actually traveled in one of the most inhospitable areas on earth.

Having the travelers go eastward also poses another problem. After crossing the Arabian Desert, the travelers would have found themselves on the shores of either the Persian Gulf or the Arabian Sea. And eastward, beyond, they would have had the broad expanse of the Indian and Pacific oceans to cross. It would have made more sense for Joseph to describe the travelers as going the much shorter distance westward across the Mediterranean and the Atlantic — but that would have contradicted the Indian tradition.

This also underscores another difference between *The Book of Mormon* and *View of the Hebrews*. Ethan Smith thought that the Ten Tribes had migrated to the New World by traveling eastward across Asia and then crossing over the Bering Strait. But Joseph apparently felt that giving an account of a trip across the immense Asian continent would take too much time and detract from the aim of his book. Moreover, he surely knew that it would be hard for him to give a convincing account of the various Asian peoples that his characters would have met on their travels. It should not be surprising, then, for Joseph to have reasoned that the simplest way of getting his characters to the New World was to have them go by boat from a place not far from where they had started.

We can also note that Joseph, at this point in the story he was telling, might have taken an idea from one of Ethan's sources. In *A Star in the West*, Elias Boudinot had made the following conjecture about the travels of the Ten Tribes to the New World:

> They proceeded till they came to a great water or river, which stopped their progress, as they had no artificial means of passing it.... How long they remained here, cannot now be known; but finally, God again appeared for them, as he had done for their fathers of old at the Red Sea by giving them some token of his presence, and encouraging them to go on....[2]

Something like this happens in *The Book of Mormon*. Going eastward from the Red Sea, Lehi and his family would have arrived, as we noted, on the shores of either the Persian Gulf or the Arabian Sea:

> And we did sojourn for the space of many years, yea, even eight years in the wilderness.... And we beheld the Sea, which we called Irreantum, which being interpreted, is, many waters....
> And it came to pass that ... after ... the space of many days, the voice of the Lord came unto me....
> And ... the Lord spake unto me, saying: ... thou shalt construct a ship, after the manner which I shall shew thee, that I may carry thy people across these waters [*B.M.*, p. 42; 1 Nephi 17:4–8].

So Joseph had his characters go, with the help of God, by boat across the Indian and Pacific oceans, a distance of some 16,000 miles, to the New World.

At this point, we might note what Ethan Smith and Joseph Smith each had to say about the significance of the land to which the travelers were going. First, Ethan:

> ... we justly infer, that God *would* in his holy providence provide some suitable place for their safe keeping, *as his outcast tribes*, though long unknown to men as such. There is no avoiding this conclusion.... God surely must have provided a place for their safe keeping, as a distinct people, in some part of the world, during that long period. They must during that period, have been unknown to the Jews as Israelites; and consequently unknown to the world as such ... [*V.H.*, p. 73].

So Joseph Smith had his *Book of Mormon* characters say:

> And it came to pass that the Lord spake unto me, saying: ... ye shall ... be led to a land of promise; yea, even a land which I have prepared for you ... [*B.M.*, p. 9; 1 Nephi 2:19, 20].

> And behold, it is wisdom that this land should be kept as yet from the knowledge of other nations: for behold, many nations would overrun the land, that there would be no place for an inheritance.... Wherefore, ... inasmuch as they which the Lord God shall bring out of the land of Jerusalem shall keep his commandments, they shall prosper upon the face of the land; and they shall be kept from all other nations, that they may possess this land unto themselves ... [*B.M.*, p. 60; 2 Nephi 1:8, 9].

In both books the Lord provides the land so that the newcomers would be kept to themselves, unknown and not bothered by the other nations of the world.

Ethan Smith also said of America:

> ... Christians in our land may well bless God that it is their happy lot to live in this land...; this protecting realm, an asylum of liberty and religion.... And ... this land of liberty ... [*V.H.*, p. 245].

While Joseph Smith had his character, Lehi, say:

> ... we have obtained a land of promise, a land which is choice above all other lands.... Yea, the Lord God hath covenanted this land to me.... And ... it shall be a land of liberty ... [*B.M.*, p. 60; 2 Nephi 1:5-7].

Making an interpretation of Biblical prophecy, Ethan Smith had also said of America:

> And the places from which they are recovered are noted; among which are *"the isles of the sea;"* or lands away over the sea.... Certainly then, from America! [*V.H.*, pp. 232, 233].

In *The Book of Mormon*, we thus find Nephi's brother, Jacob, also referring to America as an "isle of the sea":

> ... we have been led to a better land, ... and we are upon an isle of the sea [*B.M.*, p. 85; 2 Nephi 10:20].

The stage was now set for Joseph to follow Ethan Smith's ideas about what had happened to the "Israelites" after their arrival in the New World.

Chapter 12

The Prophecies

Much of the first part of *The Book of Mormon* is devoted to "prophecies" uttered by various characters. From the standpoint of Joseph's own time, some of these prophecies were merely statements about historical events, including the discovery of America by Columbus, the European settlement of the New World, the Revolutionary War, and some local events that were making news at about the time Joseph was dictating his latter-day revelation. Alexander Campbell put his evaluation of these foretellings succinctly: "How easy to prophecy of the past or of the present time."

Joseph appears to have derived many of the other prophecies in *The Book of Mormon* from the speculations he found in *View of the Hebrews.* Some of these speculations were based on Ethan Smith's ideas about Indian history. Others relate to the Vermont minister's conjectures about the relationship of Indians, Jews, and the American people to biblical prophecy.

An example of this type of prophecy occurs very early in *The Book of Mormon*, evidently derived from several references that Ethan had made to the apostle Paul's metaphor of the olive tree:

> This restoration is a great event in the prophets; and we find it in the New Testament. Paul (in his epistle to the Romans, chap. xi.) notes their being grafted again into their own olive tree, as a notable event of the last days ... [*V.H.*, p. 63].

Upon reading this, Joseph might have turned to Romans 11:13–24:

> ... I speak to you Gentiles.... For if the firstfruit *be* holy, the lump *is* also *holy*; and if the root *be* holy, so *are* the branches. And if some of the branches be broken off, and thou, being a wild olive tree, wert graffed in among them, and with them partakest of the root and fatness of the olive tree; Boast not against the branches.... For if thou wert cut out of the olive tree which is wild by nature, and wert graffed ... into a good olive tree: how much more shall these, which be the natural *branches*, be graffed, into their own olive tree?

Joseph would also have read the following in *View of the Hebrews*, in which Ethan elaborated upon Paul's metaphor of the olive tree:

Israel were excommunicated that the gentiles might take their place. But it was to be thus, only "till the fulness of the gentiles be come in," and then Israel shall be grafted in again, and their promised restoration be accomplished [*V.H.*, p. 62].

So, in *The Book of Mormon*, 600 years before Paul, we find Nephi saying:

Yea, even my father spake much concerning the Gentiles, and also concerning the House of Israel: That they should be compared like unto an olive tree, whose branches should be broken off, and should be scattered upon all the face of the earth.... And after that the House of Israel should be scattered, they should be gathered together again; or, in fine, that after the Gentiles had received the fulness of the Gospel, the natural branches of the olive tree, or the remnants of the House of Israel, should be grafted in, or come to the knowledge of the true Messiah, their Lord and their Redeemer [*B.M.*, pp. 22–23; 1 Nephi 10:12–14].

Ethan Smith had applied the metaphor of the olive tree to the American Indians, since he believed them to be the Israelite branch of the Hebrew family. Joseph evidently was quite taken with this idea. He used it in the excerpt just given and also devoted several pages elsewhere to a tedious elaboration of it.[1]

Note also the reference to the Messiah in this excerpt from *The Book of Mormon*. Through prophecy, the characters in that book "knew" about Jesus 600 years before his appearance in Palestine. This will come up again.

In *The Book of Mormon*, Nephi has a rather lengthy prophetic vision that is remarkably similar to an image that Ethan Smith gave. Significantly, the Vermont minister devised this image to illustrate his interpretation of Isaiah 18, which, as we noted, Joseph warily avoided referring to directly. In *View of the Hebrews* we find:

Behold this man of God, then, wrapt in the visions of the Almighty, casting an eye to faith down the lapse of time to the days of the final restoration of his long rejected brethren. He finds presented in a vision, away over the Mediterranean, and the Atlantic, far in the west, or going down of the sun, the continent of their long banishment. He also beholds in vision a great nation arising there in the last days; a land of freedom and religion. He hears the whisper of the Spirit of inspiration, directing him to address that far sequestered and happy land, and call their attention to the final restoration of his people [*V.H.*, pp. 237].

While still in Palestine, Nephi, a "man of God" in *The Book of Mormon*, likewise looks down the "lapse of time" in a prophetic vision and sees his people in the land across the ocean:

And it came to pass that the angel said unto me, Look, and behold thy seed, and also the seed of thy brethren! And I looked and beheld the land of promise; and I beheld multitudes of people ... [*B.M.*, p. 26; 1 Nephi 12:1].

Nephi then sees the arrival of the Europeans:

> And it came to pass that I beheld many multitudes of Gentiles, upon
> the land of promise.... And it came to pass that I, Nephi, beheld that they
> did prosper in the land ... [*B.M.*, p. 29; 1 Nephi 13:14–20].

And, after he arrives in the New World, Nephi continues the pattern set by
Ethan Smith and tells his brethren of his vision of a great gentile nation (which
is obviously supposed to be the United States of America):

> ... the Lord God will raise up a mighty nation among the Gentiles, yea,
> even upon the face of this land ... [*B.M.*, p. 57; 1 Nephi 22:7].

Nephi then makes a prophecy (as we shall see in detail later) that the
gentiles of the "mighty nation" would assist in the restoration of the branch of
the house of Israel (i.e., the American Indians) that they will find in the New
World. And, of course, since *The Book of Mormon* is to be preached to the
gentiles of the mighty nation, his prophecy has the effect of being an address to
"call their attention to the final restoration of his people."

So, as it turns out, Joseph included Isaiah 18 in *The Book of Mormon*
after all. But, rather than quoting that prophetic chapter directly, he had
Nephi make a corresponding series of prophecies. And, more specifically and
of particular significance, he seems to have patterned Nephi's prophecies after
Ethan Smith's interpretive image of Isaiah 18.

In his prophetic vision, Nephi also sees the "abominable church,"
which, as we saw, was an allusion to the Catholic Church. Closely tied in with
this was another concept derived from *View of the Hebrews*. Ethan had said:

> Look at the origin of those degraded natives of your continent.... Send
> them the word, the bread of life. You received that book from the seed of
> Abraham. All your volume of salvation was written by the sons of Jacob.
> And by them it was transferred from Jerusalem to the lost heathen world,
> and to you.... Remember then your debt of gratitude of God's ancient
> people for the word of life. Restore it to them ... [*V.H.*, p. 249].

Here, Ethan was emphasizing that the Bible had come from God's
ancient people to the gentiles, and because of that, the American gentiles
should repay the debt and restore the Bible to the remnant of God's ancient
people who were the Native Americans. Joseph apparently liked this line of
argument, because he included it in Nephi's prophetic vision as if it would
come to pass:

> And the angel of the Lord said unto me, Thou hast beheld that the Book
> proceeded forth from the mouth of a Jew; and ... it contained the plainness
> of the Gospel of the Lord; ... wherefore, these things go forth from the Jews
> in purity, unto the Gentiles ... [*B.M.*, p. 30; 1 Nephi 13:24–25].
>
> And it came to pass that I beheld the remnant of the seed of my brethren,
> and also the book of the Lamb of God, which had proceeded forth from the

mouth of the Jew; and I beheld that it came forth from the Gentiles, unto the remnant of the seed of my brethren ... [*B.M.*, p. 31; 1 Nephi 13:38].

Ethan Smith was not concerned solely with the American Indian branch of the Hebrew family; he also included the Jewish branch of that family in his contemplations. His book begins with the Jewish-Roman war and the resulting destruction of Jerusalem and dispersion of the Jews. Ethan makes clear that he believed these calamities occurred because the Jews had crucified Jesus:

> The Jews had their strong objections against the evidences which God saw fit to furnish of the Divinity of Christ.... These were not such as they would have chosen [*V.H.*, p. 168].
>
> The Jews became carnal; crucified the Lord of glory; and they fell under the denunciations and the full execution of his wrath.... And the denunciation was fulfilled [*V.H.*, p. 14].
>
> ... this remarkable people have been singularly depressed, and in ages past, made a taunt, reproach, and by-word, trodden down, scattered and peeled ... [*V.H.*, pp. 67–68].

In *The Book of Mormon*, Nephi therefore includes descriptions of what the future has in store for his Jewish brethren who remained in the Old World:

> And as for they which are at Jerusalem, saith the prophet, shall be scourged by all the people, saith the prophet, because they crucify the God of Israel, and turned their hearts aside, rejecting signs, and wonders, and the power and glory of the God of Israel; and because they turned their hearts aside, saith the prophet, and have despised the Holy one of Israel, they shall wander in the flesh, and perish, and become a hiss and a byword, and be hated among all nations ... [*B.M.*, p. 51; 1 Nephi 19:13, 14].

Furthermore, as we shall see, Ethan Smith also said that the Jews would come to believe in Christianity and would return to the land that had been convenanted to their fathers. And, as we shall also see, Nephi prophesies this. Referring to the House of Israel, Ethan Smith said:

> In Isaiah xi. the ... Millennium follows... "And it shall come to pass in that day that the Lord shall set his hand again ... to gather the remnant of his people ... from the isles of the sea. And he shall ... assemble the outcasts of Israel ... from the four corners of the earth." Here..., God is going, in the last days, to make a ... recovery from ... the four quarters of the earth [*V.H.*, p. 56].

It should be noted that "islands of the sea" is used in the King James wording of Isaiah 11, but that Ethan Smith changed it to "isles of the sea" in the above excerpt. Note also that, rather than saying "four corners of the earth" in his elaboration, as it is in the King James Version, the Vermont minister said "four quarters of the earth." He probably did this because "four corners" would not be an appropriate term for a spherical world.

We find Nephi prophesying in *The Book of Mormon* (but himself attributing it to another *Book of Mormon* prophet):

> ... that day cometh, saith the prophet...; yea, then will he remember the isles of the sea; yea, and all the people which are of the House of Israel, will I gather in, saith the Lord, according to the words of the Prophet Zenos, from the four quarters of the earth [*B.M.*, pp. 51–52; 1 Nephi 19: 15, 16].

Note that Joseph had Nephi use the phrases "isles of the sea" and "four quarters of the earth" just as Ethan did. This raises another point. When Nephi "reads" Isaiah 11 some time later, he used the King James wordings, i.e., "islands of the sea" and "the four corners of the earth." It would seem that Joseph used Ethan's book one time and the Bible, the other.

Since Ethan Smith was dependent upon the prophet Isaiah for many of his ideas, it should not be surprising that Isaiah also plays an important part in *The Book of Mormon*. Joseph quoted Isaiah extensively in his latter-day "revelation"; for example, Isaiah 48 and 49, as "read" by Nephi. Here the King James Version of the Bible is used with only a few changes. After he finishes reading these chapters, Nephi elaborates upon them to his brethren. Most of this elaboration echoes Ethan Smith's speculations.

At least twice, Ethan specifically referred to Isaiah 49, emphasizing that the prophecies in the chapter were to be fulfilled both literally and "mystically." In his view, the prophecies would come about literally when the Israelites and the Jews were physically restored to the land of their inheritance. He believed that Isaiah 49 would be fulfilled mystically when the Israelites and the Jews came to accept a spiritual belief in Christ. The Vermont minister was particularly emphatic about his because, according to him, many people of his own time made a "pretense" (his word) of applying only a mystical sense to the prophecies. These people held that the prophecies would be realized simply with the conversion of the Hebrew family to Christianity; i.e., they felt that there needed to be no physical restoration of the Hebrew family to the land of their fathers. Ethan Smith felt the need to refute this interpretation.

We therefore find that after Nephi reads Isaiah 49, some of his brothers make a pretense of asking if the prophecies were to be interpreted only "according to the spirit and not the flesh." Nephi, not surprisingly, responds to this exactly as Ethan Smith had. The prophecies, he says, are to be taken both "according to the flesh" (he also uses the word "temporally") and "spiritually." These, of course, directly correspond to Ethan's "literally" and "mystically."

In addition to Ethan Smith's elaboration on Isaiah 49, Nephi echoes several other parts of *View of the Hebrews*. It appears that Joseph had taken various statements that Ethan made about certain things and put them in the form of a series of prophecies for Nephi to give his brothers. The list is remarkably long. Ethan noted that the Jews had been scattered among the gentile nations of the world and were persecuted and hated; Nephi prophesies that this will occur. Ethan reported that efforts were currently being made to meliorate the condition of the Jews and to prepare them for the restoration; Nephi prophesies what Ethan reported. Ethan observed that the American people had reduced the Indian branch of the Hebrew people to a "deplorable situation" and had taken their lands; Nephi prophesies what Ethan had observed. Ethan asserted that the prophecies refer to the American Indians (the tribes of Israel); Nephi asserts that the prophecies refer to the seed of his people (who are a part of the tribes of Israel, and will become the American Indians). Ethan Smith pleaded with his fellow Americans to take steps to convert the Indians to Christianity and restore them to their rightful inheritance; Joseph's Nephi prophesies that this plea will be fulfilled.

The comparisons between *View of the Hebrews* and Nephi's prophecies are shown in parallel form in the following table. It is important to continue to remember that Joseph seems to have put into his own words the ideas derived from Ethan's book.

View of the Hebrews	*The Book of Mormon* (pages 56–57; 1 Nephi 22:1–14)
[After having noted Isaiah 49] To give a mystical import to all these prophecies, and say they will be fulfilled only in the conversion of these ancient people..., is to take a most unwarrantable liberty with the word of God. Some have made such pretense;	[After having read Isaiah 49] ... after I, Nephi, ... had read these things..., my brethren came unto me and said unto me, What meaneth these things which ye have read? Behold, are they to be understood according to things which are spiritual, which shall come to pass according to the spirit and not the flesh? [22:1].
but far be it from me to follow them! Why not as well apply a mystical sense to every prediction of future events? [p. 64] Is it not an uncommon thing for prophetic passages to receive a kind of literal fulfillment; while yet the passage most clearly looks in its ultimate ... sense to mystical fulfillment [p. 258].	And I, Nephi, sayeth unto them, Behold, they were made manifest unto the prophet, by the voice of the spirit: for by the spirit are all things made known unto the prophet, which shall come upon the children of men, according to the flesh [22:2].
Thus mystical texts often have a kind of literal fulfillment [p. 259].	Wherefore, the things of which I have read, are things pertaining to things both temporal and spiritual:
The ten tribes, as well as the Jews, belong to the "nation scattered and peeled..." [p. 247]. This must allude to the great dispersion of Judah, and outcast state of Israel, which strewed them over the face of the earth ... [p. 233].	for it appears that the House of Israel ... will be scattered upon all the face of the earth, and also among all nations ... [22:3].

And we find a special branch ... having been lost from the knowledge of ... the Jews [p. 71].	... [T]here are many which are already lost from the knowledge of they which are at Jerusalem.
And the places ... are noted; among which are *"the isles of the sea"* ... [pp. 232–233].	Yea, the more part of all the tribes have been led away; and they are scattered to and fro upon the isles of the sea ... [22:4].
I shall here note several additional predictions of the event, found in the prophets; ... which distinguish between the *dispersed* state of the Jews, and the *outcast* state of the ten tribes ... [p. 70].	And since that they have been led away, these things have been prophesied concerning them,
The judgements of Heaven on the Jews were still more dreadful.... Upon their ... rejecting the Saviour, the denunciation ... was fulfilled with unprecedented decision [pp. 253–254]. [The Jews] have been ... made a taunt, reproach, and byword, trodden down, scattered and peeled ... [pp. 67–68].	and also concerning all they which shall hereafter be scattered and be confounded, because of the Holy One of Israel: for against him will they harden their hearts; wherefore, they shall be scattered among all nations, and shall be hated by all men [22:5].
Considerable has been undertaken to meliorate their [the Jews'] condition, and prepare the way for their restoration [p. 68]. And numerous societies have been formed in Europe and America, to aid this great object [p. 69].	Nevertheless, after that they have been nursed by the Gentiles,
... [A]n apostrophe is made by the Most High to all nations, to stand and behold the banner of salvation erected for his ancient people.... This standard of salvation ... is a notable event in the prophets [pp. 241–242]. [Thus saith the Lord God, Behold, I will lift up mine hand to the Gentiles, and set up my standard to the people:	and the Lord has lifted up his hand upon the Gentiles and set them up for a standard,
and they shall bring thy sons in their arms and thy daughters shall be carried upon their shoulders	their children shall be carried in their arms, and their daughters shall be carried upon their shoulders,

(Isaiah 49:22, to which Ethan Smith had specifically referred – p. 63).]

And beside this, it is said that people [the Jews] shall (as a distinct nation) be restored to the land of their fathers, and shall dwell in temporal prosperity there ... [p. 64].

behold, these things of which are spoken, are temporal: for thus is the covenants of the Lord with our fathers;

Such texts have a special allusion to the lost tribes of the house of Israel [p. 260, after again referring to Isaiah 49].

and it meaneth us in the days to come, and also all our brethren which are of the House of Israel [22:6].

The writer might fill a chapter in illustrating the wrongs which the Indians have suffered from the people in our land; in noting their reduced and deplorable situation ... [p. 227] a chief, from the Indian nations at the west ... [said], "...this fine country, and this great water were once ours.... At last the white people came..., they drove us back ... into the wilderness.... They have destroyed our game. Our people are wasted away. And we live miserable and wretched" [pp. 133–134].

And it meaneth that the time cometh that after all the House of Israel have been scattered and confounded, that the Lord God will raise up a mighty nation among the Gentiles, yea, even upon the face of this land; and by them shall our seed be scattered [22:7].

The writer ... might adduce many evangelical motives ... to enforce the duty of saving the remnant of the natives of our continent from extinction, and from wretchedness [p. 227]. [W]e are the people especially addressed and called upon to restore them ... [pp. 229–230]. Ho thou nation of the last days, ... pity, instruct and save my ancient people and brethren; especially that *outcast* branch of them, who were the natives of your soil ... [p. 247].

And after that our seed is scattered, the Lord God will proceed to do a marvellous work among the Gentiles, which shall be of great worth unto our seed;

Let now the wings of your *liberty, compassion,* and *blessed retreat,* bear him from his dreary wilds to the temple of God [p. 249]. [...(A)nd they shall bring thy sons in their

wherefore, it is likened unto the[ir] being nourished by the Gentiles, and being carried in their arms, and upon their shoulders [22:8].

arms, and thy daughters shall be carried upon their shoulders (Isaiah 49:22, to which Ethan Smith had referred — p. 63).]

Rejoice, then ye distinguished people in your birthright, and engage in the work by Heaven assigned.... For you ... this honor is reserved.... Inform them that by embracing this true seed of Abraham, you and multitudes of other Gentiles have become the children of that ancient patriarch.... Unfold to them ... the entail of the covenant; ... and so all Israel shall be saved [pp. 248–250].

And it shall also be of worth unto the Gentiles; and not only unto the Gentiles, but unto all the House of Israel, unto the making known of the covenants of the Father of Heaven unto Abraham, saying, In thy seed shall all the kindreds of the earth be blessed [22:9].

... [T]he Almighty had often made bare his holy arm [p. 13]. That all this shall be, when the new covenant is made with the house of Israel and the house of Judah.... Thus it is an event to take place under the last, the gospel dispensation [p. 60].

Wherefore, the Lord God will proceed to make bare his arm in the eyes of all the nations, in bringing about his covenants and his Gospel, unto they which are of the House of Israel [22:11].

Thus the prophetic writings do clearly decide, that both Israel and the Jews shall in the last days ... be literally restored to their own land of Palestine, and be converted to the Christian faith [p. 64]. "...[T]hus saith the Lord God; now will I bring again the captivity of Jacob, and have mercy upon the whole house Israel.... When I have ... again ... gathered them out of their enemies' lands...; then shall they know that I am the Lord their God..." [p. 55].

Wherefore, he will bring them again out of captivity, and they shall be gathered together to the lands of their inheritance; and they shall be brought out of obscurity, and out of darkness; and they shall know that the Lord is their Saviour and their Redeemer, the mighty one of Israel [22:12].

In Isaiah xiv. is a prediction of the destruction ... of the mystical Babylon of the last days [p. 62]. "And ... great Babylon came ... before God to give unto her the cup of ... the fierceness of his wrath." In the desolation of Gog and his bands; faction draws the sword of extermination....

And the blood of that great and abominable church, which is the whore of all the earth, shall turn upon their own heads: for they shall war among themselves, and the sword of their own hands shall fall upon their own heads, and they shall be drunken with their own

"...[E]very man's sword shall be against his brother" [p. 45]. ... [A]t the slaughter of Gog and his bands ... "ye shall drink blood till ye be drunken..." [pp. 243-244].

blood [22:13].

Prophetic notice is ever given relative to that period, that the salvation of the friends of Zion shall be ushered in with a proportionable destruction to her enemies ... [p. 243].

And every nation which shall war against thee, O house of Israel, shall be turned one against the other.... And all that fight against Zion, shall be destroyed [22:14].

Note that Ethan brought in the idea of the war with "mystical Babylon" during the "last days." Josiah Priest had equated "mystic Babylon" with the Catholic Church in his book *Wonders of Nature and Providence Displayed*, which was published in Albany, New York, in 1825 (and a copy of which was available in the Manchester library). Since there are other connections between Josiah Priest's book and *The Book of Mormon*, we should not be surprised to find that Joseph seems to have blended Priest's views on this particular subject with those of Ethan Smith.

It is interesting that one of the other links to *Wonders of Nature* occurs in *The Book of Mormon* very shortly after Nephi gives his brothers the above prophecies. Two of those brothers, Laman and Lemuel, are a rebellious sort, and their father, Lehi, admonishes them to follow the way of the Lord more closely. In the previous chapter a part of this admonishment was presented to show how Joseph alluded to the Indian sons in the dust and to the unknown people awakening. In another part Joseph had Lehi say this to his sons:

> Awake! and arise from the dust, and hear the words of a trembling parent, whose limbs ye must soon lay down in the cold and silent grave, from whence no traveler can return ... [*B.M.*, p. 61; 2 Nephi 1:14].

At first glance, the latter part of this passage is reminiscent of Shakespeare. The relevant verse appears in *Hamlet*, Act III, scene 1: "But that the dread of something after death, the undiscovered country from whose bourn no traveller returns...."

In *The Book of Mormon*, then, as in *Hamlet*, death is described as being a place from which no traveler can return. The imagery is the same, even if the wording is not exactly so. But this is where Josiah Priest's *Wonders of Nature* comes in. In it we find the following:

> ... my time was short, and I had some preparation to make before I went to "that bourne from whence no traveller returns."[2]

It appears then that Joseph could have been quoting Shakespeare secondhand, modifying the *Wonders of Nature* version but slightly: "from whence no traveller can return" for "from whence no traveller returns."

But there is more. Not long after saying "from whence no traveler can return," Lehi says something else which is also similar to material in Josiah Priest's book. Priest had reported on a dialogue between a Deist and a Christian:

> D. ... If there has been no law, according to the bible, there would have been no moral evil. It is, therefore, a fair question to ask, Why did God give a law to man?
>
> C. ... If ... no law had been given, man would have passed the boundaries of good, and have performed actions which, in themselves were evil, without being amenable for his conduct, and while justice would have been incapable of punishing a violator of what was right.[3]

Echoing this interchange between Priest's Christian and Deist, Joseph had Lehi say:

> And if ye shall say there is no law, ye shall also say there is no sin. If ye shall say there is no sin, ye shall also say there is no righteousness [B.M., p. 64; 2 Nephi 2:13].

And soon after, Jacob, another of Lehi's sons, says:

> ... wherefore, he [God] hath given a law; and where there is no law given, there is no punishment; and where there is no punishment, there is no condemnation ... [B.M., p. 81; 2 Nephi 9:25].

There are other similarities between *Wonders of Nature* and *The Book of Mormon* which will be shown in the following chapters.

Shortly before making the above statement, Jacob reads chapters 50 and 51 of Isaiah. He then gives some elaborations, which, for the most part, are a rehash of Nephi's embroiderings on Isaiah 49. One point however, is interesting because of its similarity to something that Ethan said. The Vermont minister had expressed the following view:

> ... Christians in our land may well bless God that it is their happy lot to live in this ... protecting realm, an asylum of liberty and religion; a land so distant from the seat of anti-christ.... And their devout gratitude to Heaven ought to rise, for the blessing of having their existence so near the period alluded to in this sublime prediction, when this land of liberty is beginning to feel her immunities compared with the establishments of tyranny and corruption in the old continent [V.H., p. 245].

So Ethan Smith held that he and his fellow American gentiles were blessed to live in a land of liberty that is free from the tyrannical and corrupt kings of the old world. We therefore find Jacob saying:

> But behold, This land, saith God, shall be a land of thine inheritance; and the Gentiles shall be blessed upon the land. And this land shall be a land

of liberty unto the Gentiles; and there shall be no kings upon the land, which shall raise up unto the Gentiles. And I will fortify this land against all other nations ... [*B.M.*, p. 84; 2 Nephi 10:10–12].

Not long after this, Nephi reads chapters two through fourteen of Isaiah — using the King James Version of the Bible and making only a few minor changes. Then, Nephi gives a prophecy of the future history of the Jews up to the "last days" and of the appearance of Jesus. Most of the events that Nephi describes are in the Bible, but regardless of the source this material shows the Mormon prophet's eclecticism. Still, Ethan Smith had mentioned almost every event that Nephi does, and in some of the prophecies Nephi even uses Ethan's terminology. Here are the parallels.

View of the Hebrews	*The Book of Mormon* (pages 103–4; 2 Nephi 25:10–18)
... the Babylonian captivity of the Jews ... [p. 48].	... those which are carried away captive into Babylon [25:10].
... the restoration from the seventy years captivity in Babylon [p. 54].	... And ... they shall return again ... and be restored to the lands of their inheritance [25:11].
Our Lord proceeds; "And ye shall hear of wars and rumors of wars..." [p. 21].	But, behold, they shall have wars, and rumors of wars;
There God, manifest in the flesh, made his appearance on earth ... [p. [p. 13].	and when the ... only begotten of the Father ... shall manifest himself unto them in the flesh,
And ... in ... rejecting him ... [p. 14].	behold, they will reject him ... [25:12].
The Jews ... crucified the Lord of glory ... [p. 14].	Behold, they will crucify him ... [25:13].
The Roman army, before they left Jerusalem, not only demolished the buildings there, but they even dug up their foundations [p. 42].	And ... behold, Jerusalem shall be destroyed again...:
Tremendous indeed must the lot of those be, who reject the Messiah, and are found fighting against the Son of God [p. 39].	for wo unto them that fight against God and the people of his church [25:14].
... [T]he Jews ... have been singularly	Wherefore, the Jews shall be scattered

depressed, and in ages past, ...
scattered and peeled ... [pp. 67–68].

among all nations...;

... [T]he destruction of ... the mystical Babylon of the last days ... [p. 62].

yea, and also Babylon shall be
destroyed ... [25:15].

... [T]he Jews shall, in the last days,
before the Millennium, be ... converted to the Christian faith [p. 64].

... [A]nd after that they have been
scattered ... for the space of many
generations, ... they shall be persuaded to believe in Christ ... [25:16].

... God sets his hand a second time
to gather his Hebrew family from all
nations and regions beyond the
sea ... [p. 242].

[A]nd the Lord will set his hand
again the second time to restore his
people from their lost and fallen
state [25:17].

In the year 60, another pretended
Messiah appeared.... It would be
too unwieldy to mention all the vile
impostors of this period. They were
a just retribution ... upon the Jews,
for having rejected and put to death
the true Messiah: and they fulfilled
the warning ... of a host of deceivers
of that period [p. 21].

Wherefore, he shall bring forth his
words ... for the purpose of convincing them of the true Messiah,
who was rejected by them: ... that
they need not look forward any
more for a Messiah to come, for
there should not any come, save it
be a false Messiah, which should
deceive the people ... [25:18].

After prophesying the future of the Jews, Nephi prophesies that of
his own people. Much of what he says had already been foretold and appears
again later on — perhaps because Joseph was trying to pad out his book. There
is, however, one passage that has some interesting correspondences with *View
of the Hebrews*. Ethan Smith had made the following remarks:

> "I will hiss for them." God is represented as *hissing* for a people ... [*V.H.*,
> p. 235].
> An apostrophe is made by the Most High to all nations, to stand and
> behold the banner of salvation now erected for his ancient people ... [p. 241].
> This standard of salvation ... is a notable event in the prophets [p. 242].

We find that Nephi has combined these concepts and put them into the mouth
of God:

> ... and my words shall hiss forth unto the ends of the earth, for a standard
> unto my people, which are of the House of Israel [*B.M.*, p. 115; 2 Nephi
> 29:2].

In this case, as in so many others, it seems that it is actually Ethan
Smith's words that hiss forth unto the ends of the earth — in *The Book of
Mormon*.

Chapter 13

The Division

The similarities between *View of the Hebrews* and *The Book of Mormon* become especially significant when one examines what each has to say about the events that supposedly occurred after the ancient immigrants arrived in the New World.

The Vermont minister had proposed that the Israelite immigrants had divided into two groups:

> The probability then is this; that the ten tribes, arriving in this continent with some knowledge of the arts of civilized life; finding themselves in a vast wilderness filled with the best of game, inviting them to the chase; most of them fell into a wandering idle hunting life. Different clans parted from each other, lost each other and formed separate tribes. Most of them formed a habit of this idle mode of living, and were pleased with it. More sensible parts of this people associated together, to improve their knowledge of the arts; and probably continued thus for ages. From these the noted relics of civilization discovered in the west and south, were furnished [*V.H.*, p. 172].

In effect patterning *Book of Mormon* events after Ethan Smith's theory, Joseph had his Israelite family of Lehi divide into two parts. One of these was led by Nephi, and corresponds to Ethan's civilized group. The other, led by Nephi's brother Laman, corresponds to Ethan's idle hunters.

Ethan Smith also theorized that the idle hunters became "savage and wild," were "intent on the destruction" of their civilized brethren, and eventually became the American Indians. The Vermont minister also proposed that the civilized part of these people separated themselves from the savage, built cities, pursued the mechanic arts, and kept their religious traditions by following the law of Moses. In all these things Joseph seems to have followed Ethan's ideas.

The following table puts in parallel form some extracts which clearly show the likelihood that Joseph derived these ideas from *View of the Hebrews*. The excerpts from *The Book of Mormon* are all relatively close to one another. The significance of this is that there is a definite sequence of concepts in *The Book of Mormon* similar to material in Ethan Smith's book. Note also that Joseph further developed the story line of his book by using some

Indian "traditions" that Ethan had related. Besides using these traditions for plot ideas, the Mormon prophet may have also felt that they would give his book a certain feel of authenticity.

View of the Hebrews	*The Book of Mormon* (pages 71-73; 2 Nephi 5:1-24)
It is highly probable that the more civilized part of the tribes of Israel, after they settled in America, became wholly separated from the hunting and savage tribes of their brethren ... [pp. 172-173].	Behold, it came to pass that I, Nephi, did cry much unto the Lord ... because of the anger of my brethren.... And ... the Lord did warn me, that I, Nephi, should depart from them, and flee into the wilderness, and all they which would go with me [5:1, 5].
Thus situated, and struggling to maintain their existence, and to maintain their religious traditions ... [p. 189]. Who that reads the law of Moses, can doubt the origin of these Indian traditions? [p. 120].	And we did observe to keep the judgements, and the statutes, and the commandments of the Lord, in all things, according to the law of Moses [5:10].
... [T]he Indians have a tradition ... "that the Indians lost their credit; offended the Great Spirit ..." [p. 115] ... he (the Great Spirit) often held councils ... with the red men (i.e. in ancient times;) gave them laws to be observed—but that in consequence of their disobedience, he withdrew from and abandoned them to the vexations of the bad spirit, who had since been instrumental of all their degeneracy ... [pp. 162-163].	And behold, the words of the Lord had been fulfilled unto my brethren, which he spake concerning them..., saying: That inasmuch as they will not hearken unto thy words, they shall be cut off from the presence of the Lord. And behold, they were cut off from his presence. And he caused the cursing to come upon them ... because of their iniquity ... 5:19-21].
The Indians in other regions have brought down a tradition, that their former ancestors, away in a distant region from which they came, were white [p. 206].	For behold...; as they were white, and exceeding fair and delightsome,
Yea, we cannot so well account for their evident degeneracy in any other way, as that it took place under a vindictive Providence ... [p. 172].	that they might not be enticing unto my people, therefore the Lord did cause a skin of blackness to come upon them. And thus saith the Lord God, I will cause that they shall be

loathsome to thy people. And the Lord spake it, and it was done [5:21-23].

The probability then is this; ... finding themselves in a vast wilderness filled with the best of game, ... most of them fell into a wandering idle hunting life [p. 172].

And because of their cursing which was upon them, they did become an idle people, ... and did seek in the wilderness for beasts of prey [5:24].

In the following set of parallels, it is evident that Joseph derived from *View of the Hebrews* several of his ideas about the animosity between the civilized and the savage factions of his *Book of Mormon* people. Also, note again Joseph's use of Indian "traditions" that Ethan had given.

View of the Hebrews	*The Book of Mormon*
... [T]he better part of the ... tribes of Israel here ... became ... under rage of their savage brethren [p. 188].	... [T]heir hatred was fixed,
And nothing appears more probable than that ... the greater part of their brethren became savage and wild [p. 173]. ... [M]ost of them fell into a wandering idle hunting life [p. 172].	and they were led by their evil nature, that they became wild, and ferocious, and a bloodthirsty people; feeding upon beasts of prey, ... and wandering about in the wilderness ...;
... [A] better part of Israel ... were situated in the midst of savage tribes from their own race, who ... were intent on the destruction of this better part of their brethren [p. 189].	and they were continually seeking to destroy us [pp. 144-145; Enos 20].
"... They are represented by the prophet as ... having given to them instead of a sweet smell, a stench; ... instead of well set hair, baldness; instead of a stomacher, a girding of sackcloth.... In all these particulars, ... the prediction of the prophet is amply fulfilled in this people [the Indians]. And ... we might suppose that their shaving their heads with a razor, leaving one small lock on the crown, could constitute the baldness hinted ..." [p. 111].	... [T]hey were ... full of ... filthiness..., with a short skin girded about their loins, and their heads shaven ... [pp. 144-145; Enos 20]. ... and they had their heads shaved, that they were naked [p. 176; Mosiah 10:8].

... [T]he Indians have a tradition "that the book which the white people have was once theirs...; but that other people got it from them..." [p. 115].

... [T]he Lamanites..., believing in the tradition of their fathers ... that they were wronged by ... Nephi...: They were wroth with him, because he departed into the wilderness ... and took the records which were engraven on the plates of brass; for they said that he robbed them [pp. 176–177; Mosiah 10:11–16].

... [T]he Indian cruelties to our people have been manifestly occasioned by the injuries they have received from various of our people, and by their own traditionary notions, which they think accord with these injuries, that the white people ... are the accursed people, and may well be exterminated [p. 132].

Now, the Lamanites..., believing in the tradition of their fathers, which is this: Believing ... that they were wronged in the wilderness by their brethren.... And thus they have taught their children, that they should hate them, and that they should murder them, ... and do all they could to destroy them [pp. 176–177; Mosiah 10:11–17].

In the next to the last pair of the above parallels, Ethan Smith mentioned an Indian "tradition" that the Indians were supposed to have had a "book." The Vermont minister proposed that this was the *Book of Moses* (the first five books of the Old Testament). The brass plates mentioned in the corresponding passage from *The Book of Mormon* were supposed to contain, among other things, most of the Old Testament scriptures, including, specifically, the five books of Moses.

In the last pair of parallels, Ethan described the Indians as having had "traditionary notions" about "injuries" they had received from the white man, and that they sought to "exterminate" the white man in accordance with those notions. Joseph transferred these ideas to his Lamanites (who were supposed to become the Indians) by giving them traditions of their being "wronged" by the white Nephites. Moreover, he used these "traditions" to justify the attempts of the Lamanites to destroy their white brethren, just as Ethan's Indians did.

Ethan Smith proposed that the ancient immigrants to the New World had increased their numbers over the years and had spread over the land. According to his view, the civilized part of these people built cities and fortifications, developed the "mechanic and civil arts," and continued thus for many years. In these things, again, Joseph followed the groundwork laid down by the Vermont minister. Here, in parallel form, are some relevant excerpts.

View of the Hebrews

The Book of Mormon

This fact shows that these ancient American inhabitants were not wholly unacquainted with the use of

... [W]herefore, we withstood the Lamanties, ... and began to fortify our cities.... And we multiplied

metals [p. 196]. In ... a large mound in Marietta ... were found three large circular bosses ... composed of copper, overlaid with a thick plate of silver [p. 197].
... [I]n the tomb of a Peruvian prince, massy gold was found ... [p. 204]. Some remains of iron articles ... are found ... [p. 193]. This hypothesis accounts for the ancient works, forts, mounds, and vast enclosures, as well as tokens of a good degree of civil improvement.... These ... people ... for a long time retained their knowledge of the mechanic and civil arts ... [p. 173].

exceedingly, and spread upon the face of the land, and became exceeding rich in gold, and in silver, and in precious things, and in fine workmanship of wood, in buildings, and in machinery, and also in iron, and copper, and brass, and steel, making all manner of tools ... [p. 147; Jarom 8].

And the hugeness of these works indicates a vast population [p. 198]. The prediction implies that Israel ... should ... wander ... from sea to sea; from the northern frozen ocean, to the southern ocean at Cape Horn; and from the Pacific to the Atlantic [p. 82].

And it came to pass that they did multiply and spread, and did go forth from the land southward, to the land northward..., from the sea south, to the sea north, from the sea west, to the sea east. [p. 412; Helaman 3:8].

Different clans parted from each other, lost each other, and formed separate tribes [p. 172]. The Indians being in tribes, with their heads and names of tribes, affords further light on this subject [p. 111].

And the people ... did separate one from another into tribes. ... And every tribe did appoint a chief, or a leader over them; and thus they became tribes, and leaders of tribes [p. 468; 3 Nephi 7:2-3].

As lengthy as *The Book of Mormon* is, it contains very little description of the buildings and structures that the Nephites were supposed to have erected; the descriptions it does have are similar to descriptions that occur in *View of the Hebrews.* For example, Ethan Smith asserted that the Indians had temples similar to the one in Jerusalem:

> You find them with their temples, (such as they be), their holy of holies in their temple, into which it is utterly prohibited for a common person to enter [*V.H.*, p. 77].

> They had a temple dedicated to the Great Spirit, in which they preserved the eternal fire [*V.H.*, p. 134].

> Who taught the untutored savages to have a temple of Yohewah: a holy of holies in it, into which no common people may enter, or look? [*V.H.*, p. 264].

Ethan Smith held that the Indians had temples similar to the one in Jerusalem; Joseph gave one to the characters in his book. If the Mormon prophet did not know what it looked like, Pastor Smith had provided a lengthy description of the Jerusalem temple of which this is but a part:

> The temple was, in many respects, the most astonishing fabrick ever beheld.... In the front were spacious and lofty galleries, with cedar wainscot, resting on uniform rows of white marble columns. Josephus asserts that nothing could exceed the interior of this house of God, for exquisit workmanship and elegance. Its solid plates of gold seemed to strive to outdazzle the rising sun. ... And the grandeur of the internal workmanship of the magnificent dome did not fail of being fully equal to its external magnificence. Nothing suberb, costly, or elegant, was spared. The different parts of the world had seemed to vie with each other, to pour their most costly treasures into this wonderful treasury of heaven. ... The richest Babylonian tapestry, of purple, blue, and scarlet, and of exquisit workmanship, waved within these doors.... The temple had a huge eastern gate of pure Corinthian brass, — a metal in the highest esteem.... The most precious stones, spices, and perfumes; everything that nature, art or riches could furnish, were stored within these stupendous and hallowed walls [V.H., pp. 16–17].

Joseph answered Ethan's question about who had taught the Indians to build a temple like the one in Jerusalem:

> And I, Nephi, ... did teach my people that they should build buildings; and that they should work in all manner of wood, and of iron, and of copper, and of brass, and of steel and of gold, and of silver, and of precious ores, which were in great abundance. And I, Nephi, did build a temple; and I did construct it after the manner of the temple of Solomon, save it were not built of so many precious things; for they were not to be found upon the land; wherefore, it could not be built like unto Solomon's temple. But the manner of the construction was like unto the temple of Solomon; and the workmanship thereof was exceeding fine [B.M., p. 72; 2 Nephi 5:14–16].

In the above descriptions of the Indian temples, note that Ethan Smith used the term, "Great Spirit." The Vermont minister frequently used this term in his descriptions of the beliefs of the Indians. The following is one example:

> Here we learn that those far distant savages have (as have all other tribes) their Great Spirit, "who made everything..." [V.H., p. 103].

In The Book of Mormon, the Lamanites are described as believing in a Great Spirit also. Reflecting the foregoing passage from View of the Hebrews, we find that, after several generations have passed, a Nephite asks a Lamanite:

> Believest thou that this Great Spirit ... created all things...? And he saith, Yea, I believe that he created all things ... [B.M., p. 275; Alma 18:28–29].

Joseph mentioned this "Great Spirit" only in one short section of *The Book of Mormon*, as if he were simply presenting it to show that his Lamanites believed in a Great Spirit just like the Indians. The problem is that, according to modern scholarly consensus, the term "Great Spirit" was invented by the European settlers in America to describe their own god to the Indians. Some of the Indians subsequently took up the term for their own use. Therefore, its use in *The Book of Mormon*, purportedly a pre-Columbian record, is anachronous.

Another set of Indian religious "traits" that Ethan gave in *View of the Hebrews* appears to have suggested to Joseph that he give a similar set to some of the people in his book. Ethan has offered these traits as some of the observations of James Adair, and he presented them on two different pages. As the following parallels demonstrate, Joseph seems to have applied this set of religious traits to the Zoramites, a part of the Nephites who had separated from their brethren. In *The Book of Mormon*, we find that a Nephite named Alma visits the Zoramites and is disturbed by what he sees.

View of the Hebrews (pages 77, 99)	*The Book of Mormon* (pages 311–312; Alma 31:12–25)
You find them with their temples, ...	Now, when they had come into the land, behold, ... they found that the Zoramites had built synagogues ... [31:12].
their holy of holy in their temples ... [p. 77] ... the Indians have but one God, ... whom they call the ... holy Spirit, who dwells above the clouds ... [p. 99].	Therefore, whosoever desired to worship, must go ... and stretch forth his hands towards heaven, and cry with a loud voice, saying: Holy, holy God; we believe that thou ... art holy, and ... that thou art a spirit ... [31:14–15].
The Indians thus please themselves ... with the idea that God has chosen them from the rest of mankind as his peculiar people [p. 99]. ... [T]he Indians have but one God ... who is the only object of worship [p. 99].	Holy God, we believe that thou hast separated us from our brethren; ... we believe that thou hast elected us to be thy holy children; and also thou made it known unto us that there shall be no Christ [31:16].
They tell you that Yohewah once chose their nation from all the rest of mankind, to be his peculiar people [p. 77]. He assures that the Indians ... call all other people the accursed people; and have time out of mind been accustomed to hold	... [A]nd thou hast elected us that we shall be saved, whilst all around us are elected to be cast by thy wrath down to hell; for the which holiness, O God, we thank thee ... [31:17].

them in great contempt.... This, he
says, has been the occasion of their
hating other people ... [p. 99].

The Indians thus please themselves ... that God has chosen
them ... [p. 99]. The high priest,
when addressing his people, ... calls
them "the beloved and holy people ..." [p. 77].

And again: We thank thee, O God,
that we are a chosen and a holy
people. Amen [31:18].

He assures that the Indians are in-
toxicated with religious pride....
Their ancestors they boast to have
been under the immediate government of Yohewah, who was with
them ... [p. 99].

... Now when Alma saw this his
heart was grieved.... Yea, and he
also saw that their hearts were lifted
up unto great boasting, in their
pride [31:24-25].

The particulars of the Indian religious traits that Ethan quoted from
Adair are certainly similar to those of the Zoramites in *The Book of Mormon*.
Moreover, according to *The Book of Mormon*, the Zoramites later joined the
Lamanites against the Nephites — perhaps as an attempt by Joseph to explain
the Indian traits given by James Adair. The problem with this is that Adair's
evaluation of the religious beliefs of the Indians was inaccurate. Adair undoubtedly projected into his observations things he wished to see to confirm
his belief in Indian monotheism.

Chapter 14

The Wars

The first three "books" of *The Book of Mormon* contain an overabundance of prophecies. The next three do not contain much of anything at all. Although they cover a period of nearly 400 years, each consists of but one chapter and skips lightly over events. It is not until we reach "The Book of Mosiah" that we find a detailed chronicle. The year is about 124 B.C., and the Nephites have separated into two main groups, which have lost contact with one another. Mosiah, the king of one group, sends an expedition, which finds the other in bondage to the Lamanites. Limhi, the king of the other group, tells the leader of the expedition that he himself had sent out an expedition to try to find Mosiah's group, but without success.

More than once, Ethan Smith suggested that America was the location of the "valley of dry bones" that the prophet Ezekiel had seen in one of his visions. Joseph seems to have taken this idea and combined it with some descriptions of Indian antiquities discovered in Ohio that he read about in *View of the Hebrews*. The result was that Limhi's expedition discovers a land "covered with dry bones," which was apparently supposed to be in the same general area as Ohio. It also appears that Joseph went to Ethan's source for some of this material. One passage from that source is included in the following parallels. In this case it was *Archaeologia Americana*, published in Worcester, Massachusetts in 1820. Note that "our nothern lakes" (the Great Lakes) are mentioned in the *Archaeologia Americana* excerpt. The "many waters" in the corresponding *Book of Mormon* passage are apparently also supposed to be the Great Lakes.

View of the Hebrews	*The Book of Mormon*
Methinks I hear every person whisper his full assent, that upon the suppositions made, we have found the most essential *pile* of the prophet Ezekiel's valley of dry bones! [p. 79]. ... [I]n the *vast wilderness of America*, a literal wilderness ... where the dry bones of the outcasts	... [A]nd they were lost in the wilderness. Nevertheless, they did find a land which had been peopled; yea, a land which was covered with dry bones ... [p. 200; Mosiah 21:26].

159

of Israel have for thousands of years been scattered [p. 257].

[It is also made possible that this ancient people ... made their first settlement around the waters of our northern lakes.... Mr. Atwater ... says ... "...It is indeed nothing but one vast cemetary of the beings of past ages. Man and his works, the mammoth, tropical animals ... are all found here reposing together...." (*Archaeologia Americana*, pp. 4–5).] Not far from this tumulus was a ditch ... [with] "a great quantity of human bones" [*V.H.*, p. 195].

... [A]nd they ... returned to this land, having travelled in a land among many waters; having discovered a land which was covered with bones of men, and of beasts, &c.,

Relative to the ancient forts and tumuli, the writer ... says; "... They were once forts, cemetaries, temples, altars, ... towns, villages ..." [pp. 188–189].

and was also covered with ruins of buildings of every kind;

And the hugeness of these works indicates a vast population [p. 198].

having discovered a land which had been peopled with a people which were as numerous as the hosts of Israel [p. 172; Mosiah 8:8].

On the [skeleton's] breast lay a piece of copper ... [which] appeared to have been ... a kind of breast-plate [p. 195].

And for a testimony that the things that they have said is true ... they have brought breast-plates, which are ... of brass, and copper ... [p. 172; Mosiah 8:9–10].

The handle of a small sword ... was here found.... The blade was gone by rust [p. 194].

And again: They have brought swords, the hilts thereof hath perished, and the blades thereof were cankered with rust ... [p. 172; Mosiah 8:11].

Limhi's expedition had found the bones of the Jaredites, a people who were supposed to have killed themselves off in wars before Lehi and his followers arrived in the New World.

After telling about Limhi's expedition, Joseph regressed his story several years to the time when Limhi's father, "Noah," was king. Again, Ethan had said something that might have had a bearing:

> Some of the Creek Indians called a murderer Abe; probably from Abel, the first man murdered.... And they called one who kills a rambling enemy

Noabe; probably from Noah, importing rest, and Abe. —He thus puts his rambling enemy to rest [V.H., p. 91].

Here was the idea of a man named "Noah," and the idea of someone putting his enemy to "rest." Furthermore, Ethan Smith had implied that the ancestors of the Indians were acquainted with the name "Noah."

We find the same name in *The Book of Mormon*. King Noah is an unrighteous and corrupt ruler who is leading his people down the same path he is following, so the Lord sends a prophet named Abinadi to prophesy against the wickedness of King Noah and his people. King Noah has Abinadi "put to rest":

And he said unto him, Abinadi, we have found an accusation against thee, and thou art worthy of death. ... And ... King Noah ... delivered him up, that he might be slain [B.M., p. 190; Mosiah 17:7–12].

From examples such as this, one might see how Joseph could have picked up some plot ideas from various comments that Ethan Smith made. In any case, Joseph then followed Ethan Smith's maxim that God would visit his wrath upon those who behave unrighteously. King Noah is killed and his people are put into bondage by the Lamanites. But Noah's son, Limhi, is more righteous than his father was, and he leads his people back along the path to righteousness. God therefore rewards them by allowing them to escape the Lamanites and join the other branch of the Nephites.

Ethan Smith also elaborated upon some things that Humboldt had reported:

Here tradition had given this people an ancient mysterious founder. His present votaries were the Mozcas. He lived at Sogamozo, inhabiting a temple.... It ... seems not unnatural to say, their ancient mysterious lawgiver was Moses, from whom the devoted Mozcas may have derived their name....

Our author proceeds; "But the Mexican small colonies, wearied of tyranny, gave themselves republican constitutions [V.H., pp. 180–181].

We might now wonder if Joseph took his ideas of King Mosiah from Ethan's comments about the founder of the Mozcas. To begin with, the Vermont minister had thought that the Mozcas might have derived their name from Moses. Joseph, of course, could not use *the* Moses as a character in his book. But he could modify the name to "Mosiah." Both the founder of the Mozcas and King Mosiah were associated with a temple, for it was at a temple that Mosiah was named king:

... the people gathered ... to the temple to hear the words which King Benjamin should speak unto them [B.M., p. 155; Mosiah 2:1].

It came to pass that when king Benjamin had made an end of all these things, and had consecrated his son Mosiah, to be a ruler and a king over his people ... [B.M., p. 167; Mosiah 6:3].

Ethan Smith had also said that the founder of the Mozcas was a law-giver, and that is what we find Mosiah to be in *The Book of Mormon*:

> ... king Mosiah ... established laws, and they were acknowledged by the people; therefore they were obliged to abide by the laws which he had made [*B.M.*, p. 221; Alma 1:1].

Ethan Smith had associated the Mozcas with the establishment of a republican form of government. We therefore find that King Mosiah, citing the tyranny and wickedness of King Noah, eventually does away with the monarchy and establishes a republican form of government for his people:

> Now I say unto you, that because all men are not just, it is not expedient that ye should have a king or kings rule over you.... And now I say unto you, ... therefore choose you by the voice of this people, judges, that ye may be judged according to the laws which hath been given you by our fathers.... [*B.M.*, p. 219; Mosiah 29:16–25].

Curious similarities such as these might show how Joseph could have derived plot ideas from *View of the Hebrews*. At the same time, they show how Joseph might have loosely followed some of the traditions of the New World natives so his book would have an air of authenticity about it.

The next, and longest, "book" in *The Book of Mormon* is that of Alma. Since it emphasizes the wars between the savage and civilized factions of the branch of Israel in the New World, perhaps it is fitting that it is the longest book in Joseph Smith's latter-day revelation. After all, this warfare is precisely what Ethan Smith emphasized:

> It is highly probable ... that the more civilized part continued for many centuries; that tremendous wars were frequent between them and their savage brethren ... [*V.H.*, pp. 172–173].

In *The Book of Mormon* we find that there are "tremendous" wars between the Nephites and the Lamanites (who are often joined by renegade Nephites). As long as the Nephites follow the way of the Lord, they have little trouble winning. We thus find many of the Lamanites adding their skeletons to Ethan's "valley of dry bones":

> And it came to pass that ... the Lamanites and the Amlicites began to flee before them...; yea, they were met on every hand, and slain.... And ... their bones have been found, and they have been heaped up on the earth [*B.M.*, p. 227; Alma 2:35–38].

> And thus [there was] a tremendous battle...; yea, and tens of thousands of the Lamanites were slain and scattered abroad [*B.M.*, p. 302; Alma 28:2].

To support his theory about the wars, Ethan Smith gave lengthy descriptions of numerous Indian forts and mounds that had been found, especially in Ohio. His source for this material was *Archaeologia Americana*:

> 'These military works, — these walls and ditches cost so much labour in their structure; those numerous ... mounds, which owe their origin to a people far more civilized than our Indians, but far less so than Europeans; are interesting on many accounts to the antiquarian, to the philosopher, and the divine.... They were once forts, cemetaries, temples, altars, camps, towns, villages, race grounds, and other places of amusement, habitations of chieftains, videttes, watch towers, and monuments" [*V.H.*, pp. 188–189].

Ethan Smith then made his own interpretation of the "antiquities":

> These certainly are precisely such remains as naturally might have been expected to be furnished by a better part of Israel in their *"outcast"* state, in a vast wilderness, with the degree of civilization which they possessed when banished from Canaan; and were situated in the midst of savage tribes from their own race, who had degenerated to the hunting life, and were intent on the destruction of this better part of their brethren. Thus situated, and struggling to maintain their existence, and to maintain their religious traditions, they would naturally form many of the very things above enumerated, walled towns, forts, temples, altars, habitations of chieftains, videttes, and watch-towers.... The whole process of the hypothesis stated in relation to these two branches of the descendants of Israel, when finding themselves lodged in this vast wild continent, is natural and easy [*V.H.*, p. 189].

Joseph seems to have applied Ethan's hypothesis to the wars between the Nephites and the Lamanites, as the following parallels show.

View of the Hebrews	*The Book of Mormon*
... [T]he better part of the ... tribes of Israel here ... became ... under the rage of their savage brethren [p. 188] ... [A] better part of Israel ... were situated in the midst of savage tribes from their own race, who ... were intent on the destruction of this better part of their brethren [p. 189].	... [F]or he had hardened the hearts of the Lamanites, and blinded their minds, and stirred them up to anger, insomuch that he had gathered together a numerous host, to go to battle against the Nephites [p. 357; Alma 48:3].
Thus situated, and struggling to maintain their existence, and to maintain their religious traditions, they would naturally form ... walled towns, forts, ... and watch-towers [p. 189]. A square fort ... encompasses forty acres by a wall of earth ... [p. 192].	... Moroni, on the other hand, had been preparing the minds of the people to be faithful unto the Lord their God; yea, he had been strengthening the armies of the Nephites, and erecting small forts...; throwing up banks of earth round about...,

Four or five miles southerly from this is a stone fort enclosing forty acres or upwards [p. 192].

and also building walls of stone to encircle them about [Alma 48:7–8].

It is highly probable ... that the more civilized part continued for many centuries; that tremendous wars were frequent between them and their savage brethren ... [pp. 172–173].

... [Y]ea, and in fine, their wars never did cease for the space of many years with the Lamanites ... [p. 359; Alma 48:22].

There is a fort ... whose walls are ten feet high.... The walls are as nearly perpendicular as they could be made with earth [pp. 190–191]. This mound has been ... explored. Some things found.... A great quantity of heads, either for arrows or spears ... [p. 194].

... [A]nd they had cast up dirt round about, to shield them from the arrows and stones of the Lamanites [p. 359; Alma 49:2].

On the [skeleton's] breast lay a piece of copper.... The whole appeared ... as a kind of breast-plate [p. 195].

... [A]nd they had also prepared themselves with shields, and with breast-plates ... [p. 360; Alma 49:6].

The handle of a small sword or a large knife was here found [p. 194].

Thus they were prepared ... with Their swords and slings ... [p. 361; Alma 49:20].

At some distance from this fort ... is another circular fort ... with walls from twenty-five to thirty feet in height, with a ditch just under them [p. 191].

... [T]he Lamanites could not get into their forts of security ... because of the highness of the bank which had been thrown up, and the depth of the ditch which had been dug round about ... [p. 361; Alma 49:18].

Not far from this tumulus [earthwork] was a semi-circular ditch.... At the bottom lay "a great quantity of human bones." These are supposed to the remains of men slain in some great battle [p. 195].

Now when they found that they could not obtain power over the Nephites..., they began to dig down their banks of earth...; but ... they were swept off by the stones and arrows which were thrown at them; and instead of filling up their ditches by pulling down the banks of earth, they were filled up ... with their dead and wounded bodies [p. 361; Alma 49:22].

This ... tumulus has been opened to ascertain that it contained many thousands (probably) of human skeletons [p. 198].

Thus the Nephites had all power over their enemies...; and more than a thousand of the Lamanites were slain ... [pp. 361–362; Alma: 49:23].

At four different places ... are watchtowers on elevated ground [p. 191].

... Moroni did not stop making preparations for war. ... And he caused ... towers to be erected that overlooked those works of pickets ... [pp. 362–363; Alma 50:4].

It is curious that similar structures were usually described in *View of the Hebrews* whenever *The Book of Mormon* has descriptions of structures built by its characters. Moreover, the *Book of Mormon* structures are described in a context conforming to the hypotheses that Ethan Smith made about the structures he described. If Joseph used *View of the Hebrews* as a reference book, all he had to do was provide characters and action for Ethan's settings.

We had previously suggested that Joseph might have gone to Ethan's sources for further information after reading *View of the Hebrews*. One of Ethan's sources, *Archaeologia Americana*, contains a lengthy description and diagrams of earthworks in Ohio. The author of this account was Caleb Atwater, of the Ohio Historical Society. In the last parallel above, "pickets" are mentioned in *The Book of Mormon* excerpt. Ethan made no mention of pickets in the material that he quoted, but pickets are mentioned elsewhere in the Atwater description:

> Halfway up the outside of the inner wall is a place distinctly to be seen, where a row of *pickets* once stood, and where it was placed when this work of defence was originally erected.[1]

Since the earthworks described in *The Book of Mormon* are so similar to those in Ohio that Ethan Smith had described, one might wonder if Joseph meant them to be considered the same. Joseph might have reasoned that the earthworks could eventually be used as evidence for the historical veracity of his latter-day revelation.

It does appear that on at least one occasion Joseph went along with the idea that the earthworks described in *The Book of Mormon* were those in Ohio. In 1842, the *Times and Seasons* published a description of the Ohio earthworks that had appeared in Charles Thompson's book, *Evidences in Proof of the Book of Mormon*. Preceding the description, Thompson stated:

> I will next introduce the description of some of these ancient fortifications and military works of defense, as recorded in the American Antiquities, by Josiah Priest, and also introduce a history of the building of these fortifications and works of defense, as recorded in *The Book of Mormon*; and I will here remark, that *The Book of Mormon* was published in A.D. 1830, and the American Antiquities, by Josiah Priest, was not published until 1833, three years after.[2]

Here Thompson stated that the earthworks found in Ohio were those described in *The Book of Mormon*; Joseph did not "correct" that statement. (Although Thompson emphasized that Priest's book was published after the initial publication of *The Book of Mormon*, Priest's source for the description of the earthworks was Atwater's paper that was published in *Archaeologia Americana* in 1820.)

There is a problem with all this. According to the traditional view of *Book of Mormon* geography, the earthworks were in the "land south," below a "narrow neck of land" that was between the "sea east" and the "sea west." This "narrow neck of land" is supposed to be either the Isthmus of Panama or the Isthmus of Tehuantepec in southern Mexico. In either of these cases, the "land south" is far from Ohio where the Atwater earthworks are located.

However, as shown in Appendix B, the traditional view of *Book of Mormon* geography itself has problems. The travels of *The Book of Mormon* peoples seem unrealistic compared to the distances they were supposed to have traversed. Thus Limhi's expedition, in searching for Mosiah's people, starts out (in the traditional view) in South or Central America, and ends up near the Great Lakes in North America. But the description of the trip would hardly seem to indicate that the expedition traveled such a great distance. There is a kind of provincialism in the accounts of the travels of the *Book of Mormon* peoples. Rather than crossing continents, they seem to be simply taking trips to places a few counties away, with scarcely any mention of the natural obstacles they would have had to confront if they had crossed continents.

So how can one make sense out of all this? For one thing, we can begin with the earthworks. They are the only structures described in sufficient detail in *The Book of Mormon* to permit one to equate them, at least provisionally, with similar actual structures. Thus one could use the reality as a starting point and try to find if the surrounding geography fits that of *The Book of Mormon*.

Turning back to *View of the Hebrews*, therefore, we find that many of the earthworks described by Ethan are on the river Scioto:

> On the waters of the Scioto, at Circleville, Ohio, is a notable instance of these military works [*V.H.*, p. 194].
>
> On the river Scioto, mounds are frequently found, usually on hills with fair prospects to the East [*V.H.*, p. 195].

Can the Scioto be equated with anything in *The Book of Mormon*? Possibly; the earthworks described in *View of the Hebrews* are near a river Scioto and those described in *The Book of Mormon*, a river Sidon. (See page 250 for related information.)

The similarity between the two rivers does not end there. By looking at a map of Ohio, Joseph would have seen that the Scioto is north-south oriented. The river Sidon in *The Book of Mormon* is also north-south oriented because it is described as having an east and a west bank:

> And it came to pass that the Amlicites came upon the hill Amnihu, which was east of the river Sidon ... [*B.M.*, p. 225; Alma 2:15].

And thus he cleared the ground, or rather the bank, which was on the west of the river Sidon ... [*B.M.*, p. 227; Alma 2:34].

Moreover, Ohio itself can be described as being southwards of a "narrow neck of land." The narrow neck of land might have been between Lake Erie and Lake Ontario. The Great Lakes are, in a sense, inland seas and a pair of them might represent the "sea east" and the "sea west." If Joseph did have the Great Lakes in mind as these *Book of Mormon* seas, he was simply taking a page from the Bible. The Sea of Galilee and the Dead Sea are both called "seas," though they do not amount to a thimble in a bucket when compared with the Great Lakes.

This perhaps shows that Joseph's ideas about the geography of *The Book of Mormon* evolved. Before his book turned into a new "revelation" from God, Joseph may have sought to have it explain how the mounds in Ohio came to be. There was a popular interest in these ancient remains and he might have believed that a book providing such an explanation would turn a good profit, especially if it provided action and told a story. In support of this, we might also note that the hill Cumorah, in New York State, is reasonably close to the area in question. The flight of the Nephites to that hill during the final battle would make a lot more sense if they were originally supposed to be in "Ohio" rather than in far distant Central or South America.

After the book changed into a new "revelation," there would have been a few reasons for Joseph to change its geography. In particular, the legend of Quetzalcoatl, which played an important part in the development of Joseph's religious ideas, had its origin in Central America. Apparently, he also wanted his Nephites to have a greater and more advanced civilization than the simple mounds in Ohio would suggest. Again, Central and South America would be better suited because, as he learned from reading *View of the Hebrews*, those areas did have the kind of architectural remains he envisaged for his Nephites.

When Joseph apparently shifted the conceptual setting of his story to Central and South America, he left the remains of the Jaredites in Ohio, which extended the distance that Limhi's expedition had to go to find them — though the text was not changed to reflect the greater distance. The hill Cumorah was also left where it was in New York State, thus causing the Nephites to make their long flight to the place of their final battle with the Lamanites.

So why did Joseph go along with (or perhaps even originate) Thompson's statement that the mounds in Ohio were the same as those in *The Book of Mormon*? Perhaps because many people were criticizing his latter-day revelation and he felt he needed something substantial as evidence. The Ohio earthworks were the only actual structures that could be specifically related to structures described in *The Book of Mormon*.

Chapter 15

The Backsliding

In *View of the Hebrews*, Ethan Smith often emphasized that those who rebelled against God would suffer the consequences. His feelings about this can be summed up by the following:

> They found the sentiment in their ancient oracles fulfilled; "The Lord is with you while ye be with him; but if ye forsake him, he will cast you off" [*V.H.*, p. 14].

This precept is the theme of *The Book of Mormon*. Very early in his latter-day revelation, Joseph's character, Lehi, makes this clear to his sons:

> ... the Lord ... hath said, that inasmuch as ye shall keep my commandments, ye shall prosper in the land; but inasmuch as ye will not keep my commandments, ye shall be cut off from my presence [*B.M.*, p. 61; 2 Nephi 1:19–20].

In *View of the Hebrews*, Joseph would have found several ideas about the branches of the Hebrew people being with God and then forsaking him — and receiving the appropriate punishments. In Chapter 11, we noted what Ethan Smith said about Judah and the ten tribes in this respect. Of particular interest to Joseph, Pastor Smith had also said similar things about the ancient inhabitants of America. The Vermont minister had suggested that the more civilized part of those people had survived for many centuries and had practiced their religious traditions. He then hypothesized that eventually, "as a holy vindictive Providence would have it, and according to ancient denunciations, all were left in an *'outcast'* savage state." Specifically, Ethan said that ultimately "the savage tribes ... annihilated their more civilized brethren."

These ideas could have led Joseph to reason that the civilized part must have more or less been with God for many centuries after their arrival in the New World, or else they would not have lasted so long. Further, if they were eventually "annihilated" by their savage brethren, it must have been because they, too, finally forsook the Lord and were cast off by him. As we saw, Joseph would have found the outline for this very idea in *View of the Hebrews*:

And we find a special branch of that ancient people ... having been lost from the knowledge of the known descendants of Abraham, the Jews. Allusion is made to their ancient redemption; and to their subsequent and fatal rebellion, till God "was turned to be their enemy, and he fought against them"; — or cast them out of his sight [*V.H.*, p. 71].

In developing his story, Joseph incorporated into the character of the Nephites a gradually increasing rebelliousness and apostasy until finally the Lord casts them off. The Nephites always have ample warning, of course — that was a part of the pattern. The process begins relatively early in *The Book of Mormon* when Nephi's brother, Jacob, admonishes some of his fellow Nephites for their iniquities. He does this by comparing them with the Lamanites. Joseph seems to have picked up this idea from *View of the Hebrews.* Ethan Smith had noted several "excellent traits" of the Indians and had castigated his fellow whites for not being of the same moral character.

Joseph thus had some of his white Nephites be less righteous than their darker brethren, the Lamanites. Furthermore, as the following parallels demonstrate, he applied to the Lamanites some of the same excellent traits that Ethan had reported in the Indians (who are supposed to be the descendants of the Lamanites).

What is particularly significant about these parallels is that, with one exception, the excerpts from *View of the Hebrews* are all close together, encompassing pages 173–176, and form part of a specific sequence of ideas and descriptions. In *The Book of Mormon*, Jacob admonishes his fellow Nephites by using corresponding ideas and descriptions that are, except for the one, even in the same order as are the equivalents in Ethan's book. To be sure, Joseph modified the wording of the ideas and related them to the perspective of his characters; nevertheless, the underlying sense is much the same. Note specifically that Ethan reiterated his theory that the savage tribes were guilty of "extirpating" their more civilized brethren. In *The Book of Mormon*, Jacob correspondingly "foresees" that extirpation.

View of the Hebrews	*The Book of Mormon* (page 128; Jacob 3:3–9)
But however vindictive the savages must have been ... in extirpating their more civilized brethren;	... the Lamanites ... shall scourge you even unto destruction ... except ye repent ... [3:3–4].
yet it is a fact that there are many excellent traits in their original character.... [U]pon the base slanders uttered against the Indians; ... a man may truly say, many Christians are not so ... sincere....	Behold, the Lamanites your brethren, whom ye hate, because of their filthiness and the cursings which hath come upon their skins, are more righteous than you;
They rarely deviate from certain maxims.... They manifest ... a	for they have not forgotten the commandment of the Lord ...

submission in what they apprehend
to be the appointment of Providence
[pp. 173-175].

A chief of the Delaware ... said ...
[a] Long time ago ... it was a good
custom among his people to take
but one wife, and that for life [p. 104].

that they should have, save it were
one wife; and concubines they
should have none ... [3:5].

... they are ... loving and affection-
ate to their wives and relations,
fond of their children....

Behold, their husbands love their
wives, and their wives love their
husbands, and their husbands and
wives love their children ... [3:7].

To blacken the characters of these
people, their enemies assert that
they are scarce human. But it is
we ... who ought to blush for
having been less men, and more
barbarous than they [pp. 175-176].

Wherefore, ... revile no more
against them, because of the darkness of their skins; neither shall ye
revile against them because of their
filthiness; but ye shall remember
your own filthiness ... [3:9].

Other passages in View of the Hebrews may have helped Joseph to
develop these ideas even further. For example:

> Among the ... traditions of those wild natives, he gives the following....
> "...[T]he Great Spirit, ... in consequence of their disobedience, ... withdrew
> from and abandoned them to the vexations of the bad spirit, who had
> since been instrumental of all their degeneracy...."
> 'They believe that notwithstanding the offences of his red children, he
> continues to shower down on them all the blessings they enjoy..." [V.H.,
> pp. 162-163].

Joseph echoed this passage, but made the blessings of the Great Spirit
conditional upon repentance. We therefore find that the Lamanites are

> ... a wild ... people; ... and the curse of God had fell upon them because
> of the traditions of their fathers; notwithstanding, the promises of the Lord
> were extended unto them, on the conditions of repentance ... [B.M., p. 270;
> Alma 17:14-15].

Notice that some of the terms in the two excerpts are either the same or
similar. Both have the word "tradtions." View of the Hebrews has "wild
natives," while The Book of Mormon has "wild people." Moreover, after
appearing in the View of the Hebrews excerpt, the word "notwithstanding"
stands out noticeably in the Book of Mormon extract. Furthermore, the following passage from The Book of Mormon shows that the "traditions" of the
Lamanites came about because their fathers, like Ethan's Indians, were disobedient:

Wherefore, the word of the Lord was fulfilled which he spake unto me, saying: That inasmuch as they will not hearken unto thy words, they shall be cut off from the presence of the Lord [*B.M.*, pp. 72–73; 2 Nephi 5:20].

Ethan Smith had advocated sending missionaries to convert the Indians to Christianity, and Joseph had some of his Nephite religious leaders prose-lytize the Lamanites for the same reason. As a result some of the Lamanites become receptive to the preachings of these religious leaders, accept the word of the Lord, and are counted among the Nephites. Conversely, many Nephites become unrighteous and are numbered among the Lamanites.

As the story developed, Joseph apparently felt it necessary to have most of the Nephites eventually backslide. The ultimate destruction of the civilized faction had to occur because they had abandoned God. Moreover, Joseph would not have been at a loss for ideas on how to orchestrate this fate. He would have found a model in Ethan's comments about the destruction of Jerusalem during the Roman-Jewish war. To begin with, Ethan Smith had said:

> The Jews became carnal.... Their ... prophets had long thundered against them solemn denunciations, that if ever they should become of the char-acter which they did impiously assume, the most signal judgements of God should cut them off [*V.H.*, p. 14].

Substitute "Nephites" for "Jews" and we have a good description of events in *The Book of Mormon*. The Nephites have prophets who denounce their iniquities. They become a carnal people and God cuts them off.

There are many substantial examples tending to show that Joseph used the model that Ethan provided. For example, about 6 B.C., according to the *Book of Mormon* chronology, we find a converted Lamanite named Samuel prophesying against the Nephites in one of their main cities. Joseph could have derived some of the ideas for this prophecy from the New Testa-ment, but not all of them. Regardless of the source, they demonstrate Joseph's eclecticism (and his disregard for chronology, since he had Samuel pre-empt Jesus). Here are the comparisons in parallel form:

View of the Hebrews	*The Book of Mormon* (pages 441–444; Helaman 13, page 447; Helaman 15)
... [H]e ascended the walls, and in a voice still more tremendous than ever, he exclaimed, "Wo, wo to this city ... and this people!" [p. 26].	... [H]e went and got upon the wall thereof ... and cried with a loud voice ... [13:4] ... yea, wo unto this great city ... [13:12] ... yea, wo unto this people ... [13:24].
A meteor, resembling a sword hung over Jerusalem.... This reminds one of the sword of the destroying angel, stretched over Jerusalem ... [p. 24].	... [T]he sword of justice hangeth over this people ... [13:5].

Here were the city and temple to be destroyed ... [p. 17]. The Jews ... had a measure of iniquity filled up; a full ripeness for destruction [p. 29].

Yea, heavy destruction awaiteth this people, and it surely cometh unto this people ... [13:6].

"For nation shall rise against nation; and ... in divers places, ... famines, and pestilences ..." [p. 21].

... [T]hus saith the Lord, ... I will visit them with the sword, and with famine, and with pestilence;

... Jesus Christ *came* in awful judgement ... [p. 15] He forewarned that this cup of divine indignation should be poured on *that generation* [p. 18].

yea, I will visit them in my fierce anger ... [13:8–10].

Here were the *city* and *temple* to be destroyed, for the infidelity, malice, hypocrisy, and persecution of the Lord of glory (in himself, and in his followers) which characterized its rulers and people. Here a measure of unprecedented atrociousness was just filled up, which should bring down wrath upon them to the uttermost [p. 17].

... [Y]ea, your heart is not drawn out unto the Lord, but they do swell with great pride, unto boasting, and unto great swelling, envyings, strifes, malice, persecutions, and murders, and all manner of iniquities: For this cause hath the Lord caused that a curse should come upon the land ... [13:22–23].

"O Jerusalem...! thou that killest the prophets, and stonest them that are sent unto thee!" [p. 18].

... [Y]e do cast out the prophets, and do mock them, and cast stones at them, and do slay them ... [13:24].

How prone are men to court deception. Christ had said to the Jews, "I am come in my Father's name, and ye receive me not. If another should come in his own name, him will ye receive" [p. 21].

... [I]f a prophet come among you, ... ye ... cast him out.... But ... if a man shall come among you and shall say, Do this, and there is no iniquity, ... ye will receive him, and ye will say that he is a prophet ... [13:27].

"O Jerusalem.... Behold, your house is left unto you desolate..." [pp. 18–9].

... [B]ehold, ... your houses shall be left unto you desolate [15:11].

... [A]s our Lord denounced: "Wo to them that give suck in those days" [p. 32].

... [Y]our women shall have cause to mourn in the day that they shall give suck: ... yea, and wo unto them which are with child ... [15:2].

Ethan Smith's chapter on the destruction of Jerusalem seems to have provided Joseph with further ideas upon which to model events in *The Book of Mormon*. For example, the Vermont minister said:

> A spirit of faction now appeared in Jerusalem. — Two parties first, and afterwards three raged there; each contending with deadly animosity for precedence.... These abandoned murderers plundered in the city.... They slew their brethren of Jerusalem, as though they had been wild animals. They scourged and imprisoned the nobles, in hopes to terrify them to become of their party; and many who could not be thus won, they slew....
>
> To add to the horrid calamities of the time occasioned by the bloody factions, Judea was infested by bands of robbers and murderers, plundering their towns and cutting in pieces such as made any resistance, whether men, women or children [*V.H.*, pp. 28-29].

Joseph apparently decided that since the Jews had to contend amongst themselves with "factions" and with "bands of robbers and murderers," his Nephites would have to do so as well. Ethan's descriptions of the two groups were very similar; the Mormon prophet combined the "factions" and the "bands of robbers and murderers" into one organization:

> ... yea, they began to seek to get gain, that they might be lifted up one above another; therefore they began to commit secret murders, and to rob, and to plunder, that they might get gain. — And now behold, those murderers and plunderers were a band which had been formed by Kishkumen and Gadianton. And now it had come to pass that there were many, even among the Nephites, of Gadianton's band.... And they were called Gadianton's robbers and murderers ... [*B.M.*, p. 423; Helaman 6:17-18].

Like the "factions" that Ethan Smith described, this band was responsible for murdering some of the leaders of the people. Moreover, Joseph went on to describe some dissenters from the Nephites who went into the mountains and became part of Gadianton's band:

> ... and thus in time, yea, even in the space of not many years, they became an exceeding great band of robbers.... Now behold, those robbers did make great havoc, yea, even great destruction among the people of Nephi, and also among the people of the Lamanites [*B.M.*, p. 438; Helaman 11:26-27].

And in so doing he followed the descriptions that Ethan had given.

Ethan made it quite clear that a good deal of the blame for the fall of Jerusalem lay with the squabbling of the Jewish factions:

> Slaughter, conflagration and plunder ensued. A portion of the center of the city was burned, and the inhabitants became as prisoners to the two furious parties. The Romans here saw their own proverb verified: ... "Whom God will destroy, he gives up to madness" [*V.H.*, p. 31].

Joseph apparently followed Ethan's lead, and had Mormon say that the Gadianton band would play an important part in the eventual destruction of the Nephites.

> And behold, in the end of this book, ye shall see that this Gadianton did prove the overthrow, yea, almost the entire destruction of the people of Nephi [*B.M.*, p. 411; Helaman 2:13].

But, as we shall see, there is a discrepancy concerning this remark.

If Joseph got the idea for the bands of robbers and murderers from Ethan's book, it appears he got some ideas for their specific nature from a controversy that was storming throughout New York State while *The Book of Mormon* was forming in his mind. In September of the year 1826, a printing office in the town of Batavia was set on fire by a group of masked men. At the time of this incident, the office was being used to print an exposé of Freemasonry written by William Morgan, a Mason who was angered because he had been excluded from the Batavia chapter of the organization. A few days after the burning of the office, Morgan was arrested under a dubious charge prompted by another Mason and brought to Canandaigua, only nine miles from Joseph's home. Morgan was acquitted, but then kidnapped and apparently taken to Fort Niagara. He was never seen again, and it was presumed that he had been murdered by the Masons because of his indiscretions.* His kidnappers were arrested, tried, and convicted, but given light sentences.

These incidents precipitated a furor of anti-Masonic activity which increased to fanatical proportions in the months and years that followed. Non-Masons viewed Freemasonry as a danger to society and subversive to law and order. Newspapers printed scathing denunciations of the organization, and anti-masonic political parties were formed. Pamphlets and books exposing the secrets of the Masons abounded, including Morgan's book, which was published after his disappearance.

To understand how the Masonic controversy may have influenced Joseph, one must be familiar with the rhetoric expressed in the anti-Masonic publications of the time. The *Wayne Sentinel*, one of the newspapers published in Joseph's hometown, provides several examples of this rhetoric. The following appeared in the September 26, 1828, issue:

> The Free-masons are, therefore, radically and essentially, demagogues, jacobites, conspirators, assassins, infidels, traitors, and atheists. Their band of union is formed of the broken cement of existing order—their secret is the watchword of sedition and rebellion—their object is anarchy and plunder—...unless they are suppressed, there will soon be neither religion, morals, literature, nor civilized society left!

The following appeared in the Canandaigua *Ontario Phoenix* of July 16, 1828, and was reprinted two days later in the *Wayne Sentinel*:

---

*It is interesting to note that Joseph eventually took Morgan's widow as one of his plural wives. See Brodie, pp. 436–7.

Resolved, That however beneficial secret societies and combinations may have been considered in the dark ages of the world, as bonds of union, and shields of protection to their members, ... yet in this enlightened age and century, where the private rights and the civil liberty of our citizens as guaranteed by a free constitution and an impartial administration of justice, they become not only useless to their members, but dangerous to the government.

The *Palmyra Freeman* of September 2, 1828, contained the following:

Almost two years ago a free citizen was taken violently from the protection of the laws, carried one hundred and fifty miles, confined in a magazine, and there deliberately murdered. This was done by a *"secret society"* to vindicate its *"secret laws"*....

We cannot contemplate the overwhelming power of Free-masonry, without trembling for the safety of our country. Freemasonry must be put down or freedom must be banished from her last abode.... The people must submit or resist.... The hour of trial is at hand. Free men have everything to lose — everything to preserve. Their country, her laws and her institutions, demand action — early and energetic action. The power to do evil must be withdrawn from masonic hands.

Even many former Masons got on the anti-Masonic bandwagon. The following, which appeared in the *Ontario Phoenix* of June 4, 1828, was written by one such:

I am fully prepared to say, that it is born IMMORAL and IRRELIGIOUS, and its tendency is DANGEROUS to the Free insitutions of OUR COUNTRY.

The furor even caused other secret societies to become suspect. The following is from a letter which appeared in the Rochester *Anti-Masonic Enquirer* of Jan. 20, 1829. Here, the Phi Beta Kappa Society is condemned:

... *I am decidedly opposed to all combinations and secret associations whatsoever....* The natural tendency of all Secret societies is evil; and I am grieved and surprised, that the seeds of secret combinations should be sown in this seminary of education.

The *Palmyra Freeman* of March 18, 1828, printed the following resolutions of the Anti-Masonic Convention:

Resolved, ... that the existence of any society in this country whose objects, principles, and measures are secret and concealed, is not merely useless, but hostile to the spirit of our free institutions.

Resolved, That the bare existence of secret Societies in these United States justify fears, jealousies, and suspicions as to their objects, in the breasts of the uninitiated, which have a tendency to distract society and sow ill will and dissentions in community....

> *Resolved*, That the obligation in one of the degrees of Free Masonry to protect a brother, "right or wrong," and to preserve his secret inviolate, even in cases of Murder and Treason, has a tendency to unnerve the arm of justice, and to afford protection to the vicious and profligate from the punishment due their crimes.

The following is from an anti-Masonic pamphlet that was published in central New York:

> Secret societies are dangerous to any government. ... In one day they might strike a death blow to the liberties of our happy land.... If secret societies in America become so corrupt as to enter into an extensive combination, to destroy the property of their fellow citizens, to drag them from their homes, to rob them of their liberties, and even to murder them in cold blood..., then what may we not expect![1]

This rhetoric about the Masons could also be applied to the Gadianton bands in *The Book of Mormon* — even down to the frequent use of the terms "secret society" and "secret combinations." Here are some examples of these terms from *The Book of Mormon*:

> ... and thus the judgements of God did come upon these workers of darkness and secret combinations ... [*B.M.*, p. 329; Alma 37:30].

> And it came to pass ... there was continual peace established in the land, all save it were the secret combinations which Gadianton the nobler [sic; "robber" in subsequent editions] had established in the more settled parts of the land ... [*B.M.*, pp. 413–414; Helaman 3:23].

> ... for so great had been the spreading of this wicked and secret society, that it had corrupted the hearts of all the people ... [*B.M.*, p. 555; Ether 9:6].

The Gadiantons of *The Book of Mormon* have other similarities with the popular rhetoric about the Masons. Morgan, for example, had stated in his book that the Masons claimed an ancient origin for their organization. The *Palmyra Freeman* of March 18, 1828, stated likewise:

> Among the many impious assertions which Masons make in favor of their institution, is that of its *antiquity*. They assert that it was founded during the reign of King Solomon.

In *The Book of Mormon*, we find that a leader of the Gadianton bands makes a similar claim:

> And behold, I am Giddianhi, and I am the Governor of this the secret society of Gadianton; which society, and the works thereof, I know to be good; and they are of ancient date, and they have been handed down unto us [*B.M.*, pp. 457–458; 3 Nephi 3:9].

It is interesting to note that one of those who had conspired against Morgan was a Mason named Giddins (or Giddings). To save his own neck, this Giddins testified against his co-conspirators during the trial, but his testimony did not improve his contemporaries' opinion of him. The following appeared in an 1829 book describing the anti-Masonic excitement:

> Giddins, whose statements, unless confirmed by other circumstances, are not entitled to any credit whatsoever — who was himself an accomplice, and if to be believed, the most guilty one of the whole, as will by and bye appear....[2]

One might wonder if Joseph derived the name of Giddianhi from Giddins. And, while on the subject of names, there is this to be said: Some analyzers of Mormonism have suggested that Joseph might have derived the names Mormon, Moroni, and several others from that of Morgan, whose abduction and apparent murder brought on the anti-Masonic furor.

Morgan had also noted that the Masons wore lambskins in their ceremonies:

> The Master returns to his seat ... and gets a lambskin or white apron, presents it to the candidate, and observes, Brother, I now present you with a lambskin or white apron: it is ... the badge of a Mason.[3]

So we find the Gadiantons likewise wearing lambskins:

> And it came to pass that they did come up to battle; ... and they were girded after after the manner of robbers; and they had a lambskin about their loins ... [*B.M.*, p. 460; 3 Nephi 4:7].

Morgan had also stated that the Masons had signs, passwords, etc.:

> The signs, due guards, words, passwords, and their several names comprise pretty much all the secrets of Masonry.[4]

And we find that the Gadiantons likewise had secret signs:

> And it came to pass they they did have their signs, yea, their secret signs, and their secret words; and this that they might distinguish a brother who had entered into the covenant ... [*B.M.*, p. 424; Helaman 6:22].

In the *Palmyra Freeman* of March 18, 1828, it was stated that the Masons had secret oaths:

> ... the morals and precepts of the institution ... afford but a precarious security against the violation of our laws, or the taking of the lives of our citizens, when placed in conjunction with an exposition of its *secret* and *cut-throat* OATHS.

In *The Book of Mormon*, the Gadiantons likewise have secret oaths:

> Now behold, those secret oaths and covenants ... were put into the heart of Gadianton, by the same being who did entice our first parents ... [*B.M.*, p. 424; Helaman 6:26].

The *Wayne Sentinel* of March 14, 1828 had an article stating that the Masons took oaths to assist other Masons in difficulty. The following is the oath as it was given:

> I promise and swear, that I will aid and assist a companion Royal Arch Mason wherever I shall see him engaged in any difficulty so far as to extricate him from the same, whether he be right or wrong....

And, in the anti-Masonic pamphlet from which we quoted earlier, we find:

> What are we to think of professed Christians who will support this institution in its absolute claims, and bind themselves to it stronger and stronger by additional oaths? ... If ... members of the church of Christ will go forward and take this sacriligious oath and bind themselves under additional obligations to be secret keepers, to be silent on the crimes and abominations of the institution, does it look as if they intended ever to give it up?[5]

The basic ideas in the above two extracts are combined and paralleled in *The Book of Mormon*. Some of the Nephites, who are supposed to be followers of the "church of Christ," apostatize and join the Gadiantons. Moreover, they take oaths to protect their fellow Gadiantons whether "right or wrong":

> But behold, satan did stir up the hearts of the more parts of the Nephites, insomuch that they did unite with those bands of robbers, and did enter into their covenants and their oaths, that they would protect and preserve one another, in whatsoever difficult circumstances they should be placed in, that they should not suffer for their murders, and their plunderings, and their stealings [*B.M.*, p. 424; Helaman 6:21].

If any doubt remains that Joseph had the Masons in mind when he described the Gadiantons of *The Book of Mormon*, it should be removed by allusions in that book to the Masons of his own time. For example, he had Moroni prophesy that *The Book of Mormon* would come forth in a day (i.e., in Joseph's day) when such an organization would be in existence:

> And it shall come in a day when the blood of saints shall cry unto the Lord, because of secret combinations and the works of darkness [*B.M.*, p. 534; Mormon 8:27].

Again, Joseph had Nephi make a similar prophecy of the existence of such an organization in his, Joseph's, own time:

> And there are also secret combinations, even as in times of old, according
> to the combinations of the Devil, for he is the founder of all these things;
> ... yea, and he leadeth them around by the neck with a flaxen cord ...
> [*B.M.*, p. 108; 2 Nephi 26:22].

Notice the reference to the flaxen cord about the necks of the members of the "secret combinations." Morgan stated in his book that the Mason initiate had "a rope called a Cable-Tow, round his neck."[6]

Joseph not only provided "prophecies" about the Freemasonry of his own time, he gave his reader a warning of the potential danger of the organization to society. This was in the same spirit as the following item which appeared in the *Palmyra Freeman* of December 2, 1828:

> Our government and Country will be destroyed, unless the people put
> down Masonry root and branch.

And also the following in the same issue:

> But what must a discerning world now ... think of the Masonic institu-
> tion. And what will the people of this country think of themselves ten or
> twenty years hence, if they should suffer themselves to be duped, and do
> not unite hand and heart, to put down a *Secret Society*, which, if again
> suffered to get fairly the ascendancy, will crush them and their liberties
> together.

We therefore find Moroni telling the readers of *The Book of Mormon*:

> ... whatsoever nation shall uphold such secret combinations, to get power
> and gain, until they shall spread over the nation, behold, they shall be
> destroyed; ... wherefore, O ye Gentiles, it is wisdom in God that these
> things should be shewn unto you, that thereby ye may ... suffer not that
> these murderous combinations shall get above you...; wherefore, the Lord
> commandeth you, when ye shall see these things come among you, that
> ye shall awake to a sense of your awful situation, because of this secret
> combination which shall be among you.... For it cometh to pass that whoso
> buildeth it up, seeketh to overthrow the freedom of all lands, nations, and
> countries; and it bringeth to pass the destruction of all people ... [*B.M.*,
> p. 554; Ether 8:22-25].

We might at this point ask why Joseph imbued his Gadiantons with the popular conceptions of the Masons of his own time.

There are several possibilities, and they are not mutually exclusive. First, Joseph appears to have felt that the newspaper accounts of the Masons were similar to the descriptions of the Jewish factions and bands of robbers and murderers that Ethan Smith had reported on in his *View of the Hebrews*. The second possibility is that Joseph might have thought that his book would be more popular if he took advantage of the anti-Masonic furor. Thirdly, Martin Harris, the man who footed the bill for the publication of *The Book of*

Mormon, belonged to the Wayne County Anti-Masonic Convention. Joseph might have thought that his benefactor would be a little freer with his money if the book conformed to the popular sentiment about the Masons.

But there is something else that might have caused Joseph to connect the ancient Americans and the Masons of his own time. This item appeared in Atwater's paper in *Archaeologia Americana*:

> Near Portsmouth, a flourishing town at the mouth of the Scioto, a medal was found in alluvial earth, several years since, ... a number of feet below the surface, belonging, probably, to a recent era of time. This medal, I regret to state, is not in my possession, but it has been described to me.... It was Masonick; the device on one side represented a human heart with a sprig of cassia growing out of it; on the other side was a temple with a cupola and spire, at the summit of which was a half moon, and there was a star in front of the temple. There were Roman letters on both sides of the medal, ... probably abbreviations. That this medal had a European ... origin, there is little doubt, and belonged to a recent era of time.[7]

Considering the furor over Masonry occurring in his neighborhood, this surely would have interested Joseph. Though Atwater had concluded that the medal was of recent origin, his comments might have given Joseph the seed of an idea. The finding of a "Masonick" medal so close to the ancient earthworks might have suggested to the Mormon prophet the idea of a Masonic organization in ancient America when those structures had been built. The bands of robbers and murderers, an idea likely derived from *View of the Hebrews*, would make excellent "masons." They, along with the Lamanites, would assure that the Nephites would have "neither religion, morals, literature, nor civilized society left!"

However, Joseph made a blunder by having his book refer so frequently to the Masons. These references tag the book as a product of the early nineteenth century. Furthermore, the book's rhetoric and warnings call all the more attention to it, since the anti-Masonic furor eventually died away and Freemasonry once more became a respected instititution. Joseph Smith himself, in fact, became a Mason in 1842, and, ever the eclectic, he incorporated many Masonic rituals, symbols, garments, etc., into the ceremonies of his developing church.[8] Moreover, he made his church a "secret society" despite all the condemnations of such organizations previously written into *The Book of Mormon*.

Chapter 16

The Arrival of Jesus

Joseph incorporated into his book the idea that the ancient inhabitants of America believed in the Christian gospel. This might seem curious since those people supposedly came to the New World even before Christianity appeared in the Old World. But it is not so curious when we realize that Joseph could easily have derived the concept from material he found in *View of the Hebrews*. For example, Ethan Smith had said:

> It seems the Spanish missionaries found such traces of resemblance between some of the rites of the religion of the natives of Mexico, and the religion which they wished to introduce, that our author says, "they persuaded them that the gospel had in very remote times, been already preached in America...." It is a noted fact that there is a far greater analogy between much of the religion of the Indians, and Christianity, than between that of any other heathen nation on earth and Christianity [*V.H.*, p. 187].

Pastor Smith did not describe the rites of the Mexican Indians which the missionaries found to be so similar to those of Christianity. Those rites were not unique, being found around the world before the appearance of Christianity. One such was the eating of a food that was supposed to represent the body of a god. In the Old World, the Mithrans, the Dionysians, and the Attisians had such rites.

The passage above could have caused this question in Joseph's mind: If the ancient Americans came to the New World before the time of Jesus, how did they come to practice rites similar to those of Christianity? Joseph also would have found it interesting that the missionaries had used these similarities to persuade the Indians that the gospel had been previously preached in America. Reflecting upon this, Joseph might have realized that including such a concept would make his book more relevant. He thus had his characters learn through prophecy that Jesus would appear on the earth. Reflecting the passage from *View of the Hebrews*, he had Nephi prophesy:

> And ... in the latter days, when our seed shall have dwindled in unbelief, ... then shall the fullness of the Gospel of the Messiah come unto the Gentiles, and from the Gentiles unto the remnant of our seed; and at that

day, shall the remnant of our seed know ... and come to the knowledge of their forefathers, and also to the knowledge of the Gospel of their Redeemer, which was ministered unto their fathers by him ... [*B.M.*, p. 36; 1 Nephi 15:13–14].

Having incorporated the Christian gospel into the history of his ancient Americans, Joseph seems to have wanted them also to know when Jesus himself appeared on earth and fulfilled his ministry. Therefore he had Samuel the Lamanite prophesy of certain signs showing when those events would occur. In particular, Joseph seemed to want to provide signs heralding the death of Jesus on the cross — especially since Ethan had hinted that such had occurred in the New World. In the first edition of *View of the Hebrews*, we find:

> The earthquake, at the time of our Savior's giving up of the ghost, which rent the rocks, may be said thus to have opened many mouths (perhaps over the face of the earth) tacitly to proclaim *the event*. It may be said in figure; — "The stones cried out!" In our subject, we find a powerful corresponding evidence of the truth of revelation, extending through a wild continent ... [*V.H.*, 1st edition, p. 166].

Joseph apparently liked the idea that the earthquake at the time of the crucifixion was felt "over the face of the earth." That would have to include America — Ethan's "wild continent." So he put almost the very words of Ethan Smith into the mouth of his *Book of Mormon* prophet, Samuel:

> ... yea, at the time that he shall yield up the ghost, ... the earth shall shake and tremble, and the rocks which is upon the face of the earth ... shall be broken up; yea, they shall be rent in twain ... [*B.M.*, pp. 446–447; Helaman 14:21–22].

Further incentive to include the earthquakes may have resulted from Joseph's reading other books, particularly Francisco Clavigero's *History of Mexico*, which Ethan had cited. Clavigero was an eighteenth century Mexican historian who had access to important manuscript "histories" of America composed by various Indian writers.[1] He wrote his *History of Mexico* in Spanish, and it was subsequently translated into Italian and then into English. The American editions were published in Richmond, Virginia, in 1806, and in Philadelphia in 1804 and in 1817. In his *History*, Clavigero recounted legends of certain devastating earthquakes told by the Indians, to which he added some personal speculations:

> At present they plough those lands over which ships formerly sailed, and now they sail over lands which were formerly ploughed: earthquakes have swallowed some lands, and subterranean fires have thrown up others.... In our America, all those who have observed with philosophic eyes the peninsula of Yucatan, do not doubt that that country has once been the bed of the sea; and on the contrary, in the channel of Bahamma many indications show the island of Cuba to have been once united to the continent of

Florida. In the strait which separates America from Asia many islands are found, which probably were the mountains belonging to that tract of land which we suppose to have been swallowed up by earthquakes.... We imagine, however, that the sinking of that land, and the separation of the two continents, has been occasioned by those great and extraordinary earthquakes mentioned in the histories of the Americans, which formed an aera almost as memorable as that of the deluge. The histories of the Toltecas fix such earthquakes in the year 1 Tecpatl; but, as we know not to what century that belonged, we can form no conjecture of the time that great calamity happened....

... How great then must the convulsion have been which was occasioned by those extraordinary and memorable earthquakes, mentioned in the histories of America, when the world was thought to have been coming to an end![2]

C.F. Voleny expressed similar ideas in his *View of the Soil and Climate of the United States of America* (1804, Philadelphia), pp. 97–101; also, De Witt Clinton wrote of similar matters in his *Discourse Delivered Before the New York Historical Society* (1812, New York), pp. 58–60. From reading of such conjectures, Joseph might well have been encouraged to include in his book an account of devastating earthquakes.

So, Joseph, reacting to Ethan's suggestion, had earthquakes devastate the New World at the time of the crucifixion. Moreover, he seems to have used as a model Ethan's description of the destruction of Jerusalem. Quoting from Josephus, the Vermont minister had stated the following:

"A heavy storm burst upon them, during the night; violent winds arose, with most excessive rains, with constant lightning, most tremendous thunders, and dreadful roarings of earthquakes. It seemed as if the system of the world had been confounded for the destruction of mankind. And one might well conjecture that these were signs of no common event" [*V.H.*, p. 23].

In *The Book of Mormon*, Joseph provided a similar description to herald the earthquakes in the New World:

And ... there arose a great storm, such an one as never had been known in all the land; and there was also a great and terrible tempest; and there was terrible thunder, insomuch that it did shake the whole earth as if it was about to divide asunder; and there was exceeding sharp lightnings, such as never had been known in all the land [*B.M.*, p. 470; 3 Nephi 8:5–7].

The two books show a similar context for the storms. In Ethan's they herald the destruction of Jerusalem; in Joseph's, the destruction of the New World cities. But Ethan apparently gave Joseph still other ideas for the devastation of the cities:

Our Savior added; "And great earthquakes shall be in divers places."

These significant warnings too were accomplished in those days. Two are recorded by Tacitus; one at Rome in the reign of Claudius; another at Apamea, in Syria, where were many Jews. So destructive was the one at the latter place, that the tribute due the Romans was for five years remitted. One also was terrifick at Crete; one at Smyrna; one at Miletus; one at Chios, and one at Samos.... Tacitus and Eusebius inform, that Hieropolis and Colosse, as well as Laodicea, were overthrown by earthquakes. Another is noted at Rome; one at Campania; and others tremendous are mentioned as taking place at Jerusalem in the night, just before the commencement of the last siege of that city [V.H., pp. 22–23].

This apparently impressed Joseph, for he used a similar cataclysm in his own book. Possibly from also reading Clavigero or one of the other authors mentioned above, he also described great changes in the face of the land:

And the city of Zarahemla did take fire; and the city of Moroni did sink into the depths of the sea...; and the earth was carried up upon the city of Moronihah, that in the place of the city there became a great mountain; and there was a great and terrible destruction in the land southward. But behold, there was a more great and terrible destruction in the land northward: for behold, the whole face of the land was changed, because of the tempest, and the whirlwinds, and the thunderings, and the lightnings, and the exceeding great quaking of the whole earth; ... and many great and notable cities were sunk ... and many were shook til the buildings thereof had fallen to the earth...; and thus the face of the whole earth became deformed, because of the tempests, and the thunderings, and the lightnings, and the quaking of the earth [B.M., pp. 470–471; 3 Nephi 8:8–17].

Ethan Smith held that the earthquakes he had described were a fulfillment of the prophecies of Jesus in Matthew 24. Joseph could have turned to that chapter and found the following in verse 29:

Immediately after the tribulation of those days shall the sun be darkened, and the moon shall not give up her light....

Reading on, Joseph would have also found this in Matthew 27:45:

Now from the sixth hour there was darkness over all the face of the land unto the ninth hour.

Josiah Priest, in his *Wonders of Nature*, also mentioned that darkness:

Some people have said, that the above-mentioned darkness might have been occasioned by a natural eclipse of the sun.... But there could be no natural or regular eclipse of the sun on the day of Christ's crucifixion; as the moon was full on that day, and consequently in the side of the heavens opposite to the sun. And therefore, the darkness at the time of his *crucifixion* was quite *supernatural*.[3]

All of these ideas concerning a darkness seem to have come together in Joseph's mind. There was a darkness at the crucifixion — a supernatural darkness! Ethan Smith had suggested that the earthquake at the time of the crucifixion had been felt over the face of the earth. If the earthquake, why not then the darkness?

Thus the inhabitants of the New World experience the darkness when Jesus was crucified. Joseph seems to have derived some specific details for this from Priest's *Wonders of Nature*. In that book, Priest had presented a speculation by Adam Clarke on the nature of the darkness which afflicated the Egyptians in Exodus 10:21-23:

> *Darkness* which *may be felt.* — Probably this was occasioned by a super-abundance of aqueous vapors floating in the atmosphere; which were so thick as to prevent the rays of the sun from penetrating through them; an extraordinary thick mist, supernaturally i.e. miraculously brought on....
>
> So deep was the obscurity; and probably such was its nature, that no artificial light could be procured, as the thick clammy vapors would prevent lamps, &c. from burning; or even if they could be ignited, the light, through the palpable obscurity, could diffuse itself to no distance from the burning body....
>
> ... [T]he darkness with its attendant horrors lasted for three days.[4]

We find in *The Book of Mormon*:

> And it came to pass that there was thick darkness upon all the face of the land, insomuch that the inhabitants thereof which had not fallen, could feel the vapor of darkness; and there could be no light, because of the darkness, neither candles, neither torches; neither could there be fire kindled with their fine and exceeding dry wood, so there could not be any light at all; and there was not any light seen, neither fire, nor glimmer, neither the sun, nor the moon, nor the stars, for so great were the mists of darkness which were upon the face of the land.
>
> And it came to pass that it did last for the space of three days that there was no light seen ... [*B.M.*, pp. 471-472; 3 Nephi 8:20-23].

Note the similarity in the descriptions. In both books, the darkness could be felt. In both books, the darkness is described as being due to a thick vapor. In both books, fires could not be lit for artificial light because of the vapor. In both books, there is a mist so thick that the light of the sun could not penetrate it. And finally, in both books the darkness lasts for three days.

Joseph was not careful on that last point. The darkness in *The Book of Mormon* was apparently supposed to represent the time from the death of Jesus on the cross until the time of the resurrection. But this period of time was actually less than two days — from late Friday afternoon to Sunday morning — and not three whole days.

The next event in *The Book of Mormon* seems also to have had its origin in *View of the Hebrews*. Applying the preaching of the forerunner, John, to the Israelites in America, Ethan Smith had stated the following:

> ... it is *in a sense literally true*. The voice, which restores Israel, is heard in the *vast wilderness of America* ... [*V.H.*, p. 257].

Jesus, of course, would be the one to restore Israel. The passage therefore hints at the idea of the voice of Jesus being heard in the New World. At this point, Joseph apparently remembered something that he had read in Ethan's description of the destruction of Jerusalem:

> The last and most fearful sign Josephus relates; that one Jesus, son of Ananus ... exclaimed, "A *voice from the east — a voice from the west — a voice from the four winds — ...* a *voice against the whole people....* Wo, *wo, to ... this people!*" [*V.H.*, pp. 25–26].

The emphasis makes the words stand out and they could have caught Joseph's eye. That a man named Jesus said these words suggests the other, better known, Jesus. The passage also hints at a disembodied voice being heard over the land.

The ideas in the two passages are combined in *The Book of Mormon*:

> And it came to pass that there was a voice heard among all the inhabitants of the earth upon all the face of this land, crying, Wo, wo, wo, unto this people.... Behold, I am Jesus Christ ... [*B.M.*, pp. 472, 473; 3 Nephi 9: 2, 15].

The omnipresent voice of Jesus proceeds to explain why the cities were destroyed. Echoing Ethan Smith's explanation about Jerusalem, the voice declares that the New World cities were destroyed because of the iniquities of the inhabitants. Going back to Ethan's description of the destruction of Jerusalem, we also find the Vermont minister quoting Jesus:

> His tender feelings of soul then melted in a most moving apostrophe: "O' Jerusalem, Jerusalem: thou that killest the prophets, and stonest them that are sent unto thee! How often would I have gathered thy children together, even as a hen gathereth her chickens under her wings; and ye would not! Behold, your house is left unto you desolate ..." [*V.H.*, pp. 18–19].

In *The Book of Mormon*, we find the disembodied voice of Jesus saying:

> ... O ye people of the house of Israel, who have fallen; yea, O ye people of the house of Israel; ye that dwell at Jerusalem, as ye that have fallen; yea, how oft would I have gathered you as a hen gathereth her chickens, and ye would not.... O house of Israel, the places of your dwellings shall become desolate ... [*B.M.*, p. 474; 3 Nephi 10:5–7].

The next event in *The Book of Mormon* is quite remarkable and again Joseph apparently found the idea for it in *View of the Hebrews*. Ethan Smith had given a lengthy discussion on the legend of Quetzalcoatl, of which the following is a part:

On the pyramid of Choulula was an altar dedicated to Quetzalcoatl, or *the serpent of green feathers*; as the name imports. Of their tradition relative to this Quetzalcoatl, the writer says; "this is the most mysterious being of the whole Mexican mythology." ...

The character to whom their most noted altar was dedicated, whose name imported a serpent of green feathers, was at the same time (in their own description) "a white and bearded man." ...

"He introduced the custom of piercing the lips and ears; and lacerating the rest of the body with prickles and thorns." "He appeased by his penance divine wrath." ...

"The saint (this legislator) had chosen his place of retirement — on the volcano Catcitepetl, or *speaking mountain....*"

"The reign of Quetzalcoatl was a golden age of the people of Anahuac. The earth brought forth without culture the most fruitful harvests. But this reign was not of long duration."

"The Great Spirit offered Quetzalcoatl beverage, which in rendering him immortal, inspired him with a taste for travelling...."

"He preached peace to men and would permit no other offerings to the Divinity than the first fruits of the harvests."

"He disappeared, after he had declared to the Choululans that he would return and govern them again, and renew their happiness" [*V.H.*, pp. 204–205].

Ethan Smith had quoted this particular description of Quetzalcoatl from *Archaeologia Americana*, but some of his other sources had also mentioned this "most mysterious being." One of these was Clavigero, who reported many of the same legends, as well as some that Ethan had not. Clavigero also stated the following:

Dr. Siguenza imagined that the *Quetzalcoatl*, deified by those people, was no other than the apostle St. Thomas, who announced to them the Gospel.[5]

Ethan Smith appears to have disagreed with Dr. Siguenza. The following is his speculation on who this Quetzalcoatl was:

Though their ancient "legislator" is called by a name importing *the serpent of green feathers*; yet he was an *ancient man*, a *white man and bearded*; ... who ... taught them many things. Who could this be but *Moses*, the ancient legislator in Israel? ...

The name of *the serpent of the green plumage* being given to this legislator, leads the mind to Moses' *brazen serpent* in the wilderness....

His appeasing divine wrath, may have a striking allusion to the system of the Mosaic sacrifices, including also the mediation of Moses as a type of Christ, and God's turning away his fierce wrath from Israel at his intercession, as was repeatedly the case [*V.H.*, pp. 206–207].

Dr. Siguenza had proposed that Quetzalcoatl was St. Thomas, the apostle. Ethan Smith thought that Quetzalcoatl was Moses but represented

Moses as a "type of Christ." Joseph may have thought, if Quetzalcoatl, as Moses, was a "type of Christ," why not remove Moses from the picture entirely and have Quetzalcoatl be Christ himself?

Joseph apparently felt that a good case could be made for the concept. As related by Ethan, the Spanish missionaries had "persuaded" the natives that the gospel had, "in very remote times, been already preached in America." Dr. Siguenza had suggested that St. Thomas/Quetzalcoatl preached the gospel to the natives of the New World. But Joseph, developing his own idea of Quetzalcoatl, might have reasoned that no one would have been better suited to preach the gospel to the inhabitants of the New World than Jesus himself.

This would make an inspiring addition to *The Book of Mormon*. Christ in the New World! That concept would surely captivate many readers. Who was to say that Christ had not been in the New World? It was obvious that no one knew who Quetzalcoatl, this "most mysterious being," was. To be sure, there were traditions about Quetzalcoatl not compatible with the Christian view of Jesus, but Joseph might have reasoned that these could be explained as distortions to the legend over the years. Ethan used the same argument when he made Quetzalcoatl Moses:

> It has generally been the fact, that events in pagan mythology, which are founded on ancient revelation, have yet been confused, and blended with much fable.... While considerable fable is involved in this historic tradition of the Choululans; it appears to offer a singular facility to trace it to the inspired records of Israel [*V.H.*, p. 206].

Joseph very likely believed that the same argument could be used to make Quetzalcoatl Jesus. Moreover, he apparently felt that the traditions about this mysterious being included some that could be considered similar to beliefs about Jesus. Ethan himself had said something that suggested this when he equated "the serpent of green plumage" with Moses' "brazen serpent." This could have brought to Joseph's mind the words of Jesus in John 3:14:

> And as Moses lifted up the serpent in the wilderness, even so must the Son of man be lifted up.

This association of Jesus with the serpent of Moses must have impressed Joseph, for we find in *The Book of Mormon*:

> ... Moses ... hath spoken concerning the coming of the Messiah. Yea, did he not bear record, that the Son of God should come? And as he lifted up the brazen serpent in the wilderness, even so shall he be lifted up which should come [*B.M.*, p. 430; Helaman 8:13–14].

By including this passage, Joseph perhaps thought he could prepare the way for an eventual use of the legend of Quetzalcoatl, the serpent of green ("brazen") plumage, as evidence for the coming of Christ to the New World as described in *The Book of Mormon*.

It was noted in Chapter 9 that a Mormon writer, Sidney Sperry, stated that *View of the Hebrews* had nothing comparable to the ministry of Jesus in the New World as told in *The Book of Mormon*. Mormon literature, however, states that the legend of Quetzalcoatl proves *The Book of Mormon*.

The legend of Quetzalcoatl originated too late to have been the result of a coming of Jesus to the New World as described in *The Book of Mormon* — a fact Joseph could not have known (and Mormon literature usually ignores). There is additional material on this in Appendix B.

After conceiving the idea of having Jesus appear to the ancient inhabitants of the New World, Joseph needed to find an appropriate means for that appearance. He found it in Matthew 24:30, to which Ethan had referred:

> And then shall appear the sign of the Son of man in heaven: and then shall all the tribes of earth mourn, and they shall see the Son of man coming in the clouds of heaven with power and great glory.

We find in *The Book of Mormon*:

> And it came to pass..., they cast their eyes up again towards Heaven; and behold, they saw a man descending out of Heaven: and he was clothed in a white robe....
>
> And it came to pass that ... he spake unto the people, saying: Behold, I am Jesus Christ ... [*B.M.*, pp. 476–477; 3 Nephi 11:8–10].

One of the traditions about Quetzalcoatl was that the Great Spirit offered him a beverage. Joseph perhaps wanted to make this a point of evidence for his book, because it is paralleled in one of the first things that Jesus says after his appearance in the New World:

> ... and behold, ... I have drank out of that bitter cup which the Father hath given me ... [*B.M.*, p. 477; 3 Nephi 11:11].

Moreover, the beverage that Quetzalcoatl received from the Great Spirit gave him a "taste for travelling." So we find that Jesus also has places to go when it is time for him to leave:

> And verily, verily, I say unto you, That I have other sheep, which are not of this land.... I have received a commandment of the Father, That I shall go unto them, and that they shall hear my voice, and shall be numbered among my sheep ... [*B.M.*, p. 486; 3 Nephi 16:1–3].

One finds that Joseph's conception of Jesus has very little originality. Joseph's Jesus quotes with little change three chapters of Matthew, most of Isaiah 52, the whole of Isaiah 54, and the whole of Malachi 3 and 4, as well as portions of other chapters from the Bible — from the King James Version, of course. Apparently "Mormon" thought it was more important that the "gentiles" receive these portions of the Bible (which they already had) than some of the more enlightening pronouncements that Jesus was supposed to have given to the ancient inhabitants of America.

Joseph's Jesus also gives some prophecies about the restoration of the Hebrew people in the latter days, but these are merely a rehash of prophecies given earlier in the book. Probably in an attempt to pad out his material, Joseph had Jesus give several versions of the prophecies over the space of about five chapters. These prophecies were essentially derived from Ethan Smith's views. Here are some examples:

View of the Hebrews	*The Book of Mormon* (3 Nephi)
If God will restore them at last as his Israel, ... he surely must have provided a place for their safe keeping, as a distinct people, in some part of the world.... They must during that period, have been unknown to the Jews as Israelites ... [p. 73]. And we find a special branch of that ancient people ... having been lost from the knowledge of the known descendants of Abraham, the Jews [p. 71].	... [T]his is the land of your inheritance; and the Father hath given it unto you. — And not at any time hath the Father given me commandment that I should tell it unto your brethren at Jerusalem.... But, verily, I say unto you, that ... it is because of their iniquity, that they know not of you. And verily, ... the other tribes hath the Father separated from them; and it is because of their iniquity, that they know not of them [pp. 385–386; 3 Nephi 15:13–20].
The evidence discovered among the various tribes of Indians, of the truth of their Hebrew extraction ... seems almost like finding, in the ... wilds of America, various scraps of an ancient Hebrew Old Testament ... inscribed on some durable substance ... [p. 167, first edition]. [W]e are the people especially addressed, and called upon to restore them; or bring them to the knowledge of the gospel ... [pp. 229–230]. Assure them ... the Great Spirit ... now calls them by you to come and receive his grace by Christ..., and to whom the people must be gathered [p. 249]. God is going, in the last days, to make a ... recovery ... from the four quarters of the earth [p. 56].	And I command you that ye shall write these sayings after I am gone, that ... my people at Jerusalem ... may receive a knowledge of you ... and also of the other tribes which they know not of, that these sayings which ye shall write, shall be kept, and shall be manifested unto the Gentiles, that through the fulness of the Gentiles, the remnant of their seed ... may be brought in, or may be brought to a knowledge of me. ... And then will I gather them in from the four quarters of the earth ... [pp. 486–487; 3 Nephi 16:4–5].
Isai. xlix. "... Behold, these shall come from *far*; and lo, these from the north, and from the *west*, and	Ye remember that I spake unto you, and said that when the words of Isaiah should be fulfilled.... And

these from the land of Sinim...."
Such texts have a special allusion to
the lost tribes of the house of Israel
[p. 260]. When I have ... gathered
them ... then shall they know that I
am the Lord their God ... [p. 55].

then shall the remnants which shall
be scattered abroad upon the face of
the earth, be gathered in from the
east, and from the west, and from
the south, and from the north; and
they shall be brought to the knowledge of the Lord their God, who
hath redeemed them [p. 486; 3
Nephi 20:11-13].

Among the other things that Jesus "reveals" is a warning to the "Gentiles" (i.e., the American people): If they do not accept the "blessing" of *The
Book of Mormon*, then the "remnant" of Israel (the Indians) would overwhelm
them:

> ... then shall ye which are a remnant of the house of Jacob, go forth
> among them; ... and ye shall be among them, as a lion among the beasts of
> the forest, and as a young lion among the flocks of sheep, who if he goeth
> through, both treadeth down and teareth in peices ... [*B.M.*, p. 497; 3 Nephi
> 20:16].

But Jesus then proceeds to echo the following words of Ethan, as shown
here in parallel form.

View of the Hebrews

The Book of Mormon
(page 499; 3 Nephi 21:2-4).

Should it be ... that the aborigenes
of our continent are the descendants
of the ten tribes of Israel; ... we are
the people addressed ... [p. 229].
The writer might fill a chapter in
illustrating the wrongs which the
Indians have suffered from people in
our land ... [p. 228].

... verily, I say unto you, That when
these things ... shall be made known
unto the Gentiles, that they may
know concerning this people which
are a remnant of the house of Jacob,
and concerning this my people
which shall be scattered by them;

He also beholds in vision a great
nation arising there in the last days;
a land of freedom and religion [p.
237]. Ho thou nation of the last
days.... Were not your fathers sent
into that far distant world, not only
to be ... built up a great protecting
nation;

... for it is wisdom in the Father
that they should be established in
this land, and be set up as a free
people by the power of the Father,

but also to be the instruments of
gathering, or recovering the miserable remnants of my *outcasts* there,

that these things might come forth
from them unto a remnant of your
seed, that the covenant of the Father

in the last days? [pp. 247-248]
Look at the origin of those degraded
natives of your continent, and fly to
their relief. — Send them the heralds
of salvation. Send them the word,
the bread of life.... Unfold to them
their superlative *line* of the entail of
the covenant ... [p. 249].

may be fulfilled which he hath
covenanted with his people, O
house of Israel.

Jesus then continues with a promise for the gentiles:

> But if they will repent, and hearken unto my words, ... I will establish my
> church among them, and they shall ... be numbered among this the remnant
> of Jacob, unto whom I have given this land for their inheritance, and they
> shall assist my people, the remnant of Jacob; and also as many of the house
> of Israel as shall come, and they may build a city, which shall be called the
> New Jerusalem ... [*B.M.*, p. 501; 3 Nephi 21:22-23].

And there is one of the reasons Joseph modified Ethan's exhortation.
Instead of helping to return the remnant, the Indians, to Palestine, the American people would help build a new Jerusalem in America. Joseph apparently
wanted to establish a powerful church-state — with himself at the head, of
course — in his own country. He was well on the way towards accomplishing
this aim when he met an early death at the hands of a blood-thirsting mob.

Chapter 17

The Final Years

After he had Jesus depart from the New World, Joseph gave its inhabitants a period of peace and religion. This, he pronounced, was because the survivors of the cataclysms accepted the gospel and behaved in a righteous manner. But Joseph's characters were not left in their happy state for long. Again, Ethan Smith seems to have set the pattern:

> The reign of Quetzalcoatl was a golden age of the people of Anahuac. The earth brought forth without culture the most fruitful harvests. But this reign was not of long duration [V.H., p. 205].

The characters in Joseph's book have a "golden age" under the spiritual reign of Christ:

> And how blessed were they, for the Lord did bless them in all their doings; yea, even they were blessed and prospered, until an hundred and ten years had passed away: And the first generation from Christ had passed away, and there was no contention in all the land [B.M., p. 515; 4 Nephi 18].

After a few generations of living in harmony under the spiritual reign of Jesus, the ancient Americans again begin to backslide. What follows is familiar. The Nephites again forsake God, dwell on worldly things, form factions, and contend with one another. The Lamanites again rebel against the will of God and pursue their wars of hatred against the Nephites. God forsakes the greater portion of the New World inhabitants and abandons them to self-destruction. Ethan Smith had established the theme:

> They found the sentiment in their sacred oracles fulfilled, "The Lord is with you while ye be with him; but if ye forsake him, he will cast you off" [V.H., p. 14].

Mormon, one of the few of the Nephites who remain righteous, says:

> But behold, I was without hopes, for I knew the judgements of the Lord

which should come upon them; for they repented not of their iniquities, but did struggle for their lives, without calling upon the Being who created them [*B.M.*, p. 526; Mormon 5:2].

At this point, Joseph made a change in the story of the Nephites. Although earlier his character, Mormon, had said that the Gadianton bands were a major cause of the downfall of the Nephites, in his description of that downfall he made no mention of them. Instead, he had the Nephites meet their demise solely at the hands of the Lamanites. Ethan Smith had provided the scenario in his theory:

> But the savage tribes prevailed; and in process of time their savage jealousies and rage annihilated their more civilized brethren. And thus as a holy vindictive Providence would have it, and according to ancient denunciations, all were left in an *"outcast"* savage state [*V.H.*, p. 172].

According to the *Book of Mormon* chronology, the year was supposed to be about A.D. 385:

> And it came to pass that we did march forth to the land of Camorah, and we did pitch our tents round about the hill Camorah.... And it came to pass that my people ... did now behold the armies of the Lamanites a marching towards them; and with that awful fear of death which fills the breasts of all the wicked, did they await to receive them. And it came to pass that they came to battle against us, and every soul was filled with terror, because of the greatness of their numbers.... And it came to pass that my men were hewn down ... [*B.M.*, p. 529; Mormon 6:4–10].
>
> And now it came to pass that after the great and tremendous battle at Camorah, ... behold, the Lamanites have hunted my people, the Nephites, down from city to city, and from place to place, even until they are no more; and great has been their fall; yea, great and marvellous is the destruction of my people, the Nephites. And behold, it is the hand of the Lord which hath done it [*B.M.*, p. 532; Mormon 8:2–7].

The hill Camorah ("Cumorah" in current editions) was the hill in New York State from which Joseph purportedly obtained the gold plates of *The Book of Mormon*.

The saga was now complete. Having been annihilated by their more numerous savage brethren, the Nephites met the same end as Ethan's "civilized tribes."

The Book of Mormon was supposed to have been written by Mormon, one of the last of the Nephites, and one of the few who remained faithful to the Lord. Joseph seems to have derived the idea for Mormon from an individual who was mentioned in *View of the Hebrews*. Again, Ethan Smith was quoting Humboldt:

> He adds; "How is it possible to doubt that a part of the Mexican nation had arrived at a certain degree of cultivation, when we reflect on the care

with which their hieroglyphic books were composed, and kept; and when we recollect that a citizen of Tlascala in the midst of the tumults of war, took advantage of the facility offered him by our Roman alphabet, to write in his own language five large volumes on the history of a country, of which he deplores the subjection?" [V.H., p. 182].

Similarly, in *The Book of Mormon*, we find the Nephites keep records with care and that Mormon writes the history of his people in the midst of war as did the citizen of Tlascala. Like that citizen, Mormon also deplores what has happened to his people:

> ... I should not suffer the records which had been handed down by our fathers, which were sacred, to fall into the hands of the Lamanites, ... therefore I made this record out of the plates of Nephi, and hid up in the hill Camorah, all the records.... And it came to pass that they came to battle against us.... And my sould was rent with anguish, because of the slain of my people ... [B.M., pp. 529–530; Mormon 6:6–16].

The above passage from *View of the Hebrews* also helps us to understand why Joseph made certain claims about the writing of *The Book of Mormon*. Note that the citizen of Tlascala wrote his history in a foreign script because of its facility. We find much the same thing is in *The Book of Mormon*. The Nephites were Hebrew, and one would expect that their records should have been written in Hebrew. But instead they were written in "reformed Egyptian" because of *its* facility.

> And now behold, we have written this record according to our knowledge in the characters, which are called among us the reformed Egyptian, being handed down and altered by us, according to our manner of speech. And if our plates had been sufficiently large, we should have written in the Hebrew; but the Hebrew hath been altered by us also; and if we could have written in the Hebrew, behold, ye would have had none imperfection in our record [B.M., p. 538; Mormon 9:32–33].

In the first place, *The Book of Mormon* does not appear to have been written by someone trying to make the most of limited writing space, but instead by someone trying to produce a book of impressive proportions.

In the second place, Mormon stated that the plates were written in "reformed Egyptian" because the plates were not "sufficiently large" to be written in Hebrew. This does not seem reasonable. Egyptian hieroglyphics, even in the hieratic and demotic forms, are not very conservative of space.

In the third place, Mormon's ancestors were supposed to have been Hebrews and to have lived in Jerusalem. As Hebrews, their scriptures would have been written in their own "holy" script and not in that of the pagan and hated Egyptians. Joseph probably did not fully understand the animosity that existed between the two peoples. He even had the records that Lehi brought from Jerusalem written in the "language of the Egyptians."

In effect, Mormon appears to be saying that it is better to write an imperfect, wordy book in a pagan script, than a perfect, concise book in a holy script.

Actually, it is not hard to figure out why Joseph did not want to claim that the plates were written in Hebrew. If he did claim they were written in that language, someone might have challenged him to produce a sample of writing from them so that his translation could be independently confirmed. This would have placed him in an uncomfortable situation since at that time he did not know any Hebrew.

But why did he claim they were written in "reformed Egyptian"? Again, we can turn to Ethan Smith's book. Remember that the Vermont minister quoted Humboldt as stating:

> ... we reflect on the care with which their hieroglyphic books were com-
> posed, and kept ... [V.H., p. 182].

Here, the books of the natives of Mexico are described as written in hieroglyphics. On the next page, Ethan again quoted Humboldt:

> "The people, however, who traversed Mexico, left behind them traces of
> cultivation and civilization.... The Taultecs ... built cities, made roads,
> and constructed those great pyramids, which are yet admired.... They
> knew the use of hieroglyphic paintings ..." [V.H., p. 183].

In the above description, New World pyramids are mentioned, and shortly thereafter hieroglyphics. Earlier in his book, Ethan had quoted Humboldt as comparing these New World pyramids with those in Egypt:

> "They suffice to prove the great analogy between these brick monu-
> ments ... and the pyramids of Menschick Dashour, near Sackhara in Egypt"
> [V.H., p. 179].

Ethan Smith himself said:

> Various authors unite ... in stating the great similarity between those
> Mexican pyramids, and those to Egypt [V.H., p. 180].

And he gave his reason for such thinking:

> Israel knew the pyramids of Egypt. It is with great probability supposed,
> that during their servitude there, they aided in building those stupendous
> monuments ... [V.H., p. 180].

Since Ethan described the New World pyramids as being similar to those of Egypt, did Joseph assume that the New World hieroglyphics were likewise similar to those of Egypt? If not at this point, he would have had only to read a little further to find that Ethan had made just such an assumption:

> Whence could have been derived the knowledge of the accurate hiero-

glyphic paintings, which this most learned author exhibits as found among some of the Indians; unless they had learned them from people to whom the knowledge of hieroglyphics had been transmitted from Egypt, its original source? [*V.H.*, p. 185].

This surely would have interested Joseph. If he said that the plates were written in Hebrew, he could be challenged to provide a sample of writing from them. But he had another option. Because of the hieroglyphics that had been found in the New World, it could be said (or so he thought) that its natives had once been familiar with the Egyptian writing system. If he said that the plates were written in Egyptian, no one would be able to challenge his "divinely" given ability to "translate" them. In Joseph's time, Egyptian was a language about which very little was known.

At this point the Mormon prophet could have taken yet another idea from Ethan. Recall that the citizen of Tlascala "took advantage of the facility offered him by our Roman alphabet" to write his history. This might have indicated to Joseph that the hieroglyphics in their original form did not have the facility to be used for writing a history. If this was so, they would need to be modified or "reformed" toward that end. For Joseph's purpose, this would be even better. If it would be difficult for anyone to challenge his translation of ordinary Egyptian writing, it would be impossible for anyone to challenge his translation of a reformed version.

So Joseph claimed that the plates were written in reformed Egyptian. As we saw in Part One of this book, he even provided some characters which he said he had copied from the plates. Of course, nobody could translate the characters. Nobody, that is, except Joseph — or so he claimed. He could "translate" the characters, he said, because he had the "means."

Concerning this means, we find Moroni, Mormon's son, saying:

> But the Lord knoweth the things which we have written, and also that none other people knoweth our language; and because that none other people knoweth our language, therefore he hath prepared means for the interpretation thereof [*B.M.*, p. 538; Mormon 9:34].

In *The Book of Mormon*, the "means for the interpretation" were called the "interpreters." But Joseph, some time after he dictated *The Book of Mormon*, called them the "Urim and Thummim" — and those terms appear in *View of the Hebrews*:

> In resemblance of the Urim and Thummim, the American Archimagus wears a breastplate made of a white conch shell with two holes bored in the middle of it, through which he puts the ends of an otter skin strap, and fastens a buck horn white button to the outside of each, as if in imitation of the precious stones of the Urim [*V.H.*, p. 150].

Ethan Smith had stated that the Urim and Thummim were stones and that there were two of them. We find in *The Book of Mormon* that the "means" to interpret likewise consists of two stones:

> And it came to pass that the Lord said unto the brother of Jared, Be-
> hold, ... these two stones will I give unto thee, and ye shall seal them up
> also, with the things which ye shall write; ... wherefore I will cause in mine
> own due time that these stones shall magnify to the eyes of men, these
> things which ye shall write [Ether 3:21–24].

Joseph declared that he found the Urim and Thummim in the hill
Cumorah along with the gold plates:

> With the records was found a curious instrument which the ancients
> called "Urim and Thummim," which consisted of two transparent stones set
> in the rim of a bow fastened to a breast-plate.[1]

There is a problem here, though. As we saw in Part One of this book,
Joseph apparently did not apply the terms Urim and Thummim to the interpreters until about three years after *The Book of Mormon* was published. Why
this was so, we can only guess. Perhaps before he developed his book into a
new "revelation" from God, he merely picked up on the idea of a magical
device from Ethan's description of the breastplate of the Indian archimagus. At
the time, it appears he simply envisioned using this magical device (the spectacles) to translate the plates. Some time later, though, perhaps to give more of
a biblical basis for his claims, he called it the Urim and the Thummim.

In the Bible, the Urim and Thummim seem to have been used as lots to
determine the will of God (see, for example, 1 Samuel 14:41–42 of the Revised
Standard Version, which is more detailed than the King James Version).

(Ethan Smith's assumptions concerning the relationship of the Egyptian
hieroglyphics to those of the New World natives were fallacious. The Egyptian
writing system now poses few problems for Egyptologists, and in recent years
much progress has been made in translating the New World glyphs. The
characters in the two writing systems are quite dissimilar, and the languages
that they represent have no linguistic relationship with one another.)

Towards the end of the exhortation that he put into the mouth of the
prophet Isaiah, Ethan Smith voiced a plea that the American people take his
message to the Indians. This seems to have induced Joseph to have his character, Mormon, finish his portion of the Nephite record with a message that
has much the same aim as Ethan's plea. In *The Book of Mormon*, "Mormon" is
addressing the descendants of the Lamanites, but with the understanding that
the direct recipients of the message, the "Gentiles" (the American people),
would carry his message to those descendants, i.e., the Indians.

Although much of Ethan Smith's wording is changed in *The Book of
Mormon*, the basic sense of each parallel between these two messages remains.
Both Ethan and Mormon seek to inform the Indians of their heritage in the
Hebrew family. Both try to induce the Indians to return to God and to rise
above their lowly pursuits. Both seek to bring the Indians to a belief in Christ.
Both state that the gentiles received the scriptures from the Jews and are to
restore the scriptures to the Indians. Both note the works that God had done
for the forefathers of the Indians and both affirm that the Indians are of the
covenant.

Here are the parallels. The excerpts from Ethan Smith's plea are from page 249 and the top of page 250 in *View of the Hebrews*. To facilitate the comparisons, I have arranged them in the order in which the corresponding passages appear in *The Book of Mormon*. In the modern editions of *The Book of Mormon*, Mormon's message takes up the whole of Mormon 7. Significantly, almost every verse in that chapter has a counterpart in Ethan's plea. It is also significant that the Vermont minister based his appeal upon his interpretation of Isaiah 18.

View of the Hebrews (pages 249-250)	*The Book of Mormon* (pages 530-531; Mormon 7)
Go, thou nation highly distinguished in the last days; save the remnant of my people.	And now, I would speak somewhat unto the remnant of this people...,
Look at the origin of those degraded natives of your continent.... Teach them the story of their ancestors; ... of Abraham, Isaac and Jacob....	that they may know of the things of their fathers; yea, I speak unto you, ye remnant of the house of Israel; and this is the words which I speak: [7:1].
Teach them their ancient history....	Know ye that ye are of the house of Israel [7:2].
Tell them the time draws near, and they must now return to the God of their salvation.	Know ye that ye must come unto repentance, or ye cannot be saved [7:2].
Sublimate their views above the savage pursuits of the forests. Elevate them above the wilds of barbarism and death....	Knew ye that ye must lay down your weapons of war, and delight no more in the shedding of blood ... [7:4].
Teach them the story of their ancestors.... Tell them ... they must return to the God of their salvation ... and receive his grace by Christ....	Know ye that ye must come to the knowledge of your fathers, and repent of all your sins and iniquities, and believe in Jesus Christ ... [7:5].
	[Verses 6 and 7 are an expansion of of verse 5].
Send them the heralds of salvation. Send them the word, the bread of life. You received that book from the seed of Abraham. All your volume of salvation was written by	Therefore ... lay hold upon the Gospel of Christ, which shall ... come unto the Gentiles from the Jews, which record shall come from the Gentiles unto you [7:8].

the sons of Jacob. And by them it
was transferred from Jerusalem ...
to you.... Restore it to them....

Elevate them ... by showing them what has been done for their nation; and what is yet to be done by the God of their fathers in the line of his promise.	For behold, ... if ye believe this, ye will know concerning your fathers, and also the marvellous works which were wrought by the power of God among them; [7:9].
Teach them the story of their ancestors; ... of Abraham, Isaac and Jacob.... Unfold to them their superlative *line* of the entail of the covenant....	and ye will also know that ye are a remnant of the seed of Jacob; therefore ye are numbered among the people of the first covenenant ... [7:10].

With this, Joseph had almost completed his "history" of the Nephites. It concludes with Mormon's son, Moroni, expounding upon a few subjects. One of these was the prophecy that the Nephites would cry out from the dust in the latter days. In Chapter 11 we saw that Joseph likely derived this from *View of the Hebrews*.

Chapter 18

The Book of Ether

One of the last "books" within *The Book of Mormon* is "The Book of Ether." It purports to be the abbreviated history of a people who came to the New World shortly after the confusion of languages at the tower of Babel. The story of these people, called the Jaredites, follows much the same pattern as that of the descendants of Lehi. Soon after their arrival in the New World, the Jaredites divide into rival factions and exterminate themselves after several generations of nearly continuous warfare.

The story of the Jaredites adds little to the remainder of *The Book of Mormon*, and one might tend to give it little attention. Yet, it raises a few points that seem to indicate something of how *The Book of Mormon* developed. For one, it shows inconsistencies in its relationship with the rest of the book. These inconsistencies are such that they might indicate that Joseph made a major revision in the work as a whole but failed to resolve some of the resulting loose ends. One possibility is that the story of the Jaredites was an early version of the main part of the book that Joseph later revised to make into a separate story. This suggestion is strengthened by the fact that the story of the Jaredites exhibits patterns similar to those in the story of the Nephites.

Still, if "The Book of Ether" does represent an early version of *The Book of Mormon*, one might ask why Joseph did not discard it after making his revision. In answer to that, it is possible that Joseph wanted to satisfy the various schools of thought then being expressed about the ancient inhabitants of the New World. He probably felt that the Nephite story would achieve acceptance from those who believed the Indians to be of Hebrew descent, but he would also have been aware of the belief that the New World had been inhabited for a longer period than he described. Some of Joseph's contemporaries thought that another race of people had existed in the New World before the arrival of the Indians. Joseph might have read the following, which appeared in the *Palmyra Herald* of February 19, 1823:

> The Indians are reported the aborigines of North America; — but I doubt the truth of this proposition. The fortifications and the remains of antiquity in Ohio and elsewhere, clearly prove them to be the work of some other people than the Indians....
> The first settlers of North America were probably the Asiatics, the

201

descendants of Shem—Europe was settled by the children of Japeth. The Asiatics, at an early period, might easily have crossed the Pacific Ocean, and made settlements in North America.... The descendants of Japeth might afterwards cross the Atlantic, and subjugate the Asiatics, or drive them to South America.

... What wonderful catastrophe destroyed at once the first inhabitants, with the species of the mammoth, is beyond the researches of the best scholar and greatest antiquarian.

In one of Ethan Smith's sources, the *Archaeologia Americana*, Joseph might have found some more ideas along this same line. For example, in the preface to the 1820 volume is the following:

More recent examination has confirmed an opinion previously formed, that the works described in this publication were erected by a race of men widely different from any tribe of North American Indians known in modern times. It is also made probable, that this ancient people emigrated from Asia [and] made their first settlement around the waters of our northern lakes....[1]

In a letter in the preface of *Archaeologia Americana* shortly after the above, Caleb Atwater, author of the paper on the earthworks in Ohio, said of that region:

It is indeed nothing but one vast cemetary of the beings of past ages. Man and his works, the mammoth, [and] tropical animals ... are all found here reposing together in the same formation.[2]

Since some authorities did believe that an earlier race of men, unrelated to the Indians, had once existed in the New World, Joseph possibly felt it prudent to include in his book at least a brief account of such a people. Perhaps he thought that if he did so, fewer objections would be made to his latter-day revelation. Following this line of reasoning, he might have chosen to take his early version of *The Book of Mormon* story and revise it to create a "different race of men" from those in the main part of the book.

It is interesting to note that the foregoing excerpts from the *Palmyra Herald* and the *Archaeologia Americana* each mention mammoths, a species of elephant, in the same context as the ancient inhabitants of the New World. It might have been because of these mentions that Joseph gave his Jaredites elephants:

... and they also had horses, and asses, and there were elephants and cureloms and cumoms; all of which were useful unto man, and more especially the elephants, and cureloms, and cumoms [*B.M.*, p. 556; Ether 9:19].

As an aside, one wonders why the English words for "cureloms" and "cumoms" were excluded from Joseph's "gift" of translating the plates. What is most likely, is that Joseph was allowing for the unnamed "tropical animals" that Atwater had mentioned or other animal remains that might be found.

In any case, we have already seen how the comments by Atwater, above (and his paper, to which Ethan Smith referred), apparently caused Joseph to describe similar finds by Limhi's expedition.

Among the objects that Limhi's expedition supposedly brought back were twenty-four gold plates upon which was inscribed the story of the Jaredites. With the aid of the interpreters, King Mosiah eventually translates the plates — but therein lies an inconsistency. In the last chapter, we saw that God was described as having given the interpreters (the stones) to one of the ancient inhabitants of America with the instructions that they were to be hidden with the records of his people. The person said to have received them was the brother of Jared, the founder of the Jaredites. One could therefore assume that the "interpreters" were supposed to have been hidden with the gold plates containing the history of the Jaredites. Joseph, however, represented Mosiah as possessing the interpreters before the forty-three travelers discovered the land of the Jaredites. He had King Limhi ask the leader of Mosiah's expedition if there was anyone who could translate ancient languages. The answer was:

> ... I can assuredly tell thee, O king, of a man that can translate the records: for he hath wherewith that he can look, and translate all records that are of ancient date; and it is a gift from God. And the things are called interpreters ... [*B.M.*, pp. 172–173; Mosiah 8:13].

The man with the interpreters is Mosiah; but Joseph provided no account of how they came into his possession.

According to "The Book of Omni," a large stone with engravings on it had been found years before. Mosiah's grandfather, who was also named Mosiah, translated the engravings on the stone by the "gift and power of God" — but there is no mention of "interpreters." This stone also contains an account of the Jaredites.[3] Curiously, "The Book of Ether" makes no mention of the engraved stone. According to that text a man named Ether wrote the history of the Jaredites on the gold plates that Limhi's people found.

There is, then, a blank concerning the interpreters. God gives them to the brother of Jared at the time the Jaredites are brought to the New World. Then, some 2000 years later, the second Mosiah has them in his possession with no explanation of how he got them. An apologist might say that the interpreters were found with the engraved stone. But if that were so, then why wasn't it mentioned? Surely it would have been important enough. Moreover, why is there no mention of the engraved stone in "The Book of Ether"?

The answers to these questions might be found in the suggestion that Joseph made a major revision in his book. If the story of the Jaredites was Joseph's first version of *The Book of Mormon*, the Mormon prophet might have originally intended to claim to have found the interpreters along with the gold plates of the *Jaredite* record. However, when he revised his book and made the story of the Nephites the main part, Joseph neglected to make the modifications that would have been necessary to show how Mosiah had come by the interpreters. Moreover, the two different accounts of the finding of the

Jaredite records might also indicate that Joseph had experimented with various versions as he was revising. Perhaps the Mosiah who translated the record on the stone was from one version, while the Mosiah who translated the gold plates was from another.

There is yet more evidence of a major revision. In the first edition of *The Book of Mormon* we find:

> And now Limhi was again filled with joy, on learning from the mouth of Ammon that king Benjamin had a gift from God, whereby he could interpret such engravings ... [*B.M.*, p. 200].

Mosiah, not Benjamin, was king at that time. In the later editions of *The Book of Mormon* the passage (Mosiah 21:28) was corrected to read "Mosiah."

Significantly, the same error occurs in "The Book of Ether." There we find the following:

> And the Lord commanded the brother of Jared to ... write the things which he had seen: and they were forbidden to come unto the children of men, until after that he should be lifted up on the cross: and for this cause did king Benjamin keep them ... [*B.M.*, pp. 545–546].

In later editions, this passage (Ether 4:1) was corrected to read "Mosiah" instead of "Benjamin."

Such errors certainly might have occurred if Joseph had made a major revision. They are what might have resulted if he revised the relationship of "The Book of Ether" to the rest of *The Book of Mormon*, but failed to attend to all the connections and references.

For Joseph to revise "The Book of Ether" so that its characters were a "different race of men" from others in *The Book of Mormon*, required suitable new ideas. Some of these ideas seem to have come from *View of the Hebrews*. For example, Ethan Smith had claimed that the Indians had a legend similar to the story of the tower of Babel:

> They tell you of the confusion of languages once when people were building a great high place ... [*V.H.*, p. 77].

Since, according to the Bible, mankind spread out over the earth from the tower of Babel, Joseph apparently saw that this would be a good starting point for his Jaredites. Perhaps he thought that the Indian legend about the confusion of languages could be used as "evidence" for his story.

So Joseph had his Jaredites come from the tower of Babel:

> ... Jared came forth with his brothers and their families, with some others and their families, from the great tower, at the time the Lord confounded the language of the people ... [*B.M.*, p. 539; Ether 1:33].

Joseph also seems to have applied to the Jaredites some of Ethan's remarks concerning the Ten Tribes. For example, the Vermont minister had looked to the Apocrypha for information:

> The writer adds; "But they took this counsel among themselves, that they would leave the multitude of the heathen, and go forth into a further country, where never man dwelt; that they might there keep their statutes which they never kept (i.e. uniformly as they ought) in their own land...."
>
> ... God indeed determined to separate them from the rest of the idolatrous world, and banish them by themselves, in a land where no man dwelt ... [V.H., pp. 74–75].

And so we find in "The Book of Ether":

> And it came to pass that Jared spake again unto his brother, saying, Go and inquire of the Lord whether he will drive us out of the land, ... And who knoweth but the Lord will carry us forth into a land which is choice above all the earth. And if it so be, let us be faithful unto the Lord, that we may receive it for our inheritance [B.M., p. 540; Ether 1:38].
>
> And it came to pass that the Lord commanded them that they should go forth into the wilderness, yea, into that quarter where there never had man been [B.M., p. 541; Ether 2:5].

The ideas are similar. Ethan Smith's Ten Tribes took counsel that they might go to another land; so did the Jaredites. Ethan's Ten Tribes vowed to keep their (religious) statutes; Joseph's Jaredites vowed to be faithful to the Lord. According to Ethan, God sent the Ten Tribes into a land "where no man dwelt"; similarly, God sent the Jaredites into "that quarter where there never had man been."

Even the initial direction is the same in the two books. Ethan said:

> Their journey then, was to the north, or north-east [V.H., p. 75].

We find in "The Book of Ether":

> And it came to pass that Jared, and his brother, and their families ... went down into the valley which was northward ... [B.M., p. 540; Ether 2:1].

Jared and his followers eventually reach the ocean. To cross it, they build "barges" at the Lord's direction. These barges are to be completely enclosed, but Jared's brother asks for a means which would give light to the dark interiors. Interestingly enough, Joseph's preoccupation with stones comes to the fore at this point:

> ... O Lord, ... touch these stones, O Lord, with thy finger, and prepare them that they may shine forth in darkness; and they shall shine forth unto us in the vessels which we have prepared, that we may have light while we cross the sea.... And it came to pass that when the brother of Jared had said

these words, behold, the Lord stretched forth his hand and touched the stones one by one with his finger ... [*B.M.*, pp. 543–544; Ether 3:4–6].

Once the Jaredites arrive in the New World, the familiar pattern emerges. They divide into factions and wage war against each other. We also find another familiar note — as related by Moroni, who is telling the story of the Jaredites:

And it came to pass that they formed a secret combination, even as they of old; which combination is a most abominable and wicked above all, in the sight of God. ... And now I, Moroni, do not write of their oaths and combinations, for it hath been made known unto me that they are had among all people, and they are had among the Lamanites, and they have caused the destruction of this people of which I am now speaking, and also the destruction of the people of Nephi ... [*B.M.*, p. 554; Ether 8:18–21].

As noted previously, Mormon had said a little more than half way through *The Book of Mormon* that the "secret combinations" would prove to be a major cause of the downfall of the Nephites. We saw, however, that the secret combinations, or secret societies, were not mentioned when that downfall was finally described. In any case, although the secret societies have no part in the description of the annihilation of the Nephites, they do have one in the description of the annihilation of the Jaredites. This may be another indication that Joseph made a revision in his story.

The conclusion can only be that Joseph made a revision in his "history" of ancient America. As to the question of why he made such a revision, the answer might lie in the lost 116 pages. He needed to replace those pages somehow, but there is evidence that he did not do so until he finished the rest of the book.[4]

A little more than half way through *The Book of Mormon*, Joseph had Mormon state that the secret society of Gadianton was to cause the destruction of the people of Nephi. Yet when Joseph got around to describing this destruction he made no mention of any secret society. One might thus conclude that, some time before completing the book, Joseph decided to downplay the secret society insofar as the Nephites were concerned, instead making it the cause of the downfall of the Jaredites. When he was dictating "The Book of Ether," however, he left the loose end from the earlier version by having Moroni state that Gadianton's secret society was also the cause of the downfall of the Nephites.

Like the Nephites and the Lamanites who were supposed to come after them, the Jaredites have their final battle at the hill Cumorah:

And it came to pass that the army of Coriantumr did pitch their tents by the hill Ramah; and it was that same hill where my father Mormon did hide up the records unto the Lord, which were sacred [*B.M.*, p. 571; Ether 15:11].

There is here a small but possibly interesting coincidence. The hill Cumorah was in Manchester, New York, near the farm of Joseph's parents. In

Orsamus Turner's *History of the Pioneer Settlement of Phelps and Gorham's Purchase* which gives a history of the settlement of Western New York, we find the following about Manchester:

> Township 12, R.2, originally a part of Farmington, now Manchester; settlement commenced as early as 1793. Stephen Jared, Joel Phelps, and Joab Gillett, were the first settlers.[5]

One of the first settlers in Joseph's hometown of Manchester was a man by the name of Jared, while, according to *The Book of Mormon*, the first settlement in the New World was led by a man also named Jared. Furthermore, the *Book of Mormon* people who were called by this man's name met their demise in a battle on the land that was to become Manchester, New York. Did the name of the latter-day Jared find its way by association into Joseph Smith's latter-day revelation?

Part Four

Turmoil in Zion

Chapter 19

The Curse of Cain

Joseph Smith was hardly the sort to content himself with leadership of a tiny rag-tag religious sect. His imagination and his desire to improve his lot in life pushed him to seek greater heights. Inevitably, in seeking those heights he would look beyond the inauspicious beginnings of his church and develop rather grander plans for its future. His church could become a powerful, far-reaching, and wealthy organization — one that he seems to have viewed as ultimately providing the basis for a veritable empire with himself at the head.

Joseph took the first direct step towards this end when he sent Oliver Cowdery on a mission to the western frontier in the autumn of 1830. As well as having Oliver preach among the Indians and settlers, the Mormon prophet also gave him responsibility for finding a suitable location where the new "Zion" could be built. Like its namesake in the Old World, the American Zion would, as Joseph planned it, be looked upon as a "city of God" by his followers.

Oliver did not shirk his responsibility. After leaving Kirtland he and his party journeyed several hundred miles, eventually reaching western Missouri. There, in Jackson County, in the vicinity of Independence, Oliver felt that he had found an admirable location for Zion. On the banks of the Missouri River and near the fringes of civilization, Independence consisted of little more than a few scattered cabins; yet, despite its comparative isolation, the region was also a gateway to the western plains and held great promise of future development and prosperity. Moreover, Oliver saw another favorable portent for the establishment of the church there. Having been uprooted from their original lands, many of the Indian tribes of the eastern states were passing through the area in their enforced westward migration. To Oliver, the availability of the Indians would give the fledgling church an ample opportunity to work toward the fulfillment of some of the prophecies in *The Book of Mormon*.

While Oliver remained in Missouri, Parley Pratt returned to Kirtland in May of 1831. That June, influenced by Pratt's enthusiastic report, Joseph organized a party and set out to see "the promised land" for himself. On his arrival, he declared that it was indeed the new Zion, and he accordingly approved a site upon which Zion's temple would be built. That done, he went back to Kirtland at Sidney Rigdon's appeal. After his followers had suitably built up Zion, he planned to return and make it his headquarters.

210

The next two years saw a steady growth in the church. The missionary program that Joseph instituted brought in a steady stream of converts, many of whom the Mormon prophet sent on to the branch of the church in Missouri. With this influx of new members, Zion became a relatively large settlement. It even had its own newspaper, *The Evening and the Morning Star*, with William W. Phelps, one of the Mormon leaders, its editor.

The church in Zion, like the one in Kirtland, was organized in the form of a religious commune. With Sidney Rigdon's help, Joseph patterned this system along the lines of the primitive communism described in the New Testament. Upon joining, each convert turned over all his property and the results of his labor to the church and in turn received sufficient material and goods to support himself and his family. This system did not last long, since many of the converts were without means and the more well-to-do were hesitant about giving up their substance. By the spring of 1834, the resulting difficulties caused Joseph to dissolve the communal system and to rewrite the revelation instituting it. Instead of requiring the converts to turn over all of their property, the revised revelation incorporated tithing as a means of providing support for the church.

Among the converts were several very capable men who proved to be of considerable value to Joseph. One was Brigham Young, who came to Kirtland in the autumn of 1832. Young and Joseph became good friends and the newcomer was subsequently established as a power in the church.

Joseph had difficulties with some converts. In particular, he found that apostasy was a recurrent problem. Some of his followers became disillusioned when too many of his revelations failed to materialize or dealt purely with temporal subjects. Others became suspicious of his motives. Two sons of John Johnson, for example, apostatized and gave a rather graphic demonstration of their suspicions when they joined a mob that tarred and feathered Joseph. In addition to that perpetration, one of the Johnson boys wanted to take an even more drastic action. Believing that the Prophet had been intimate with his sister, Nancy, Eli Johnson had angrily demanded that Joseph be castrated as well as tarred and feathered.[1] Fortunately for Joseph, the doctor who was asked to perform the operation had second thoughts about it.

In the summer of 1833, Joseph ordered the construction of a temple in Kirtland. He also ordered the Missouri branch of the church to raise the money to build the temple in Zion. To back up his order, he received a revelation from the Lord which declared that the reward for the church in Zion would be great if the Saints there complied. But if they did not, the "Lord" promised:

> ... I will visit her according to all her works, with sore affliction, with pestilence, with plague, with sword, with vengence, with devouring fire. Nevertheless, let it be read this once to her ears, that I the Lord have accepted of her offerings; and if she sin no more none of these things shall come upon her....[2]

When Joseph received this revelation, he did not know that the original Jackson County settlers had already afflicted Zion with vengeance and with fire.

Almost from the beginning, the Mormon newcomers had been a source of irritation to the first settlers in Jackson County. That frontier breed liked things the way they were, while the Mormons seemed to be bent on change. One touchy subject, for example, concerned plans the Mormons had for converting the Indians and bringing them into the white man's society. In addition, the Mormons considered themselves a chosen people, and sometimes were not diplomatic towards their Missouri neighbors. Those neighbors angrily reported; "We are daily told ... that we, (the gentiles), of this country are to be cut off, and our lands appropriated by them for inheritances."[3]

What exacerbated the situation was that most of the Mormons were Northern immigrants to a slave state. The native Missourians did not want outsiders barging in and putting strange ideas about freedom into the heads of their slaves. In the same vein, the Missourians especially did not want free blacks coming into Missouri and showing the slaves that there was another life. When some Mormon converts who were free blacks tried to immigrate to Independence, they found that a Missouri law required them to have a certificate of citizenship from another state before they could enter Missouri.

To prevent any further difficulties in similar cases, William Phelps reprinted the law along with some carefully worded comments in *The Evening and the Morning Star* for July, 1833. The results were quite different from Phelps' expectations, for the original Jackson County settlers apparently took it as an invitation for free blacks to come to Missouri, with instructions on how to do so legally. Angered by this apparent contempt for their mores, the Missourians gathered together and demanded that the Mormons stop coming to their state and that those already there sell their property and leave. To accentuate their demands, they burned down the printing office of *The Evening and the Morning Star* and tarred and feathered two Mormon leaders. Under continued harassment from the Jackson County natives over the next few months, most of the Mormons abandoned Zion and settled across the Missouri River in neighboring Clay County.

It was Oliver Cowdery who brought Joseph news of the Missouri events. Shocked and crushed, Joseph realized the gravity of the situation but was powerless to do much about it. He vacillated for several months until, in February of 1834, he learned that the governor of Missouri, Daniel Dunklin, was going to take action on petitions from the Mormons requesting help in restoring them to their lands. Though the governor was willing to help them in regaining their lands, the Missouri Mormons realized that they were badly outnumbered by the original settlers and would be simply run off again. In desperation, they sent word to Joseph that they would be able to keep their recovered lands only if he could raise an army to protect them. The Mormon prophet found the idea of such a military operation appealing, so he set to work gathering the needed volunteers.

Despite prodding revelations from the Lord and despite considerable recruiting among the faithful, Joseph had little luck in getting his volunteers. After two months of recruiting he had only about two hundred men, a force he had to be satisfied with because the Missouri Mormons were becoming increasingly desperate. In May, he therefore started for Missouri with "Zion's Camp," as the army was called.

Zion's Camp turned out to be a failure. Hampered by poor planning, it was severely weakened when many of the men in its ranks were stricken with cholera. Furthermore, when the Jackson County Missourians heard of the coming of the army, they reacted with such vehemence that the governor abandoned his plan of restoring the Mormon lands. Realizing the hopelessness of a military victory, Joseph and his men stayed on the opposite side of the Missouri River while he and some other Mormon leaders negotiated with the Missourians. During the negotiations, the old settlers offered to buy all the Mormon lands at twice the appraised value. This offer, however, was unacceptable to the Mormons since it woul mean abandoning the site that God had decreed was to be the location of the temple in Zion.

With the failure of the negotiations, Joseph ordered his army to return to Kirtland. To salve the feelings of his men, he promised them that "within three years they should march to Jackson County and there should not be a dog to open his mouth against them." He also told the High Council of Zion that the redemption of Zion would occur by September 11, 1836.[4] All these promises came to naught, for Joseph was never able to reclaim Zion.

The failure of Zion's Camp must have been a severe blow to Joseph, not only from a military but also from a religious standpoint. He had committed himself and his church on the location of his "city of God" and he certainly must have felt that his credibility as a prophet of the Lord might very well suffer if he could not reclaim Zion. Yet a military solution was out of the question — for the time, at least. The only way to reclaim Zion reasonably soon, he must have thought, would be to placate the native Missourians by giving them no cause for further resentment. It followed, then, that he had to justify the institution of slavery to the members of his church since that institution was what had caused most of the trouble in the first place. It was perhaps with such an idea in mind that Joseph wrote the following and had it published in the *Messenger and Advocate* of April, 1836:

> I am aware, that many who profess to preach the gospel, complain against their brethren of the same faith, who reside in the south, and are ready to withdraw the hand of fellowship because they will not renounce the principle of slavery and raise their voice against everything of the kind. This must be a tender point, and one which should call forth the candid reflection of all men, and especially before they advance in an opposition calculated to lay waste the fair states of the South, and set loose, upon the world a community of people who might peradventure, overrun our country and violate the most sacred principles of human society, — chastity and virtue....
>
> After having expressed myself so freely upon the subject, I do not doubt but those who have been forward in raising their voice against the South, will cry out against me as being uncharitable, unfeeling and unkind — wholly unacquanted with the gospel of Christ. It is my privilege then, to name certain passages from the bible, and examine the teachings of the ancients upon the matter, as the fact is uncontrovertable, that the first mention we have of slavery is found in the holy bible, pronounced by a man who was perfect in his generation and walked with God. And so far from that prediction's being averse form the mind of God it remains as a

lasting monument of the decree of Jehovah, to the shame and confusion
of all who have cried out against the south, in consequence of their holding
the sons of Ham in servitude!

"And he said cursed *be* Canaan; a servant of servants shall he be unto
his brethren. And he said, Blessed *be* the Lord God of Shem; and Canaan
shall be his servant. — God shall enlarge Japheth, and he shall dwell in the
tents of Shem; and Canaan shall be his servant" — Gen. 8:25, 26, 27.

... I can say, that the curse is not yet taken off the sons of Canaan,
neither will be until it is affected by as great power as caused it to come....[5]

The idea of a curse against the lineage of Ham seems heavy on Joseph's
mind. It was at this time that Joseph was "translating" a work that, as it turned
out, also dealt with such a curse.

In the summer of 1835, a traveling showman by the name of Michael
Chandler had arrived in Kirtland with an exhibit of Egyptian mummies and
papyri. Wanting to have the papyri translated and finding that no scholar
could help him, Chandler had sought out Joseph because he had heard that the
Mormon prophet had a supernatural ability to translate ancient records. His
trip to Kirtland did not reveal to him the secrets he hoped to learn from the
papyri, but he did leave a town a little wealthier than when he arrived.

The reason for Chandler's pecuniary gain was possibly the result of a
longing that Joseph may have had to give substance to his claim that he had
the ability to translate unknown languages. Whereas he had declared that he
had translated *The Book of Mormon* from a set of ancient records, he had no
tangible relic that he could show to the world as proof of what he said. But
there, in Chandler's papyri, Joseph saw a set of genuine literary artifacts from
an ancient civilization. If they were his and if he "translated" them no one
could say they did not exist, as so many had said of the gold plates. Joseph
offered to buy them from Chandler. Apparently seeing a chance to turn a good
profit, the showman accepted Joseph's offer, but only if the mummies, of
which there were four, were included in the arrangement. Joseph acceded and
he bought two of the mummies while some of his followers bought the others.

After Joseph examined the papyri, he declared that one of them contained the writings of the biblical Joseph and that another contained the
writings of Abraham. He eventually "translated" the papyrus that he claimed
was the record of Abraham and published it in 1842 in the *Times and Seasons*.
It was subsequently included in *The Pearl of Great Price*, one of the Mormon
doctrinal works.

Among other things, *The Book of Abraham* provided the basis for the
so-called "Negro Doctrine" of the Utah church. According to the doctrine, the
Negro race had inherited the curse of Cain through Canaan and was therefore
denied the priesthood — that is, until recently when the church abrogated the
doctrine.* The Negro Doctrine was even more restrictive than might at first
seem apparent, for in the Mormon religion every adult male (indeed, every
Mormon boy upon reaching the age of twelve) is expected to become a

The Reorganized Church has never accepted either the Negro Doctrine or The Book of
Abraham; *what is said here applies to the Utah church.*

member of the priesthood. The Negro Doctrine therefore excluded Negroes from becoming fully participating members of the church. Needless to say, the civil rights movement of the nineteen-sixties and seventies brought attention to this fact and the church was frequently charged with being a racist organization.

But the real significance of *The Book of Abraham* is that an examination of it provides an interesting parallel to an examination of *The Book of Mormon*. Like *The Book of Mormon*, *The Book of Abraham* was the product of an eclectic mind and reflects the beliefs and literature of Joseph's own time (some parallels are shown in Appendix D). As we shall see, recent findings about *The Book of Abraham* provide revealing testimony about Joseph's ability as a translator of unknown languages.

The first part of *The Book of Abraham* is patterned after the account of Abraham's wanderings as given in Genesis 11 and 12. Some changes are apparent and some new material has been added. The new material about the Pharaoh of Egypt eventually came to be used by the church to deny blacks the priesthood.

> Now this king of Egypt was a descendant from the loins of Ham, and was a partaker of the blood of the Canaanites by birth. From this descent sprang all the Egyptians, and thus the blood of the Canaanites was preserved in the land. The land of Egypt being first discovered by a woman, who was the daughter of Ham, and the daughter of Egyptus, which in the Chaldean signifies Egypt, which signifies that which is forbidden. When the woman discovered the land it was under water, who afterward settled her sons on it; and thus, from Ham, sprang that race which preserved the curse in the land. Now the first government of Egypt was established by Pharaoh the eldest son of Egyptus, the daughter of Ham.... Noah, his father, ... cursed him pertaining to the priesthood.[6]

From his letter in the *Messenger and Advocate* of April, 1836, we have already seen that Joseph declared that the Negro race had inherited the curse of Canaan. Though the letter was written after Joseph had acquired the papyri, the belief was not new. It was frequently used by Southerners to justify slavery. In an attempt to amend the difficulties he had caused in Missouri, W.W. Phelps had even voiced the argument in the *Messenger and Advocate* before Joseph ever saw the papyri:

> Is or is it not apparent from reason and analogy as drawn from a careful reading of the scriptures, that God causes the saints, or people that fall away from his church to be cursed in time, with a *black skin*? Was or was not Cain, being marked, obliged to inherit the curse, he and his children, forever? And if so, as Ham, like other sons of God, might break the rule of God, by marrying out of the church, did or did he not have a Canannite wife, whereby some of the *black seed* was preserved through the flood, and his son, Canaan, after he laughed at his grandfather's nakedness, heired three curses; one from Cain for killing Abel; one from Ham for marrying a black wife, and one from Noah for ridiculing what God had respect for?[7]

Joseph therefore appears to have used the common belief that the descendants of Ham had inherited a curse through Ham's wife. He did add the idea that the curse involved a denial of the right of the priesthood to those descendants. Though *The Book of Abraham* does not state that the descendants of Ham were cursed with a black skin, in his letter in the *Messenger and Advocate*, quoted earlier, Joseph did unequivocally make the Negro a descendant of Ham. That line of reasoning falls apart on an examination of the facts; it also shows a conformity to a questionable belief of his own time; i.e., that the curse of Cain was a black skin, and that the curse was carried on by Ham's wife.

The Bible does not state that Cain was cursed with a black skin nor does it state that Ham's wife was a descendant of Cain. In any case, the curse of Cain was that he would be a vagabond (which hardly fits the settled Egyptians). Moreover, whatever it was, the mark that God placed on Cain, rather than a curse, was a warning that the bearer was not to be harmed. Of the peoples whom the Bible names as the descendants of Ham — various people of Palestine, Arabia, and northern Africa — none belonged to the Negro race. The most notable of these people were the Egyptians, the Canaanites, and the Babylonians; all of whom belonged to a branch of the Caucasian race. The idea that Ham was associated with blackness might have derived from a name that the ancient Egyptians applied to their land. They called their land Khemet, which means "the black land." However, the blackness referred to here was not of skin color, but of the rich Nile mud laid down during the annual floods.

That raises another point. Joseph claimed that the word "Egypt" was derived from a Chaldean word, "Egyptus." But the ancient Egyptians never called their land "Egypt," nor is that word of Chaldean origin. It was derived from *Aegyptus*, a comparatively late Greek word for the land of the Nile. Joseph might have picked up the name "Egyptus" from the Jewish historian, Flavius Josephus, as that was the name of an individual in one of his works.

The *Book of Abraham* passage that denys the priesthood to the descendants of Ham also causes problems because of the inconsistent ways the way the church had applied it. Until recently, the Utah church denied the priesthood to blacks, even though it cannot be shown that blacks are descended from either Ham or from the ancient Egyptians. Yet the church had no prohibition against giving the priesthood to modern Egyptian converts, though most modern Egyptians are descended from the ancient Egyptians upon whom the curse was supposedly placed.

The Bible also raises a problem for the doctrine. According to the "revelations" in *The Book of Abraham*, Abraham knew that all those of Egyptian blood were cursed regarding the priesthood. According to Genesis 16, however, Abraham took his wife's Egyptian handmaiden as a second wife because his first wife bore him no children. And therein lies the problem. It would hardly seem reasonable for Abraham to have taken for a wife a woman whose children for him would be denied the priesthood. Until the abrogation of the Negro Doctrine, present-day Mormons were against mixed marriages for that very reason. This brings up another inconsistency. The Arabs are supposed to be the descendants of Ishmael, a son whom the Egyptian woman bore for Abraham. Because of that, the Arabs should have been denied the priesthood.

Yet the present-day Mormon church had no regulation against giving the priesthood to any Arab convert.

Furthermore, Joseph appears to have had no intention of promulgating any such thing as the Negro Doctrine. There is no record of his making any statement restricting the Negro from entering the priesthood, nor from participating in any church ceremony. In 1836, Joseph even signed the Elder's license of a black man by the name of Elijah Abel.[8]

It is possible that Joseph did not intend the priesthood that he referred to in *The Book of Abraham* to be the Aaronic or the Melchizedic priesthoods, which are the important ceremonial priesthoods in the Mormon Church; rather, he might have had the "Patriarchal" priesthood in mind. That has been proposed by H. Michael Marquardt, who points out that in the passage in question it is not God who cursed Ham pertaining to the prieshood, but the Patriarch, Noah.[9]

If this is all so, how did the Negro Doctrine arise? One must look to Brigham Young, for it was apparently he who first applied the *Book of Abraham* passage to blacks. Here is what Young had to say on the matter in 1852:

> ... the Lord told Cain that he should not receive the blessings of the priesthood nor his seed, until the last posterity of Able had received the priesthood, until the redemption of the earth. If there never was a prophet, or apostle of Jesus Christ spoke it before, I tell you, this people that are commonly called Negroes are the children of old Cain ... they cannot bear rule in the priesthood ... until the times of the restitution shall come....[10]

Elsewhere, Young stated:

> When all the other children of Adam have had the privilege of receiving the Priesthood, and of coming into the kingdom of God, and of being redeemed from the four quarters of the earth, and have received their resurrection from the dead, then it will be time enough to remove the curse from Cain and his posterity....[11]

Young also stated that if the church should give the priesthood to blacks before the rest of mankind had received it, the church itself would receive the curse:

> ... suppose we ... declare that it is right to mingle our seed, with the black race of Cain, that they shall come in with us and be pertakers of all the blessings God has given to us. On that very day, and hour we should do so, the priesthood is taken from this Church and kingdom and God leaves us to our fate ... — we should receive the curse which has been placed upon the seed of Cain....[12]

Thus, with Brigham Young's words, the Negro Doctrine was established in the church.

During his lifetime, Joseph never received a challenge to his "translation" of the Egyptian papyri. The science of Egyptology was then in its infancy and a great many people, including Joseph, no doubt, did not know that

Champollion had recently learned how to decipher Egyptian hieroglyphics. Furthermore, even though the writing system was no longer a mystery, learning how to read it took much painstaking study and it was to be several years before the science of Egyptology would have many savants. For these reasons, when Joseph's papyri eventually disappeared, reportedly in the great Chicago fire of 1871, they had not yet been examined first hand by experts.

But Joseph had unknowingly provided a means by which Egyptologists would eventually be able to make at least a partial investigation of his claims as a translator of ancient records. The three facsimiles that he included in *The Book of Abraham* provided enough of a glimpse of what some parts of the papyri looked like to raise serious doubts about the validity of Joseph's translation — at least to non-Mormons.

The first real challenge to Joseph's translation of the papyri came in 1861 when a French traveler named Jules Remy published a book entitled *A Journey to Great Salt Lake City*. This book included the verdict of a French Egyptologist named Theodule Deveria who had examined *The Book of Abraham* facsimiles published in the *Pearl of Great Price*. According to Deveria, the facsimiles represented ordinary Egyptian funeral documents. That explanation, of course, was completely at odds with Joseph's.

An even more important challenge came in 1912, when the Rev. F.S. Spalding, the Episcopal Bishop of Utah, published a book entitled *Joseph Smith, Jr., as a Translator*. Spalding had submitted the facsimiles to several Egyptian scholars and had included their comments in his book. The consensus of these Egyptologists was that the facsimiles represented common Egyptian funeral documents and Joseph's explanations of them were fallacious. James H. Breasted, of the Haskell Oriental Museum in the University of Chicago, for example, stated:

> To sum up then, these three facsimiles of Egyptian documents in the "Pearl of Great Price" depict the most common objects in the mortuary religion of Egypt. Joseph Smith's interpretations of them as part of a unique revelation through Abraham, therefore, very clearly demonstrates that he was totally unacquainted with the significance of these documents and absolutely ignorant of the simplest facts of Egyptian writing and civilization.[13]

Through the years, similar comments were made by other Egyptologists who examined the facsimiles, but the Mormons generally refused to accept these pronouncements. They held that no valid judgment of Joseph's ability as a translator could be made without the original papyri. Thus the matter became a stalemate.

But it was not to remain that way. In the 1960s, some new evidence was found which provided a striking confirmation of the explanations that the Egyptologists had previously given for the facsimiles. The first piece of this evidence was a manuscript which was brought to light after having been hidden away in the church archives for well over a century. The manuscript was entitled "Grammar and Aphabet [sic] of the Egyptian Language" and it turned out to be Joseph's working paper for the translation of the papyri.

As significant as it was, the bringing to light of Joseph's "Grammar and Aphabet" was spectacularly overshadowed when some of Joseph's original papyri were discovered in the New York Metropolitan Museum of Art in 1966. In November of 1967, the Museum transferred the eleven pieces of papyri to the church authorities in Salt Lake City. Several Egyptologists have subsequently studied the papyri and Joseph's Egyptian "Grammar" and have confirmed that Joseph's "translation" of the papyri was without foundation and that the papyri are Egyptian funeral documents having nothing to do with the biblical Abraham. (Appendix D has further information about the papyri and Joseph's "Grammar and Aphabet.")

In June of 1978, the leaders of the Utah church announced the abrogation of the Negro Doctrine. They are not admitting that they made this change because of what has been learned about Joseph's translation of *The Book of Abraham*; nor are they acknowledging that translation was incorrect. According to the "revelation" that the president of the church said he had received, and in apparent disregard for Brigham Young's prophecy, the time had come for the Negro to gain full admittance to the ceremonies, blessings, and offices of the church.

Chapter 20

Steppingstones to Disaster

When the average person thinks of Mormonism in its historical context, what usually comes to mind is polygamy. That topic predominates in the popular view primarily because of the notoriety it generated in the days of Brigham Young and his followers in Utah. During that period, the editors of newspapers and periodicals back East and in Europe saw in the institution of plural marriage the makings of a scandal they could sensationalize. The resultant publicity persisted for several decades, often in the form of lurid articles and whimsical cartoons. The notoriety lessened in the late 1800s when church leaders bowed to secular political pressure and disallowed "God ordained" polygamy so that Utah could become a state. Nevertheless, polygamy has ever since been a part of the folklore of Mormonism.

Although Mormon polygamy became best known under Brigham Young in Utah, perhaps its greatest significance, and irony, is that it indirectly led to the death of the founder of the religion.

Joseph was a very earthy sort despite the religious facade he presented to the world. An occasional rough and ready wrestling match with a willing convert gave him an enjoyable diversion, while it shocked the sensibilities of the more spiritually inclined. Despite his "word of wisdom," Joseph liked an occasional nip at the bottle – also to the discomfort of some of his followers.[1] But Joseph was at his earthiest when his eye fell upon a comely woman. Although he apparently cared deeply for his wife, Emma, he could not content himself with one woman, especially after his marriage lost its bloom. Consequently, if his position as God's earthly representative facilitated an approach to the more desirable of the young women in his flock, Joseph was not one to look the other way. The resulting escapades got him into trouble more than once. (We have already noted that Joseph narrowly escaped castration when an irate Eli Johnson felt that the Prophet had been too intimate with his sister, Nancy.)

Joseph would tell the women that he had had a revelation from God declaring that it was lawful for a man to have more than one wife. He did not put this revelation into writing, however, until 1843, and until then only a select few of his close followers knew of it. For several years, Joseph even tried to keep his first wife, Emma, in the dark about his experiments in plural marriage – not always with success.

Though Joseph claimed that he had received the revelation from God, his marital forays did not meet with approval from some of his coreligionists. For example, his relationship with a certain young woman named Fanny Alger, who in 1835 apparently became one of the first of his plural wives, led to a falling out with Oliver Cowdery. In a letter to his brother, Oliver stated the following:

> When he was there we had some conversation in which in every instance I did not fail to affim that what I said was strictly true. A dirty, nasty, filthy affair of his and Fanny Alger's was talked over in which I strictly declared that I had never deviated from the truth on the matter, and as I supposed was admitted by himself.[2]

If Oliver and Joseph had collaborated in the authoring of *The Book of Mormon*, Oliver might have felt that Joseph was endangering what they had worked together for. Be that as it may, the friction between Oliver and Joseph in the Fanny Alger matter was partly the cause of Oliver's excommunication from the church in 1838.

Of those in the church hierarchy who knew about the new revelation, Oliver appears to have been in the minority in condemning it. Some of the other church members also took advantage of "the Principle." The inevitable result was that the rumor mills began turning in the neighboring gentile communities. Eventually, the General Assembly of the church felt the need to make a resolution on the matter; published in the August, 1835, issue of the *Latter-Day-Saints' Messenger and Advocate*, it read in part as follows:

> Inasmuch as this church of Christ has been reproached with the crime of fornication and polygamy: we declare that we believe, that one man should have one wife: and one woman, but one husband, except in case of death when either is at liberty to marry again.[3]

Joseph was not in Kirtland when the General Assembly adopted the resolution. Moreover, there is a tradition that Oliver Cowdery had composed the resolution, which perhaps shows that he was trying to take advantage of Joseph's absence.

Despite the publication of the resolution, the rumors concerning polygamy would not die down, and in the May, 1837, issue of the *Messenger and Advocate* the Quorum of Seventies made the following statement:

> ... we will have no fellowship whatever with any Elder belonging to the quorum of the seventies who is guilty of polygamy or any offense of the kind....[4]

Nevertheless, the members of the inner circle who knew about the revelation continued to practice polygamy in secret. At this time, most of the rank and file had little idea of what was going on.

Joseph was also engaging in other activities in Kirtland which were to cause him great trouble. For one thing, in trying to expand his church he had amassed an enormous pile of debts. For another, he was involved in the volatile land speculation gripping the state of Ohio at the time. And, finally, he desperately needed hard cash to buy land in northern Missouri where he planned to resettle those followers of his who had been ousted from Jackson county.

In order to meet the mounting need for cash, Joseph and some of his associates organized the Kirtland Safety Society Bank. By printing bank notes under the name of the bank, Joseph hoped to pay off his debts and place his church on a sound financial footing. Despite his claims of solvency, the bank had little hard currency to back up the large number of notes he planned to issue. Moreover, the Ohio State Legislature, out to stop the spread of just such banks (of which Joseph's was but one), rejected the Mormon prophet's application for incorporation. But Joseph was not about to let the State Legislature frustrate his plans. By overstamping the name on the bank notes, he changed the Kirtland Safety Society Bank into the Kirtland Safety Society Anti-Banking Company. Hoping to get around the law by this means, he proceeded to issue the bank notes as if they were legal tender.

The "Anti-Banking Company" commenced operation on the second of January, 1837, with Sidney Rigdon as president and Joseph as cashier. It did not take long for the recipients of the notes to realize how worthless they were, and the resultant demands for redemption put a strain on the meager resources of the Anti-Banking Company. Less than a month after the opening of the company, Joseph was forced to stop redeeming the notes for cash. Rigdon and Joseph then resigned their positions and F.G. Williams and Warren Parrish replaced them. However, these men could do little to straighten things out.

Becoming disillusioned with the Prophet, Parrish himself resigned and began telling stories about Joseph's monetary manipulations. Apparently to save face, Joseph later accused Parrish of stealing $25,000 from the bank, but Parrish did not take over as cashier until Joseph stopped redeeming the bank notes because of a lack of funds. As Fawn Brodie has pointed out, if that amount of cash were on hand, Joseph would not have had to stop redeeming the bank notes so soon. Furthermore, Parrish remained in the Kirtland area for some time after leaving the bank but was never arrested for the so-called "theft." In any case, the bank's ledger book shows that the bank received only $20,000 for the issuance of its stock. This money was paid in over several months, some of it after Parrish resigned, so the bank likely had nowhere near that amount in its vault at one time.[5]

In the following months, Joseph was inundated with lawsuits over the failure of the Safety Society. He was also charged with operating an illegal bank, for which he was found guilty and fined $1000 plus costs. On top of this, he was still in debt. To add to his problems, his monetary machinations had caused some serious repercussions within his church. Many of his followers had lost money because of the failure of the Safety Society, and, while most were willing to forgive the financial indiscretions of their prophet, others were not. Complaints against Joseph subsequently mounted, not only over the failure of the bank, but also over other matters.

Apparently hoping that his absence would lessen some of the resentment towards him, and probably wanting to avoid some of the law suits pending against him as well, Joseph went on a mission to Canada, after which he made a visit to the Missouri Mormons. Upon his return to Kirtland, though, he found the situation no better. Considering him to be a fallen prophet, the dissidents had even organized a new church. Finally, in January of 1838, when he heard a report of a warrant for his arrest on charges of banking fraud, he abandoned Kirtland to the dissenters and headed back to Missouri with those followers who remained faithful.

Having outlived their welcome in Clay County, most of the Missouri "Saints" had moved to the relatively uninhabited northern regions of the state, where they established the town of Far West. Joseph's arrival there was greeted with joy by the Missouri Mormons, for whom the events in far away Kirtland were of little consequence.

Making Far West the new headquarters of the church, Joseph had great plans for this Mormon community. But he found that dissenters within his church were still to continue troubling him. It was at this time that Oliver Cowdery, John Whitmer, and David Whitmer were excommunicated. Even so, Joseph found that he was not rid of them as they had made claim to a large amount of land in the surrounding area that was also claimed by the church. Cowdery and the Whitmers refused to relinquish their claims and their intransigence prompted Sidney Rigdon to have more than eighty church elders sign a letter demanding that the three men and their families leave the county within three days. In turn, the three, determined to keep what they deemed to be rightfully theirs, went to Clay County to get a lawyer. On their return, they came upon their families on the road, frightened and dispossessed. The Danites, a secret society of "enforcers" within the church, had driven them from their homes with only the clothes on their backs and their blankets. Moreover, the Danites had sent them on their way with the threat that any dissenter who returned to Far West would suffer death.

Joseph was also finding that earlier problems in Missouri were returning to haunt him. Their sufferings in Jackson County had caused the Saints to build up a great deal of resentment against the native Missourians. Some of the Mormons advocated war in order to right the wrongs and to convince the Missourians of the truth of the Mormon religion. At a ceremony for the laying of the cornerstone for a new temple in Far West, Sidney Rigdon did not help matters any when he gave a speech advocating that no quarter be given in any future hostilities.

The native Missourians took umbrage at such talk, and anti-Mormon feelings began building up again. Once more, skirmishes erupted between the Mormons and the gentiles. The hostilities increased in intensity and each side began raiding the settlements of the other, plundering, burning and killing. The new governor of Missouri, Lilburn Boggs, was rabidly anti-Mormon, and did nothing to lessen the tensions. At one point (effectively giving his answer to Rigdon's speech), he even issued an order that the Mormons be either exterminated or driven from the state. The culmination of the conflict came in late October of 1838 when Joseph had several other Mormon leaders were arrested, brought to Independence, and then to Richmond. There the prophet was charged with treason, among other things, on the basis of claims by Mormon apostates that he was seeking to overthrow the state government, drive out or exterminate the native Missourians, and establish a theocracy with himself at the head. In the ensuing months, the Mormon settlers were forced to leave Missouri by crossing the Mississippi River into Illinois. There, Brigham Young took over as temporary head of the church in Joseph's absence.

In April of 1839, after spending the intervening time in the Liberty jail, Joseph and the others were put on trial. Their lawyer argued for a change of venue, which, because most of the anti-Mormon feeling had by then died down, was readily granted. As Joseph and his fellow prisoners were being taken to the county of choice, bribes assured their easy escape, and they joined their comrades in Illinois.

Initially welcomed by the citizens of Illinois, the Mormons created a new town from the wilderness and called it Nauvoo. Over the next few years the Saints increased in numbers to several thousand, partially because of a successful missionary campaign in England.

As the number of Mormons grew, they became a political force to be reckoned with, and Joseph took full advantage of the situation. By instructing his followers which candidate to vote for he was able to curry favor from the elected officials. As a result, Joseph was able to get the State Legislature to grant charters for the city of Nauvoo, which made the Mormon community virtually a legal entity unto itself and called for the organization of a militia to be named the Nauvoo Legion.

Inevitably, the political machinations, the charters, the Legion, and the separateness of the Mormons came to be resented in nearby communities. This resentment was heightened by the definite military character of the Legion, in which Joseph assumed the rank of Lieutenant General. The Mormons' neighbors became further upset when they heard rumors that Joseph intended to use the Legion to wage war on Missouri. Further friction developed when the Mormon leaders frustrated legal processes of surrounding communities and the state government. For example: if a sheriff came from a gentile town with an arrest warrant for a Mormon, the Nauvoo city council would issue a writ of habeas corpus and have the individual tried in the Mormon town. Inevitably, the individual would be found not guilty. Thus the stage was set for what was to follow.

With the loss of Zion in Missouri, Joseph was forced to enlarge the concept of the City of God. From then on, Zion was not to be simply one town, but wherever the faithful were gathered. Colonies thoughout America and the world would become "stakes" supporting and enlargening the tent of Zion that was the church.

Nevertheless, the church needed a headquarters and Joseph worked toward making Nauvoo a special monument to the glory of the religion he founded. Since he had lost the temple in Kirtland and the others were never completed, he ordered construction to begin on a new one in Nauvoo.

It was also in Nauvoo that Joseph further developed his system of plural marriage, though still in secret. Joseph was not content with simply initiating single women into the mysteries of "spiritual wifery." He also brought into his circle of wives several married women, some of whom entered the new covenant of plural marriage with the consent of their husbands, and some without their husbands' knowledge. By the time of his death, Joseph had conducted at least forty-five women through his "spiritual marriage" ceremony.[6]

Nevertheless, Joseph was not without resistance to his marital experiments. His own brother, Don Carlos, was quite puritanical in his outlook. Ebenezer Robinson, then coeditor of the *Times and Seasons* with Don Carlos, reported the following:

> In the spring of 1841, the doctrine of "spiritual wives" began to be secretly talked about.... Don Carlos Smith said: Any man who will teach and practice the doctrine of spiritual wifery will go to hell. I don't care if it is my brother Joseph.[7]

The rumors about polygamy now became widespread, and they were fed by substantial testimony. Brigham Young had tried to convince a young English girl, Martha Brotherton, to become one of his plural wives. Joseph himself argued on Young's behalf, and added, "If he turns you off, I will take you on." Martha, however, was having neither of them. She reported the matter to her parents, who angrily spread the story around Nauvoo before leaving for St. Louis. Martha later published her account in the St. Louis *Bulletin* of July 15, 1842.[8]

In another instance, Joseph approached Nancy Rigdon, the daughter of Sidney Rigdon, with a proposal for her initiation into the new order of marriage, but Nancy rejected him. The following day, Joseph dictated a letter to her in which he tried to convince her of the rightness of his actions. Nancy showed the letter to her father and told him of what had transpired. Rigdon, who had been kept in the dark about the new order of marriage, angrily confronted Joseph. After denying everything at first, Joseph finally claimed that he was merely testing Nancy's virtue. Nevertheless, it took Sidney Rigdon some time to reconcile himself with his prophet. In the meantime, the story of Joseph's failure with Nancy became ordinary Nauvoo gossip.

The rumors finally came to a head with the revelations of John C. Bennett. Bennett was an opportunist, who, shortly after his arrival in Nauvoo, had endeared himself to the Mormon prophet. Bennett gained a high standing in the town and was one of the few entrusted with the secrets of the new order of marriage. He thereupon seduced several women by citing Joseph's authority, but without going through the ceremony that Joseph required for the sake of decorum. Moreover, Bennett, who claimed to be a doctor, had promised to perform abortions to cover up the results of "spiritual wifery."

As word of his actions spread Bennett became embroiled in an ugly scandal, into which Joseph's name was inevitably brought. The scandal reached such a level that Joseph had no recourse but to excommunicate Bennett in order to be rid of him. Bennett responded to this slight by having a series of letters published in the Springfield *Sangamo Journal*. The letters, which began in the July 8, 1842, issue of the paper, were later published by Bennett in his book, *The History of the Saints; or, an Expose of Joe Smith and Mormonism*. Bennett detailed a whole list of reprehensible activities that he claimed were going on in the Mormon community, the most sensational of which were the polygamous marriages. Bennett, however, had so whitewashed and falsified

his own activities that the Mormon leaders were able to convince the
unknowing of their followers that everything Bennett said was basely false.

Though he had publicly disavowed the practice of polygamy, Joseph
found it increasingly hard to keep his matrimonial escapades from Emma, his
first wife. As she gradually learned that her suspicions were well founded,
Emma became increasingly bitter and Joseph could see no other way out
except to try to convert her to the new order of marriage. After he argued his
case, she gave grudging acceptance for a while, but then became implacably
opposed to the system of plural wives. Finally, on July 12, 1843, apparently at
the prodding of his brother, Hyrum, Joseph committed the revelation to
paper. The revelation, which eventually became Section 132 of the *Doctrine
and Covenants*, read in part as follows:

> Verily, thus saith the Lord unto you my servant Joseph.... I, the Lord,
> justified my servants Abraham, Isaac and Jacob; as also Moses, David and
> Solomon, my servants, as touching the principle and doctrine of their
> having many wives and concubines....
>
> God commanded Abraham, and Sarah gave Hagar to Abraham to wife.
> And why did she do it? Because this was the law....
>
> David also received many wives and concubines, as also Solomon and
> Moses my servants....
>
> David's wives and concubines were given unto him of me....
>
> And let mine handmaid, Emma Smith, receive all those that have been
> given my servant Joseph....
>
> But if she will not abide this commandment, she shall be destroyed,
> saith the Lord; for I am the Lord thy God, and I will destroy her, if she
> abide not in my law.[9]

Joseph's tactic was unsuccessful. When he gave Emma a copy of the
revelation she burned it in the fireplace. From then on, Joseph apparently
never broached the subject of plural wives to her again. Although according to
Joseph the Lord had promised that he would destroy Emma if she did not
accept Joseph's other wives, she lived to the age of seventy-five, while Joseph
would die in less than a year.

Having written out this revelation, Joseph had committed himself to establishing it as a doctrine of the church. In August, he had Hyrum read it to the
High Council. Dividing into opposing groups, the higher levels of the church
hierarchy subsequently became embroiled in the question of plural marraige,
while most of the rank and file were still unaware that polygamy was being
practiced by a select number of their leaders.

Although Joseph apparently always held an expansive view of himself,
that view seems to have become more exalted and visionary through the years.
Seeing himself as God's representative on earth, it appears that he felt he could
do whatever he wished.

Joseph showed an increasing disregard for the secular powers of the
state. The laws of man were not to frustrate the will of the Lord and Joseph
acted accordingly. Frequently harassed by officers of the law coming from
Missouri seeking his extradition, he had the Nauvoo City Council pass a law

requiring their arrest and trial. If they were found guilty of attempting to arrest the Mormon prophet, they were to be sentenced to life imprisonment in the Nauvoo city jail. They could not even be pardoned by the governor of Illinois without the permission of the mayor of Nauvoo — who happened to be Joseph.

But that was only a small example of the power that Joseph seemed determined to wield. In December of 1843, he wrote a petition that he intended to submit to Congress. This called for Congress to restore the Mormon lands in Missouri to the rightful owners; to make Nauvoo an independent federal territory; and to give the mayor of Nauvoo (Joseph) the power of calling up the United States Army. Joseph "prophecied" that if Congress did not heed the petition they would "be broken up as a government and God shall damn them, and there shall be nothing left of them — not even a grease spot!"[10]

In February of 1844, Joseph ordered some of his men to investigate Oregon and California as places to which his people could migrate and where he could establish his own government. He also took steps to negotiate a treaty that would give the Saints an enormous block of the Southwest, including large parts of what are now Texas, New Mexico, Oklahoma, Colorado, and Wyoming.

In March of 1844, Joseph took what was surely the most self-aggrandizing step of all. It was then that he secretly organized the "Council of Fifty" to rule over the empire that he planned to create. One of the first acts of this council was to ordain and crown Joseph as king. Aware of the furor it would cause, Joseph tired to keep his kingship a secret.[11] In the meantime, he satisfied his aspirations by taking steps to run for the presidency of the United States.

Understandably, a good many of the gentiles in the surrounding communities were perturbed about Joseph's contempt for the law and graspings toward political power. The inevitable result was that the threat of renewed violence against the Mormons at the hands of the gentiles became greater and greater. But for the moment, the greatest threat to Joseph came from within the church. Joseph's Second Counselor, William Law, was the head of the antipolygamy minority in the church hierarchy. For some time he had been saddened by the introduction of what he felt was an ungodly doctrine. Now he became more outspoken in his condemnation of the new system of marriage. The split between the two men became even wider when Law learned that his own wife had been approached by Joseph in an attempt to recruit her into his circle of plural wives.

But polygamy was not the only factor that caused Law to turn from Joseph. He was also deeply concerned about what he felt were the many other unseemly activities of the Mormon prophet. In April of 1844, he and several other like thinkers gathered together to discuss the situation. Joseph received word of the meeting and ordered one of the dissidents, Robert D. Foster, to appear before the High Council on April 20 to hear charges against him. When Joseph then learned that Foster had gathered forty-one witnesses to speak on his behalf, he called a secret meeting of the council on the eighteenth and had Foster, William Law, and some others excommunicated.

Still believing in the message of the Mormon religion, but convinced that Joseph was a fallen prophet, Law decided to organize his own reformed church. Along with others of like mind, he proceeded on this course and brought in a printing press to publish a newspaper that was to be called the *Nauvoo Expositor*.

The first and only issue of the paper came out on June 7, 1844. Through the years, Mormon writers have applied various epithets to this paper; for example, that it was "filled with vile and malicious slanders against the Prophet and the leading citizens of Nauvoo."[12] In actuality, Law was quite reserved in his editorial policy for the *Expositor*. He simply set forth the facts about what was going on in the church.

Law first stated his faith in the Mormon religion:

> We all verily believe and many of us know of a surety that the religion of the Latter Day Saints, as originally taught by Joseph Smith, which is contained in the Old and New Testaments, Book of Covenants, and Book of Mormon, is verily true; and that the pure principles set forth in those books, are immutable and eternal principles of Heaven, and speaks a language which, when spoken in truth and virtue, sinks into the heart of every honest man....

Law then proceeded to give a lengthy rebuke to the Mormon leaders for their indiscretions, charging that "many items of doctrine as now taught, some of which, however, are taught secretly, and denied openly" were "heretical and damnable in their influence."

He followed this by a description of what lay in store for young foreign women who, convinced of the truth of the Mormon gospel, made their way to America in order to live in the city of the Saints:

> But what is taught them on their arrival at this place? ... They are requested to meet brother Joseph, or some of the twelve, at some insulated point...; they meet him, expecting to receive through him a blessing, and ... in the stead thereof, they are told, after having been sworn in one of the most solemn manners, to never divulge what is revealed to them, with a penalty of death attached, that God Almighty has revealed it to him, that she should be his (Joseph's) Spiritual wife; for it was right anciently, and God will tolerate it again....

After having made the charge of polygamy against the Mormon leaders, Law brought up the following:

> The next important item which presents itself for our consideration, is the attempt at Political power and influence.... We believe it is inconsistent, and not in accordance with the christian religion. We do not believe that God ever raised up a Prophet to christianize a world by political schemes and intrigue....

Law next condemned the "doctrine of many Gods," a polytheistic concept that Joseph had brought into the church through *The Book of Abraham*. This he followed with the charge that the excommunication of himself and the others was illegal:

> On Thursday evening, the 18th of April, there was a council called, unknown to the Church, which tried, condemned and cut off brothers Wm. Law, Wilson Law, and sister law, (Wm's wife) brother R.D. Foster, and one brother Smith with whom we are unacquainted; which we contend is contrary to the book of Doctrine and Covenants, for our law condemnest no man until he is heard....

Then came a list of resolutions which affirmed the complaints and charges, and which sought to have them resolved. To the charges already mentioned, Law added charges that Joseph had engaged in financial and land manipulations for his own profit.

Finally, after giving examples of how it had been abused, Law condemned the Nauvoo Charter and advocated its repeal:

> Now we ask if the executive and judicial authorities deem it politic to submit to such a state of things in similar cases? Can, and will the constituted authorities of the federal government be quiescent under such circumstances, and allow the paramount laws of the Union to be set at defiance, and rendered negatory by the action of a court having no more co-ordinate powers, with a common justice of the peace? If such an order of things is allowed to exist, there is every reason to believe that Nauvoo will become a sink of refuge for every offender who can carry in spoils enough to buy protection. The people of the State of Illinois will, consequently, see the necessity of repealing the Charter of Nauvoo, when such abuses are practiced under it....

With the publication of the *Expositor*, Joseph's situation became precarious. He simply could not allow the charges from the dissident press to continue. Yet he knew he had little choice of action. If he brought suit against the dissidents in an attempt to silence them legally, they would be able to present witnesses to prove all too many of the charges. The resultant revelations would tear his church apart.

The Prophet apparently saw only one answer to the problem. He called together the members of the city council and had them declare the newspaper a public nuisance. Joseph, as mayor, then ordered the City Marshal and some members of the Nauvoo Legion to wreck the press of the *Expositor*, to pi the type, and to burn every copy of the paper that they could find.

It appears to have been Joseph's greatest mistake. Law and his followers fled to the neighboring non-Mormon towns of Carthage and Warsaw where they told in detail what had happened. The anti-Mormons in the area seized upon the opportunity and soon the call to avenge the destruction of the *Expositor* was echoing all the way back to Nauvoo.

On June 11th, one of Law's followers got the justice of the peace in Carthage to issue a warrant charging Joseph Smith and the members of the city council with riot in the destruction of the *Expositor*. When he was served with the warrant, Joseph had the Nauvoo Municipal Court issue a writ of habeas corpus and try himself and the others on the charges, with the result, of course, that they were found innocent.

When Thomas Ford, the governor of Illinois, heard of the destruction of the *Expositor*, he went to Carthage and sent word to Joseph that he and the others were to submit themselves to the Carthage constable for arrest. Fearing the consequences if they complied, Joseph and his brother, Hyrum, fled across the Mississippi into Iowa. Shortly thereafter, Emma sent a plea to Joseph to return. Swayed by arguments that Nauvoo would be destroyed if he did not do so, Joseph and his brother made their way back to Illinois and turned themselves in.

At the preliminary hearing, all those who were involved in the destruction of the *Expositor* were released on bail, except for Joseph and Hyrum. The two brothers were placed in a room on the second story of the Carthage jail along with two other Mormons who chose to remain with their leaders. The prisoners were allowed several visitors and one of them managed to smuggle in a single shot pistol and a revolver.

On June 27, a lynch mob attacked the jail. As part of the mob rushed up the stairs, the prisoners braced themselves against the door of their room in a desperate attempt to hold back their attackers. Gunfire echoed in the hall and the door panels splintered under the impact of the balls, forcing the four men inside to jump back. The mob then pushed the door open and fired into the room. One of the balls hit its mark and Hyrum fell dead. In a rage, Joseph sprang toward the doorway and emptied his revolver at the attackers. Then, throwing aside the useless weapon, he turned and ran to the window. There, he was struck by a bullet coming from the doorway. He leaned against the window frame for a moment, then fell through the window and landed on the ground beside a well. To make sure he was dead, some of those who had remained outside fired a volley of bullets into his motionless body.

Epilogue

After Joseph's death, the Mormon community broke into two major and several minor groups. Under the leadership of Brigham Young, the largest of these groups made its way to Utah. There, in relative isolation from the gentile world, Young built his branch of the church into a frontier empire and openly proclaimed the revelation on plural marriage. Over the years, the Utah church continued to grow and to send missionaries throughout the world. Known as the Church of Jesus Christ of Latter-day Saints, it presently numbers over five million members, including college presidents and professors, senators and congressmen, lawyers and journalists. It probably has the greatest amount of wealth per member of any church in the United States, and it certainly is one of the fastest growing.

The next largest group eventually came under the leadership of Joseph's son, Joseph Smith III. Known as the Reorganized Church of Jesus Christ of Latter Day Saints, this group established its headquarters in Independence, Missouri. Under the influence of Emma Smith initially, the Reorganized Church holds that Joseph never advocated polygamy. It also considers Joseph to have passed the leadership of the church on to his son and Brigham Young to have been a usurper. The Reorganized Church now has over 200,000 members.

Though the Utah church officially discontinued the practice of polygamy in 1890 so that Utah could become a state, several splinter sects formed to remain true to the revelation on plural marriage. It has been estimated that some thirty thousand people in the United States and Mexico now live in polygamous family relationships based upon that revelation.

Appendices

Appendix A

The "Wood Scrape"

The "Wood Scrape" is the name given to an affair that occurred around the year 1800 in the vicinity of Middletown (now Middletown Springs), Vermont. Its possible relationship to the origin of Mormonism has not been generally recognized in the literature but it has some interesting aspects that deserve to be made better known. In it one finds moneydigging, a religious cult that seems to have been a kind of primitive precursor to Mormonism, and an individual who appears to have had a connection with Oliver Cowdery's father and with Joseph Smith and his father.

An early account of the Wood Scrape can be found in *The Vermont American* of May 7, 1828, in an article entitled "The Rodsmen." However, the most detailed source of information on the Wood Scrape is in *The History of Middletown, Vermont*, which was published in Poultney in the year 1867 by its author, Barnes Frisbie. Frisbie had done much research on the Wood Scrape by interviewing several elderly people who had lived in the area when the affair occurred. The results of his research appear on pages 43–64 of his book, from which we shall take some pertinent extracts. He begins:

> About the year 1800, occurred ... the "Wood scrape," a term not expressive perhaps of what is meant by it, but a name which has always been given by the people to a strange affair in which the Wood families, then living here, were the leading actors. It was a religious delusion, and at the time was the cause of great excitement here, and of a good deal of notoriety in this part of the state....

Frisbie proceeded to describe some difficulties that one Nathaniel Wood was having with the Congregational Church in the year 1789. As a result of these difficulties, Wood was excommunicated from the church, but this merely encouraged him to gather followers and set up meetings of his own:

> His peculiar religious doctrines will appear as we proceed. Suffice it to say, for the present, that he regarded himself and his followers as modern Israelites or Jews, under the special care of Providence; that the Almighty would not only specially interpose on their behalf, but would visit their enemies, the Gentiles (all outsiders), with his wrath and vengeance.

In this condition we find Nathaniel Wood and his followers when the hazel rod was introduced, and the moneydigging commenced; but the Woods did not commence it, that honor belongs to a man of another name; but they were in a condition to adopt this man's rod notions, which they did with great effect in their work of deluding the people.

It is at this point that we get the first connection with Mormonism and with a mysterious individual named Winchell:

> A man by the name of Winchell, as he called himself when he came here, was the first man who used the hazel rod. From what we have learned of him, he was, undoubtedly, an expert villain. He sought to accomplish his purposes by working upon the hopes and fears of individuals, and by a kind of sorcery, which he performed with great skill. The time he came here I cannot give, but it was, undoubtedly, sometime in the year 1799. He was a fugitive from justice from Orange county, Vermont, where he had been engaged in counterfeiting. He first went to a Mr. Cowdry's, in Wells, who then lived in that town, near the line between Wells and Middletown.... Cowdry was the father of Oliver Cowdry, the noted Mormon, who claimed to have been one of the witnesses to Joe Smith's revelations, and to have written the book of Mormon, as it was deciphered by Smith from the golden plates. Winchell, I have been told, was a friend of Cowdry's, but this I cannot be positive, they were intimate afterwards; but Winchell staid at Cowdry's some little time, keeping himself concealed, and it is the opinion of some with whom I have conversed that he commenced his operations of digging for money in Wells, but I have been unable to determine as to that....

Both Wells and Middletown are adjacent to Poultney, where Ethan Smith published his *View of the Hebrews* some years after these events. At the time of the Wood Scrape, the Cowdery family lived in Wells and it was there that Oliver Cowdery was born. The Cowdery family afterwards moved to Middletown, then to Poultney after the death of Oliver's mother and the remarriage of his father.[1]

To continue with Frisbie's narrative:

> Winchell next turns up in Middletown, at Ezekiel Perry's, in the fall or forepart of the winter of 1799.... Here he staid all winter, keeping himself from the public eye, practicing his arts of deception as he had opportunity to do so, without attracting too much attention; and here he began to use the hazel rod.... He would tell fortunes, and do other wondrous things with it. In the spring of 1800, feeling, perhaps, a little more secure from those who desired to find him and bring him to justice, he gathered quite a number about him from the immediate neighborhood, and told them there was money buried in that region, and with his rod he could find it; and told them if they would assist in digging it out, and forever keep it a secret, he would give them a part of the money. This they agreed to, and were all eager to commence digging.

Frisbie went on to describe one of Winchell's money digging operations. In this instance, Winchell had led the money diggers to a place where he said a treasure was buried. After they had dug for a while, the money diggers came to the level in which the treasure was supposed to be, but it "moved" away from them under the power of a "divinity" who guarded it. Frisbie then stated that "Winchell managed to get what little change these men had while they were digging, probably under the expectation, on their part, that they all would soon have money enough."

Frisbie continued:

> Soon after this affair Winchell made the acquaintance of the Woods.... Jabez D. Perry ... gave me this account of Winchell.... I have found ... witnesses, to sustain Mr. Perry....
>
> As I have said, ... they then commenced using the Hazel rod and digging for money, which was in the spring or early in the summer of 1800.... Winchell was with them, but it was not generally known, he being concealed — the Woods were the ostensible managers.... Jacob Wood, ... one of the sons of Nathaniel, was the leader in the use of the rod. "Priest Wood," his father, seemed to throw his whole soul into the rod delusion, but *his* use of the rod was mostly as a medium of revelation....

Frisbie gave some descriptions of the money digging activities of the Woods and then stated:

> The rods-men, (such as they were called,) became so infatuated as to give up nearly their whole time to this scheme. All the believers became wild fanatics. Besides those in Middletown in this movement, there were several families in the south-east part of Poultney...; also several families in the north-east part of Wells.... These were also digging for money, and were known as belonging to the rod-men.

Further on, Frisbie continued:

> I shall now introduce the letter to which I have alluded. It is from Rev. Laban Clark, D.D., a man over ninety years old, as I am informed, who resides in Middletown, Connecticut....
>
> "In the year 1801, I traveled in the north part of Vermont, and in lower Canada.... In December I went to Poultney for my first appointment there.... I went thence to Middletown, where I preached in the house of Mr. Done.... He told me that many people in America were, unknown to themselves, Jews, and these divining rods would designate who they were. I asked him to let me see one of the rods.... I asked him to learn by it whether I were a Jew. The rod immediately pointed towards me...."

On his next trip to Poultney, Clark met Done again and heard "Priest Wood" give a lecture. He continued with the following:

> "After eight weeks I had another appointment to preach in the same place.

When I inquired of Bro. Done respecting the rods.... He told me the rods were able invisibly to remove gold and silver. He said they had found that there was a vast quantity of it in the earth, and the rods could collect it to one place.... I then asked him if they had any person who understood refining gold? He said they had one who understood it perfectly well. "Where is he," I said. "He keeps himself secreted in the woods," he replied. I asked his name, and he told me it was Wingate. I remembered at once; it was the name of a man who was detected about two years before in Bradford, Vt., in milling counterfeit dollars. My father having been selectman of the town at the time, I had known the case well.... I said to Bro. Done "I fear there is counterfeiting going on, and if you are not careful I fear you will be drawn into it....

"I ascertained afterwards that the eldest son of Priest Wood, called Capt. Wood, was the principal religious mover in sight while Wingate kept concealed. Wood was Wingate's outside agent, and got up the religious excitement to aid the scheme."

Clark added the following in a postscript:

"... By what I learned of them [the Woods], I have no doubt that their movement gave origin to the Mormons, the vilest sch[e]me of villainy and corruption that has ever cursed the country...."

After presenting Clark's letter, Frisbie gave the following conclusion:

... This Wingate and Winchell the name given me by Perry and others, are beyond question, one and the same person. What we get from Mr. Clark's letter, so far as it goes, of Wingate is the same I obtained from Perry of Winchell in 1862 — that is, that he was detected in counterfeiting, in Bradford, Vt., came here and was with the Woods in their movement, and kept himself concealed in the time. Perry told me that he changed his name after he came, to avoid discovery by the officers of justice....

Mr. Clark in his letter says: "By what I have heard of them (the Woods,) I have no doubt that the movement gave origin to the Mormons." ... But Mr. Clark is not the only man who has given the same opinion. I first got it from Jabez D. Perry in 1862.... After receiving the foregoing letter from Mr. Clark, I wrote him again asking him for the facts to sustain his opinion. In reply, he ... says that about 1840 he heard two Mormon preachers in Connecticut, who held to the "same or much the same doctrines which the Woods did in Middletown...."

That the system of religion promulgated by Nathaniel Wood, and adopted by his followers in 1800, was the same, or "much the same," as the Mormons adopted on the start, is beyond question.... [Frisbie then proceeded to point out some basic, but not very remarkable, similarities between the religious doctrines of the Woods and those of the Mormons.]

The question now arises, how came the Mormons by these religious doctrines of the Woods? ... This same Winchell or Wingate, the counterfeiter, who introduced the rod here, and was with the Woods in their operations, afterwards went to Palmyra, New York, the house of Joe Smith, when he (Smith) set on foot the Mormon scheme. What time Winchell went to Palmyra, I am unable to say, but he was there early enough to get Joe Smith's father to digging for money, some years before Joe was old enough to engage in the business—but Joe was at it as soon as he was old enough, and if his biographers can be relied on, he followed it until about the time he pretended to have found the gold bible. I have been told that Joe Smith's father resided in Poultney at the time of the Wood movement here, and that he was in on it, and one of the leading rods-men. Of this I cannot speak positively, for the want of satisfactory evidence, but that he was a rods-man under the tuition of this counterfeiter after he went to Palmyra has been proven to my satisfaction, at least. I have said before that Oliver Cowdry's father was in the "Wood Scrape." He then lived in Wells, afterwards in Middletown, after that went to Palmyra, and there we find these men with the counterfeiter, Winchell, searching for money over the hills and mountains with a hazel rod, and their sons Joe and Oliver, as soon as they were old enough, were in the same business....

It appears from some of the Mormon histories, that the Mormon organization first consisted of the Smith family, Oliver Cowdery and Martin Harris, the name of the counterfeiter, whether it was Wingate or Winchell, does not appear in any account that I have seen, unless he had by this time assumed another name, but he had been at Palmyra for some years and went with them from Palmyra to Ohio. He was not a man who could endure the gaze of the public, but his work was done in secret; that he was at Palmyra, acted the part I have indicated, and went off with the Mormons when they left Palmyra, has been fully proven by men who were here during the Wood affair, and afterwards removed to Palmyra, and knew him both places.

Note that Frisbie said he could not find the name of Wingate or Winchell in any of the material on the Mormons that he had researched. Nevertheless, his statements concerning Wingate/Winchell find a remarkable fit in the statements about Walters the "juggler" (see Chapter 3) that Obadiah Dogberry published in the Palmyra *Reflector*. If Frisbie had known about Dogberry's accounts of Walters, he surely would have mentioned them and would have reached the conclusion that Walters and Wingate/Winchell were the same person. His making no mention of Dogberry's articles would indicate that he had independent sources of information concerning Wingate/Winchell's activities in Palmyra—if Walters was indeed Wingate/Winchell.

At this point, it seems to be a reasonable conclusion that Walters was Wingate/Winchell. If he were not, it would be quite remarkable that two different "jugglers" would have played such similar roles in association with the Smith family and the Palmyra moneydiggers in the years before Joseph Smith had his revelations.

Appendix B

The Book of Mormon
and Ancient America

To the church that he founded, Joseph Smith left a certain viewpoint concerning the original inhabitants of the New World. According to this viewpoint, as it is given in *The Book of Mormon*, the ancient Americans were descended from a relatively small number of Hebrews who traveled to the New World from Palestine shortly after 600 B.C. This viewpoint further holds that the ancient Americans were divided into two groups: one consisting of the Nephites, who built a great civilization, and the other, of the Lamanites, who exterminated the Nephites and became the American Indians.

In this book, we have attempted to show that Joseph Smith synthesized *The Book of Mormon* from the literature and ideas of his own time. A conclusion to be drawn from this is that *The Book of Mormon* is not the factual history it purports to be. The validity of that conclusion is supported by the fact that no present-day non–Mormon archaeologist or anthropologist considers the history presented in *The Book of Mormon* to be tenable.

There is a branch of Mormon literature whose writers aver that an impressive amount of archaeological evidence exists proving *The Book of Mormon* to be an authentic history of ancient America. To those not schooled in New World archaeology and anthropology, the adductions presented by these authors can be quite convincing, so much so that if we ignored them, some readers might be confused or skeptical about the arguments of this book. Let us look at some relevant facts about the ancient Americans and examine some of the arguments made by some Mormon writers.

Published works purporting to prove *The Book of Mormon* true often demonstrate the two weaknesses of very liberal interpretation of archaeological findings and misrepresentation or apparent ignorance of relevant facts. For example, some Mormon writers have claimed that it was not known in Joseph Smith's time that elephants had once existed in the New World. These writers use that claim to justify saying that Joseph must have been divinely inspired because he described the Jaredites as having had elephants.[1] Previously in this book two different sources that had been published before *The Book of Mormon* were quoted concerning the finding of the remains of mammoths, an extinct species of elephant, in America. In 1820, we saw that one of these, *Archaeologia Americana* had the following about some finds in Ohio:

> It is indeed nothing but one vast cemetary of the beings of past ages. Man
> and his works, the mammoth, [and] tropical animals ... are all found here
> reposing together in the same formation.[2]

In the Hudson Valley near Newburgh, New York, in 1801, Charles
Wilson Peale dug up the fossil skeletons of two mastodons, an extinct species
of elephant.[3] The fossil specimens were found in the same state in which Joseph
Smith, having taken up residence, would publish *The Book of Mormon* 29
years later. The facts say that Joseph need not have been divinely inspired to
have known that elephants once existed in the Americas.

Mormon writers have also pointed to the fossil remains of horses as
evidence for the validity of *The Book of Mormon*. However, Joseph might
well have reasoned that if something as exotic as elephants had once existed in
ancient America, then why not something as mundane as horses. It is also
possible that Joseph did not know there were no horses in America when the
white man first arrived. If that were the case, he might simply have described
his ancient Americans as having had horses without giving it a second
thought. In any case, horses became extinct in the New World by about 10,000
years ago — long before *The Book of Mormon* peoples were supposed to have
arrived. It is also interesting to note that Solomon Spalding, who died in 1816,
described the pre-Columbian natives as having had horses as well as domesticated mammoths in one of his novels (see Appendix C).

Mormon writers have put forth many arguments about pre-Columbian
Indian culture and traditions in the effort to prove *The Book of Mormon* true.
They have been assisted in this by some of the same material that Joseph
originally used to develop his ideas. The legend of Quetzalcoatl is a case
in point. Mormon writers frequently point to the legend as proof that Jesus
came to the New World as described in *The Book of Mormon*. But we have
seen how Joseph may well have used the speculations about Quetzalcoatl
in the literature of his own time to conceive of the idea of having Jesus appear
to the ancient Americans.

Quetzalcoatl could not have been Jesus. There were, in fact, two
Quetzalcoatls. The first one lived in the latter part of the tenth century, almost
a thousand years after Jesus (according to *The Book of Mormon*) was in the
New World. The reign of this Quetzalcoatl is fairly well known and hardly fits
the description of Jesus in the New World that is given in Joseph Smith's latter-
day revelation. The second Quetzalcoatl lived some two hundred years after
the first, taking the name of his predecessor as his own.[4] Various writers have
claimed that Quetzalcoatl was everything from a Chinese Buddhist to a
Viking.

Most of those who try to prove the truth of *The Book of Mormon* refer
to the ruins of ancient cities in Central America and say that Joseph Smith could
not have known about them. For example, the late Joseph Fielding Smith made
the following statement:

> The Book of Mormon was published in 1830 and it was not until 1841
> that Stephens published his work on archaeological findings pertaining to
> what we now know as the Ancient Americas. This is the first writing we

have on this subject in the present day. This proves without a doubt that Joseph Smith knew nothing about the area inhabited by the people of the Book of Mormon before he translated the plates.[5]

There are several problems with that statement. In the first place, as we have already seen, several books describing many of the ruins found in Central and South America had been published before the first publication of *The Book of Mormon.* Ethan Smith's *View of the Hebrews,* the works of Humboldt, and the *Archaeologia Americana* are relevant examples. The claim that Stephens' work was the "first writing we have on this subject in the present day" is therefore untrue. Stephens' book, *Incidents of Travel in Central America, Chiapas, and Yucatan,* did describe new findings pertaining to the Maya, but Joseph Fielding Smith expanded these findings out of proportion to make it appear that prior to Stephens' book *nothing* was known about the "Ancient Americas."

Secondly, Mormon scholars cannot agree on the locations of the places mentioned in *The Book of Mormon.* Some hold that the geography of *The Book of Mormon* encompasses a relatively small area in Central America. Others believe that it includes both North and South America. Some state that the Isthmus of Panama is the "narrow neck of land" mentioned in *The Book of Mormon,* while others believe it is the Isthmus of Tehuantepec. Neither the Utah church nor the Reorganized Church takes an official stand on where The *Book of Mormon* cities were supposed to have been.

In light of that, why did Joseph Fielding Smith specifically mention Stephens' work, and why did he state that the area described by Stephens was that inhabited by the *Book of Mormon* peoples?

We can find an answer to that by going back to Joseph Smith. It would appear that Fielding Smith was influenced by statements that Joseph had made in 1842 in the *Times and Seasons.* Joseph had acquired a copy of Stephens' book and had quoted from it. Following the quote, he made this statement:

> The foregoing extract has been made to assist the Latter-Day Saints in establishing the Book of Mormon as a revelation from God.... Let us turn our subject ... to the Book of Mormon, where these wonderful ruins of *Palenque* are among the mighty works of the Nephites: — and the mystery is solved.[6]

When Joseph read Stephens' book, he apparently saw an opportunity to identify the new finds at Palenque with the "mighty works of the Nephites" and so provide new evidence for *The Book of Mormon.* He probably thought he could safely do this because he had not given detailed descriptions of any of the cities in *The Book of Mormon,* and because his geographical references were sufficiently vague so that almost any Central American ruined city could be claimed to correspond to any of those mentioned in *The Book of Mormon.* It would thus appear that Joseph Fielding Smith simply took Joseph at his word on this identification.

Many other Mormon writers have also felt the need to declare that the Mayan ruins at Palenque and in other locations are the remains of the

Nephite civilization. What is known of the Mayans makes such a stand baseless. For one thing the time frames are wrong. The Nephites were said to have come to the New World shortly after 600 B.C., but recent archaeological findings date the beginnings of Mayan culture as early as 2500 B.C.[7] The Formative period of the Mayan culture extended up to about A.D. 150, while the Proto-Classic was from about 150 to 300, and the Classic period, in which the Mayans achieved their greatest heights, was from 300 to 900. (The Nephites were said to have been exterminated about the year 385.) After A.D. 900 came the Post-Classic, in which the Mayan culture began the decline that lasted until the arrival of the white man.

Although the Mormon church of today takes no official stand on the identification of *Book of Mormon* cities with known archaeological sites, the founder of the church was not so noncommital. Michael Coe, a non–Mormon archaeologist and author, said this about the implications of Joseph's stand:

> The Nephite story ... extends from about 600 B.C. to the final annihilation in 385 A.D. This chronology means that a Book of Mormon archaeologist would necessarily have to concentrate on the Formative period in Mesoamerica. But how is one to reconcile this dating with the flat statement of Joseph Smith himself that Palenque was a Nephite city? This Maya center was built *after* 600 A.D. according to all modern scholarship, some 215 years after the Nephites had been wiped from the surface of the earth. I can only sympathize with the Mormon scholar who has to work that one out.[8]

More significant is the fact that the Mayans are not an extinct people as the Nephites are said to be. The Mayans now number some two million. The facial features of these people are much like those of their ancestors represented in the paintings and stone figures found in the ruins of their cities. Those features, and other Mayan physical traits, are hardly compatible with the supposed Hebrew ancestry of the "white and delightsome" Nephites. Here is a description of the Maya:

> In color the Maya are copper-brown. The hair is straight, black to dark brown in color, and rather coarse. The Maya are not a hairy people. The men either have no beards and moustaches, or only very sparse ones, while other parts of the body have less hair than in the case of American whites....
>
> Two other physical characteristics of the modern Maya suggest the northeastern Asiatic origin which they share with other American Indian groups: (1) the epicanthic eye fold, and (2) the Mongolian spot. The epicanthic eye fold is a fold at the inner corner of the eye which is characteristic of eastern Asiatics; it is also common among the modern Yucatan Maya. Judging by its frequency in representations of the face in sculpture and paintings, it must also have been a prevalent characteristic in ancient times.
>
> The Mongolian spot is an almost universal physical characteristic of the peoples of eastern Asia, and is also very common among Maya babies of northern Yucatan. It is a small irregular-shaped spot at the base of the

spine, which is present at birth but generally disappears before the tenth year. It is bluish to purple in color, which generally fades to slate.[9]

Semitic peoples are not noted for possessing any of these characteristics. Semitic men, for example, are relatively hairy, as are most caucasian men, and frequently grow heavy beards.

In addition to the above traits, there is another that we might note. There is a blood factor called the Diego factor, which is occasionally found in American Indians. The only Old World peoples in which this factor occurs are the eastern Asiatics (commonly called the Mongoloid race) or those with eastern Asiatic ancestry.[10]

That the Mayans, and Indians in general, have some characteristics in common with the natives of eastern Asia is not surprising to non–Mormon archaeologists and anthropologists. After all, the evidence indicates that the ancestors of the Indians came from Asia in several small, successive migrations during the last Ice Age. At that time, the sea level was 150 to 300 feet lower than at present because of the volume of the earth's water that was tied up in glacial ice. This lowering of the sea level exposed a thousand-mile-wide land bridge across the shallow and narrow Bering Strait.[11] The immigrant ancestors of the Indians established several sites by 10,000 B.C., many of which have been found by archaeologists.

Though American Indians exhibit features indicating they are related to the Mongoloids of eastern Asia, that relationship must be placed in its proper perspective. For the most part, the Indians are representative of what are termed "archaic Mongoloids," an early population of the race that had not developed the typical Mongolian features to as great an extent as are found in modern Japanese and Chinese. Furthermore, the migrations to the New World took place over many thousands of years and consisted of several diverse groups exhibiting many variations in characteristics. Thus, while the characteristics of the original inhabitants of the New World point to a basically Mongolian origin, there is a considerable diversity in their physical features. This diversity is far more than would be expected in a necessarily highly inbred population descended from a relatively few Hebrew immigrants such as described in *The Book of Mormon*.

From the study of language comes additional strong evidence against the proposition that the American Indians are of Hebrew descent. Languages change slowly through time, and divergent populations that once spoke the same language eventually speak different languages. However, the changes tend to be regular and relatively consistent so that a pattern of similarity between the various offshoot languages is preserved. It is through these regular and even predictable variations and similarities that certain languages can be shown to have had a common ancestor.

It is from such patterns that languages as far apart in space and time as English, Greek, Russian, Latin, Sanskirt, and Hittite have been identified as having a common ancestor in a postulated original language called Indo-European. For example, many words that begin with the letter "f" in English (specifically, in words derived from the original Anglo-Saxon) begin with the letter "p" in Latin or in Greek: e.g., father, pater; fish, piscis; foot, ped-; flow, pluvia; fire, pyra; etc. This is the result of a phonetic shift in the initial sound of these words that came about after the branch that led to the Germanic languages (to which English belongs) split off from the ancestral stock that also eventually gave rise to the Greek-Latin branch. There are several other examples of such patterns.[12] They show that these languages had a common linguistic predecessor spoken more than four thousand years ago.

If the American Indians were an offshoot of the Hebrews from as late as 600 B.C., their languages would still be very distinctly derived from Hebrew. It has been estimated that some two thousand languages were spoken in the Americas at the time of the arrival of Columbus, many so far apart linguistically as to appear unrelated. None of these New World languages have been found to have a definite relationship with *any* Old World language, much less Hebrew, despite attempts to find such a relationship.[13] These facts indicate that the American Indians have been linguistically separated from the Old World, and some Indian populations from others, for many thousands of years. The necessary time for such linguistic diversity to have occurred is entirely in accordance with the traditional non–Mormon view of the origin of the American Indians, and is completely at odds with the Mormon view.

Some Mormon scholars have expressed irritation with those who attempt to prove *The Book of Mormon* true by relying on a distortion of scientific findings. For example, Dee F. Green, a Mormon scientist who has had lengthy exposure to New World archaeology, stated in an article in *Dialogue*:

> Those volumes which most frequently ignore time and space and most radically distort, misrepresent, or ignore portions of the archaeological evidence are the popular Farnsworth volumes. Also inadequate, from a professional archaeologist's point of view, are the well intentioned volumes by Milton Hunter and a number of smaller pamphlets and works by various authors. On a slightly more sophisticated plane is Ferguson's *One Fold and One Shepherd*.... His knowledge of New World archaeology is better than that of Farnsworth or Hunter but still too shallow to avoid getting into trouble.[14]

John L. Sorenson, another Mormon scholar, has stated that "Most L.D.S. literature on 'archaeology and *The Book of Mormon*' ranges from factually and logically unreliable to truly kooky. In general it appears that the worse the book, the more it sells...."[15]

Much has been and is being learned about the original inhabitants of the Americas. The Mormon church itself, as noted by Michael Coe in his *Dialogue* article, has contributed to this learning. In 1952, the Utah church financed the "largest and most ambitious archaeological project ever funded by a religious institution (including the Vatican)." Coe described the program as an "unqualified success," in that it "established one of the longest and best archaeological sequences for any part of the world." But as far as providing evidence for *The Book of Mormon*, it was a complete failure. Coe went on to state:

> The bare facts of the matter are that nothing, absolutely nothing, has ever

turned up in any New World excavation which would suggest to a dispassionate observer that the Book of Mormon, as claimed by Joseph Smith, is a historical document relating to the history of the early immigrants to our hemisphere.[16]

Some Mormon writers and scholars have come to much the same conclusion. In an address to the Brigham Young University Archaeological Society in 1964, for example, Fletcher B. Hammond stated:

> There does not yet appear any artifact that we Latter-day Saints can present to the world and prove by any scientific rule—that such artifact is conclusively proof of any part of the Book of Mormon.[17]

In his *Dialogue* article, Dee F. Green stated that "Book of Mormon archaeology is largely useless—even a delusion" and concluded that it was only through faith that one could accept *The Book of Mormon* as true. The lack of supportive archaeological evidence, however, is but one facet of the matter. The truth of that book depends upon whether or not the Indians are of Hebrew descent. Brigham H. Roberts put it this way:

> The Hebrew origin of those races in our book is so unequivocably stated and so emphasized that if the said American races could be proven beyond doubt to be of other than Hebrew origin, the claims of the Book of Mormon would be shattered.[18]

That American Indians have more racial characteristics in common with eastern Asiatics than with Hebrews has caused some Mormons to modify their views and to contend that not all American Indians are the descendants of the *Book of Mormon* peoples. Dee F. Green, for example, states:

> Another myth which needs dispelling is our Lamanite syndrome. Most American Indians are neither descendants of Laman nor necessarily of Book of Mormon peoples. The Book itself makes no such claim, and there is ample evidence in the archaeological record to show that this hemisphere was widely populated by people of Asiatic stock crossing the Bering Strait long before Book of Mormon peoples were supposed to have arrived on the scene.[19]

This approach has its problems too. Even though *The Book of Mormon* does not explicitly state that all American Indians are descendants of the people described in it, the implication is there that they are supposed to be. America, according to *The Book of Mormon*, was a place "where there never had man been" before the arrival of the Jaredites, for example. Several of the prophecies in *The Book of Mormon* state that the "Lamanites" would be scattered by what were to be the European settlers. If all the Indians the white man scattered were those of Asiatic origin (as seems to have been the case) rather than the Lamanites of *The Book of Mormon*, then those prophecies fail.

Joseph Smith himself stated that the Indians were Lamanites. In his autobiography, he described the destruction of the Nephites by the Lamanites and declared that "the remnants are the Indians that now inhabit this country."[20] The Cowdery history of the church, which Cowdery wrote with Joseph's help, also makes that clear. In his description of the 1823 vision, Cowdery stated that the angel gave "a history of the aborigines of this country, and said they were literal descendants of Abraham."[21]

Furthermore, if the New World was "widely" populated by Asiatics even before the *Book of Mormon* peoples were supposed to have arrived, then why are they not mentioned in the book? The *Book of Mormon* peoples were supposed to have increased their numbers to the millions, yet during the one thousand years (three thousand, if one includes the Jaredites) of their migrations and explorations there is no tale or record of their having run into any of the "other" Native Americans. Archaeologists have found innumerable sites belonging to American natives, but have found none that can be identified as belonging to the *Book of Mormon* peoples.

Dee F. Green's perspective also raises a religious issue. The Mormons, according to their religious tenets based upon prophecies in *The Book of Mormon*, are supposed to inform the Lamanites of their heritage in the Hebrew family and bring them into the church. The importance of this tenet is such that one of the first things Joseph Smith did after organizing his church was to send missionaries to the Lamanites, i.e., the American Indians. But if "most American Indians are neither descendants of Laman nor necessarily of Book of Mormon peoples," and those who are — if any — cannot be identified as such, how are the Mormon missionaries to work toward the fulfillment of the prophecies?

Appendix C

The Spalding Theory

The Spalding theory of the origin of *The Book of Mormon* was in vogue for many decades of the nineteenth century. It has subsequently re-surfaced at times — most recently in 1977 when new evidence for it was claimed to have been found. The new evidence, it turned out, was invalid, though it had been accepted by many people. A new piece of documentation relating to the Spalding theory turned up as this book was being completed. It involves Ethan Smith and might explain how the Spalding controversy began in the first place.

The Spalding theory on the origin of *The Book of Mormon* had its start in 1834 when Eber D. Howe published his book, *Mormonism Unvailed*. In it, Howe presented several statements given by relatives and acquaintances of one Solomon Spalding claiming that *The Book of Mormon* was based on a romance that Spalding had written before his death in 1816. The first of these, as Howe gave them, was by John Spalding, Solomon Spalding's brother:

> Solomon Spalding was born in Ashford, Conn. in 1761.... After he left school, he entered Plainfield Academy.... He next commenced the study of Law, in Windham county, in which he made little progress, having in the mean time turned his attention to religious subjects. He soon after entered Dartmouth College, with the intention of qualifying himself for the ministry, where he obtained the degree of A.M. and was afterwards regularly ordained. After preaching three or four years, he gave it up, removed to Cherry Valley, N.Y., and ... in the year 1809 removed to Conneaut, in Ohio. The year following, I removed to Ohio, and found him engaged in building a forge. I made him a visit in about three years after; and found that he had failed, and considerably involved in debt. He then told me he had been writing a book, which he intended to have printed, the avails of which he thought would enable him to pay all his debts. The book was entitled "Manuscript Found," of which he read me many passages. — It was an historical romance of the first settlers of America, endeavoring to show that the American Indians are the descendants of the Jews, or the lost tribes. It gave a detailed account of their journey from Jerusalem, by land and sea, till they arrived in America, under the command of NEPHI and LEHI. They afterwards had quarrels and contentions,

247

and had separated into two distinct nations, one of which he denominated Nephites and the other Lamanites. Cruel and bloody wars ensued, in which great multitudes were slain. They buried their dead in large heaps, which caused the mounds so common in this country. Their arts, sciences and civilization were brought into view, in order to account for all the curious antiquities, found in various parts of North and South America. I have recently read the Book of Mormon, and to my great surprize I find nearly the same historical matter, names, &c. as they were in my brother's writings. I well remember that he wrote in the old style, and commenced about every sentence with "and it came to pass," or "now it came to pass," the same as in the Book of Mormon, and according to the best of my re-collection and belief, it is the same as my brother Solomon wrote, with the exception of the religious matter. — By what means it has fallen into the hands of Joseph Smith, Jr. I am unable to determine. JOHN SPALDING."[1]

Howe also included statements given by John Spalding's wife, Solomon Spalding's partner, an employee, and some others who knew Spalding. They all related that, except for the religious material, *The Book of Mormon* contained much the same story and had many of the same names that appeared in Spalding's romance. Spalding's partner, Henry Lake, included the following in his remarks:

> ... I spent many hours hearing him read said writings, and became well acquainted with its contents.... One time, when he was reading to me the tragic account of Laban, I pointed out to him what I considered an incon-sistency, which he promised to correct; but by referring to the Book of Mormon, I find to my surprise that it stands there just as he read it to me then. — Some months ago I borrowed the Golden Bible.... About a week after, my wife found the book in my coat pocket, as it hung up, and com-menced reading it aloud as I lay upon the bed. She had not read 20 minutes till I was astonished to find the same passages in it that Spalding had read to me twenty years before, from his "Manuscript Found." Since that, I have more fully examined the said Golden Bible, and have no hesitation in saying that the historical part of it is principally, if not wholly taken from the "Manuscript Found." I well recollect telling Mr. Spalding, that the so fre-quent use of the words "And it came to pass," "Now it came to pass," rendered it ridiculous....[2]

After giving the testimonies of Spalding's relatives and acquaintances, Howe went on to relate that he sent a messenger to inquire of Spalding's widow, who lived in Massachusetts, concerning the disposition of the manu-script:

> She states that Spalding had a great variety of manuscripts, and recollects that one was entitled the "Manuscript Found," but of its contents she has no distinct knowledge. While they lived in Pittsburgh, she thinks it was once taken to the printing office of *Patterson & Lambdin*; but whether it was ever brought back to the house again, she is quite uncertain; if it was,

however, it was then with his other writings, in a trunk which she had left in Otsego County, N.Y....

The trunk referred to by the widow, was subsequently examined, and found to contain only a single M.S. book, in Spalding's handwriting.... This is a romance purporting to have been translated from the Latin, found on 24 rolls of parchment in a cave, on the banks of Conneaut Creek, but written in a modern style, and giving a fabulous account of a ship's being driven upon the American coast, while proceeding from Rome to Britain, a short time previous to the Christian era, this country then being inhabited by the Indians. This old M.S. has been shown to several of the foregoing witnesses, who recognise it as Spalding's, he having told them that he had altered his first plan of writing, by going farther back with the dates, and writing in the old scripture style, in order that it might appear more ancient. They say that it bears no resemblance to *"Manuscript Found."*[3]

Howe subsequently proceeded to explain how he felt Spalding's romance became *The Book of Mormon*:

It was inferred at once that some light might be shed upon this subject, and the mystery revealed, by applying to Patterson & Lambdin, in Pittsburgh. But here again death had interposed a barrier. That establishment was dissolved and broken up many years since, and Lambdin died about eight years ago. Mr. Patterson says he has no recollection of any such manuscript being brought there for publication, neither would he have likely to have seen it, as the business of printing was conducted wholly by Lambdin at the time. He says, however, that many M.S. books and pamphlets were brought to the office about that time which remained upon their shelves for years, without being printed or even examined. Now, as Spalding's book can no where be found, ... there is the strongest presumption that it remained there in seclusion, till about the year 1823 or '24, at which time *Sidney Rigdon* located himself in that city. We have been credibly informed that he was on terms with Lambdin, being seen frequently in his shop....

We are, then, irresistibly led to the conclusion: — that Lambdin, after having failed in business, had recourse to the old manuscripts in his possession, in order to *raise the wind*, by a book speculation, and placed the "Manuscript Found," of Spalding in the hands of Rigdon, to be embellished, altered, and added to, as he might think expedient; and three years' study of the bible we should deem little enough time to garble it, as it is transferred to the Mormon book ... and in a miraculous way to bring it before the world.... And where could a more suitable character be found than Jo Smith, whose necromantic fame and arts of deception, had already extended to a considerable distance? ...[4]

Thus began the Spalding theory. Time has seen various versions of how Spalding's manuscript might have come into Joseph's hands. Some have held that Joseph himself purloined the manuscript since the Otsego County location of the trunk was only about thirty miles from Bainbridge, New York. Joseph spent some time in Bainbridge before he was supposed to have acquired the gold plates. In any case, both Sidney Rigdon and Joseph Smith vehemently denied that *The Book of Mormon* was based on Spalding's romance.

For several decades after Howe published his book, new witnesses came forward to testify that *The Book of Mormon* was based on Spalding's romance. New witnesses also turned up to provide further "evidence" of Rigdon's complicity in the affair. Rather than diminishing memories of past events, the passage of time seemed instead to sharpen recollections. Unfortunately, the recollections of these witnesses did not always tally with each other.

The Spalding theory received a minor setback in 1884 when the person who inherited Howe's papers discovered among them the manuscript that was found in the trunk by Howe's associates. The manuscript was given to Oberlin College in Ohio, and the Mormons immediately published it with the declaration that the Spalding theory could at last be put to rest. Howe, however, had honestly described this manuscript when he published his book amost fifty years earlier; the crux of the Spalding theory actually depended upon there being a second manuscript, and obviously if Joseph had got hold of a second manuscript, it would not have been in the trunk.

Though the Mormons declared there were no similarities between the Spalding manuscript and Joseph Smith's latter-day revelation, there in fact are some. The similarities, however, though interesting, are not compelling. Both books describe a sea voyage; both describe wars between two factions of ancient Americans; both describe the use of earthwork forts; both relate that sacred writings were preserved among the records of their respective peoples; and both describe the ancient inhabitants of America as possessing horses and elephants. (In Spalding's work there are mammoths, and also "mammoons," which Spalding described as being bigger than elephants and very useful; *The Book of Mormon* describes the Jaredites as having, in addition to elephants, "cureloms and cumons ... which were useful unto man.") The earthworks in Spalding's work were the same ones by the Scioto River that Charles Thompson said were described in *The Book of Mormon* (see pp. 165–166).

The people in Spalding's manuscript are not described as being descended from the Israelites. Moreover, Spalding had the ship, a Roman ship, come to the New World merely to provide someone who could write the history of the natives in Latin, which Spalding could then claim to have translated. It is also noteworthy that the term "And it came to pass" is used only once in the manuscript.

The next big event concerning the Spalding theory came in 1977 when Wayne L. Cowdrey (a distant relative of Oliver Cowdery), Howard A. Davis, and Donald R. Scales announced that they had proof that *The Book of Mormon* was based on a second manuscript of Spalding's.[5] The proof consisted of twelve pages of manuscript copy that they claimed were part of that long-lost second manuscript. According to these men, the twelve pages were part of the manuscript copy of *The Book of Mormon* in the possession in the Utah church. The different handwritings in the remainder of this copy could be identified as belonging to various of Joseph Smith's scribes, but that on the twelve pages could not be so identified. Cowdrey, Davis, and Scales contended that this handwriting matched Spalding's in the Oberlin manuscript.

The three handwriting experts called in were not unaminous in their opinions. One dropped out and refused to make any comment, one declared that the handwriting in the two documents was the same, while another declared that it was not the same. This last expert, Howard C. Doulder, concluded that any similarities were due to the different writing style of the time when compared with that of today. This difference could cause someone used to the modern style to attribute the similarities in the samples of the older writing to the same hand, though they were actually from different hands.

Moreover, shortly after the three researchers made their claims public, the church archivists found another sample of handwriting identical to that in the *Book of Mormon* manuscript pages in question. It was found in a manuscript dated June, 1831, which contained some of Joseph Smith's revelations and could not have been written by Solomon Spalding.

The church also published handwriting samples from the Spalding and *Book of Mormon* manuscripts. There were differences that the layman could easily observe.[6]

Although the claims of these recent researchers have proved invalid, that does not mean there is nothing to the Spalding theory. It is conceivable that Joseph Smith or one of his associates did acquire a copy of a second Spalding manuscript. *The Book of Mormon* could then have had its beginning in that manuscript as an essentially nonreligious book. Ethan Smith's ideas could then have been brought in also to provide a significant embellishment and a religious background. Such a scenario would explain why Spalding's acquaintances were able to find similarities between *The Book of Mormon* and Spalding's manuscript.

There is another possibility that could explain those similarities. The following article, which was recently uncovered, originally appeared in the Cleveland *Plain Dealer* of April 24, 1887, long before anybody had noticed similarities between *View of the Hebrews* and *The Book of Mormon*.

THE BOOK OF MORMON

A Puritan Minister Partly Responsible for its Production.

How a Congregational Clergyman in New England Elaborated His Theories Regarding the Lost Tribes of Israel in a Book Which was Never Published and Eventually Found Its Way into the Hands of Solomon Spaulding – Rev. Ethan Smith's Semi-Historical Romance Identified With the Story as Told in the Book of Mormon.

The recent conference of the Josephites or monogamous Mormons at Kirtland, O., and the extended reports of their proceedings in the PLAIN DEALER has renewed public interest in the peculiar faith to which members of this church subscribe. The origin of the Book of Mormon has never been clearly established. The Latter Day Saints, of course, accept the statements of Joe Smith and believe it to be an inspired work. The general public, however, are hardly as credulous and regard the alleged Bible as a fraud.... The Spaulding theory, with which everyone at all acquainted with the subject is familiar, has the most advocates. They hold that Spaulding's manuscript of his romance "The Manuscript Found" fell into the hands of Joe Smith, Sidney Rigdon and others and from that fanciful work was constructed the Book of Mormon.

If this theory be true it will astonish orthodox people to learn that a Congregational divine, one of the foremost of his time in New England, is responsible for the introduction of the "twin relic of barbarism" — as the Utah church has been called — in this country. Rev. Ethan Smith, who died at an advanced age in the early "forties," was one of the lights of the Congregational church in new England.... One of his pet hobbies was the belief that the North American Indians were descended from the lost tribes of Israel.... Rev. Dr. Smith wrote a work on this subject, which after completion, he decided not to publish, fearing that it might injure his reputation as a theological writer. This book was an elaboration of the theory Dr. Smith had so long maintained. Taking as its foundation the migration of the lost tribes of Israel to the western continent, it described the hegira from Palestine, the establishment of the Jews in what is now Central America and Mexico, the founding of a great empire and its gradual decline and fall. It told of magnificent cities inhabited by an enlightened and Christian people. The author claimed for them a civilization equal to that of Egypt or Jerusalem.

Hundreds of years passed and the history of the eastern Jews was repeated on the western continent. Quarrels between the various tribes sprang up, bloody wars were waged and the process of disintergration began. Gradually the people were scattered, their cities destroyed and all semblance to a nation was lost. Thousands perished by pestilence and the sword and the remnants of a once mighty nation relapsed into a state of barbarism. Their descendants, Dr. Smith claimed, were the Indians of North America and the Aztecs of Mexico. This is almost exactly similar to the story told in the Book of Mormon.

Solomon Spaulding was a warm admirer of Dr. Smith and when a young man studied under his tuition. He became interested in his theories regarding the settlement of America, and in return Dr. Smith took the young student into his confidence and granted him a perusal of his unpublished book. Spaulding was deeply impressed with the truth of this theory and pursued his investigations even farther than Dr. Smith had ventured. Taking the latter's views as expressed in his book Spaulding some years later wrote his famous "Manuscript Found," which afterward fell into the hands of Joe Smith and was reconstructed into the Book of Mormon. Indeed, it is not at all unlikely that Dr. Smith's original manuscript, which it is said Spaulding had in his possession, suffered a similar fate. At any rate it has never been seen since.

These facts are told the PLAIN DEALER by a grandson of Dr. Smith, now residing in this city. He states that the Book of Mormon differs very slightly as far as its general outline is concerned, from the historical romance written by his grandfather sixty or seventy years ago, and he is quite certain that the Mormon faith is founded on the production of that worthy pastor's fertile imagination.

Perhaps Ethan Smith's grandson was merely joining others who were "uncovering" the origin of *The Book of Mormon*. Still, his words deserve consideration.

To be sure, there are some problems with what is said in the article, (though there is nothing in it that is impossible). The statement that Solomon Spalding and Ethan Smith were acquainted might possibly be true. Both men became Congregational ministers and both attended Dartmouth College, in Hanover, New Hampshire. Spalding entered as a sophomore and graduated with the class of 1785. Since he was not licensed to preach until October 9, 1787, however, in Windham, Connecticut, he likely continued his ministerial studies until that date.[7] Ethan Smith entered Dartmouth in 1786 after a course of study in Belchertown, Massachusetts.[8] (Ethan Smith's grandson was in error about his grandfather's being the senior of the two; Spalding was actually about a year older.) Ethan Smith, then, was studying for the ministry at about the same time as Spalding, and their locations, Windham and Belchertown, were about fifty miles apart.

Given the foregoing, one might consider the possibility that both men took a term of instruction together under some noted minister, and so met. Or, perhaps they became acquainted at some religious gathering that took place under the auspices of the Congregational Church. Through these or other circumstances, they might have become friends. And, since he appears to have had a greater knowledge of religion, Ethan Smith might have helped Spalding with his studies.

Let us go back in time and presume that Ethan Smith and Solomon Spalding do meet and become good friends. Let us also presume that their friendship continues and they correspond with each other. Occasionally, this correspondence consists of the trading of ideas and information about the ancient inhabitants of America, especially after Spalding moves to Ohio and becomes intrigued by the ancient earthworks there. This trading of ideas stimulates both men to write romances about the ancient Americans.

Spalding aims to publish his romance at a profit. But Ethan Smith feels it would not be suitable to publish his since such a "frivolity" might injure his reputation as a religious writer. Instead, he accumulates more evidence in support of his theories about ancient America with the goal of eventually publishing them in a more serious and acceptable form — what would become *View of the Hebrews*.

Meanwhile, Spalding is not having much luck with his story. He writes to his old friend, Ethan Smith, and relates monetary problems and an inability to produce a publishable romance. The New England minister, thinking he might help, sends a draft of his story to Spalding. He tells Spalding that he is free to use it as he sees fit, but that he does not want his own name to be in any way associated with it. Spalding takes Ethan Smith's manuscript and combines it with his own ideas. He reads it to his family and acquaintances. They think it is better than his previous attempts. He tries to get the manuscript published in Pittsburgh, but does not succeed, and short time later dies. The manuscript disappears, perhaps being discarded when the printing firm goes out of business.

Ethan Smith finds his way to Poultney, Vermont, where, in 1823, he publishes the first edition of his *View of Hebrews*. There he gets to know a young man who is particularly interested in his ideas about the ancient Americans and their descendants, the Indians. The young man is Oliver Cowdery. Oliver asks Pastor Smith for permission to read some of the relevant books he has accumulated over the years. The minister is impressed with the studious young man and allows him free access to his library. With increasing interest, Oliver reads all of the books and pamphlets dealing with ancient America or with the idea of the Hebrew origin of the Indians. Included in this material is Boudinot's *A Star in the West*, Adair's *History of the American Indians*, Clavigero's *History of Mexico*, and the *Archaeologia Americana*.

Ethan Smith also allows Oliver to look through his accumulated notes and papers. In so doing, Oliver comes across a draft of the Vermont minister's by-now-forgotten romance. Oliver asks Ethan Smith about it and the latter states that it is only a frivolity he indulged in many years before and has no real value. Oliver tells the minister that he liked reading it and asks if he might have it. The minister, thinking nothing of it, grants the request.

In 1825, Ethan Smith publishes the enlarged edition of his *View of the Hebrews* and Oliver leaves Poultney for New York State, carrying with him a copy of the book and also the draft of Ethan Smith's old romance.

In New York, Oliver meets up with a relative of his, Joseph Smith. The two get the idea of using Ethan Smith's romance as the basis of a history of ancient America that they can sell for a profit. After a period of work on the book, events cause them to modify it, adding considerably more material, especially from *View of the Hebrews*. After the book is published, they establish a new religion based on it and send out missionaries.

A few years later, a Mormon missionary arrives in Conneaut, Ohio, selling copies of *The Book of Mormon*. The family and former friends of Solomon Spalding are astounded to find in it many of the things they had heard Spalding read from his manuscript several years before. In this way, the Spalding theory began.

The above sketch is purely speculative. If true, however, it would explain much. There is another reasonable argument one could put forth in its favor. Ethan Smith, we know, was intensely interested in the ancient Americans and in the religious implications of those ancient Americans' being of Hebrew origin. He must have heard of *The Book of Mormon* and under ordinary circumstances one would expect that he would have investigated it. Having done this, he surely would have noted its resemblance to his *View of the Hebrews* — even supposing that he did not write any such romance as we have described above. That being the case, one would expect to hear Ethan Smith's voice through the corridors of time declaring that *The Book of Mormon* was formed from his *View of the Hebrews*. Yet, there is not to be found one comment by Ethan Smith concerning *The Book of Mormon* or concerning Mormonism — at least none that this writer has learned about.

Granted the connections traced in this book, why was Ethan Smith silent concerning *The Book of Mormon*? Was it because he did not want it known that he was in any way responsible for the origin of a religious "imposition" held in such contempt by so many non–Mormons of the time. Would he especially have not wanted it known if Mormonism actually did have its beginning in a romance he had written so long before? Ethan Smith placed a considerable value upon his reputation. He might well have thought that it would be ruined if people learned of a close connection between an early frivolous work of fiction of his and *The Book of Mormon*.

If he did so think about his reputation, we can speculate why he kept quiet about his involvement. Perhaps he thought the Spalding revelation would silence the new religion. Later, when he heard of Joseph Smith's death, he may have thought that event would do likewise.

If *The Book of Mormon* actually did have its start in an early fiction of his about the ancient Americans, Ethan Smith died in 1849 without telling anyone. How, then, did Ethan Smith's grandson know about it? And why did he take so long in reporting it? Quite possibly and quite reasonably, the grandson might have learned about it while going through his grandfather's papers many years after the old gentleman had passed away. In those papers the grandson might have found some correspondence with Solomon Spalding in which the draft of the romance was mentioned. And, not knowing about Oliver Cowdery, the grandson quite reasonably, though erroneously, assumed that the path from Ethan Smith's romance to *The Book of Mormon* was through Spalding and his manuscript.

Appendix D

The Book of Abraham

In Chapter 19 we examined the historical conditions that prompted Joseph Smith to produce *The Book of Abraham*. In this Appendix, we shall examine the book in more detail and judge the validity of the Mormon prophet's claim that he translated it from Egyptian papyri he had acquired in 1835.

Joseph Smith first published the book, along with three facsimiles of the papyri, in two installments in the *Times and Seasons* during March of 1842. *The Book of Abraham* was subsequently included in *The Pearl of Great Price* (which will be used here for the *Book of Abraham* excerpts).

Much of the material one finds in *The Book of Abraham* could have been derived from the literature of Joseph's own time. One of the first verses in the book, in fact, reflects an early writing of Oliver Cowdery's: in the *Patriarchal Blessing Book, No. 1*, under the date of December, 1833 (two years before Joseph acquired the papyri), Oliver commented:

> ... we diligently sought for the right of the fathers, and the authority of the holy priesthood, and the power to administer the same; for we desired to be followers of righteousness and the possessors of greater knowledge.... After this, we received the high and holy priesthood....[1]

In *The Book of Abraham* we find Abraham saying almost the same thing:

> ... I sought for the blessings of the fathers, and the right whereunto I should be ordained to administer the same; having been myself a follower of righteousness, desiring also to be one who possessed great knowledge..., I became ... a High Priest, holding the right belonging to the fathers [Abraham 1:2].

The first part of *The Book of Abraham* is patterned after the account of Abraham's wanderings as given in Genesis 11 and 12, but with some changes and added material. Among the additions is a dissertation on the nature of the universe and celestial bodies that Abraham gives to the Egyptians. Jerald and Sandra Tanner have suggested that the writings of Josephus might have inspired Joseph to include this touch in *The Book of Abraham*, since Josephus

256

had related a tradition that Abraham had taught the Egyptians the science of astronomy. Josephus had stated:

> He communicated to them arithmetic, and delivered to them the science of astronomy. For before Abram came into Egypt, they were unacquainted with some parts of learning; for that science came from the Chaldeans into Egypt....[2]

This tradition is not found in the Bible. Moreover, it is simply not true; the science of Egyptology has determined that the Egyptians were acquainted with mathematics and astronomy long before the time of Abraham. Nevertheless, this spurious tradition related by Josephus is reflected in *The Book of Abraham*:

> And the Lord said unto me: Abraham, I show these things unto thee before ye go into Egypt, that ye may declare these words [Abraham 3:15].

The "things" referred to here were the secrets of astronomy. In the explanation of Facsimile No. 3, Joseph stated, "Abraham is reasoning upon the principles of astronomy in the king's court." So Joseph, echoing Josephus, claimed that Abraham taught astronomy to the Egyptians.

Fawn Brodie noted that the astronomical ideas in *The Book of Abraham* appear to have had their source in Thomas Dick's *Philosophy of a Future State*. The second edition of this book was published in 1830, and Oliver Cowdery quoted a rather lengthy excerpt from it in the *Messenger and Advocate* of December, 1836.

In a study he published, Clarence F. Packard has presented evidence that an additional source for Joseph's ideas on astronomy was *The Six Books of Proclus, The Platonic Successor, on the Theology of Plato*, translated by Thomas Taylor and published by him in 1816.[3] Taylor added a seventh book of his own to make up for one that was lost; most of the similarities in *The Book of Abraham* are from Taylor's seventh book.

Joseph's wording of the explanation of Figure No. 5 in Facsimile No. 2 has several concepts from Volume 2 of Taylor's book (to which the following page numbers refer). Both call the planets "governors" (p. 140); both refer to the sun as a planet (p. 146); both declare that the sun gets its light from another source (p. 145); both use the term "grand key" (p. 142); both talk of power given to the sun (p. 145); finally, the total number of Taylor's worlds is fifteen (p. 146), and he used the term "fixed stars and planets" (p. 145), while Joseph's explanation has "fifteen other fixed planets or stars."

In Chapter Three of *The Book of Abraham* (henceforth "Abr."), there are further similarities with the esoteric astronomy of Taylor's and Dick's books. Dick speaks of the systems of the universe which revolve around one common center that may be termed "THE THRONE OF GOD" (Dick, pp. 249, 250); in Abr. 3:2 are described the stars near "The throne of God." Dick declares that that "grand central body may be considered as the capital of the universe" (Dick, p. 250); after again alluding to Taylor's stellar "governors," the author of Abr. 3:3 describes a "great" stellar body near God that governs the world. Taylor describes the relative motions of the planetary spheres (Taylor, pp. 141, 144); Abr. 3:5 does likewise. Finally, Taylor describes the progression of time among the universal bodies (Taylor, p. 144); Abr. 3:6–8 does likewise.

More than just astronomical ideas in *The Book of Abraham* seem to have derived from Taylor and Dick. Ideas about the "intelligences" inhabiting the universe likely also came from these sources. Dick speaks of the gradations of intellect which people the universal system (Dick, p. 219); Abr. 3:18 does likewise. Dick and Taylor declare that the intellect or thinking principle was unbotten and eternal (Taylor, p. 116; Dick p. 101); Abr. 3:18 does likewise. Dick describes a superior intellect far above others (Dick, p. 220); Abr. 3:19 does likewise. Dick describes God as ruling the "intelligences" of the universe (Dick, pp. 118, 196); so does the author of Abr. 3:21, even duplicating the term "intelligences." Dick describes the "intelligences" of the highest order (Dick, p. 250); Abr. 3:24 does likewise, again using the term "intelligences."

Dick states that among the higher order of intelligences "the glorified body of the Redeemer may have taken its principle station" (Dick, p. 250); Abr. 3:24 states, "And there stood one among them [the intelligences] that was like unto God...," a reference to Jesus.

From his studies of Hebrew, Joseph had learned that the word translated as "God" in Genesis was actually a plural form. This could have encouraged him, in preparing *The Book of Abraham*, to follow Taylor's remarks about the existence of lesser gods. Taylor proposed that these "junior gods" organized the world from pre-existing matter[4]; Joseph did a rewrite of creation in Genesis that is in accordance with Taylor's ideas. In the following, the "one ... who was like unto God," or Jesus, directs the "gods" to form the heavens and the earth from pre-existing material. For the sake of brevity, we will give only the first part of the rewrite of Genesis:

> ... And there stood one among them that was like unto God, and he said unto those who were with him: We will go down, and we will take of these materials, and we will make an earth whereon these may dwell.... And they went down at the beginning, and they, that is the Gods, organized and formed the heavens and the earth.... And they (the Gods) said: Let there be light; and there was light.... And the Gods called the light Day, and the darkness they called Night ... [Abraham 3:24–4:5].

Thus Mormonism seems to have been changed from a monotheistic religion to a polytheistic one.

As was mentioned in Chapter 19, some early Egyptologists declared the facsimiles in *The Book of Abraham* to be of Egyptian funeral documents; most Mormons did not accept these pronouncements. In the 1960s there occurred a series of events of particular signifigance in regard to *The Book of Abraham*. The first of these harks back to the following statement in which Joseph Smith described his activities during the month of July, 1835:

> The remainder of the month, I was continually engaged in translating an

Alphabet of the Book of Abraham, and arranging a grammar of the Egyptian language as practiced by the ancients.[5]

In 1965, a Mormon named Grant Heward managed to acquire a reproduction of one of Joseph's manuscripts. The manuscript was entitled "Grammar and Aphabet [sic] of the Egyptian Language." Mr. Heward, who had taught himself the Egyptian writing system, felt that he could use the manuscript to prove the validity of *The Book of Abraham*. But he found out otherwise, finding instead that the manuscript was "full of nonsense and doubletalk."[6] Feeling obligated to bring what he had learned into the open, he had his findings printed. Mr. Heward has since been excommunicated from the church.

In 1966, a very significant event occurred when some of Joseph's original papyri were "found" in the New York Metropolitan Museum of Art. In November of 1967, the Museum turned the papyri, which consisted of eleven pieces, over to the church authorities in Salt Lake City. They, in turn, gave the papyri to the Mormon scholar, Dr. Hugh Nibley, for study.

Shortly thereafter, Dr. Nibley began to publish a series of articles on the papyri in the *Improvement Era*, a Mormon periodical. These articles, which began in the January, 1968, issue, ran for about two years and, though full of fanciful conjectures about the relationship of the papyri to *The Book of Abraham*, never included a translation of them.

Another Mormon periodical, *Dialogue: A Journal of Mormon Thought*, which was not under the control of the church, did print translations of the papyri. These translations were by John Wilson, Richard Parker, and Klaus Baer, non–Mormon Egyptologists of good repute.[7] Using photos of the papyri that *Dialogue* had acquired, these scholars verified the pronouncements made by the earlier Egyptologists: The Joseph Smith papyri are common Egyptian funeral documents and make no mention of the Biblical Abraham. Furthermore, the papyri were found to date from a time considerably after that of Abraham.

One important question was whether the particular piece of papyrus that Joseph claimed was the source for *The Book of Abraham* was among those recovered. It was important to know this since it was apparent that not all of the papyri Joseph was known to have had were among those found in the Metropolitan Museum. Also, following the discovery of the papyri, several Mormon writers have attempted to show that the papyrus in question was in fact not among those recovered.

It was Grant Heward who was one of the first to determine that the papyrus in question was included among those the Museum turned over to the church. Shortly after the church received the papyri, Heward obtained photographs of them.[8] He proceeded to compare the photos with his copy of Joseph's "Grammar and Aphabet" and soon found what he sought. The "Grammar" manuscript also contained Joseph's draft of part of *The Book of Abraham*. The pages of this draft consisted of a series of Egyptian hieratic characters in the lefthand margin and, to the right, the "translation" into the part of the *Book of Abraham* text that was supposedly derived from each character. Mr. Heward found that the hieratic characters were from the first

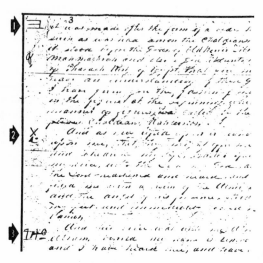

Figure 1. To the left is column one of the Joseph Smith Papyrus No. XI. To the right is page three (also labeled page "q") from Joseph Smith's "Grammar and Aphabet" manuscript of *The Book of Abraham*. The numbers show the corresponding characters from the two documents.

two rows of the piece of papyrus that came to be labeled No. XI (according to the numbering of the papyrus pieces that were later pictured in the *Improvement Era* of February, 1968). As is shown in the example in Figure 1, these characters were even copied in the same order. They were read from right to left from the papyrus and entered into their vertical positions on the left column of the draft of *The Book of Abraham*.[9]

The manuscript copy of the "Grammar and Aphabet" carried only a "translation" of Abraham 1:4 through 2:2, but Mr. Heward had learned that photos of another draft of *The Book of Abraham* were in the Brigham Young University. He went there, examined the photos, and found that this draft covered Abraham 1:1 through to 2:18. The head of this draft reads, "Translation of the Book of Abraham written by his own hand upon Papyrus and found in the Catacombs of Egypt." As with the other draft of *The Book of Abraham*, the pages of this manuscript consist of a series of hieratic characters down the left margin with a "Translation" to the right. Mr. Heward found that the characters of this more extensive draft were to be found on papyrus No. XI also, this time down into line four of the text, and that the characters were the same in the corresponding parts of the two manuscripts.[10]

But why do the manuscripts go no further than Abraham 2:18? The answer appears to be that, since they are in the handwriting of the scribes that Joseph used while in Kirtland, these manuscripts represent the extent of the work that Joseph did on the book before he was forced to leave there in 1838. Moreover, it is interesting to note that the longest manuscript includes Abraham 1:1 through 2:18, which is the exact extent of what was printed in the first installment of *The Book of Abraham* in the March 1, 1842, *Times and*

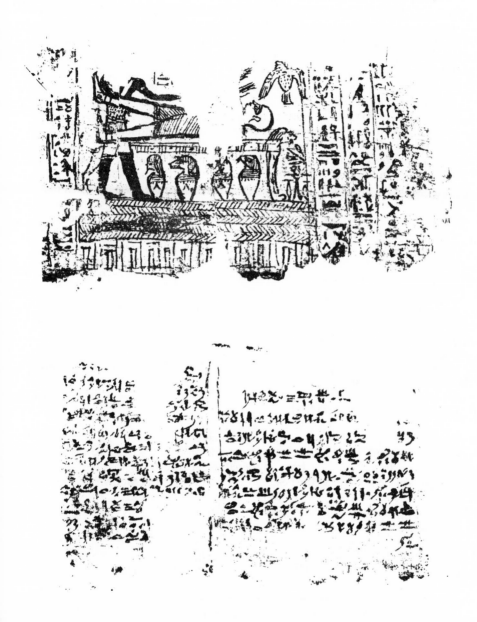

Figure 2. Top, the Joseph Smith Papyrus No. I, the original for Facsimile No. 1. Bottom, the Joseph Smith Papyrus No. XI, one of the "Book of Breathings" fragments.

Seasons. Thus, that manuscript apparently provided the basis for that installment. In order to get the second installment printed, it seems that Joseph had
to finish translating the papyrus. This is confirmed by the following statement
that Joseph made in the *History of the Church* under the date of March 8,
1842: "Recommenced translating from the Records of Abraham for the tenth
number of the Times and Seasons...."

There is some additional and important evidence that Papyrus No. XI is
the same one that Joseph said was the source for *The Book of Abraham*. To
begin with, Joseph and his scribes had pasted the long rolls of papyrus onto
paper and then cut them into shorter sections, apparently to make the papyrus
easier to work with. An examination of the recovered pieces of papyrus
reveals that the one designated as No. XI matches up with the one designated
No. I (see Figure 2), which contains the illustration that provided the source
for Joseph's Facsimile 1 in *The Book of Abraham*. It could be determined that
these pieces were once a part of the same roll for several reasons: the physical
size and match of the pieces, the match of the parts of a rough plan for the Zion
temple that was drawn on the paper backing, and the match of the individual
fibers of papyrus, which, as one of the Egyptologists put it, are as distinctive as
fingerprints. Furthermore, because of the Egyptian text, it was determined that
the piece of papyrus designated as No. X was also a part of the original roll to
which numbers I and XI belonged.[11]

The fact that the original for Facsimile 1 was a part of the same papyrus
roll that contained papyrus No. XI is important because in the book Abraham
makes this statement:

> And it came to pass that the priests laid violence upon me, that they
> might slay me ... upon this altar; and that you may have a knowledge of
> this altar, I will refer you to the representation at the commencement of this
> record [Abraham 1:12].

The representation that is referred to here is Facsimile No. 1 (see Figure
3). Furthermore, in Abraham 1:13–14 there is another reference to the same
facsimile. The author of the book is therefore in effect stating that the original
for Facsimile No. 1 was at the beginning of the papyrus roll that was supposed
to provide the text for *The Book of Abraham*. Since Papyrus No. XI is demonstrably a part of that roll, that piece of papyrus must be a part of what Joseph
claimed was the source for *The Book of Abraham*.

Thus, not only do Joseph's drafts of *The Book of Abraham* provide
evidence that papyrus No. XI was supposed to be the source of the text for the
book, Joseph's comments within the book provide further evidence.

It is worth noting that the deteriorated condition of the papyrus is reflected in Joseph's manuscript copy of *The Book of Abraham*. Parts of papyrus
XI are broken off and some of the characters are missing. It appears that this
was the case even when Joseph first acquired the papyri; one of the individuals
to whom the Mormon prophet showed them reported that some parts were
entirely lost, "but Smith is to translate the whole by divine inspiration and that
which is lost ... can be interpreted as well as that which is preserved."[12] What is
interesting about this is that the characters entered in the lefthand margin of

Figure 3. The *Book of Abraham* Facsimiles. Facsimile No. 1 is in the upper left, Facsimile No. 2 is in the upper right, and Facsimile No. 3 is below. This Facsimile No. 1 is from the *Pearl of Great Price*. The other facsimiles are from the *Times and Seasons*, of March, 1842.

Joseph's manuscripts of *The Book of Abraham* are normal Egyptian hieratic characters derived from papyrus XI except where the gaps in that papyrus occur. Those particular characters are not hieratic and appear to have been of Joseph's own creation and entered in the manuscripts to make up for the characters that were lost.[13]

And that brings us to Joseph's translation of the papyrus. One unusual aspect of this translation is the great number of words the Mormon prophet derived from each character. In Figure 1, note the top character — the one that looks like a backwards "E"; its associated translation consists of 73 words, found in Abraham 1:13–14, and reads as follows:

> it was made after the form of a bed stead, such as was had amon[g] the Chaldeans, and it stood before the gods of Elk kener Libnah Mahmachrah [Korash] and also a god like unto that of Pharaoh king of Egypt, that you

> may have an understanding of these gods, I have given you the fassion of
> them, in the figures at the beginning, which manner of the figures is called
> by the Chaldeans Rahleenos, [which signifies hieroglyphics].

In the published version, corrections in spelling and punctuation were made
and the parts in brackets were added.

This brings us to the translation that the Egyptologists made. They
determined that Papyrus No. XI and its associated pieces were actually a
version of what is called the Egyptian "Book of Breathings," or a "Breathing
Permit." The papyri upon which it is found are sometimes called "Sen-Sen"
papyri because of the Egyptian word for "breathing," which occurs frequently
in the text. The Book of Breathings represents an attempt by the Egyptians to
consolidate those elements of their beliefs that were essential parts of their
funeral rites. It was a kind of talisman buried with the dead to assure their
well-being in the afterlife and has its basis in a literary tradition that began
quite late in Egyptian history. The Egyptologists estimated that Joseph Smith's
papyrus copy of the Book of Breathings dates from as late as the first century
A.D. — considerably after the time of Abraham.[14]

Column one, the righthand column of papyrus XI, which contains the
characters found in Joseph's drafts of *The Book of Abraham*, was a sort of
preamble to the main part of the Book of Breathings. It reads:

> *Osiris shall be conveyed into* the Great Pool of Khons — and likewise
> Osiris Hor, *justified*, born to Tikhebyt — after his arms have been *placed* on
> his heart and the Breathing Permit (which [Isis] made and has writing on
> its inside and outside) has been wrapped in royal linen and placed under
> his left arm near his heart; the rest of his mummy-bandages should be
> wrapped over it. The man for whom this book has been copied will breathe
> forever as the bas of the gods do.[15]

Restorations have been indicated by italics in this translation. Since
other examples of the Book of Breathings exist to provide the proper format,
the missing parts could be properly reconstructed. The person for whom this
particular papyrus was written was a priest named Hor, who was the son of
Tikhebyt. It was traditional in the Book of Breathings to prefix the name of the
deceased with the name of the resurrected god Osiris; hence, "Osiris Hor" in
the text.

The hieratic character which looks like a backwards "E," and from
which Joseph "translated" the 73 words given previously, actually is a part of a
group of characters that translates as the word "pool" in the above true translation.

According to Joseph, Facsimile No. 1 represented an attempt by a priest
of the god Elkenah to slay Abraham upon an altar. The Egyptologists say
something quite different. Here is how Richard A. Parker describes the
original:

> This is a well-known scene from the Osiris mysteries, with Anubis, the
> Jackel-headed god, on the left ministering to the dead Osiris on the bier. The

penciled(?) restoration is incorrect. Anubis should be jackel-headed. The left arm of Osiris is in reality lying at his side under him. The apparent upper hand is part of the wing of a second bird which is hovering over the erect phallus of Osiris (now broken away). The second bird is Isis and she is magically impregnated by the dead Osiris and then later gives birth to Horus who avenges his father and takes over his inheritance. The complete bird represents Nephthys, sister to Osiris and Isis. Beneath the bier are the four canopic jars with heads representative of the four sons of Horus, human-headed Imseti, baboon-headed Hapy, jackal-headed Duamutef and falcon-headed Kebehsenuf.[16]

Significantly, the vertical columns of characters on the side of Papyrus No. I mention the name Hor, son of Tikhebyt. This is the same name that is on Papyrus No. XI and is further proof that this Papyrus No. I was part of the same roll to which the Book of Breathings pieces belonged.[17]

Though the original for Facsimile No. 3 (see Figure 3) was not included among the papyri material recovered in 1966, the facsimile itself has been analyzed by the Egyptologists. Joseph said it represented Abraham reasoning upon the principles of astronomy to the Egyptians, but Klaus Baer gives the following interpretation of the illustration:

> "Facsimile No. 3" shows a man (5), his hand raised in adoration and a cone of perfumed grease and a lotus flower on his head (ancient Egyptian festive attire), being introduced by Maat (4), the goddess of justice, and Anubis (6), the guide of the dead, into the presence of Osiris (1), enthroned as king of the Netherworld. Behind Osiris stands Isis (2), and in front of him is an offering-stand (3) with a jug and some flowers on it. Over the whole scene is a canopy with stars painted on it to represent the sky.[18]

The facsimile, as it was originally published in the *Times and Seasons*, is clear enough to permit a translation to be made of some of the characters. The line of hieroglyphs below the illustration in that facsimile reads:

> O gods of ... gods of the Caverns, gods of the south, north, west, and east, grant well-being to Osiris Hor, justified....[19]

So this facsimile also represents a piece of papyrus that was dedicated to the deceased priest Hor. Klaus Baer has concluded that it too was a part of Joseph's "Book of Breathings" papyrus — the original for Facsimile No. 1 being at one end of the roll, while the original for Facsimile No. 3 was at the other end. He notes that other copies of the Book of Breathings have a similar arrangement.[20]

The circular piece of papyrus that provided the original for Facsimile No. 2 was what is called a "hypocephalus" (which means "under the head") because it was placed under the head of the deceased as an amulet. Enough of the characters on the facsimile have been translated to determine that this particular hypocephalus was made for an individual named Shoshenq.[21] Joseph's interpretation of the scenes it represents is erroneous.

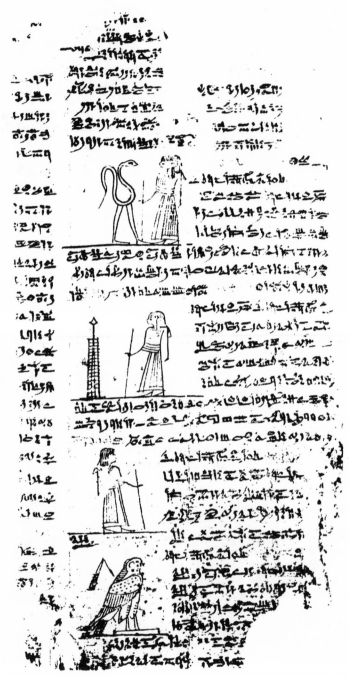

Figure 4. Joseph Smith Papyrus No. V. This is one of the papyrus fragments from the roll that Joseph Smith claimed was the record of the biblical Joseph.

In addition to the claim that one of the papyrus rolls was written by Abraham, Joseph also claimed that another was written by the biblical Joseph. It appears that this one is also among the recovered papyri. Such a determination can be made because of a description that Oliver Cowdery gave of the "record of Joseph" roll:

> The representation of the god-head — three, yet in one, is curiously drawn to give simply, though impressively, the writers views of that exalted personage. The serpent, represented as walking, or formed in a manner to be able to walk, standing in front of, and near a female figure, is to me, one of the great representations I have ever seen upon paper.... Enoch's Pillar, as mentioned by Josephus, is upon the same roll.... The inner end of the same roll, (Joseph's record,) presents a representation of the judgment....[22]

What Oliver described as a walking snake standing before a female figure can be seen on Papyrus No. V. What he called "Enoch's Pillar" is also on this piece (see Figure 4). Moreover, what is apparently supposed to be the "three, yet in one," god-head is on Papyrus No. IV.

The Egyptologists have determined that these papyrus pieces are from a roll that contained a rendition of the Egyptian "Book of the Dead." This particular copy was dedicated, as was usual, to the person with whom it was buried — in this case, a woman by the name of Ta-Sherit-Min, who was the daughter of Neskhons.[23]

Despite what has been learned about the papyri and Joseph's translation of them, the Utah church continues to accept *The Book of Abraham* as scripture. In fact, it has retained its place in the latest edition (1981) of the *Pearl of Great Price*, even though the church has abrogated the Negro Doctrine. There is not so much as a footnote in that book declaring that Joseph Smith's Egyptian papyri have been found, even though their discovery initially caused much excitement within the church. Furthermore, most Mormons are quite unaware of what has been learned about the papyri.

There are pragmatic reasons for this. In the first place, the church was under enormous pressure and was frequently accused of being a racist organization because of its "Negro Doctrine." If it had retained that doctrine, the findings about the Egyptian papyri would have been continually publicized by civil rights advocates who wanted to make an issue of the inequality of blacks in the church. One way out was for the church to receive a revelation giving the priesthood to the blacks, thus relieving the pressure and drawing attention away from the papyri and *the Book of Abraham*.[24]

In the second place, if the church admitted that *The Book of Abraham* was not a divine revelation, it would have serious implications for *The Book of Mormon*. Since an angel supposedly took the plates for *The Book of Mormon* from Joseph after he translated them, the correctness of that translation could not be judged by scholars. With *The Book of Abraham*, however, we have the original documents Joseph said he translated, and we can consequently make a judgment about his ability to translate ancient records — including, by implication, *The Book of Mormon*. Since, by all ordinary criteria, that judgment indicates that Joseph did not have such an ability, the church has in effect been forced to take the position that ordinary criteria do not apply.

Some believers have declared that one cannot draw any conclusions about the validity of *The Book of Mormon* from conclusions drawn from Joseph's translation of *The Book of Abraham*. Nonetheless, both have been shown to have a basis in the literature and ideas of the early nineteenth century. Even without current information about Joseph's translation of the Egyptian papyri, this should be sufficient to give one a suspicion that both books were products of an eclectic mind itself a product of the early nineteenth century. What has been learned about Joseph's translation of the Egyptian papyri should be enough to confirm that suspicion.

Chapter Notes
and Bibliography

Chapter Notes

Prologue

1. When I examined and took photos of them in the summer of 1977, the original records of the church were in the possession of the Poultney Historical Society. The records were apparently stolen from the museum when it was closed during the following winter, but the Society still has photocopies of the original, as well as a transcription of the births, baptisms, etc. that the WPA made from the records during the thirties.

2. See Stanley R. Gunn, *Oliver Cowdery — Second Elder and Scribe* (Salt Lake City: Bookcraft, 1962), p. 19.

3. Under the date of May 26, 1810, there is a note that a vote was taken "to give Mrs Keziah Cowdry a letter of recommendation." In 1787, while the Cowdery family lived in Reading, Vt., Oliver's grandfather was chosen as one of the four deacons of the Congregational Church of that town. This would seem to establish that the family had a Congregationalist background. See Gunn, p. 14.

4. Ethan Smith was installed as minister of the church on Nov. 21, 1821, according to the church records.

5. Ethan Smith, *View of the Hebrews*, 2d ed. (Poultney, Vt.: 1825), pp. 228, 230, 245–249.

6. *The Historical Record*, Vol. 6, Nos. 3–5 (May, 1887), p. 196. This Mormon periodical was published in Salt Lake City.

Chapter 1

1. Orsamus Turner, *History of the Pioneer Settlement of Phelps and Gorham's Purchase* (Rochester, N.Y.: 1851), pp. 213–214. Printers' assistants in those days were called "devils." The "balls" were of printer's ink.

2. See William Warren Sweet, *The Story of Religions in America* (New York: 1930), pp. 316–318.

3. From an interview with Daniel Hendrix published in the St. Louis *Globe Democrat*, Feb. 21, 1897.

4. *History of Lee County* (Chicago: 1881), p. 387.

5. Wilhelm Wyl (von Wymetal), *Mormon Portraits* (Salt Lake City: 1886), Vol. 1 (*Joseph Smith the Prophet, His Family and Friends*), p. 25.

6. In a pamphlet, *An interesting Account of Several Remarkable Visions...*, first published in Edinburgh in 1840.

7. *The Book of Mormon*, 1830 ed., p. 121 (2 Nephi 33:1). Henceforth, the abbreviated form, *B.M.*, will be used for the references.

8. *B.M.*, p. 564 (Ether 12:23–24).

9. Milton V. Backman, Jr., *Joseph Smith's First Vision* (Salt Lake City: Book-craft, 1971), pp. 48–49.

10. Lucy Mack Smith, *Biographical Sketches of Joseph Smith the Prophet and His Progenitors for Many Generations* (Liverpool, England: 1853), p. 85.

11. According to an article of his that was published in the Lockport *Daily Courier*, May 5, 1854, Turner left the Palmyra area in 1822. A lower limit for the time frame of the camp meeting might be set by the fact that the "Deeds of Ontario Co. Bk G, 345" show that the Methodists did not acquire their property in the woods on the Vienna Road until July of 1821. See Wesley P. Walters, "A Reply to Dr. Bushman," *Dialogue: A Journal of Mormon Thought*, Vol. 4, No. 1 (Spring, 1969), p. 99.

12. *B.M.*, p. 112 (2 Nephi 28:3–4). The contentions between the various denom-inations that are referred to in this prophecy figure prominently in the Mormon accounts of the religious excitement.

13. *A Book of Commandments for the Government of the Church of Christ* (Zion [Independence], Mo.: 1833), p. 10.

14. *Doctrine and Covenants*, Sec. 5:2–4. The first edition of this book was published in 1835. Joseph changed several of his revelations. See Jerald and Sandra Tanner, *The Case Against Mormonism* (Salt Lake City: Modern Microfilm Co., 1967) Vol. 1, pp. 130–191.

15. David Whitmer, *An address to All Believers in Christ* (Richmond, Mo.: 1887) p. 57.

Chapter 2

1. "History of Joseph Smith," *Times and Seasons*, Vol. 3, No. 10 (March 15, 1842), p. 727. This history was published in installments in the *Times and Seasons*, and was derived from an autobiography that Joseph supposedly began in 1838. It was later incorporated with some changes and additions into the *History of the Church*.

2. *Ibid.*, Nos. 10, 11 (March 15 and April 1, 1842), pp. 728, 748.

3. *Ibid.*, No. 11, pp. 748–749.

4. Fawn Brodie, *No Man Knows My History* (New York: Alfred A. Knopf, 1945), pp. 23–25. A qualification, of course, would be the autobiography that Joseph is said to have begun in 1838. However, the earliest known extant manuscript copy of that biography dates from 1839.

5. For a survey of the lack of mention of the first vision in both Mormon and non-Mormon literature, see James B. Allen, "The Significance of Joseph Smith's 'First Vision' in Mormon Thought," *Dialogue: A Journal of Mormon Thought*, Vol. 1, No. 3, (Autumn, 1966), pp. 30–35. *Dialogue* is a Mormon periodical, but not under church control.

6. For a transcript of this account, see Dean C. Jessee, "The Early Accounts of Joseph Smith's First Vision," BYU *Studies*, Vol. 9, No. 3 (Spring, 1969), pp. 278–280.

7. *Ibid.*, p. 284, 286.

8. For examples, see Jerald and Sandra Tanner, *The Case Against Mormonism*, Vol. 1, pp. 119–128.

9. Oliver Cowdery, "Letter III," *Latter Day Saints' Messenger and Advocate*, Vol. 1, No. 3 (Dec., 1834), pp. 42–43.

10. Oliver Cowdery, "Letter IV," *Latter Day Saints' Messenger and Advocate*, Vol. 1, No. 5 (Feb., 1835), p. 78.

11. *Ibid.*

12. In the *Messenger and Advocate*, Vol, 1, No. 1 (Oct., 1834), p. 13, Oliver stated: "That our narrative may be correct, and particularly the introduction, it is proper to inform our patrons, that our brother J. Smith, jr. has offered to assist us. Indeed, there are many items connected with the fore part of this subject that render his

labor indispensible. With his labor and with authentic documents now in our possession, we hope to render this a pleasing and agreeable narrative ... that shall be founded
upon facts."

13. For further information on the study, including all source material, see
Wesley P. Walters, "New Light on Mormon Origins from the Palmyra (N.Y.) Revival,"
originally published in the *Evangelical Theological Society*, Vol. 10, No. 4 (Fall, 1967),
pp. 227–244. A somewhat revised version was published in *Dialogue: A Journal of
Mormon Thought*, Vol. 4, No. 1 (Spring, 1969) pp. 60–81.

14. *The Methodist Magazine.*, Vol. 8 (April, 1825), 159f.

15. Walters, "New Light...," *Dialogue*, pp. 66–67. Though Joseph stated that the
"excitement" occurred "in the place" where he lived, some Mormon writers have expanded Joseph's "neighborhood" to a large enough area to cause the figures for the actual
neighborhood to be swamped, and also by referring to revivals in other parts of the
state.

16. William Smith, *William Smith on Mormonism*, (Lamoni, Iowa: 1883), pp.
5–7.

17. Lucy Smith, *Biographical Sketches...*, p. 90.

18. Lucy Smith, "Preliminary Manuscript." p. 86. Quoted from a typed copy.
The original is in the Utah church archives. This particular quote was crossed out in the
original and was followed by the account of the man laboring in the neighborhood,
previously quoted.

19. *Ibid.*, p. 87.

20. The date is on Alvin's gravestone in the General John Swift Memorial Ceme-
tery in Palmyra.

21. *Deseret Evening News*, Vol. 27, No. 11 (Jan. 20, 1894).

22. *Ibid.*

23. Noted in Vol. 2 of the "Session Records" of the Palmyra Presbyterian
Church. See BYU *Studies*, Vol. 10, No. 4 (Summer, 1970), pp. 483–484. Wesley P.
Walters brought these records to light. Unfortunately, Vol. 1, which would show when
the family members joined the church, is missing.

24. See Chapter 1, note 11.

25. Fayette Lapham, "The Mormons," *Historical Magazine*, Vol. 8, 2d ser.,
No. 5 (May, 1870), pp. 305–306. The well was the one in which Joseph found his peepstone.

26. Mitchell Bronk, "The Baptist Church at Manchester," *The Chronicle: A Baptist Historical Quarterly*, Vol. 11, No. 1 (Jan., 1948), p. 24.

27. "History of Joseph Smith," *Times and Seasons*, Vol. 3, No. 12 (April 15,
1842), p. 753.

28. Lucy Smith, "Preliminary Manuscript," p. 77. Punctuation has been added
for clarity.

29. These statements will be covered in more elaborate detail in the upcoming
chapters.

Chapter 3

1. Eber D. Howe, *Mormonism Unvailed* (Painesville, Ohio: 1834), p. 261. The
italics are in the original.

2. *Ibid.*, p. 248.

3. Some Mormon writers appear to have misrepresented the facts and falsified
information about the statements. See Rodger I. Anderson, "Joseph Smith's Early Reputation Revisited," *Journal of Pastoral Practice*, Vol. 4 (1980), No. 3, pp. 71–108, and
No. 4, pp. 72–105.

4. This was his pen name. His actual name was Abner Cole.

5. "Gold Bible, No. 3," Palmyra *Reflector*, Feb. 1, 1831.

6. "Gold Bible, No. 5," Palmyra *Reflector*, Feb. 28, 1831.

7. Howe, pp. 232–233.

8. The original of this letter is in the Amistad Research Center, Dillard University, New Orleans.

9. "Gold Bible, No. 5," Palmyra *Reflector*, Feb. 28, 1831. See Appendix A for a possible identification of Walters.

10. "The Book of Pukei," Palmyra *Reflector*, June 12 and July 7, 1830.

11. Joseph Lewis, "Review of Mormonism," *Amboy Journal*, June 11, 1879.

12. *B.M.*, p. 444 (Helaman 13:35–37).

13. Howe, pp. 259–260.

Chapter 4

1. From Isaac Hale's affidavit that was published in the *Susquehanna Register*, May 1, 1834, and by Howe, pp. 262–263.

2. As given in "The Original Prophet, By a Visitor to Salt Lake City" (Charles Marshall), *Fraser's Magazine*, Vol. 7, No. 38, n.s. (Feb., 1873), pp. 229–230. The bracketed words are Marshall's.

3. "History of Joseph Smith," *Times and Seasons*, Vol. 3, No. 13 (May 2, 1842), p. 772.

4. Lucy Mack Smith, *Biographical Sketches...*, p. 92.

5. *Latter Day Saints' Messenger and Advocate*, Vol. 2, No. 1 (Oct., 1835), pp. 200–201.

6. This testimony reads as follows: "Horace Stowel sworn. Says he see prisoner look at hat through stone, pretending to tell where a chest of dollars were buried in Windsor, a number of miles distant; marked out size of chest in the leaves on ground." As given by Bishop Tuttle in the *New Schaff-Herzog Encyclopedia*, also titled *A Religious Encyclopedia: or Dictionary of Biblical, Historical, Doctrinal, and Practical Theology* (New York: 1883), Vol. 2, p. 1576.

7. Brodie, pp. 405–407.

8. From the letter by Dr. William Purple published in the *Chenango Union*, May 3, 1877, as quoted by William Mulder and A. Russell Mortensen, *Among the Mormons* (New York: Alfred A. Knopf, 1958), pp. 35–38.

9. Francis W. Kirkham, *A New Witness for Christ in America* (Independence, Mo.: Press of Zion's Print and Publishing Co., 1951), Vol. 1, pp. 385–386.

10. "Mormonites," *Evangelical Magazine and Gospel Advocate*, n.s. 2 (April 9, 1831), p. 120.

11. Wesley P. Walters, "Joseph Smith's Bainbridge, N.Y., Court Trials," *Westminster Theological Journal*, Vol. 36, No. 2 (Winter, 1974), p. 140.

12. Dr. Hugh Nibley, *The Myth Makers* (Salt Lake City: Bookcraft, 1967), pp. 155–156. As previously noted, these 1830 trials of Joseph Smith occurred in connection with his trying to organize his church in the Bainbridge area.

13. *Ibid.*, p. 142.

14. From a notarized statement by Wesley P. Walters, dated Oct. 28, 1971. The bills are now in the Chenango County Supervisor's office in Norwich, New York.

15. The statement was published in conjunction with the trial notes in the *Utah Christian Advocate*, January, 1886.

16. Clarence E. Pearsall, *The History and Genealogy of the Pearsall Family in England and America* (San Francisco: 1928), Vol. 2, Section 10, p. 1151. The late Stanley S. Ivins located this material.

17. *Ibid.*

18. *Ibid.*, Section 2, p. 1143.

19. *Ibid.*, p. 1144.

20. Burt Bridgman and Joseph C. Bridgman, *Genealogy of the Bridgman Family* (1894), pp. 129, 116, 118–119; cited by Walters, "Joseph Smith's Bainbridge, N.Y., Court Trials," p. 141.

21. *Deeds*, Lib. 45, 400, Ontario County Court House, Canandaigua, N.Y.; as given by Walters, "Joseph Smith's Bainbridge, N.Y., Court Trials," p. 142.

22. *Ibid.*, p. 132.

23. The original of this letter is in the Turner Collection of the Illinois State Historical Library in Springfield, Ill. Mr. Walters discussed this letter, and provided a photocopy of it, in an article, "From Occult to Cult with Joseph Smith, Jr.," in the *Journal of Pastoral Practice*, Vol. 1, No. 2 (Summer, 1977), pp. 121–137.

24. *Laws of the State of New York, Revised and Passed...*, revisors William P. Van Ness and John Woodworth (1813), Vol. 1, p. 114, cited by Walters, "From Occult to Cult...," p. 124.

25. Donna Hill, *Joseph Smith: The First Mormon*, (New York: Doubleday, 1977), pp. 67–68.

Chapter 5

1. "Gold Bible, No. 4," Palmyra *Reflector*, Feb. 14, 1831.

2. Josiah Priest included an excerpt from the first edition of Ethan Smith's book in his *Wonders of Nature and Providence, Displayed*, which was published in 1825 in Albany. According to its still extant book list, the Manchester library had Priest's book shortly after it was published. The remains of the rental library are now held by the Ontario County Historical Society in Canandaigua, N.Y.

3. See Gunn, p. 14.

4. In the *Book of Commandments* (p. 19), Joseph referred to Oliver's ability with the divining rod, saying that Oliver had "the gift of working with the rod." In the *Doctrine and Covenants*, Joseph changed this to "the gift of Aaron" (Section 8:6–7).

5. Howe, p. 260.

6. Joel Tiffany, "Mormonism—No. II," *Tiffany's Monthly*, Vol. 5, No. 4 (August, 1859), p. 163. Harris made the comment in an interview that he had with Tiffany.

7. *On the Mormon Frontier: The Diary of Hosea Stout*, ed. by Juanita Brooks (Salt Lake City: University of Utah Press, 1964), Vol. 2, p. 593.

8. Howe, pp. 242–243.

9. Fayette Lapham, "The Mormons," *Historical Magazine*, Vol. 8, 2d ser., No. 5 (May, 1870), p. 307.

10. Dean Jessee, "Joseph Knight's Recollection of Early Mormon History," BYU *Studies*, Vol. 17, No. 1 (Autumn, 1976), p. 31. Punctuation has been added for clarity.

11. *Susquehanna Register*, May 1, 1834. Also Howe, p. 263.

12. Howe, pp. 243–244.

13. "History of Joseph Smith," *Times and Seasons*, Vol. 3, No. 13 (May 2, 1842), p. 772.

14. Jessee, "Joseph Knight's Recollection...," p. 32.

15. *Susquehanna Register*, May 1, 1834. Also Howe, pp. 263–264.

16. Howe, pp. 234–235.

17. *Ibid.*, p. 235.

Chapter 6

1. Jessee, "Joseph Knight's Recollections...," pp. 32–33.

2. Lucy Mack Smith, *Biographical Sketches...*, p. 101.

3. Joel Tiffany, "Mormonism—No. II," pp. 165–166.

4. This was in the *Evening and Morning Star*, Vol. 1, No. 8, (Jan., 1833), p. 2: "The Book of Mormon ... was translated by the gift and power of God, by an unlearned man, through the aid of a pair of interpreters, or spectacles—(known, perhaps, in ancient days as Teraphim, or Urim and Thummim)...."

5. Howe, pp. 260–261.

6. John A. Clark, *Gleanings by the Way* (New York: 1842), p. 223.

7. Tiffany, "Mormonism—No. II," pp. 168–169.

8. *View of the Hebrews* (1825 ed.), p. viii. Clark, *Gleanings...*, pp. 223–224.

9. *B.M.*, p. 578 (Moroni 7:16–17).

10. Clark, *Gleanings...*, p. 224.

11. Howe, pp. 254–256.

12. *Ibid.*, p. 254.

13. Lucy Mack Smith, *Biographical Sketches...*, p. 102–103.

14. Tiffany, "Mormonism—No. II," pp. 164, 167.

15. *Susquehanna Register*, May 1, 1834. Also Howe, p. 254. Several other individuals also related that Joseph said the first one to see the plates would be a young child.

16. From their letter entitled "Mormon History," published in the *Amboy Journal* (Amboy, Ill.), April 30, 1879.

17. Clark, *Gleanings...*, pp. 229–230.

18. This was Charles Anthon, a professor of classical studies at Columbia. For further information, see Stanley B. Kimball, "The Anthon Transcript: People, Primary Sources, and Problems," BYU *Studies*, Vol. 10, No. 3 (Spring, 1970), pp. 325–352.

19. Howe, pp. 270–272.

20. "History of Joseph Smith," *Times and Seasons*, Vol. 3, No. 13 (May 2, 1842), p. 773.

21. In 1980, the situation was further confused when a piece of paper was "uncovered" which contained an arrangement of characters similar to that described by Anthon, but it was found to be a forgery.

22. *B.M.*, p. 538 (Mormon 9:32–34).

23. *B.M.*, p. 111 (2 Nephi 27:15–19).

Chapter 7

1. *Susquehanna Register*, May 1, 1834. Also Howe, p. 269.

2. *Amboy Journal*, April 30, 1879.

3. *Ibid.*, May 21, 1879.

4. *Ibid.*, June 11, 1879.

5. *Doctrine and Covenants*, Sec. 10:45.

6. Lucy Smith, *Biographical Sketches...*, pp. 124–126.

7. See Chapter 2, note 23.

8. *Doctrine and Covenants*, Sec. 5:30–34.

9. David Whitmer, *An Address to All Believers in Christ* (Richmond, Mo.: 1887), p. 30.

10. *Susquehanna Register*, May 1, 1834. Also Howe, pp. 265–266.

11. Whitmer, *An Address...*, p. 12.

12. *Saints' Herald*, Oct. 1, 1879, p. 289, as quoted in the *Saint's Herald*, Vol. 109, No. 22 (Nov. 15, 1962), p. 15. The *Saints' Herald* is a publication of the Reorganized LDS Church.

13. *Millennial Star*, Feb. 6, 1882, as quoted in the *Saints' Herald*, Nov. 15, 1962, p. 16.

14. *Chicago Inter-Ocean*, Oct. 17, 1886, as quoted in the *Saint's Herald*, Nov. 15, 1962, p. 16.

15. From a letter written by Emma, presently in the archives of the RLDS church, as quoted in the *Saints' Herald*, Nov. 15, 1962, p. 15.

16. Howe, pp. 240, 241, 247.

17. *B.M.*, p. 586 (Moroni 10:4).

18. *B.M.*, p. 403, p. 249.

19. *B.M.*, p. 290.

20. *B.M.*, p. 204.

21. *B.M.*, p. 140, p. 248.

22. *B.M.*, p. 244 (Alma 8:18–19).

23. *B.M.*, p. 564 (Ether 12:25–26).

24. *B.M.*, p. 533 (Mormon 8:17).

Chapter 8

1. In the *Times and Seasons*, Vol. 3, No. 9 (March 1, 1842), p. 707, Joseph said the following: "... each plate was six inches wide and eight inches long and not quite so thick as common tin.... The volume was something near six inches in thickness...." With these dimensions, the plates would have had a volume of 288 cubic inches. Gold has a density of 19.3 grams per c.c., or .69 lbs. per cubic inch. Therefore the plates would have weighed 198 lbs.

2. Wilford C. Wood, *Joseph Smith Begins His work*, Vol. 1, forepart, "Memorandum made by John H. Gilbert, Esq."

3. From a letter by Stephen Burnett to Lyman E. Johnson, dated 15 April, 1838. This letter was copied on May 24, 1838, into pages 64–68, of a letter-book that is presently in the Joseph Smith Collection in the L.D.S. Church Archives, Salt Lake City, Utah.

4. "History of Joseph Smith," *Times and Seasons*, Vol. 3, No. 21 (Aug. 15, 1842), pp. 897–898.

5. Anthony Metcalf, in an interview with Martin Harris, *Ten Years Before the Mast* (Malad City, Idaho., 1888), pp. 70–71.

6. From a sworn statement by G.J. Keen, 14 April, 1885, given by Charles Shook, *The True Origin of the Book of Mormon* (Cincinnati: 1914), pp. 58–59.

7. As quoted by Wayne Cutter Gannel in a master's thesis, Brigham Young University, 1955, "Martin Harris, Witness and Benefactor to the Book of Mormon"; a copy is presently in the Church Historian's Office, Salt Lake City.

8. Wood, forepart.

9. *Book of Commandments*, Chap. 25, verse 14.

10. "Mormonites," *Evangelical Magazine and Gospel Advocate*, April 9, 1831, p. 120.

11. *Ibid.*

12. Wesley P. Walters, "From Occult to Cult with Joseph Smith, Jr.," *The Journal of Pastoral Practice*, Vol. 1, No. 2, (Summer, 1977), p. 135.

13. *Ibid.*, p. 129.

14. Jesse, "Joseph Knight's Recollection...," p. 38.

Chapter 9

1. Brodie, pp. 46–48; footnote, p. 47. It was from reading Mrs. Brodie's book several years ago that I became curious about the relationship between *View of the Hebrews* and *The Book of Mormon*.

2. A longer version of Roberts' study has recently come to light. Titled "Book of Mormon Difficulties," it shows a few more similarities between the two books, provides lengthier commentaries, and deals with other aspects of the origin of *The Book of Mormon*. A photo reprint of the study is available from the Modern Microfilm Co., Salt Lake City.

3. Kirkham, *A New Witness...*, Vol. 2, pp. 391–392.

4. Hugh Nibley, "The Comparative Method," *The Improvement Era*, Vol. 62, No. 10 (October, 1959), pp. 744–745.

5. Roy E. Weldon and F. Edward Butterworth, *Criticisms of The Book of Mormon Answered* (Independence, Mo.: Herald House, 1973), p. 15. The page number referenced by Weldon is in error. It should be page 171.

6. Sidney B. Sperry, *Answers to Book of Mormon Questions* (Salt Lake City: Bookcraft, 1967), p. 178.

7. *Ibid.*

8. *Ibid.*, pp. 178–179.

9. Charles Thompson, *Evidences in Proof of the Book of Mormon* (Rochester, N.Y.: 1841), pp. 57–58.

10. In the volume entitled, *The Book of the Prophet Isaiah, Chapters 1–39,* commentary by A.S. Herbert (London: Cambridge University Press, 1973), p. 118.

Chapter 10

1. Joseph made an error in this prophecy by saying that the *Book of Mormon* people were descendants of the Jews. Technically, only the descendants of the tribe of Judah can be called Jews. An actual Israelite would not have made such an error.

2. David Millard, *The True Messiah Exalted, or, Jesus Christ Really the Son of God Vindicated* (Canandaigua: 1818), p. 1. Canandaigua is nine miles from Joseph's home.

3. Alexander Campbell, *The Sacred Writings of the Apostles and Evangelists of Jesus Christ, Commonly Styled the New Testament* (Bethany, Va.: 1823), second edition, p. x.

4. *The Christian Baptist*, Vol. 2, No. 7 (Feb. 7, 1825), p. 156; Vol. 2, No. 11 (June 6, 1825), p. 254; Vol. 4, No. 4, (Nov. 6, 1826), p. 96.

5. *Ibid.*, Vol. 2, No. 12 (July 4, 1825), p. 273.

6. *The Christian Baptist*, Vol. 3, No. 1 (Aug. 1, 1825), p. 4, from the stereotype edition of 1848, p. 174.

7. Josiah Priest, *Wonders of Nature and Providence, Displayed* (Albany, N.Y.: 1825), p. 249.

Chapter 11

1. See Joseph Fielding Smith, *Essentials in Church History* (Salt Lake City: Deseret, 1959), p. 63.

2. Elias Boudinot, *A Star in the West* (Trenton: 1816), p. 73.

Chapter 12

1. *B.M.*, pp. 131–139 (Jacob 5).

2. *Priest*, p. 464. Jerald and Sandra Tanner found this particular item.

3. *Ibid.*, p. 133.

Chapter 14

1. *Archaeologia Americana,* published by the American Antiquarian Society (Worcester, Mass: 1820) Vol. 1, p. 145.
2. *Times and Seasons,* Vol. 3, No. 5, (Jan. 1, 1842), p. 640.

Chapter 15

1. John G. Stearns, *An Appendix to "An Inquiry into the Nature and Tendency of Speculative Free Masonry"* (Cazenovia, N.Y.: 1828), pp. 40–41.
2. Henry Brown, *A Narrative of the Anti-Masonick Excitement* (Batavia, N.Y.: 1829), p. 43.
3. William Morgan, *Illustrations of Masonry,* 3d ed. (New York: 1827), p. 26.
4. *Ibid.,* p. 38.
5. Stearns, *An Appendix...,* pp. 44–45.
6. Morgan, *Illustrations...,* p. 13.
7. *Archaeologia Americana,* pp. 117–118.
8. See Brodie, pp. 279–282. See also *Mormonism—Shadow or Reality?,* pp. 484–492.

Chapter 16

1. Among these was a history by Ixtlilxochitl. This history was not formally published until after the publication of *The Book of Mormon.* Some Mormon writers have used this fact as evidence that Joseph could not have had access to it, but Clavigero's use of it shows that it need not have been published in its entirety in order for parts of it to have been previously published in other works.
2. Clavigero, *History of Mexico* (Philadelphia: 1817), Vol. 3, pp. 112–114.
3. *Priest,* p. 355.
4. *Ibid.,* pp. 527–528. Jerald and Sandra Tanner found this particular item.
5. Clavigero, Vol. 2, p. 13.

Chapter 17

1. *Times and Seasons,* Vol. 3, No. 9 (March 1, 1842), p. 707.

Chapter 18

1. *Archaeologia Americana,* pp. 3–4.
2. *Ibid.,* p. 5.
3. *B.M.,* p. 150 (Omni 20–22).
4. The revelation that ordered Joseph to replace the missing 116 pages by translating from the plates of Nephi is dated May, 1829. Near the end of the translation process it was learned that there were to be three witnesses to the book; but the section in which that appears is near the beginning of the book. The most likely conclusion is that Joseph did not replace the lost 116 pages until near the end of the translation process.
5. Turner, *History of the Pioneer Settlement...,* p. 209.

Chapter 19

1. Eli's suspicions may have had a basis in fact since Nancy Marinda Johnson was later listed as one of Joseph's plural wives. See Brodie, pp. 119, 439.

2. *Doctrine and Covenants*, Section 97.

3. *The Western Monitor*, Fayette, Mo., August 2, 1833.

4. Joseph's promise to the men was reported by Reed Peck, one of the volunteers, in a manuscript dated 1839. The manuscript was published in 1899 by Lu B. Cake, *Peepstone Joe and the Peck Manuscript.* The date for the redemption of Zion was given in a letter by Joseph to the High council. It was printed in the *History of the Church*, Vol. 2, p. 145.

5. *Messenger and Advocate*, Vol. 2, No. 7 (April, 1836), pp. 289–290.

6. *The Book of Abraham* 1:21–26.

7. *Messenger and Advocate*, Vol. 1, No. 6 (March, 1835), p. 82.

8. "Records of Certificates of Membership and Ordination…," p. 61, in the LDS Church Historical Department, Salt Lake City. For information concerning Elijah Abel, see Tanner, *Mormonism—Shadow or Reality?*, pp. 267–272.

9. John W. Fizgerald, Dee Jay Nelson, and H. Michael Marquardt, *Discrimination: Is It of God?*, p. 125.

10. Brigham Young Addresses, Ms. d, Box 48, folder 3, dated Feb. 5, 1852, LDS Church Historical Dept., as given by Tanner, *The Changing World of Mormonism* (Chicago: Moody Press, 1980), p. 312.

11. *Journal of Discourses*, Vol. 2, p. 143.

12. Brigham Young Addresses, Feb. 5, 1852.

13. F.S. Spalding, *Joseph Smith, Jr., as a Translator* (Salt Lake City: 1912), pp. 26–27.

Chapter 20

1. For documentation on Joseph's drinking habits, see LaMar Peterson, *Hearts Made Glad* (Salt Lake City, 1975).

2. A photo of the letter is in Jerald and Sandra Tanner's *The Mormon Kingdom* (Salt Lake City: Modern Microfilm Co., 1969), Vol. 1, p. 27.

3. *Messenger and Advocate*, Vol. 1, No. 11, p. 163.

4. *Ibid.*, Vol. 3, No. 8, p. 511.

5. See D. Paul Sampson and Larry T. Wimmer, "The Kirtland Safety Society: The Stock Ledger Book and the Bank Failure," BYU *Studies*, Vol. 12, No. 4 (Summer, 1972), pp. 427–436. These authors suggest that Parrish may have been responsible for the failure of the bank, but they concede that the ledger does not indicate any dishonesty on Parrish's part.

6. See Brodie, Appendix C, for documentation concerning these women.

7. *The Return*, Vol. 3, No. 2 (Feb. 1891), p. 28.

8. Martha Brotherton's account was also published in Bennett's *History of the Saints*, 1842, pp. 236–240.

9. It should be noted that in *The Book of Mormon* it is stated: "Behold, David and Solomon truly had many wives and concubines, which thing was abominable before me, saith the Lord" (p. 127; Jacob 2:24). This contradicts the revelation on plural marriage which states that the wives of David and Solomon were given to them "of the Lord." Nevertheless, Joseph seems to have had an idea about polygamy even while dictating *The Book of Mormon*. Shortly after the aforementioned verse is the following: "For if I will, saith the Lord of Hosts, raise up seed unto me, I will command my people; otherwise they shall hearken unto these things" (p. 127; Jacob 2:30). Mormon polygamists used this verse to reconcile *The Book of Mormon* with Joseph's revelation on plural marriage, though they had to ignore the earlier verse to do so.

10. *Millennial Star*, Vol. 22 (1860), p. 455.

11. For a fuller discussion of the subject, see Klaus J. Hansen, *Quest for Empire: The Political Kingdom of God and the Council of Fifty in Mormon History* (East Lansing: Michigan State University Press, 1967).

12. Joseph Fielding Smith, *Essentials in Church History* (Salt Lake City: Deseret, 1950), p. 365.

Appendix A

1. Hiland Paul and Robert Parks, *History of Wells, Vermont* (Rutland, Vt.: 1869), p. 79.

Appendix B

1. See Dewey Farnsworth and Edith Wood Farnsworth, *Book of Mormon Evidences in Ancient America* (Salt Lake City: Desert, 1953), pp. 140, 173.

2. *Archaeologia Americana*, p. 5. The other source was the *Palmyra Herald* of Feb. 19, 1823.

3. See L. Sprague de Camp, *Elephant* (New York: Pyramid, 1964), p. 55–56. See also *Encyclopaedia Britannica* under Peale, Charles Wilson, in the Micropaedia.

4. See Michael Coe, *The Maya* (New York: Praeger, 1966), pp. 118, 120, 129. The two Quetzalcoatls also went by the name Kukulcan, which likewise means the "feathered serpent."

5. Farnsworth, p. 172.

6. *Times and Seasons*, Sept. 15, 1842, p. 914.

7. See *Science News*, April 24, 1976, p. 261. See also Norman Hammond, "The Earliest Maya," *Scientific American*, March, 1977, pp. 116–133.

8. *Dialogue: A Journal of Mormon Thought*, Summer, 1973, p. 45.

9. Sylvanus G. Morley and George W. Brainerd, *The Ancient Maya* (Stanford, Calif.: Stanford University Press, 1956), pp. 23–24.

10. See Theodosius Dobzhansky, *Genetics of the Evolutionary Process* (New York: Columbia University Press, 1970), p. 286.

11. See William G. Haag, "The Bering Strait Land Bridge" (*Scientific American*, Jan., 1962), in the Readings from Scientific American series, *New World Archaeology: Theoretical and Cultural Transformations* (San Francisco: W.H. Freeman, 1974), pp. 263–267.

12. See Mario Pei, *The Families of Words* (New York: St. Martin's Press, 1962), for a more thorough study of the subject.

13. See Gordon R. Wiley, *An Introduction to American Archaeology* (Englewood Cliffs, N.J.: Prentice-Hall, 1966) Vol. 1, pp. 16–19. See also Ives Goddard, "Barry Fell Reexamined," *Biblical Archaeologist*, Sept. 1978, pp. 85–88. The only exception would be that of the Inuit language, which is represented in Arctic Siberia as well as in Arctic North America. A few tentative suggestions have been made deriving certain American Indian languages from certain Asian languages, but these are far from definite.

14. *Dialogue*, Summer, 1969, p. 74.

15. *Ibid.*, p. 81.

16. *Ibid.*, Summer, 1973, p. 46.

17. Quoted in *Mormonism — Shadow or Reality?*, p. 102.

18. Brigham H. Roberts, *New Witnesses for God*, (1909), Vol. 3, p. 40.

19. *Dialogue*, Summer, 1969, p. 78.

20. *Times and Seasons*, Mar. 1, 1842, p. 707.

21. *Latter-Day Saints' Messenger and Advocate*, Feb. 1835, p. 80.

Appendix C

1. Howe, pp. 278–280.
2. *Ibid.*, p. 282.
3. *Ibid.*, pp. 287–288.
4. *Ibid.*, pp. 289–290.
5. See their book, *Who Really Wrote the Book of Mormon?* (Santa Ana, Calif.: Vision House Publishers, 1977).
6. See "Mormon Critic Discounts Latest Attack on Book," *The Salt Lake Tribune,* July 10, 1977, p. C 25. See also, "Mormon Manuscript Claims: Another look," *Christianity Today,* Oct. 21, 1977, pp. 38–39.
7. Rev. George T. Chapman, *Sketches of the Alumni of Dartmouth College* (Cambridge: 1867), p. 39.
8. William Sprague, *Annals of the American Pulpit* (New York: 1857), Vol. 2, pp. 297–298.

Appendix D

1. As given in the *Improvement Era*, Sept., 1968, p. 20.
2. William Whiston, *Josephus, the Jewish Historian*, rev. by Samuel Burder (New York: 1821), Vol. 1, p. 24.
3. Clarence F. Packard, *The Mystery Religions of Paganism, Freemasonry, and Mormonism* (1965).
4. Thomas Taylor, *The Six Books of Proclus* (London: 1816), Vol. 1, p. 361; Vol. 2, pp. 130, 136, 142.
5. *History of the Church*, Vol. 2, p. 238.
6. Statement by Grant Heward, published in *Mormonism — Shadow or Reality?*, p. 358.
7. John Wilson, professor of Egyptology at the University of Chicago, "The Joseph Smith Papyri: A Summary," *Dialogue*, Summer, 1968, pp. 67–85. Richard A. Parker, professor of Egyptology at Brown University, "The Joseph Smith Papyri: A Preliminary Report," *Dialogue*, Summer, 1968, pp. 86–88; also his translation, "The Book of Breathings," appeared in the same issue on pp. 98–99. Klaus Baer, professor of Egyptology at the University of Chicago Oriental Institute, "The Breathing Permit of Hor," *Dialogue*, Autumn, 1968, pp. 109–134.
8. Since the photos Mr. Heward acquired were relatively poor, he took them to the offices of the *Desert News* in an attempt to see theirs. The church authorities, upon learning that outsiders had photos of the papyri, apparently decided it would be in their own interest to publish their photos first, which they did in the February, 1968, *Improvement Era.*
9. Joseph was right to read the line in that direction, for that is the way the Egyptian reads; not only was he familiar with this method of writing from his study of Hebrew but the short last line of papyrus text clearly begins on the right.
10. Mr. Heward published his findings in an article, "The Source of *The Book of Abraham* Identified," coauthored with Jerald Tanner in the summer, 1968, *Dialogue*, pp. 92–98.
11. See Baer's article in *Dialogue*. As well as using the photos supplied by *Dialogue*, Professor Baer made use of those published in the *Improvement Era*, which were apparently of better quality. Just before his article went to press he was able to see the original papyri and examine the paper backing and the papyrus fibers.
12. William S. West, *A Few Interesting Facts Respecting the Rise, Progress, and Pretensions of the Mormons* (1837), pp. 5–6.
13. See the article by Heward and Tanner in *Dialogue*, p. 95, and Baer, pp. 130–132.

14. See Parker, p. 86.

15. Baer, pp. 119–120.

16. Parker, p. 86.

17. Baer, pp. 116–117.

18. *Ibid.*, p. 126.

19. *Ibid.*, p. 127.

20. *Ibid.*

21. Baer, p. 127. One of Spalding's scholars had determined this as early as 1912.

22. *Messenger and Advocate*, Vol. 2, No. 3, Dec., 1835, p. 236.

23. Parker, p. 87.

24. The missionary activities of the church provided an added complication for the Negro Doctrine. In some areas, such as Brazil, many of the converts had mixed ancestry, though they could easily pass for white. Since even one drop of Negro blood supposedly disqualified an applicant for the priesthood, enforcement of the Negro doctrine would have been a burdensome task for the church.

Bibliography

Archaeologia Americana, Vol. 1. American Antiquarian Society. Worcester, Mass.: 1820.

Backman, Milton V., Jr., *Joseph Smith's First Vision*. Salt Lake City: Bookcraft, 1971.

Boudinot, Elias. *A Star in the West*. Trenton: 1816.

Bridgman, Burt, and Joseph C. Bridgman. *Genealogy of the Bridgman Family*. Hyde Park, Mass.: 1894.

Brodie, Fawn. *No Man Knows My History*. New York: Alfred A. Knopf, 1945.

Brooks, Juanita (ed.). *On the Mormon Frontier: The Diary of Hosea Stout*. Salt Lake City: University of Utah Press, 1964.

Brown, Henry. *A Narrative of the Anti-Masonick Excitement*. Batavia, N.Y.: 1829.

Campbell, Alexander. *The Sacred Writings of the Apostles and Evangelists of Jesus Christ, Commonly Styled the New Testament*. Bethany, Va.: 1828.

Cake, Lu B. *Peepstone Joe and the Peck Manuscript*. New York: 1899.

Chapman, George T. *Sketches of the Alumni of Dartmouth College*. Cambridge: 1867.

Clark, John A. *Gleanings by the Way*. New York: 1842.

Clavigero, Francisco. *History of Mexico*. Philadelphia: 1817.

Coe, Michael. *The Maya*. New York: Praeger, 1966.

Cowdrey, Wayne L.; Howard Davis, and Donald R. Scales. *Who Really Wrote the Book of Mormon?* Santa Ana, Calif.: Vision House Publishers, 1977.

Dick, Thomas. *Philosophy of a Future State*. Brookfield, Mass.: 1830.

Dobzhansky, Theodosius. *Genetics of the Evolutionary Process*. New York: Columbia University Press, 1970.

de Camp, L. Sprague. *Elephant*. New York: Pyramid, 1964.

Farnsworth, Dewey, and Edith Wood Farnsworth. *Book of Mormon Evidences in Ancient America*. Salt Lake City: Deseret, 1953.

Frisbie, Barnes. *The History of Middletown, Vermont*. Poultney, Vt.: 1867.

Gunn, Stanley R. *Oliver Cowdery — Second Elder and Scribe*. Salt Lake City: Bookcraft, 1962.

Hansen, Klaus J. *Quest for Empire: The Political Kingdom of God and the Council of Fifty in Mormon History*. East Lansing: Michigan State University Press, 1967.

Hill, Donna. *Joseph Smith: The First Mormon*. New York: Doubleday, 1977.

History of Lee County (Illinois). Chicago: 1881.

Howe, Eber D. *Mormonism Unvailed*. Painesville, Ohio: 1834.

Kirkham, Francis W. *A New Witness for Christ in America*. Independence, Mo.: Press of Zion's Print and Publishing Co., 1951.

Metcalf, Anthony. *Ten Years Before the Mast*. Malad City, Idaho: 1888.

Millard, David. *The True Messiah Exalted, or, Jesus Christ Really the Son of God Vindicated*. Canadaigua, N.Y.: 1818.

Morgan, William. *Illustrations of Masonry*, 3d ed. New York: 1827.

283

Morley, Sylvanus, and George W. Brainerd. *The Ancient Maya*. Stanford, Calif.: Stanford University Press, 1956.

Mulder, William, and A. Russell Mortensen. *Among the Mormons*. New York: Alfred A. Knopf, 1958.

Nibley, Hugh. *The Myth Makers*. Salt Lake City: Bookcraft, 1967.

Paul, Hiland, and Robert Parks. *History of Wells, Vermont*. Rutland, Vt.: 1869.

Pearsall, Clarence E. *The History and Genealogy of the Pearsall Family in England and America*. San Francisco: 1928.

Pei, Mario. *The Families of Words*. New York: St. Martin's Press, 1962.

Peterson, LaMar. *Hearts Made Glad*. Salt Lake City: 1975.

Pratt, Orson. *An Interesting Account of Several Remarkable Visions....* Edinborough, Scotland: 1840.

Priest, Josiah. *Wonders of Nature and Providence, Displayed*. Albany: 1825.

Shook, Charles. *The True Origin of the Book of Mormon*. Cincinnati: 1914.

Smith, Ethan. *View of the Hebrews; or the Tribes of Israel in America*, 1st ed. Poultney, Vt.: 1823 (2d. ed., 1825).

Smith, Joseph, Jr. *A Book of Commandments for the Government of the Church of Christ*. Zion (Independence), Mo.: 1833.

————. *The Book of Mormon*. Palmyra, N.Y.: 1830. (There are subsequent editions.)

————. *Doctrine and Covenants*. Kirtland, Ohio: 1835, (There are subsequent editions.)

————. *The Pearl of Great Price*. Salt Lake City: 1921.

Smith, Joseph Fielding. *Essentials in Church History*. Salt Lake City: Deseret, 1959.

Smith, Lucy Mack. *Biographical Sketches of Joseph Smith the Prophet and His Progenitors for Many Generations*. Liverpool, England: 1853.

Smith, William. *William Smith on Mormonism*. Lamoni, Iowa: 1883.

Spalding, F.S. *Joseph Smith as a Translator*. Salt Lake City: 1912.

Spalding [also spelled "Spaulding"], Solomon. *The "Manuscript Found."* Salt Lake City: 1886.

Sperry, Sidney B. *Answers to Book of Mormon Questions*. Salt Lake City: Bookcraft, 1967.

Sprague, William. *Annals of the American Pulpit*, Vol. 2. New York: 1857.

Sterns, John G. *An Appendix to "An Inquiry into the Nature and Tendency of Speculative Free Masonry."* Cazenovia, N.Y.: 1828.

Sweet, William Warren. *The Story of Religions in America*. New York: 1930.

Tanner, Jerald, and Sandra Tanner. *The Case Against Mormonism*, 3 vols. Salt Lake City: Modern Microfilm Co., 1967.

————. *The Changing World of Mormonism*. Chicago: Moody, 1980.

————. *Mormonism—Shadow or Reality?* Salt Lake City: Modern Microfilm Co., 1972.

Taylor, Thomas. *The Six Books of Proclus, the Platonic Successor, on the Theology of Plato*. London: 1816.

Thompson, Charles. *Evidences in Proof of the Book of Mormon*. Rochester, N.Y.: 1841.

Turner, Orsamus. *History of the Pioneer Settlement of Phelps and Gorham's Purchase*. Rochester, N.Y.: 1851.

Weldon, Roy E., and F. Edward Butterworth. *Criticisms of the Book of Mormon Answered*. Independence, Mo.: Herald House, 1973.

West, William S. *A Few Interesting Facts Respecting the Rise, Progress, and Pretensions of the Mormons*. 1837.

Whitmer, David. *An Address to All Believers in Christ*. Richmond, Mo.: 1887.

Wyl, Wilhelm (von Wymetal). *Mormon Portraits*. Salt Lake City: 1886.

Articles

Allen, James B. "The Significance of Joseph Smith's 'First Vision' in Mormon Thought." *Dialogue: A Journal of Mormon Thought,*" Vol. 1, No. 3 (Autumn, 1966), pp. 30–35.

Anderson, Rodger I. "Joseph Smith's Early Reputation Revisited." *Journal of Pastoral Practice,* Vol. 4, (1980), No. 3, pp. 71–108, and No. 4, pp. 72–105.

Bachman, Daniel W. "A Look at the Newly Discovered Joseph Smith Manuscript." *Ensign,* Vol. 10, No. 7 (July, 1980), pp. 69–73. Deals with Harris transcript.

Backman, Milton V., and James B. Allen. "Membership of Certain of Joseph Smith's Family in the Western Presbytarian Church of Palmyra." *Brigham Young University Studies,* Vol. 10, No. 4 (Summer, 1970), pp. 482–484.

Baer, Klaus. "The Breathing Permit of Hor." *Dialogue: A Journal of Mormon Thought,* Vol. 3, No. 3 (Autumn, 1968), pp. 109–134.

Benton, A.W. "Mormonites." *Evangelical Magazine and Gospel Advocate,* n.s. 2 (April 9, 1831), p. 120.

Bronk, Mitchell. "The Baptist Church at Manchester," *The Chronicle: A Baptist Historical Quarterly,* Vol. 11, No. 1 (Jan., 1948), pp. 17–30.

Cadwell, Edwin. Letters concering Mormonism. *Amboy Journal,* Amboy, Ill. May 21, July 9, 1879.

Cowdery, Oliver. Numbered "Letters." Beginning in *The Latter Day Saints' Messenger and Advocate,* Vol. 1, No. 1 (Oct., 1834), p. 13, and continuing for several issues. Contains the Cowdery history of the church.

Dogberry, Obadiah. "The Book of Pukie." Beginning in the June 12, 1830, Palmyra *Reflector* and continuing for several issues.

————. "Gold Bible." Beginning in the Jan. 6, 1831, Palmyra *Reflector,* and continuing for several issues.

"1829 Lucy Mack Smith Letter Displayed." *Ensign,* Vol. 12, No. 10 (Oct., 1982), pp. 70–73.

Hill, Marvin. "Joseph Smith and the 1826 Trial: New Evidence and New Difficulties." *Brigham Young University Studies,* Vol. 12, No. 2 (Winter, 1972), pp. 223–233.

Historical Record. "The Twelve Apostles," Salt Lake City, Vol. 6, Nos. 3–5 (May, 1887), p. 195ff.

Jessee, Dean C. "The early Accounts of Joseph Smith's First Vision." *Brigham Young University Studies,* Vol. 9, No. 3 (Spring, 1969), pp. 278–280.

————. "Joseph Knight's Recollections of Early Mormon History." *Brigham Young University Studies,* Vol. 17, No. 1 (Autumn, 1976), pp. 29–39.

————. "Lucy Mack Smith 1829 Letter to Mary Smith Pierce." *Brigham Young University Studies,* Vol. 22, No. 4 (Fall, 1982), pp. 455–465.

Kimball, Stanley B. "The Anthon Transcript: People, Primary Sources, and Problems." *Brigham Young University Studies,* Vol. 10, No. 3, (Spring, 1970), pp. 325–352.

Lancaster, James E. "By the Gift and Power of God." *Saints' Herald,* Vol. 109, No. 22 (Nov., 1962), pp. 14–32.

Lapham, Fayette. "The Mormons." *Historical Magazine,* Vol. 8, 2d ser., No. 5 (May, 1870), pp. 305–306.

Lewis, Joseph and Heil. Letters concerning Mormonism. *Amboy Journal,* Amboy, Ill. April 30, June 4, June 11, July 30, Aug. 6, 1879.

Marshall, Charles. "The Original Prophet, By a Visitor to Salt Lake City." *Fraser's Magazine,* Vol. 7, No. 38, n.s. (Feb., 1873), pp. 229–230.

Nibley, Hugh. "The Comparative Method." *The Improvement Era,* Vol. 62, No. 10 (Oct., 1959).

Parker, Richard A. "The Book of Breathings." *Dialogue: A Journal of Mormon Thought,* Vol. 3, No. 2 (Summer, 1968), pp. 98–99.

————. "The Joseph Smith Papyri: A Preliminary Report." *Dialogue: A Journal of Mormon Thought,* Vol. 3, No. 2 (Summer, 1968), pp. 86–88.

Peterson, J.W. "Another Testimony." *Deseret Evening News,* Vol. 27, No. 11 (Jan. 20,
  1894), p. 11. Interview with William Smith that was reprinted from *Zion's Ensign,*
  date not given.
St. Louis Globe Democrat. "The Origin of Mormonism," Feb. 21, 1897.
Sampson, D. Paul, and Larry T. Wimmer. "The Kirtland Safety Society: The Stock
  Ledger Book and the Bank Failure." *Brigham Young University Studies,* Vol. 12,
  No. 4 (Summer, 1972), pp. 427–436.
Smith, Joseph, Jr. "History of Joseph Smith." Beginning in the *Times and Seasons,* Vol.
  3, No. 10 (March 15, 1842), p. 726, and continuing in subsequent issues.
"Mormonism." *Susquehanna Register,* May 1, 1834. Contains affidavits made by Joseph
  Smith's in-laws and acquaintants in the Harmony, Pa., area.
Tiffany, Joel. "Mormonism—No. II." *Tiffany's Monthly,* Vol. 5, No. 4 (Aug., 1859),
  pp. 163–170.
Turner, Orsamus. "Then and Now Interesting Reminiscences," *Lockport Daily Courier,*
  May 5, 1854.
Tuttle, Daniel, Bishop. "Mormons." *A Religious Encyclopedia: or Dictionary of Bibli-
  cal, Historical, Doctrinal, and Practical Theology,* ed. by Philip Schaff. Vol. 2,
  pp. 1575ff. New York: 1883.
Walters, Wesley P. "From Occult to Cult with Joseph Smith, Jr." *Journal of Pastoral
  Practice,* Vol. 1, No. 2 (Summer, 1977), pp. 121–137.
_____. "Joseph Smith's Bainbridge, N.Y., Court Trials." *Westminster Theological
  Journal,* Vol. 36, No. 2 (Winter, 1974), pp. 123–155.
_____. "New Light on Mormon Origins from the Palmyra (N.Y.) Revival." *Evangeli-
  cal Theological Society,* Vol. 10, No. 4 (Fall, 1967), pp. 227–244. A somewhat
  revised version was published in *Dialogue: A Journal of Mormon Thought,* Vol.
  4, No. 1 (Spring, 1969), pp. 60–81.
_____. "A Reply to Dr. Bushman." *Dialogue: A Journal of Mormon Thought,* Vol.
  4, No. 1 (Spring, 1969).
Wilson, John. "The Joseph Smith Papyri: A Summary." *Dialogue: A Journal of
  Mormon Thought,* Vol. 3, No. 2 (Summer, 1968), pp. 67–85.

Manuscripts and Records

Poultney Congregational Church Records, Poultney, Vt. Poultney Historical Society.
Roberts, Brigham H. "Book of Mormon Difficulties." University of Utah, Marriott
  Library, Western Americana Section. Salt Lake City, 1921.
Smith, Lucy Mack. "Preliminary Manuscript." Church Archives, Salt Lake City. Draft
  for Lucy Smith's *Biographical Sketches....*

Index

A

Abel, Eljah, 217

Abraham, 130, 146, 190, 199. *See also Book of Abraham*.

Adair, James, 106, 108, 135, 157, 158, 235

Alger, Fanny, 221

Alma, 162

Amboy Journal, 81, 82

America: Ethan Smith's role for, 58, 111, 115; Isaiah 18 applied to, 112; a land of liberty, 137, 148, 149; likened to two great wings, 113; prophecy of, 139, 140; Ten Tribes, to help convert, 129; valley of dry bones in, 159. *See also* American people; Nation of last days.

American people, 138, 142, 191, 192; mission for, 115, 116

Americans, ancient: lost from knowledge of Jews, 130; speculations about, 17; to speak from the dead, 131. *See also* Indians, American; Parallels, *Book of Mormon* and *View of the Hebrews*.

"And it came to pass": in *B.M.*, 91; in Spalding's manuscript, 248, 250

Angel(s), 24, 33, 59, 70, 246

Another book of God, 118

Anthon, Professor Charles, 275 (n18); Harris visit to, 74–76, 78; on Harris visit, 75. *See also* Characters, transcript of.

Anthony, Professor, 76. *See also* Anthon, Professor Charles.

Anticatholicism, 123–125

Antimasonry, 174ff

Apostasy, 123

Archaeologia Americana, 159, 160, 163, 165, 166, 180, 187, 202, 239, 241

Atwater, Caleb, 165, 166, 180, 202

B

Babel, 89, 204

Babylon, mystic(al), 123, 146, 147, 150

Backman, Milton V., Jr., 17

Baer, Klaus, 259, 265

Bainbridge, N.Y., 38, 42, 48, 53, 64, 249, 250; Emily Pearsall from, 47, 52; 1830 trial in, 50, 100, 101; 1826 trial, in, 42ff; Joseph Smith attended school in, 15, 43, 53; treasure hunting in, 43, 46

Bands of robbers and murderers, 173, 174, 207

Baptist Church, Joseph Smith and, 30, 31, 81

Benjamin, King, 161

Bennett, John C., 225

Benton, A.W., 52, 64; on 1826 trial 49, 50; on 1830 trial, 100, 101

Bible, 126; errors in, 120, 121; faulty translation of Isaiah 18 in, 113; King James Version of, quoted in *B.M.*, 90, 91, 189; more to be written, 119

Boggs, Lilburn, 223

Book of Abraham, 214ff; 256ff; doctrine of many gods from, 228; published in *Times and Seasons*, 214, 256; manuscript (drafts) of, 259, 260; polytheism in, 258. *See also* Facsimile(s), *Book of Abraham*; Papyri; Papyrus, *Book of Abraham*; Parallels, *Book of Abraham*...

"Book of Breathings," 264. *See also Papyrus, Book of Abraham*.

Book of Commandments...: revelation in, changed, 19

"Book of Ether," 89, 201ff

"Book of Lehi," 93

Book of Mormon, 7, 8, 17, 103–207; anachronisms in, 91; "and it came to pass" in, 91; anticatholicism in, 123, 124; antimasonry in, 174ff; beginning as nonreligious book, 33, 57, 59; capability of Joseph Smith to produce, 12–30; discrepancies in, 174, 194, 206; exhortation to accept, 89; faults of, 90–92; geography in, 166, 241; grammatical errors in, 90–91; Harris trip worked into, 79; inconsistencies in, 201, 203; Joseph Smith projected in, 16; manuscript of, 99; padding in, 90; Palmyra religious excitement prophecied in, 18, 271 (n1:12); plural marriage, contradicts revelation on, 279

Diego factor, 243

Divination, 57

Divining (hazel) rod, 38, 57, 235, 236, 238

Doctrine and Covenants, 226

Doctrine of many gods, 228. *See also Book of Abraham.*

Dogberry, Obadiah, 36, 37, 39, 40, 56, 58, 238

Dry bones, 159

Dunklin, Daniel, 212

E

Earthworks, 163–167, 180, 250, 253. *See also* Mounds.

East Poultney, Vt., 5; *See also* Poultney.

Egyptian Hieroglyphics, 75, 195, 197

Egyptologists, 218, 219, 258, 259, 264, 267

1820 vision. *See* Vision, first.

1823 vision. *See* Vision, second.

1826 trial. *See* Trial, 1826.

1830 trial. *See* Trial(s), 1830.

Elephants, 202, 239, 240, 250

Enchantment, 40, 42, 45

Ephraim, stick of, 132, 134

Ether. *See* "Book of Ether."

Evangelical Magazine and Gospel Advocate, 49, 100

Evening and the Morning Star, 211, 212

Evidences in Proof of the Book of Mormon (Thompson), 113, 165

Excitement, religious, 22, 28, 58, 89, 272 (n15); conflicting dates for, 25–27; no mention of, in early account, 24; prophecy of, in *B.M.*, 18, 271 (n1:12). *See also* Vision, first.

Expositor. See Nauvoo Expositor.

Ezekiel: alluded to by Lehi, 133; two sticks of, 132; valley of dry bones of, 159

F

Facsimile(s), *Book of Abraham*, 256, *263*; Egyptian funeral documents, representations of, 218; No. 1, 261, 262, *263*, 265; No. 2, 257, *263*, 265; No. 3, 257, *263*, 265; parallels with sources, 257. *See also* Papyrus, *Book of Abraham*; Papyri.

Factions, savage and civilized. *See* Civilized tribes; Savage tribes, Parallels, *Book of Mormon* and *View of the Hebrews.*

Far West, 223

First vision. *See* Vision, first.

Ford, Thomas, 230

Fortifications, 201. *See also* Earthworks; Mounds.

Fraser's Magazine, 48, 49

Freemasonry. *See* Masonry; Antimasonry.

Frisbie, Barnes, 234ff

G

Gadianton, 173, 176, 207; discrepancy about, in *B.M.*, 174, 194. *See also* Gadianton bands.

Gadianton bands, 173, 176, 178; masonry, similarity with, 174ff.

General Assembly of the Church, 221

Gentile(s), 12, 110, 111, 123, 191. *See also* Parallels, *Book of Mormon* and *View of the Hebrews.*

Giddianhi, 176, 177

Giddins, 177

Gilbert, John: on Harris testimony, 96; on manuscript, 99

Glass, 38, 62. *See also* Stone; Seer stone.

Glass-looking, 65

God, 18, 19; in vision, 22. *See also* Supreme Being.

Gold bible, 36, 39, 58, 69, 72; would bring Millennium, 70

Gold plates. *See* Plates.

Gospel, 193; corrupted, 124; preached in America in remote times, 181, 188

"Grammar and A[l]phabet of the Egyptian Language," 218, 259, 260

Grammatical errors in *B.M.*, 90, 91

Grandin, Egbert B., 99

Great Spirit, 110, 111, 116, 187, 189, 190; in *B.M.*, 155–157; Indians disobedient to, 152, 170

Green, Dee F., 244, 245, 246

H

Hale, Alva, 40, 46, 65, 73

Hale, Emma, 35, 42, 43, 61, 62; the right person, 62, 63, 74; marriage of, to Joseph Smith, 63, 64. *See also* Smith, Emma.

Hale, Isaac, 63, 64, 65, 73; on Pennsylvania money digging, 42, 43; on translation, 86

Ham, curse against, 214, 215, 216

Hamlet in *B.M.*, 147

Harmony Methodist Episcopal Church: Joseph attempted to Join, 81–83

Harmony, Penn., 35, 43, 45, 61, 65, 74, 84; money digging in, 40, 42

Harris, Abigail, 71, 72

Harris, Lucy, 71, 83

Harris, Martin, 73; Anthon, visit to, 74–76; anti-masonic convention, and, 179, 180; belief of, in Joseph, 74, 78, 79; excommunicated, 75, 98; object of, to make money, 71–72; 116 pages and, 80, 83; never saw plates, 96, 97, 98; on money diggers and plates, 72; on plates, 59, 72; printing *B.M.*, paid for, 99; religious views of, 69; Shakerism, belief in, 98; on spectacles, 68; testimony of, 94, 95; took dictation, 79; on